Writing Manhood in Black and Yellow

ASIAN AMERICA
A series edited by Gordon H. Chang

The increasing size and diversity of the Asian American population, its growing significance in American society and culture, and the expanded appreciation, both popular and scholarly, of the importance of Asian Americans in the country's present and past—all these developments have converged to stimulate wide interest in scholarly work on topics related to the Asian American experience. The general recognition of the pivotal role that race and ethnicity have played in American life, and in relations between the United States and other countries, has also fostered this heightened attention.

Although Asian Americans were a subject of serious inquiry in the late nineteenth and early twentieth centuries, they were subsequently ignored by the mainstream scholarly community for several decades. In recent years, however, this neglect has ended, with an increasing number of writers examining a good many aspects of Asian American life and culture. Moreover, many students of American society are recognizing that the study of issues related to Asian America speak to, and may be essential for, many current discussions on the part of the informed public and various scholarly communities.

The Stanford series on Asian America seeks to address these interests. The series will include works from the humanities and social sciences, including history, anthropology, political science, American studies, law, literary criticism, sociology, and interdisciplinary and policy studies.

Writing Manhood in Black and Yellow

RALPH ELLISON, FRANK CHIN,
AND THE LITERARY POLITICS
OF IDENTITY

Daniel Y. Kim

STANFORD UNIVERSITY PRESS
STANFORD, CALIFORNIA
2005

Stanford University Press
Stanford, California
© 2005 by the Board of Trustees of the Leland Stanford Junior
University. All rights reserved.

Printed in the United States of America on acid-free, archival-quality
paper

Library of Congress Cataloging-in-Publication Data

Kim, Daniel Y.
Writing manhood in black and yellow : Ralph Ellison, Frank Chin, and
the literary politics of identity / Daniel Y. Kim.
    p.   cm. — (Asian America)
    Includes bibliographical references (p.) and index.
    ISBN 0-8047-5108-0 (acid-free paper) — ISBN 0-8047-5109-9 (pbk. :
acid-free paper)
        1. Chin, Frank, 1940—Criticism and interpretation. 2. American
literature—Minority authors—History and criticism. 3. Ellison, Ralph—
Criticism and interpretation. 4. African American men in literature.
5. Asian Americans in literature. 6. Group identity in literature.
7. Masculinity in literature. 8. Gay men in literature. 9. Race in
literature. 10. Men in literature. I. Title. II. Series.
    PS3553.H4897Z74 2005
    810.9'920693–dc22   2005009124

Typeset by BookMatters in 11/14 Adobe Garamond

Original Printing 2005

Last figure below indicates year of this printing:
14   13   12   11   10   09   08   07   06   05

To Jen

Contents

Acknowledgments

Nothing like this ever gets done without a lot of people helping out. I feel blessed to have had the love and support of many wonderful teachers, students, friends, and colleagues along the way, and also of my family. I would like to suggest here the great debt of gratitude I owe to all of them.

I thank my professors at Berkeley for showing me what kind of teacher and scholar I wanted to become. Carolyn Porter, Sau-ling Wong, and Mitchell Breitwieser served as my mentors when this project began as a dissertation. They taught me *how* I ought to think—with rigor, precision, passion and humaneness—without ever telling me *what* to think, without ever demanding that my thoughts be a mirror to their own. I have come to value more and more the sense of intellectual independence they fostered in their students. David Lloyd, D. A. Miller, Sue Schweik, and Kaja Silverman were also important teachers for me at Berkeley—indeed they were formative. I was lucky to be part of a great cohort of Asian Americanist graduate students: Tina Chen, Mark Chiang, Jeannie Chiu, David Eng, Candace Fujikane, Viet Nguyen, Karen Su, and Dorothy Wang. They invited and challenged me—along with Sau-ling Wong—to see what was powerful about the Asian American literary tradition. Finishing graduate school would simply not have been possible without Alyson Bardsley, Greg Forter, and Seth Moglen—friends and intellectual companions of the highest order. And I am grateful to Daniel Benveniste for what I learned from him.

For being essential to the sense of community I have enjoyed in Providence and at Brown University, I thank Tim Bewes, Laura Chrisman, Elliott Colla, Philip Gould, Matthew Gutman, Jose Itzigsohn, Neil Lazarus, Robert Lee, Robert Scholes, Leonard Tennenhouse, and Esther Whitfield. Indelibly part of my life here has been Josefina Saldaña, a woman of miraculous intellectual and personal exuberance. Arthur Riss—a seeming curmudgeon whose intellectual generosity and analytic perspicacity are second to none— made me remember at crucial times why I do what I do. I'm grateful to have had the friendship of Stuart Burrows, a true mensch. My cup runneth over with appreciation for Ravit Reichman, whose intelligence, kindness, and spirit are boundless. Madhu Dubey is one of the most remarkable people I have ever met—what her friendship and intellectual mentorship have meant to me I cannot even hope to convey.

I thank Jim Egan, Ellen Rooney, and David Savran for reading early versions of this book and helping it develop; Kandice Chuh, Arthur Riss, and Josefina Saldaña for their insightful comments on individual chapters. Tamar Katz has shaped this book more than she probably knows: my prose and my ideas have become, I hope, clearer and smarter because of her influence. Olakunle George, who has read every page of this study, offered sage words of advice and encouragement when I was most in need of them. Madhu Dubey read much of this book as it was being written; the feedback and support she provided were truly phenomenal. For being exemplars of intellectual integrity and commitment, I thank Nancy Armstrong, Mary Ann Doane, Evelyn Hu-Dehart, and Ellen Rooney. They are colleagues whom I greatly admire, both for their research and for the tireless work they've put toward creating and developing intellectual communities at Brown that have been vital to my work.

I am grateful to have received the Henry Merritt Wriston Fellowship from Brown University, which enabled me to take a year's sabbatical that was crucial to the writing of this book. I am also deeply appreciative of the faculty fellowship provided by the Pembroke Center.

I would also like to acknowledge the following scholars, all of whom have been important interlocutors for me in various ways: Patricia Chu, Kandice Chuh, Yoonmee Chang, James Lee, Rachel Lee, Lisa Lowe, Gary Okihiro, Fred Moten, Hyungji Park, Tony Peffer, Karen Shimikawa, Min Song, and Kenneth Warren.

I could not have asked for a more rewarding teaching experience than the one I've had at Brown. My undergraduates believe that the knowledge they gain should be used to do good things in the world: their unjaded intellectual passion has meant a lot to me. I owe a particular debt to those who took my seminar "Race, Writing and Manhood," as they helped me develop the ideas in this book. I have had the pleasure of knowing many more extraordinary students than I can name here, but I would like to acknowledge at least those with whom I have worked most closely: Aixa Almonte, Anand Balakrishnan, Miabi Chatterji, Farng-yeong Foo, Daniel Hoffman-Schwartz, Anne Lessy, Aimee Paik, Richard So, Joanne Suh, Ben Suzuki-Graves, Victor StaAna, and Pui-ling Tam.

My graduate students at Brown have also been a real source of inspiration. I have gained much—by way of ideas, but also personally—from working with them. I would like to thank Guy Mark Foster, Jennifer Jang, Gene Jarrett, Chris Lee, Susette Min, Kasturi Ray, Eric Reyes, Cynthia Tolentino, and Sanjeev Uprety. From Yogita Goyal and Asha Nadkarni I have learned at least as much as they learned from me—how to build a raft, for one thing. Their friendship was indispensable to me as I finished this book.

At Stanford University Press, I would like to thank Anna Eberhard Friedlander and Carmen Borbón-Wu for their professionalism and their hard work, and Gordon Chang for his support. I especially thank Muriel Bell for her faith in this project.

Chris Lee was an outstanding research assistant, as was Heather Lee—Heather did an excellent job compiling the index. I am much obliged to them for their stellar efforts.

During a difficult hour, a recent one, I was buoyed by many friends and allies—all of them have my gratitude. Two of my friends, however, had the misfortune to be there for me every minute: Ravit Reichman and Pat Chu. And it must be said that there can be no advocate more ferocious or more indefatigable than Nancy Armstrong.

I have always had my family's love and support, and everything I ever do comes in some way from them. I thank my father, Jaejong Kim, my mother, June Chun, my sister, Debbie Finch, and my *halmoni*, Dong Sun Lim.

The final word of thanks must go to the lifelong companion of my head and heart, Jennifer Walrad, whose creativity, wit, and overall genius have always left me awed, and whose love has kept me going at times when I thought I could not.

Sections of some of the chapters in this book have been published previously in different versions. Parts of an earlier version of Chapter 1 appeared as "Invisible Desires: Homoerotic Racism and its Homophobic Critique in Ralph Ellison's Invisible Man," *Novel* 30 (1997): 309–28. Portions of Chapters 3 and 4 constituted "The Strange Love of Frank Chin" by Daniel Y. Kim, originally published in *Q & A: Queer in Asian America*, edited by David L. Eng and Alice Y. Howe. Copyright 1998 by Temple University. All rights reserved. Used by permission.

Preface

I only begin to wonder what it actually meant to think of myself as American—and to consider what that term might mean to others who shared my ancestry, my skin color—when I began to read books by black men. My gateway to thinking about race, in other words, were the works of writers like Richard Wright and Ralph Ellison—and, if memory serves, the first book that ever took on for me the aura of "literature" was *Black Boy*. I mention these facts not because they are somehow exceptional (my guess is that they would apply to many Asian American intellectuals of my generation) and not as a preface to an autobiographical account of the personal history that led to the writing of this book; rather, I mention them because they indicate something of this study's distinctive focus. My concern here, first of all, is something that was, in a sense, invisible to me when I first encountered works like *Native Son*—something that has increasingly come to be seen as a kind of truism: that the language of race is also a language of sex, that meditations on the effects of racism and the possibilities of its transcendence are often framed by a rhetoric of gender and sexuality. Thanks to the work of a number of recent scholars working at the intersections of gender, queer, and ethnic studies, it has generally come to be acknowledged that, as Dwight A. McBride puts it,

> Race is not simple. It has never been simple. It does not have the history that would make it so, no matter how much we may yearn for that degree of clarity. . . . The point being, if I am thinking about race, I should

already be thinking about gender, class, and sexuality. This statement, I think, assumes the very impossibility of a hierarchy or chronology of categories of identity.[1]

This book, *Writing Manhood in Black and Yellow*, attempts to further the kind of inquiry that McBride describes by analyzing African American and Asian American masculinities in a comparative framework. It also seeks to bring into focus a certain fantasy about literature that conceives of writing as the domain of racialized manhood *par excellence*. It explores certain influential narratives that men of color in the United States have often relied upon to make sense of the psychic damage that racism threatens to inflict, and it examines a particular idea of literary power that promises to undo that damage. This study does not, however, simply place black and yellow men side by side, as it were. It also hopes to confront directly the interracialism that links them together and also differentiates them—an interracialism that registers (though asymmetrically and unevenly) as identification and desire, as an uneasy libidinal charge that alternates between antagonism and solidarity.

In the focus it brings to this interracialism, it should be clear that this is a project animated by a foundational ethos of ethnic studies—a field that has been committed since its inception to, in Johnnella E. Butler's words, "the interdisciplinary and comparative study of the social, cultural, and economic expression and experience of U.S. racialized ethnic groups and of U.S. racialization."[2] Recently, a consensus has emerged among most scholars that the parameters of this field should expand to encompass the transnational cultural and economic forces that increasingly structure the workings of race: to address issues of globalization, empire, and diaspora. But even as this development has taken place, scholars have tended to maintain the field's comparative premise. Amritjit Singh and Peter Schmidt, for instance, even as they underscore the crucial significance of transnational approaches, have called for more "multiracial comparisons of, say, Asian Americans, blacks, Latinos, and whites . . . that will not treat their cultural histories as if they developed autonomously."[3]

This shift in emphasis from U.S.-centered paradigms to ones that push beyond the category of the nation, however productive it has been, has not led to an increase in the number of individual projects that examine race in comparative terms. Most works that fall under the rubric of ethnic studies exhibit a mono-racial focus, even if it is possible to think of them collectively as part of a larger intellectual project directed toward an interracialist understanding. What threatens to be lost in accepting this division of intellectual labor, however, is the opportunity for a direct critical engagement with the forces that both draw members of different racial minority groups together and also pull them apart. This book seeks to address some of those forces—psychic and ideological. The brief anecdote I began with, moreover, suggests why it is so particularly important, in my view, for Asian Americanist intellectuals to engage with the question of interracialism. To the extent that the scenario I describe is typical, it reflects a certain *belatedness* that frames the attempts of progressive Asian American intellectuals to offer their own insights about how race structures U.S. society. For the languages that seem appropriate to such an endeavor seem to be ones either authored by or shaped to fit the needs of African Americans—languages that when spoken or written by Asian Americans can take on the character of a borrowing, or even an appropriation. The interracialism this study examines, therefore, is not one that is symmetrical. It does not take shape through depictions of black and Asian men standing together in antiracist homosocial solidarity, granting each other through their mutual recognition a manhood that the racist world of white men would attempt to deny. Rather, it is an interracialism that is, in some sense, fractured by the asymmetry of African and Asian American concerns.

To put this another way, what the writers I examine in this study *share* are a set of ideologies that would tend to encourage interracial antagonism rather than solidarity. I focus primarily on the major works of two influential figures—Ralph Ellison and Frank Chin—in order to identify two interrelated strands of "minority discourse" that shape how African and Asian American men render their experiences of racism. Connecting the work of these two figures is, first of all, a common rhetoric of masculinity and sexuality—a rhetoric that depicts the violent psychic effects of living under a racist regime through a symbolic vocabulary of emasculation, feminization, and homosexualization. What they also share is a highly masculinist conception of literature in which the act of writing is seen as the privileged mode of combating a racism that seeks to effect the "castration" of men of color. Their writings thus link virility with racial and literary authenticity; moreover, they render manhood coterminous with an intense agonism that does not readily facilitate a sense of interracial solidarity.

In its emphasis on an agonistic and masculinist dimension of black-Asian interracialism, this study occupies a somewhat unusual relationship to the body of scholarly works with which it is nonetheless allied. As should be clear from its comparative scope and from the critiques it offers of ideologies for their masculinism and homophobia, this is a project animated by the coalitional and collaborative ethos that most intellectuals in the field identify as integral to ethnic studies—a political ethos that mirrors its stated commitment to a comparative approach to the study of race. In reference to the two minority groups it focuses on—African American and Asian American—this work comes out of the same concern with coalitional thinking apparent in the work of scholars like George Lipsitz, Gary Okihiro, Vijay Prashad, Penny M. Von Eschen, and Frank H. Wu. That this book gives attention to issues of gender and sexuality should also indicate its commitment to a critical practice that strives to be feminist and antihomophobic as well as antiracist: the issues I treat here would have been literally unthinkable without a rich tradition in ethnic studies that also allies itself with feminist and queer studies (about which I will have more to say shortly).

Given these allegiances, however, the critical itinerary that this book pursues might seem eccentric or counterintuitive to some readers. The approach to black-Asian interracialism that it adopts, for instance, is quite different from the one taken in the studies I have just cited. Much of this work brings to light the progressive antiracist or anti-imperialist coalitions—both real and imagined—that have emerged between Americans of African and Asian descent. Gary Okihiro, for instance, argues in his essay "Is Yellow Black or White?" that African and Asian Americans comprise a "kindred people" who not only "share a history of migration, interaction and cultural sharing, and commerce and trade" but also share a history of colonization and racist exploitation; George Lipsitz devotes a chapter of his book *The Possessive Investment in Whiteness* to a study of African American intellectuals and activists of the World War II era who "found in Asia a source of inspiration and emulation whose racial significance complicated the black-white divisions of the United States"; Vijay Prashad identifies an antiracist "polyculturalism" in the "mongrel Afro-Asian history" he traces in *Everybody Was Kung-Fu Fighting*; Penny M. Von Eschen's *Race Against Empire* examines how anti-colonial struggles in Africa and the diaspora as well as in South Asia shaped the political vision of African American activists, journalists, and intellectuals from the 1930s through the 1950s.[4] Lipsitz eloquently conveys the interracialism that this body of black-Asian scholarship illuminates:

Liberal narratives about multiculturalism and cultural pluralism to the contrary, race relations in the United States have always involved more than one outcast group at a time acting in an atomized fashion against a homogeneous "white" center. Interethnic identifications and alliances have been powerful weapons against white supremacy. All racial identities are relational; communities of color are mutually constitutive of one another, not just competitive or cooperative.[5]

For scholars in ethnic studies, works like these help conjure the political ideal toward which our writing and teaching is directed, which is to promote antiracist "interethnic identifications and alliances" that cut against the most narrow and essentialist forms of identity politics. But as many of us are aware, the forms of identity politics that were so crucial to the field's inception—those associated with cultural nationalism—can continue to take on a more than spectral presence in the minds of the students we teach and in the coalitions we try to encourage. Moreover, as recent events have made clear, nationalist forms of imagining community retain a significant interpellative power despite the emergence of a vital body of work that helps us, as the title of one such recent study puts it, to "imagine otherwise."[6] Given the persistent power of nationalist and cultural nationalist identifications, the need remains for rigorous and comparative studies of such ideologies.

What I thus offer in this book is, I believe, the first comparative study of African American and Asian American forms of literary identity politics— politics that are, in their basic shape, nationalist. By focusing primarily on select works by Ralph Ellison and Frank Chin—writers who have been chosen precisely for their emblematic and influential status in the African and Asian American literary traditions, respectively—I identify certain paradigmatic elements of the cultural nationalism forwarded by each that encourage an interracial antagonism. I trace the erasure of "the Oriental problem" in Ellison's conception of "American Negro" nationalism and disclose a latent Orientalism in the homophobic symbolism that gives structure to *Invisible Man*; I call attention to a complex competitiveness vis-à-vis African Americans that shapes Chin's cultural nationalism and suggest how the homophobia that structures it is derived in part from black-authored texts. The works I examine here, therefore, do not comprise an archive that in some straightforward way promotes the political cause of coalition building. But it is my belief that analyses of how such influential nationalist ideologies encourage African and Asian Americans to see one another in antagonistic rather than cooperative terms remain indispensable to the goal of advancing more progressive forms of interracialism, for they speak to the question of why such coalitions seem to emerge with such infrequency and difficulty.

The relationship of this book to a recently emergent and highly generative body of work by scholars working at the borders of gay/lesbian, African American, and Asian American studies also requires clarification, and doing so will require a bit more elaboration. While the field of ethnic studies has had, in Johnnella Butler's terms, a "historically ambivalent relationship to gender and sexual identity," most practitioners would agree that feminist and gay/lesbian scholarship has been part of a larger and important movement in the field toward examining the intimate connection between race and other categories of identity that exert an essentializing power in U.S. culture—preeminent among these being gender and sexuality.[7] Without presuming to offer an exhaustive mapping of a field that is rapidly expanding even as I write, it is still possible to identify several currents in it.

It is instructive to consider queer ethnic studies in relation to the productive tension that Eve Kosofsky Sedgwick has identified as constitutive of gay/lesbian studies as a whole. In *Epistemology of the Closet*, Sedgwick distinguishes between a "minoritizing view" of "homo/heterosexual definition" and a "universalizing view"—between an epistemological orientation that sees this distinction as "of active importance primarily for a small, distinct, relatively fixed homosexual minority" and one that sees it "as an issue of continuing, determinative importance in the lives of people across the spectrum of sexualities."[8] While Sedgwick argues that these two approaches are not in fact mutually exclusive, work in queer ethnic studies has tended—and for good reason—to emphasize the first approach, focusing attention on the effect of the homo/heterosexual binary on gay and lesbian subjects.

One quite important result of this work—and indeed the most pressing in everyday political terms—has been to draw critical attention to gay and lesbian subjectivities that have been marginalized and/or erased not only by the white mainstream and white gay/lesbian communities, but also by minority communities. Such studies in the African American context, according to Marlon B. Ross, generally attempt either "to uncloset the lives of famous individuals of African descent who might be suspected of having, at some point, harbored same-sexual desire or engaged in same-sexual activity" or to "expose the homophobia at work in the literatures of and histories on African-American life and culture."[9] Two important Asian American anthologies—*Asian American Sexualities* and *Q&A: Queer in Asian America*—have helped the field confront the ways in which it has tended to be—as Dana Y. Takagi put it in her 1996 essay—"mostly ignorant about the multiple ways that gay identities are often hidden or invisible within Asian American communities."[10] Firmly in this tradition as well are exemplary critiques of the homophobia that subtends cultural nationalist constructions of community by Phillip Brian Harper and David L. Eng—critiques I modify and elaborate in ways that I will discuss momentarily.[11]

Another current in queer ethnic studies—which takes its inspiration from the theoretical writings of Judith Butler—explores how the denigrated category of the homosexual of color is performatively re-signified in gay/lesbian cultural contexts. To a certain extent, this approach elaborates what Sedgwick terms a "minoritizing view" of "homo/heterosexual definition," but in ways that stress the mobility, heterogeneity, and multiplicity of queer-of-color identities rather than positing a relatively fixed sense of racialized homosexual identity. In *Disidentifications,* for instance, José Esteban Muñoz explores "the survival strategies the minority subject practices in order to negotiate a phobic majoritarian public sphere that continuously elides or punishes the existence of subjects who do not conform to the phantasm of normative citizenship"; he explores how gay and lesbian subjects of color effect a "disidentification" with the "damaged stereotypes" that the wider culture promotes, how they are able to "recycle" these demeaning images "as powerful and seductive sites of self creation."[12] David L. Eng and Gayatri Gopinath identify an archive of contemporary and diasporic Asian cultural texts that, in Eng's words, "brings together queerness and diaspora in innovative, destabilizing, and compelling ways that contest the dominant representations comprising the domestic image-repertoire."[13] I want here to stress the importance of this second current of work, as it focuses on cultural texts that exceed the representational logic that I will be examining in this study. For even as my study carefully explores and seeks to explain the persistent allure of a deeply nationalist, masculinist and homophobic vocabulary for thinking about racism and its resistance, it is not intended to deny the existence of performances and practices of antiracist resistance that move beyond that vocabulary. Neither is it intended to suggest that queers of color simply abject themselves to the demeaning representations of homosexuality promoted by the nationalist rhetorics I analyze here: indeed, the studies I have cited make clear that this is not the case.

The objective of this project, however, is to understand how an antiracist cultural politics comes to articulate itself *with* instead of *against* homophobia. This book grapples with the fact that what can look and feel like empowerment or liberation from the perspective of heterosexual men of color can easily depend on a disturbing disidentification with and a denigration of other racially and sexually stigmatized identities. While a "minoritizing view," in Sedgwick's terms, still shapes this study—as it recognizes that the destructive effects of the homophobia it critiques are experienced most directly by gay men of color—its basic perspective thus tends more to a "universalizing view": it focuses on how issues of gender and sexuality shape the racialized subjectivities of avowedly heterosexual men.

My analysis of the masculinism and homophobia that subtend cultural nationalist ideologies draws from and synthesizes the findings of prior critiques. It echoes the assertions of critics such as Phillip Brian Harper and Hazel Carby who note that African American rhetorics of authenticity tend to link racial inauthenticity with an inadequately virile masculinity.[14] Such critiques, which build upon the work of feminist scholars like Michele Wallace, tend to focus on homosexuality as a signifier of *gender*—as a symbol of a racialized manhood deemed unworthy of the name. My study adopts a different approach to male homosexuality as a signifier, stressing how disturbingly capacious and effective it is at conveying a myriad range of racism's dehumanizing effects. These effects involve not simply an (un)gendering and an injurious fracturing of subjectivity; they also involve—and here is where my particular emphasis lies—the production of sexualized forms of interracial homosocial desire.

By giving meticulous attention to the figural complexity of this homophobic symbolism—by engaging, in other words, in close readings of it—I offer analyses that read "with the grain," as it were, though they are part of a project that reads "against" it. For it is my contention that we cannot hope to understand the seductive allure that this symbolism possesses—a symbolism that links antiracism with homophobia—without bringing into focus the intricate rhetorical logics that make it work. Where previous studies have done an effective job of "outing" the homophobia of cultural nationalism, they have not attended sufficiently to the figural complexity of its articulation, a complexity that must be understood to grasp how it is able so effectively to mobilize the affective investments of its readers.

Moreover, in its careful consideration of the centrality of desire to cultural nationalist representations of homosexuality, this study explores more fully than others have how the *sexual* politics of racial identity become enmeshed in and articulated as a *literary* politics. The writers I examine depict racism as seeking to instill in black and Asian men a feminizing and "homosexual" desire—an *interracial* and mimetic desire that is directed at white men, though for Chin it will be directed also at black men. The conceptions of the aesthetic proposed by Ellison and Chin purport to provide a solution to the "homosexual" desire that white racism engenders—a solution that promises not so much to eradicate it but to enable expressions of it that are "virile" and racially "authentic." Ellison and Chin champion an ideal of literary identity that allegedly takes its cues from the vibrant, muscular, and agonistic forms of cultural expression characteristic of working-class communities of color—that gives literary form to a *vernacular*. In my analyses of these vernacular theories, I highlight the ways in which they privilege a masculinist subject, one whose power is rendered as the expression of a highly aggressive, indeed cannibalistic, homosocial desire.

Over the course of this study I demonstrate the persistence of this particular conception of the vernacular across a wide range of twentieth-century writings. It is an ideology that links Ellison to figures who are usually thought of as endorsing a wholly opposed perspective on literary politics: Richard Wright, Amiri Baraka, and Eldridge Cleaver. It is also an ideology that is reworked by Chin in his influential polemics of the 1970s, which outline the parameters of an "authentic" Asian American literary tradition. Moreover, I contend that the masculinist agonism privileged in this conception of literary and racial authenticity haunts the work of more current black critics of the vernacular. Thus even aestheticians like Houston Baker, Jr., and Henry Louis Gates, Jr., who explicitly seek to distinguish their post-structuralist accounts of the vernacular from those forwarded by black nationalists inadvertently reproduce their masculinism.

In its focus on literary ideology and literary representations, *Writing Manhood in Black and Yellow* argues for a re-thinking of the interdisciplinarity that has long been a hallmark of ethnic studies. As an "interdiscipline," ethnic studies sets itself against the methodological parochialisms of more traditionally defined disciplines;[15] it tends toward Geertzian "thick descriptions" of the racialized fabric of culture that intermingle the modes of analysis practiced in both the humanities and the social sciences. Many studies therefore tend to place a varied assortment of texts side by side, as it were, pointing out the common cultural logic they engage with. But while a federal law, a Supreme Court decision, an autobiography, a novel, and a Hollywood film might all negotiate the same underlying cultural *logic*, it does not necessarily follow that they are attempts to exercise the same modality of cultural *power*. The danger with the prevailing mode of cultural criticism is that it risks a certain ahistoricizing leveling of discourses. To recognize that writers of color are seeking to effect specifically *literary* interventions in the politics of race—as my study does—is not to resuscitate a politically regressive aesthetic ideology whose collusion with an oppressive history of racism and colonialism is well documented. It is, on the contrary, to produce a more historically sensitive account of the particular kinds of interventions in race politics that authors attempt to engage in through their works—to engage directly with the specific form of cultural power they believe they are appropriating through the act of writing literature.[16]

In order to arrive at a more precise understanding of the resistance-through-writing that these writers claim to engage in, it is helpful to consider Viet Thanh Nguyen's assertion in *Race and Resistance* that we should view Asian American cultural works from the perspective offered by the work of Pierre Bourdieu: Nguyen argues that Asian American writers and academics ought to be seen as operating within a social field in which "it is not economic capital, that is money and its investment, that matters as much as *symbolic* capital, other things besides money that we invest with value and which eventually generate an economic return."[17] This entails, in my view, investigating the terms in which writers depict the "symbolic capital" they believe themselves to gain through their literary interventions in the politics of race. For the writers I examine, this symbolic capital is tendered in the currency of aesthetics, masculinity, and desire.

By refocusing attention on the disciplinary specificity of this antiracist stance, this study reexamines from an interracial perspective what Henry Louis Gates, Jr., has described as "the onerous burden of literacy" that has played a determining role in the production of African American culture.[18] As Gates argues in "Literary Theory and the Black Tradition," the great emphasis that this tradition has placed on literacy and literature stems from the antiblack racism it sought to resist, an ideology that justified the dehumanizing treatment of Africans and African Americans by pointing to the purported nonexistence of African written languages; in this way, blacks were distinguished from "Asiatics" who had developed their written languages and literatures of their own. Writers like Ellison, Gates, and Baker have been able to remake this alleged condition of illiteracy into a kind of supraliteracy by stressing the capacity of African American writers to harness the power of a nonwritten form of cultural expression, a vernacular tradition exemplified by black music. A different "burden of literacy" has shaped the emergence of the Asian American tradition—a burden complicated by the success with which writers like Ellison had been able to codify a celebratory and resistant view of black vernacular expression. While purportedly the heirs of ancient civilizations that were—like those of the West—highly literate, Asians in the United States have generally been perceived as linguistically deficient—as non-native speakers whether they are foreign- or American-born—or as linguistically suspect. In dominant representations, as Elaine Kim has observed, "Asians either spoke English badly because they were slow and unable to grasp Western ways, or they spoke it with a flowery, almost unnatural fluency that was humorous or sinister."[19] What Asian American writers seem to face—to rework Gates's phrase—is an onerous burden of *fluency*. To such authors, the African American tradition provides a powerful model of emulation, but it also throws into relief a certain linguistic lack. For Asian Americans, unlike African Americans, have not been regarded as having developed the kind of vernacular traditions in the United States that could fortify claims to an ethnically distinct form of supraliteracy. These are the kinds of dilemmas, I contend, that must be explored in order to understand how the forms of antiracist resistance that writers of color claim to engage in through their writing might foster an antagonistic rather than collaborative sense of interracialism.

While my book does not engage directly with the multiculturalism that the advent of ethnic studies approaches has provoked, its focus on the literary politics of race from an interracial perspective—and the politics of interracialism from a literary perspective—does suggest that existing progressive critiques of this development require some supplementation. One particularly cogent and persuasive critique of what has been called "weak" or "official" multiculturalism is offered by Lisa Lowe in *Immigrant Acts*:

> Although the concept of multiculturalism registers the pressures that increases of immigrant, racial, and ethnic populations bring to all spheres, these pressures are expressed only partially and inadequately in aesthetic representations; the production of multiculturalism instead diffuses the demands of material differentiation through the homogenization, aestheticization, and incorporation of signifiers of ethnic differences.[20]

Lowe argues that multiculturalism "levels the important differences and contradictions within and among racial and ethnic minority groups according
to the discourse of pluralism." From this vantage point, "African, Asian, and
Latino cultures all become equally 'other,' are metaphorized as equally
different and whole without contradiction."[21] Obscured then are "the profound and urgent gaps, the inequalities and conflicts, among racial, ethnic,
and immigrant groups."[22] A parallel critique is offered by David Palumbo-
Liu in his introduction to a volume of essays entitled *The Ethnic Canon*.
Palumbo-Liu expresses his deep suspicion about the way in which a "an ethnic literary canon" has been incorporated into college courses: certain exemplary texts are presented "as authentic, unmediated representations of ethnicity" that students are then encouraged to read within the protocols of
traditional literary criticism; such "readings produce a mystified 'understanding' of difference that restabilizes the individual momentarily disori-
ented by this encounter with this Other," thereby reducing ethnic difference
to a category of the sublime.[23] These critics suggest that the politically qui-
escent subject that multiculturalism tends to interpellate is defined by a consumerism and an aestheticism.

While such critiques address how official multiculturalism can work to
depoliticize the study of race and ethnicity by rendering different cultures
into aesthetic commodities that are all "equally 'other'" and "equally different and whole," they need also to confront the fact that in the aesthetic
marketplace of U.S. multiculturalism—like any other marketplace—some
commodities are more equal than others. As multiculturalism brings into
view a range of racial groups, one of "the important differences within and
among them" that it might *exacerbate* rather than level is the comparatively
greater amount of symbolic value that African American culture possesses
vis-à-vis other minority cultures. For in the ethnic canon that multiculturalism inaugurates, African American texts do not simply occupy one place
among many but in fact take pride of place.

By pointing this out, I am not simply restating the need to think outside
the constraints of "the black-white binary" or lamenting how it marginalizes
Asian American concerns; rather, I am arguing that the justifiable centrality
of African American issues coupled with the idea of culture that multiculturalism enshrines can incite rather than suppress interracial conflict, tension, and opposition. For if the multicultural canon tends, as Palumbo-Liu
argues, to "mimic and reproduce the ideological underpinnings of the dom-

inant canon,"[24] then the idea of culture it proposes may not simply be the assimilative ideal of the ethnic melting pot or the homogenously heterogeneous ideal of cultural pluralism; it may in fact resemble the conception of the "Tradition" as construed by cultural conservatives from Matthew Arnold to T. S. Eliot to Harold Bloom. For these aesthetic ideologues, "inclusion" in the canon can only be gained through an agonistic struggle with those who are already deemed to be in it. This idea of writing is not only compatible with but also encouraged by the multiculturalist agenda. For the culture it envisions as a marketplace is one in which the aesthetic artifacts of different racial communities are not only placed side by side but must actively compete for consumers.

This competitive antagonism is also embedded in the aesthetic ideologies of the two male writers I study in this book, both of whom are ensconced in the "canon" of ethnic studies. Like many other writers of color, in fact, Ellison and Chin are wholly invested in the notion that what makes a writer original and not merely derivative—what makes him an "authentic" artist— is the power with which he reworks the cultural materials he has inherited, however ambivalent a resource they may be. In examining how this aesthetic posture structures the antiracist politics of Ellison and Chin, I am not simply pointing out the homophobia and masculinism that subtends it; I am arguing that this agonism is an aestheticized version of the "homosexual" desire that white racism allegedly engenders in men of color, and I am also exploring how it tends to incite a competitive antagonism among and between African and Asian Americans.

Having described the materials I treat in this study and sketched out its overall argument, I want to underscore the fact that the masculinist conception of writing-as-resistance that I examine in this study is one that is clearly nationalist in character. While scholars in a range of U.S.-centered fields have in recent years engaged in the crucial work of drawing attention to the emergence of transnational and diasporic cultural formations and the increasingly globalized character of late capitalism, few would argue that nationalism or the nation-state has somehow lost its determining force, here or elsewhere. Indeed, recent events have made abundantly clear the persistent willingness of nationalist subjects to die for their countries and to kill for them. This is by no means to question the recent scholarly interest in globalization, transnationalism, and diaspora, but simply to register my belief that nationalist imaginings of community—not to mention the economic and military power of nation-states—still shape the workings of history and should thus remain important objects of study. The arguments of this book would take a different shape, to be sure, if it were also claiming to address writings that espoused a more diasporic outlook. But while the need certainly exists for, say, a comparative study of racialized masculinities in the Asian and African diasporas, this book is not an attempt at such a study. As in any scholarly work, the force of its arguments is directed at the materials it addresses, materials that have not been looked at together in any existing study. The hope that animates it, however, is that its findings will prove useful to scholars whose own interests in the cultural politics of race, gender, and sexuality are directed toward archives different than the ones I examine here.

Writing Manhood in Black and Yellow

Introduction

While the body of the black man has long been a focal point of the racial imaginary in the United States, the body of the Asian man has tended to figure as a kind of absence. Richard Fung describes this difference in the following terms: "whereas Fanon tells us, 'the Negro is eclipsed. He is turned into a penis. He *is* a penis,' the Asian man is defined by a striking absence down there. And if Asian men have no sexuality, how can we have homosexuality?"[1] This absence is discernible, Fung argues, in the two kinds of images of the Asian man that appear in North American popular culture: "the egghead/wimp" and "the kung fu master/ninja samurai."[2] The first denies Asian male corporeality *in toto*, and the second only recognizes a body enveloped in "a desexualized Zen asceticism."[3] Even within the domain of gay pornography, an industry that trades on the hypersexualization of male bodies and the fantasies associated with them, Fung finds "narratives [that] always privilege the penis while assigning the Asian the role of bottom; Asian and anus are conflated."[4] David L. Eng takes Fung's assertion as his point of departure in his book-length study of Asian American masculinity, arguing that the subjectivities of Asian men in the United States take shape in relation to a racist imaginary that effects a *racial castration*.[5]

These studies by Eng and Fung offer illuminating insights into the construction of Asian American masculinity, some of which I echo and amplify in this book; their mono-racial focus, however, leaves unexamined the black-Asian interracialism that initiates their inquiry. While Fung freely acknowledges that his own axiomatic formulation—"Asian and anus are conflated"—

emerges from an engagement with the work of Frantz Fanon, he and Eng do not explore how the dominant presence of certain images of black masculinity throws into relief the Asian American absence they examine. This book addresses directly the complex interplay between these overlapping and often conflicting representations of racialized masculinity, bringing into focus the interracialism earlier studies have left unaddressed. To engage in a comparative analysis of this sort requires mediating between two approaches: the first involves recognizing, as Fung does, key differences in how black and Asian masculinities are shaped by white racism's identificatory dictates; the second involves identifying certain points of convergence, teasing out certain strands of what David Lloyd and Abdul JanMohamed have termed "minority discourse." Although I later elaborate on the differences that Fung points us toward, I want to begin by identifying the commonalities.

The origins of "minority discourse," according to David Lloyd and Abdul JanMohamed, are to be found in the "damage" that racism inflicts on minoritized subjects: "we must realize that minority discourse is, in the first instance, the product of damage—of damage more or less systematically inflicted on cultures by the dominant culture."[6] But as a discourse, minority discourse is not only "the product of damage," but also the narratives, symbols, images, and so forth that subjects of color might use to give representational shape to that "damage."[7] In the masculinist fictions I examine in this study, I locate a particular strain of minority discourse in the gendered and sexualized rhetoric that men of color use to underscore racism's dehumanizing effects. I identify a more or less unified set of interpretive narratives that African American and Asian American writers have relied upon to depict the psychic damage inflicted by racism. Embedded in these narratives are a whole host of metaphors that are used to crystallize racism's injurious effects: metaphors of division, feminization, and homosexualization. I place particular emphasis on a highly disturbing figuration of male homosexuality—a homophobic symbolism that proves to be at once quite malleable and precise, that functions, in fact, to give a kind of aesthetic and analytic coherence to the works I examine.

I also identify a second, closely related strand of minority discourse that figures the literary realm as a utopian site in which the un-manning damage done by racism can be reversed. I map the features of a highly masculinist *literary* identity politics that is espoused by both African American and Asian American writers. In order to delineate this discursive element, I focus on claims authors themselves make about the nature of the liberation to be gained via the aesthetic—claims that I locate in their writings *on* literature rather than in their literary writings. I do not imply that these writers succeed in becoming the racially "authentic" and wholly virile subjects they present themselves to be; rather, I analyze the paradigmatic fantasies they spin out about the "authentic" form of racialized manhood that they believe the act of writing literature enables them to personify.

In this introductory chapter, I delineate the various elements of the interconnected rhetorics of race, writing, and manhood mobilized by both African and Asian American writers. But in so doing, I explicitly acknowledge the temporal and ideological priority of *black* meditations on the central issues this book explores, a priority that Fung himself registers through his reference to Fanon. So, in this study as in his, Fanon comes first. The considerable interest that has surrounded Fanon's work in the past fifteen years or so—an interest that has centered mainly on *Black Skin, White Masks*—has come from a wide range of theoretical and critical contexts: postcolonial studies, queer studies, African American studies, and, to an extent, Asian American studies. Since Fanon's work is inextricably linked with psychoanalytic approaches that address the interaction between the racial and sexual aspects of subject-formation—an approach that my own study shares—it provides a useful point of entry into the problematics that I address here. I therefore turn first to a selective reading of *Black Skin, White Masks* in order to begin elucidating the theoretical infrastructure, as it were, of this book.

Fanon: Some Axioms

"Dirty Nigger!" Or simply, "Look, A Negro!". . .

On that day, completely dislocated, unable to be abroad with the other, the white man, I took myself far from my own presence, far indeed, and made myself an object. What else could it be for me but an amputation, an excision, a hemorrhage that spattered my whole body with black blood? But I did not want this division, this thematization. All I wanted was to be a man among other men. I wanted to come lithe and young into a world that was ours and to help to build it together.

—Frantz Fanon[8]

Scenarios like this one abound in *Black Skin, White Masks*. Indeed much of the interest that has surrounded this work in recent years stems, according to Stuart Hall, from "the association it establishes between racism and what has come to be called the scopic drive—the eroticization of the pleasure in looking and the primary place given in Fanon's text to the 'look' from the place of the 'Other.'"[9] Because of the attention that Fanon gives to racism's scopic regime, his writings are often cited as evidence for the ways in which the binary of racial difference derives its discursive shape from that of sexual difference. Lee Edelman, for instance, has argued that Fanon's rendering of white racism's visual logic suggests "a borrowing from—and a repositioning of—the scopic logic on which the prior assertion of sexual difference depends."[10]

In the passage above Fanon likens the experience of being subjected to the "look" of white racism to "an amputation, an excision." As a consequence of the interpellative hails that accompany the visual apprehension of a subject as black—"Dirty Nigger!" "Look, a Negro!"—what was hidden "in" the body is forced, figuratively speaking, to come "out"; the "hemorrhage" that results is one that "spatter[s]" the "whole body with black blood." This seeing and naming marks the body as black and as bloodied simultaneously, conflating identity with injury. To be captured by this "look" is not simply to be wounded; it is also to have one's being reduced to the wound that black identity is.

While Fanon is not anatomically specific in his evocation of this "amputation," it seems clear that he is suggesting a kind of castration. He does, after all, employ an autobiographical and consequently male persona in this passage. There is, moreover, the legacy of lynching, those rituals of racist brutality in which the castration of black men played a prominent part, that looms behind this passage. By invoking this practice, Fanon locates a subjective correlative to those male bodies dismembered and slaughtered by lynch mobs in the psyches of all black men who confront the "look" of white racism and find themselves crushed by its weight, reduced to the status of objects.

Rendered axiomatically, the claim that emerges from this passage can be put this way: *whites look at blacks in much the same way that men look at women.* The alterity that the black body signifies in the scopic regime of racial difference would presumably bear some resemblance to the alterity that the woman's body signifies in the scopic regime of sexual difference. But the fact that *Black Skin, White Masks* (like the texts my study as a whole centers on) is a deeply masculinist and homosocial text, a slight modification of this axiom is in order.[11] We might refine this claim as follows: *that white men look at black men in much the same way that men look at women—as bodies whose alterity is signaled by the wounds of castration they bear.* The black *male* experience Fanon renders, then, is one of being looked at as a body that has been castrated by the white male Other who looks—of being, in a sense, castrated by the looking itself.[12]

The psychic damage that racism inflicts on the black man, however, does not simply consist of being subjected to an emasculating racial "look" localized in white male subjects, for Fanon insists that this "look" provides the standpoint from which the black man comes to know himself. "On that day," Fanon writes, "I took myself far from my own presence, far indeed, and made myself an object." The "I" Fanon describes has taken epistemological shape through an identification with the "look" of the white man whom he is no longer able to "be abroad with." This "I," then, is the trace of a white male other that has been taken in, as it were, and become the perspective from which the black subject comes to see himself as "an object." This "I" is no longer able to see himself as "a man among other men," as possessed of a body "lithe and young." Rather, he sees himself as housed in a body that has been "amputated" and "spattered with black[ening] blood." He sees himself as "completely dislocated," as "division," as a subject lacking closure—lacking the wholeness and monadic integrity, the autonomous and autotelic sense of self that is imagined to be the sovereign birthright of white men.

Detectable here are resonances of the "to-be-looked-at-ness" that is, from the vantage point of classic psychoanalysis, a defining characteristic of normative feminine subjectivity, signaling as it does the "internalization" of a masculine "look." These resonances further affirm racism's emasculating effects. Indeed the intra-subjective alterity Fanon describes through this figure of "division" can be mapped along both axes of difference, sexual and racial. From the perspective of gender, this subject is unable to be a man because he is unable to be wholly himself—for his selfhood is divided from within, hollowed out by an epistemological identification with a white *male* Other, whose internalized and intransigent alterity monumentalizes the fractured state of his identity. From the perspective of race, the persistence "within" of that very same *white* male Other likewise marks an identity that can never be whole—can never be racially "pure," in other words, consigned as it is to the shadowy liminality of an injurious hybridity.

It would be possible to marshal the resemblances that Fanon underscores between the visual economies that underwrite racial and sexual difference towards a kind of analysis that would, in effect, identify the fundamental interarticulation of misogyny and racism, thus suturing together a feminist politics and an antiracist one. It would also be possible to extend the Lacanian trajectory of Fanon's text in order to suggest that the lack, the division, the self-alterity, and the hybridity that the man of color is forced to exemplify is actually a psychic condition that is shared, though differently, by both colonizer and colonized—to make of Fanon, as Benita Parry has characterized Homi Bhabha as doing, "a premature poststructuralist," or, as Hall puts it, "a sort of Lacanian *avant la lettre.*"[13]

These are not the ends, however, toward which Fanon directs his insights. It is important to keep in mind, as Hall reminds us, that the condition of the man of color as Fanon describes it is "a 'pathological' condition, forced on the black subject of colonialism" (27); it has, moreover, "the political question of *how to end this alienation* inscribed in it. Fanon cannot, politically, 'live with this ambivalence,' since it is the ambivalence that is killing him!" (27).[14] As Fanon himself puts it, quite plainly, "*I did not want* this division, this thematization."

The "thematization" that Fanon illustrates—which establishes a relationship of equivalence between black men and women—is one he also rejects. The image of himself that the black man has internalized, which has taken shape through an identification with the white man's "look," Fanon presents as the effect of a *faulty* optics of racial vision—a vision that *mis*construes the stigmata of racial difference as being comparable to those of sexual difference. As Fanon deploys the image of castration to evoke the condition of the man of color, he emphasizes the unnaturalness, the perversity, of that imposition. He accentuates, in other words, the disjuncture between the *figure* of castration, which he uses to evoke the psychic condition of the man of color under racism, and the "intactness" of the black male body, which is erroneously being seen as Other. (The "whole" body Fanon describe as his own is not *literally* "amputat[ed]," but only appears so when apprehended from the perspective of white racism.) While the man of color—"lithe and young," "a man among other men"—is anatomically endowed with the preeminent signifier of manhood and all that would seem to entail, he has been mistakenly and unjustly denied access to the prerogatives that ought to be his in a social order whose patriarchal and homosocial character is taken for granted.

To the extent that freedom in Fanon's text is framed in masculinist and homosocial terms, as Terry Goldie has observed, his focus remains on racism's devastating effects on men of color. As such, colonial racism is vilified as a structure that depends upon and seeks to maintain an unequal distribution of patriarchal privilege. By using this figure of castration to measure the extent of injury that colonial racism inflicts on black men, Fanon makes use of a regulative standard that is calibrated as much by gender as it is by race. Preventing the black man from enjoying an equal share of the patriarchal dispensation is the particular form of misrecognition to which he is subjected and to which he subjects himself.

Fanon shares with the two U.S. writers who are the primary focus of this book the sense that racism's most pernicious effect is to deny men of color the prerogatives that ought to be theirs as men—those privileges that ought to be their sexual birthright in a social order whose homosocial and patriarchal nature is taken for granted. Like Fanon, Ralph Ellison and Frank Chin correlate the injurious effects of racism with its tendency to align the man of color with femininity. They both seek to elucidate the ways in which white men perceive and treat the man of color as both a racial and sexual Other. The attention that Ellison and Chin give to the racist "look" tends to localize it—as does Fanon—in the interracial homosocial regard of white men. Moreover, despite the disparities in the specific traits assigned to black and Asian men respectively (differences that are to some degree historically variable, as my study will show), what links these writers is their outrage at the fact that their racial difference from white men is apprehended as analogous to a sexual difference—that black and Asian men, however distinctly, are perceived and treated by white men in ways that are comparable to the ways in which men perceive and treat women.

Ellison and Chin also share with Fanon a broadly Freudian understanding of *why* it is that white men (mis)perceive men of color in the way they do. All of these writers suggest that if racism seeks to emasculate and feminize men of color, this reflects the fact that they are forced to function under racism as objects that satisfy the sadistic and erotic desires of white men. Homosocial forms of white male racism are presented, in other words, as having a fundamentally homoerotic component. The texts I examine emphasize this homoeroticism by rendering white racism equivalent to homosexuality.

As various commentators have noted, this logic is very much apparent in the sixth chapter of *Black Skin, White Masks*, in which Fanon attempts to demonstrate that "the Negrophobic man is a repressed homosexual" (156).[15] Fanon makes this assertion in two different ways. First of all, he stresses how the black man functions as a kind of specular object for the white man. Fanon describes the "Negro myth" as containing within it those aspects of the white male self that have undergone repression, or been abjected: pre-eminent among these—and thrown into prominent relief by the white fixation with the black penis—are the biological, the sexual, and the genital:

> Every intellectual gain requires a loss in sexual potential. The civilized
> white man retains an irrational longing for unusual eras of sexual license,
> of orgiastic scenes, of unpunished rapes, of unrepressed incest. In one way
> these fantasies respond to Freud's life instinct. Projecting his own desires on
> to the Negro, the white man behaves "as if" the Negro really had them. . . .
> To suffer from a phobia of Negroes is to be afraid of the biological. For the
> Negro is only biological. (165)

Elsewhere Fanon writes: "In the remotest depth of the European unconscious an inordinately black hollow has been made in which the most immoral impulses, the most shameful desires lie dormant" (190). Lying in this hollow is the imago that Fanon terms "the biological-sexual-sensual-genital-nigger" (202). It is the erotic aspect of the white man's disavowed identification with the qualities he ascribes to this "nigger" that inspires, according to Fanon, both fear and sexual desire.

Alongside this depiction of the white man's homosexual desire, which underscores its identificatory aspect, is another that places emphasis on the sadism of white male racist practices:

> Still on the genital level, when a white man hates black men, is he not
> yielding to a feeling of impotence or of sexual inferiority? Since his ideal
> is an infinite virility, is there not a phenomenon of diminution in relation
> to the Negro, who is viewed as a penis symbol? Is the lynching of the
> Negro not a sexual revenge? We know how much of sexuality there is
> in all cruelties, tortures, beatings. One has only to reread a few pages of
> the Marquis de Sade to be easily convinced of the fact. (159)

In Fanon's text, homosexuality figures, on the one hand, as an ambivalent mimetic desire for the abjected aspects of the white male racial self and, on the other, as a sexualized sadistic pleasure that is gained through the inflicting of "cruelties, tortures, beatings" on other men. That Fanon's "outing" of the "homosexual" desire animating homosocial racism is accompanied by a homophobic revulsion is quite clear. Near the end of chapter 6, Fanon addresses himself directly to Michel Salomon—a French physician who had described "that aura of sensuality that [the Negro] gives off" (qtd. in Fanon, 201)—with the following statement: "M. Salomon, I have a confession to make to you: I have never been able, without revulsion, to hear a *man* say of another man: 'He is so sensual!' I do not know what the sensuality of a man is" (201–2).

Addressing such representations places critics who see their work as animated by both antiracist and antihomophobic concerns in a difficult position. One reader of Fanon who has responded productively to his treatment of homosexuality in *Black Skin, White Masks* is Diana Fuss. In her book *Identification Papers*, she argues that Fanon's homophobia, as well as his "resolutely masculine self-identifications," should be read as *reactive* and historically situated as a response that "take[s] shape over and against colonialism's castrating representations of black male sexuality."[16] She further identifies a more specific "refusal" in Fanon's equation of whiteness with homosexuality: "an implicit rejection of the 'primitive = invert' equation that marks the confluence of evolutionary anthropology and sexology and their combined influence on early twentieth-century psychoanalysis."[17]

Fuss's suggestions invite us to read such representations as attempting to negate and reverse white racism's emasculating effects by insisting that it is the white man whose manhood is more severely compromised by the homosocial relations engendered by racism. What is perverse, in other words, about racism is not just that it forces men of color to adopt a feminized position, but also that it institutes a hierarchical form of homosociality that enables white men to indulge, in Fanon's terms, "the most immoral impulses, the most shameful desires." If the taxonomical trajectory of racist discourse reduces the man of color to a certain *racial* type—the essence of which is encapsulated by those marks of alterity that his body bears—this trajectory is reversed in these representations that similarly reduce the racist white man to a certain *sexual* type.

Versions of this homophobic symbolism that renders white racism equivalent to homosexuality will prove vital, as I will establish in later chapters, to the literary projects in which Ralph Ellison and Frank Chin are engaged. This particular anatomization of white male desire provides *Invisible Man* with its basic narrative structure and comprises the core of its symbolic economy; a modified, more *multi*racial version of this imagery structures Chin's assertions concerning the ways in which racist popular texts cater to both the sexual and racist fantasies of white men. My own approach to Ellison's and Chin's works—like Fuss's in regards to Fanon's—will likewise stress their reactive character. The "resolutely masculine self-identifications" and the homophobic equation of the white man with homosexuality that Fuss identifies in *Black Skin, White Masks* will be evident in their works as well; and their writings also take shape "over and against" certain "castrating representations" of racial difference.

I will not be treating this symbolism as *merely* reactive, however. What is unsettling about these representations, I contend, is not just the homophobia that structures them; it is also that this homophobia proves crucial to the analytical insights they offer into the libidinal economy of homosocial racism. These texts "out" the eroticism that underwrites the hierarchical forms of homosociality that racism engenders. But in so doing, they demonstrate how disturbingly apt a signifier homosexuality is for the "perverse" forms of white male desire that racist practices satisfy. In Fanon's writings as well as Ellison's, homosexuality signifies both the specular and identificatory desires that white men harbor for black men and also the sadistic desires that they satisfy through "cruelties, tortures, beatings."

It is necessary to emphasize at this point that the white male desire Fanon vilifies in *Black Skin, White Masks* is an *interracial* homosocial desire. As such, it would seem that the palpable disgust with which he renders it—"I have never been able, without revulsion, to hear a *man* say of another man: 'He is so sensual!' I do not know what the sensuality of a man is" (201)—finds expression, in inverted form, in the paeans to the emancipatory potential of interracial fraternity that punctuate this text. Indeed, passages like the one below seem to confirm the truism that the most homophobic writings tend to be those that are the most steeped in male homosocial desire:

> On the field of battle, its four corners marked by the scores of Negroes being hanged by their testicles, a monument is slowly being built that promises to be majestic.
>
> And at the top of this monument, I can already see a white man and a black man *hand in hand*. (222; emphasis Fanon's)

Fanon's investment in the possibility of a more equitable and utopian homosociality between black and white men is also apparent from the pedagogic imperative that structures *Black Skin, White Masks*: his intent, in part, is "to show the white man that he is at once the perpetrator and the victim of a delusion" (225). The "delusion" that Fanon wishes to makes readers like M. Salomon confront and free themselves of is the interracial "homosexual" desire they harbor for the black man. Indeed, it is a mutual recognition between white man and black that marks the utopian telos toward which *Black Skin, White Masks* (much like *Invisible Man*) moves—and this despite the fact that the vast bulk of this text is devoted to anatomizing the psychic conditions that prevent such a recognition from taking place. Fanon's desire, after all, is "to be a man among other men. . . . to come lithe and young into a world that was ours and to help to build it together."

The representations I examine in this study evince a similarly profound if acutely ambivalent allegiance to this ideal of interracial fraternity that is directly proportional to their denigration of homosocial couplings that express this ideal in a radically desublimated form. What is apparent in them, in other words, is a version of the now familiar binary that Eve Kosofsky Sedgwick, in her landmark study *Between Men*, has identified as crucial to the formation and maintenance of heteronormative masculinity: the discrete distinction between homosexual and homosocial forms of same-sex desire.[18] In the texts I consider, however, this binary is used for racially specific purposes, to distinguish the perverse forms of masculinity and interracial homosocial desire that racism fosters from the more utopian forms that might emerge if white men were able to recognize themselves as, in Fanon's words, "the perpetrator[s] and the victim[s] of a delusion."

That the primary subject of this book is the work of two *writers* is not, however, incidental; the domain of literature does not assume a central place here merely because it offers a particularly illuminative perspective on a more pervasive cultural logic. For as a study of the literary ideologies that can sub-tend an antiracist politics it seeks to bring into critical focus the persistent and seductive belief that the domain of the aesthetic enables a measure of mobil-ity and freedom from the repressive constructions of minoritized masculine identity that prevail in a racist social order. It is the perspective afforded by the aesthetic that is imagined as providing a stable epistemic standpoint from which debilitating forms of interracial male homosociality can be distin-guished from those that are emancipatory, and from which compromised forms of racialized manhood can be distinguished from those that are "whole" and "authentic." We can turn once again to *Black Skin, White Masks* for a paradigmatic assertion of this aesthetic sentiment. For Fanon locates in the domain of art the kind of intersubjective vision that would enable men on either side of the racial and colonial divide to see each other as men:

> The eye is not merely a mirror, but a correcting mirror. The eye should make it possible for us to correct cultural errors. I do not say the eyes, I say the eye, and there is no mystery about what that eye refers to; not to the crevice in the skull but to that very uniform light that wells out of the reds of Van Gogh, that glides through a concerto of Tschaikowsky, that fastens itself desperately to Schiller's Ode to Joy, that allows itself to be conveyed by the worm-ridden bawling of Césaire. (202)

It is the mediating gaze afforded by the aesthetic, Fanon contends, that makes it possible for men of different races to see each other truly, that corrects for the distortions produced by the optics of racism. The more utopian and equitable form of interracial homosociality that Fanon celebrates is thus linked with a virtual visuality that the aesthetic enables—a more "authentic" optics of homosocial recognition. This vision is discernible in the works of certain European artists like Van Gogh, Tschaikowsky, and Schiller; it is also "conveyed," however, "by the worm-ridden bawling of Césaire." This racially hybrid canon of artists—all male—fleshes out in the aesthetic sphere a version of the fraternity he imagines emerging in the political sphere after a revolutionary transformation of the colonial order: "at the top of this monument, I can already see a white man and a black man *hand in hand*."

The gesture that Fanon makes in the passage above toward the utopian potential of art is more fully fleshed out in the writings of Ralph Ellison and Frank Chin, as later chapters of this study will make clear. The domain of literature, as these writers conceive of it, promises a measure of freedom from the perverse forms of interracial homosociality that racism engenders—a homosociality that allows white men to indulge their "most immoral impulses, the most shameful desires" vis-à-vis men of color, and that effects an emasculating identification of men of color with femininity. The division that Ellison and Chin posit between a racist and feminizing social order and the virilizing utopian elsewhere of art, then, might justifiably be seen as a reworking of "The Great Divide" that Andreas Huyssen has identified as a cornerstone of modernist aesthetic ideology.[19] Indeed, the agonistic impulses operant in modernist texts, which claim their "cultural authority by opposing themselves to practices and spaces disparaged as feminine,"[20] are apparent in Ellison's and Chin's aesthetic writings as well. The aesthetic postures that Ellison and Chin adopt, in other words, recapitulate, to a certain extent, the oppositional stance taken by male writers who are more conventionally thought of as modernist. But while this study will call attention to this ideological borrowing, my intent is not to enter into critical debates about the categorization or periodization of modernism as a literary movement—the issue of whether Ellison or Chin should or should not be considered modernist is not of primary concern here. By suggesting how certain modernist arguments comprise a component of the ideological framework that structures these writers' codifications of aesthetic, racial, and masculine authenticity, however, I am attempting to situate their writings in a broader cultural context. I am also seeking to emphasize the ways in which the racial and sexual identity politics that Ellison and Chin espouse articulate themselves as a *literary* identity politics.

In order then to clarify further the features of the identities that Ellison and Chin champion as "authentic," I want to re-orient the issues I have thus far been discussing around the term *hybridity*, for it constitutes a key component of the racial, sexual, and literary rhetorics I will be exploring. The issue of hybridity, as Robert J. C. Young has argued, has always been at the core of modern conceptions of race. Since this term's original meaning in racial discourse had to do with the progeny produced by interracial heterosexual unions, it testifies to the fact that "Theories of race were [and are] always covert theories of desire."[21] While Young insists that "hybridity as a cultural description will always carry with it an implicit politics of heterosexuality,"[22] in the representations I consider here it is framed much more prominently as an issue of homosocial desire.

Hybridity performs a central function in Fanon's depiction of the wounded and fissured subjectivity of the black man as it has been shaped by the scopic regime of white racism. It is, after all, a white male "look" that has, in a sense, been grafted onto the psyche of the black man that provides the perspective from which he comes to see himself as an object—that causes him to see himself as "amputated" and "spattered with black[ening] blood." As such, the epistemological violence that white racism wreaks upon the black man is registered by Fanon as the imposition of an injurious racial hybridity. Hybridity is also central to Fanon's depiction of the Negrophobic man as a "repressed homosexual." After all, this figure's homoerotic attraction to the black man—an attraction that is, in part, mimetic, and that reduces the black man to a specular object—is presented by Fanon as a hybrid desire: a desire to have those "black" qualities that the white man has abjected—those qualities possessed in abundance by the "biological-sexual-sensual-genital-nigger"—re-grafted, as it were, to the white male self.

But if Fanon thus links hybridity to the "inauthentic" forms of masculine consciousness that are characteristic of the colonial racist regime he subjects to critique in *Black Skin, White Masks,* this does not lead him to embrace, by contrast, a notion of racial purity. His ambivalence toward *negritude* is well documented and clearly expressed in *Black Skin, White Masks.* Also apparent is his commitment to an intellectual syncretism—to a different modality of hybridity expressed through his deployment of Adler, Freud, Hegel, Sartre, and so forth. There is, finally, the hybrid canon of artists he invokes to suggest the utopian possibility of aesthetic vision: Van Gogh, Tschaikowsky, Schiller, and Césaire.

Ellison and Chin similarly distinguish between different modalities of racial hybridity. They, like Fanon, suggest that it is the homosexual hybrid desire of white men that gives racism its perverse structure, that engenders the potential feminization of men of color. And the desire that they install at the heart of the aesthetic subject they prize is also, I will be arguing, a hybrid and homosocial desire, though it is one driven by a violent and appropriative impulse that is, for them, quintessentially virile. The desire that animates the literary subjectivity they champion, in other words, is an aestheticized version of the *hybrid* desire that animates the "homosexual" white male racist—but it is one that has been appropriated, re-directed against its source, and submitted to a disciplined regime of aesthetic hygiene.

While I have been, to this point, identifying certain axiomatic assertions of Fanon that resonate in the writings of Ellison and Chin, I want now to call attention to a certain crucial difference. Fanon's depiction of the white male racist as a "repressed homosexual" does not lead him to suggest that the man of color is thereby threatened with becoming homosexual himself. Rather, he contends that homosexuality among the colonized is a virtual impossibility. For the writers who are the primary subject of this study, by contrast, the homosexual of color comprises a central point of concern.

Fanon does devote considerable attention in *Black Skin, White Masks* to the sexual neuroses that afflict the colonized, but these are always rendered as diseased expressions of a *hetero*sexual hybrid desire. He anatomizes in successive chapters a pathological desire for whiteness—which he terms a desire for "lactification"—which can take the form of a black male fixation with white women or a black female fixation with white men; it apparently does not manifest itself, however, as a fixation with white objects of the same sex. While Fanon discusses in some detail the racially perverse yet sexually normative desires that colonialism engenders in black men and women, his discussion of black male same-sex desire is consigned to a single footnote in the sixth chapter that seems to deny its existence, or at least its significance.[23] It might be ventured that Fanon's inability to acknowledge the possibility of black male homosexuality may have everything to do with the fervency of the interracial homosocial desire that propels the writing of *Black Skin, White Masks*. The desire he cannot seem to name is, after all, a sexualized version of the desire that frames his lyrical evocations of a homosocial postcolonial future: "I can already see a white man and a black man *hand in hand*."

But while the black homosexual is thus disturbingly erased in *Black Skin, White Masks*, this figure features quite prominently in the works of a generation of African American writers who were greatly influenced by Fanon—writers like Amiri Baraka and Eldridge Cleaver who allied themselves with black nationalism. As Henry Louis Gates, Jr., has noted, homophobia constitutes "an almost obsessive motif that runs through the major authors of the Black Aesthetic and the Black Power movements."[24] In part this homophobia expresses itself through characterizations of the racist white man that recapitulate Fanon's findings in the sixth chapter of *Black Skin, White Masks*. Baraka's 1965 essay "American Sexual Reference: Black Male," for example, begins with the infamous proclamation: "Most American white men are trained to be fags."[25] But some of these writers would extend Fanon's homophobic symbolism to suggest that *some* African American black men are "trained" by racism "to be fags" as well. According to Michele Wallace, it was Eldridge Cleaver who first introduced "the idea that black homosexuality was synonymous with reactionary Uncle Tomism," an assertion that she characterizes as "one of his most dubious contributions" to the ideology of Black Power.[26] In the next section of this introductory chapter, I will detail precisely how the rhetoric of inauthenticity deployed by Baraka and Cleaver renders the black homosexual "synonymous with reactionary Uncle Tomism."

The writings of black nationalist writers like Baraka and Cleaver provide a crucial relay point between the works of the two writers who are the central concern of this study, Ellison and Chin. While the ascendance of Black Power, as Darryl Pinckney has observed, "nearly buried [Ellison's] reputation" in the sixties and seventies, these writers actually espoused, as I will be demonstrating, quite similar aesthetic and political views.[27] What becomes obscured by Ellison's explicitly antagonistic relationship to black nationalism is the fact that he shared with his ideological opponents the view that racial and literary forms of "inauthenticity" were linked to non-normative forms of masculinity, hybridity, and interracial homosocial desire.

My analyses of the homophobic symbolism that subtends black nationalist discourse also provide a necessary preface to the analyses that I will be later offering of Frank Chin's writings. Gates suggests that the homophobia and misogyny apparent in the writings of the major black male authors of the late sixties and seventies reflect a wider convergence of racial and sexual discourses in cultural nationalism more broadly: "national identity became sexualized in the 1960s, in such a way as to engender a curious subterraneous connection between homophobia and nationalism."[28] This sexualization of national identity is very much in evidence in the work of Frank Chin, who spearheaded an Asian American literary movement that was clearly modeled on Black Arts. He was the primary ideological spokesperson for a group of Asian American male writers who sought, in the early seventies, to project a literary vision of *Yellow* Power, as it were, one that would not "fall(s) short of the vision Malcolm X and other blacks had for their 'minority.'"[29] While this ideological debt has been noted by critics, its complexities and its ramifications have not, I contend, been sufficiently explored. Indeed, I argue that this black-Asian interracialism—which reworks the central homophobic symbolism of black nationalism, and which has both emulatory and antagonistic elements—is crucial to understanding the sexual and literary politics of the Asian American cultural nationalism inaugurated by Chin's writings.

Figurations of the Homosexual in Black Nationalist Discourse: The "White Negro" and the "Eternal [Black] Faggot"

The ideological foundations of the cultural nationalism espoused by proponents of the Black Arts movement have been subjected to several cogent critiques over the past two decades. Feminist scholars have called attention to the misogyny and masculinism of black nationalist discourse. Drawing on the work of Paula Giddings and Michele Wallace, Madhu Dubey has observed that it was "the black man [who was presented] as the true subject of black nationalist discourse."[30] Black nationalists thus maintained that the emancipation of the black race as a whole would only be achievable through the liberation of the black man from the various structures that held him down. In their rhetoric, the black woman was often presented as "an obstacle between black men and their revolutionary future."[31] Such representations tend to echo the pathologizing view of black family life offered by the much-derided Moynihan Report: as Dubey notes, they cast "the black woman as an active agent of the black man's economic and social emasculation,"[32] blaming her, in effect, for wielding an inordinate and "unnatural" amount of matriarchal power—power that should have been patriarchal, and that should have been wielded by black men. The black woman was thus linked with two other figures maligned by Black Arts writers: "the white [male] bourgeois subject, and concomitantly, . . . the middle-class Negro [male] who, as a 'link between the slave and the new man,' had to be destroyed."[33] In *Are We Not Men?*, Harper adds another figure to the list of "Others" against which black nationalist discourse projected its idealized revolutionary black male subject—the black homosexual—thereby highlighting its homophobia along with its misogyny.

To the extent that a discourse of *gender* frames black nationalism's rendering of these four figures as "obstacle[s] between black men and their revolutionary future," they are depicted as agents who effect the emasculation of black men—who deny black men the patriarchal prerogatives that ought to be theirs as men. If these figures then comprise the "Others" of the revolutionary male subject posited by black nationalism, its rhetorical maneuvers can be read as attempts to identify and neutralize the threat of emasculation posed by each. A paradigmatic rhetorical strategy that black nationalist writers adopt, then, is to depict these figures in terms that stress the *femininity* they exemplify or should exemplify. Black women are thus exhorted to adopt a more "natural" subservient role, to serve as breeders and caretakers for the revolution—to, in a sense, re-feminize themselves.

When interpreted in terms that privilege the interarticulation of race and gender, it makes sense that the three *male* figures vilified by black nationalist discourse—the black male bourgeois subject, the white male bourgeois subject, and the homosexual—are depicted in similarly feminized terms. It makes further sense that the femininity of middle-class men, both black and white, would be asserted in black nationalist rhetoric through descriptions of such men as homosexual. Indeed, as Phillip Brian Harper notes, homosexuality is "the primary signifier" for "a failed manhood"; as such, "Black Arts judgments of insufficient racial identification" carried with them the charge that racially inauthentic—and inadequately virile—black men were, in reality or in effect, homosexual.[34]

In the following, I hope to supplement Harper's account of the homophobic symbolism that subtends the black nationalist rhetoric of authenticity by moving beyond its *gendered* significance and foregrounding the issues of *desire* and *racial hybridity* that are also inscribed in it. The black homosexuality disparaged by Amiri Baraka and Eldridge Cleaver involves not only a willful acceptance of the emasculation and feminization that racism seeks to effect, it also signals a sexualized capitulation to the intrasubjective racial "division"—the hybridity—that racism seeks to impose: it is expressive of an identity that lovingly accepts and embraces the white male other "within," an identity that takes what we might call its orificial shape through a cross-gender identification with a sexually receptive femininity. For the "failed manhood" and the "inadequately developed consciousness" of the figures vilified in this rhetoric are linked with a certain fantasmatic conception of the gay male body, which helps to explain the disturbing ease with which this body comes to function as an apt symbol for the injurious hybridity to which black men are subjected by white racism's identificatory dictates.[35]

To this extent, my analyses of this symbolism in this section seek primarily to extend the reach of Harper's analyses, placing emphasis on how rhetorically effective and figuratively complex this symbolism turns out to be. In the next section, as I trace Chin's translation of this homophobic symbolism from the African American context to the Asian American one, I will be highlighting the intensified sense of racial self-loathing that would seem to emerge from this borrowing. For the subject position occupied by the homosexual in black nationalist discourse—a figure defined by a certain modality of racial hybridity that locates him in a liminal space between black and white—approximates the subject position occupied by Asian American men: both the homosexual of color and the Asian man are, in other words, figured as "yellow" men, a catachresis that would seem to have a corrosive effect on the project of cultural nationalism that Chin espouses. But before I explore the shape that this borrowing takes, I need first to analyze in some detail the ideology that is being borrowed. I thus begin my analysis of the homophobia in black cultural nationalist rhetoric by focusing on Amiri Baraka's 1965 essay, "American Sexual Reference: Black Male," which begins with the notorious proclamation "Most American white men are trained to be fags" (216).[36]

*

The homosexuality that Baraka ascribes to white men in this essay is, in the main, a characteristic of middle-class white men. By "faggotry" he refers to an effete sterility, an alienation from physicality that afflicts the white male bourgeois subject. While such subjects may enjoy a virtual monopoly over patriarchal power as a result of their class-position, they are also, as a consequence, *feminized*, as they become increasingly distanced from their corporeal selves. Black men who thus emulate this model of empowerment—those who aspire to become middle-class—will meet the same fate as they are seeking a form of integration that is "merely [a] whitening to fit the white soul's image. It is also, for the black man, a weakening" (226).

But there is another dimension to the white man's "faggotry" as defined by Baraka, one that exceeds its function as a signifier of a compromised gender and class identity; it emerges through his discussion of those white men who seem to be most removed from the values of their compatriots—the beatniks, the "white Negroes" celebrated by Norman Mailer. According to Baraka, "the alienation syndrome" that defines the identities of most American white men "is most pronounced in the sensitive, the artists, etc., because what they claim as motive for their lives they try to understand as being separate from the rest of the culture" (219). The difference between the typical white man and the beatnik, then, is not one of kind but of degree. The white Negro does not in fact stand apart from the dominant culture he appears to rebel against, according to Baraka; rather, he merely makes manifest what is latent in the larger racial unconscious:

> For a man to be living in a certain social order, in fact, to have benefited by the order (and the filth of its image) and yet to have no connection with it is unrealistic in the extreme. The artist is the concentrate, as I said, of the society's tendencies—the extremist. And the most extreme form of alienation acknowledged within white society is homosexuality. The long abiding characterization of the Western artist does not seem out of place. (219)

Why this association of the Western artist with homosexuality is not "out of place" is apparently because the artist is self-consciously aware of and indeed gives lyrical expression to a deeply felt homosocial longing that other white men repress. What homosexuality then names is the *identificatory* desire for blackness that is explicitly expressed in texts like Jack Kerouac's *On the Road*:

> The beatnik longs for experience he understands is missing from his reality. Jack Kerouac's virtuous, mysterious, sensual black is drawn from his conscious/unconscious understanding that the white man is in evil withdrawal from the sweetest feelings in life. The beatnik or white Negro, as Mailer called them, wants out of the mainstream ofay world, and sees the Negro as the image of such alienation. (228–29)

The beatnik thus stands in roughly the same relation to the normative white male subject as the pervert does to the neurotic in Freud's *Three Essays on the Theory of Sexuality*: the former acts out (at least through his writing) the unconscious fantasies that the latter represses. There are obvious echoes here of Fanon's characterization of "the Negrophobic man [as] a repressed homosexual" (156): although the beatnik is a Negro*phile*, his desire—which is exemplified by Kerouac's desire for the "virtuous, mysterious, sensual black"—also bespeaks an "irrational longing for unusual eras of sexual license, of orgiastic scenes, of unpunished rapes, of unrepressed incest" (*Black Skin*, 165). This hybrid homosocial desire Baraka also finds exemplified by "a white boy Negroes on the Lower Eastside call Superspade, in honor of his dedication," who has wholly adopted the language, the gestures, and the clothing of urban blacks (228).

Interestingly, the white male figures Baraka discusses who exemplify the bohemian "faggotry" of the White Negro are never depicted as engaging in sex with black men. The desire in question here—to use the distinction that Freud makes in *Three Essays on the Theory of Sexuality* between the two components of the sexual instinct—seems to have a homosexual *object* (which corresponds to "the person from whom sexual attraction proceeds") but not a homosexual *aim* (which is "the act towards which the instinct tends").[37] Because the homosexuality that Baraka ascribes to a Kerouac or a Superspade is so focused on *object* rather than *aim*, it comes across as rather chaste, especially as his discussion of it is contained in an essay replete with detailed inventories of the *hetero*sexual white fantasies that subtend racism. The "homosexuality" of these artists or would-be artists is expressed not through carnal acts but rather through literary depictions of interracial longing (Kerouac) or through the adoption of black cultural styles (Superspade). The *virtual* quality, then, of the "homosexuality" typified by these figures seems to be explained by Baraka's contention that they embody "the most extreme form of [an] alienation" that is pervasive among white men—an alienation specifically from their biological and sexual selves. The white bohemian, in other words, like most white American men, is so estranged from his own physicality that he cannot act out his homosexual desires corporeally and can only give expression to them in his art. To give this homophobic logic its crudest formulation: the beatnik, as the most extreme kind of white man, is such a faggot (i.e., alienated from his own body) that he cannot even be a proper faggot (i.e., fuck or be fucked by other men), and all he can do instead is be a faggot-artist.

The malleability and capaciousness of the figure of homosexuality as it is deployed by Baraka attests to its disturbing rhetorical power in underscoring both the perversity and pervasiveness of white male racism. While Leo Bersani and Lee Edelman have argued that homophobic discourse always pivots around the figure of a penetrated male body, in Baraka's essay no such image is in evidence.[38] As I will show in the next chapter, this rather labile figuration of a white male homosexuality that is both everywhere and nowhere is what gives Ellison's first novel its symbolic coherence, structuring its depiction of the libidinal economy of homosocial racism. This semiotic flexibility, I will also be demonstrating, is also what gives Chin's homophobic depiction of white racism its rhetorical power, though his deployment of this symbolism will be modified in light of the different qualities that the racist imaginary attributes to the Asian male body. But while I will be treating these writers' representations of the white racist as homosexual—and the crucial differences between them—at some length in these later chapters, I want to turn now to a consideration of the figure of the *black* homosexual. Of particular interest here is the heightened concern with "sexual aim"—with the image of homosexual copulation—that characterizes such representations.

*

The first line of Baraka's "CIVIL RIGHTS POEM" mirrors the opening of his essay, "American Sexual Reference: Black Male," though the racial identity of its referent is different:

> Roywilkins is an eternal faggot
> His spirit is a faggot
> his projection

and image, this is
to say, that if I ever see roywilkins
on the sidewalks
imonna stick half of my sandal
up his
ass[39]

What is striking about this passage is that the "faggotry" that roywilkins is alleged to embody seems, at least initially, rather noncorporeal—it is an expression of his "spirit," his "projection / and image." There is no stated reference to any sexual object toward which roywilkins's allegedly homosexual desire is directed. There is, moreover, no explicit mention of sexual aim, of any sexual act that his body performs. The implied symptom, then, of his homosexuality seems to be his attitude toward whites, a racial-political moderation that is defined elsewhere in Baraka's writings as a cowardliness.

The poem pivots, however, around the phrase, "this is to say," which suggests that the "true" meaning of roywilkin's homosexuality, depicted in insistently abstracted terms in the first four lines of the poem, is to be gleaned from the corporeal action fantasized in the concluding four lines. There is something about the "image" of roywilkins as "an eternal faggot" that incites the speaker of the poem into an act of violence. Put more prosaically, the poem basically states the following: roywilkins is such a faggot that the mere sight of him makes me want to kick his ass. But the somewhat awkward poetic embellishment given to the stock threat issued by the poem—which might more ordinarily read "imonna kick his ass" or even "imonna stick my foot up his ass"—by the phrase "half of my sandal" seems coyly to whisper a certain accusation about what the "image" of the faggot's body seems to "say": namely, that this is a man whose backside is permeable to (and perhaps in need of) another man's penetration. Implied here in other words is that roywilkins is the kind of man who is accustomed to certain men—i.e., white men—entering his body, and the joke of the poem is the speaker's imagined substitution of a different organ of penetration altogether.[40]

What I am suggesting here is that cultural nationalist writings that make use of this kind of homophobic symbolism draw upon a quite specific representation of gay male bodies that is central to the dominant conceptions of homosexuality. Enabling homosexuality to serve as a "primary signifier" of racial inauthenticity and masculine inadequacy is a pervasive homophobic fantasy about the *sexual aims—the specific acts of sexual contact*—toward which male homosexual desire is assumed to direct itself. Hovering over this poem, in other words, is the ghostly presence of a quite specific representation of gay male bodies, one that is, according Leo Bersani, "the vicious expression of a more or less hidden fantasy of males participating, principally through anal sex, in what is presumed to be the terrifying phenomenon of female sexuality."[41] In being penetrated, gay men are perceived as indulging in "the suicidal ecstasy of taking their sex like a woman."[42]

This particular fantasmatic representation of the gay male body—which links it with a "suicidal ecstasy"—lies at the heart of Eldridge Cleaver's notion that black male homosexuality, as Wallace puts it, "was synonymous with reactionary Uncle Tomism."[43] I want to turn now to Cleaver's elaboration of this idea in "Notes on a Native Son," an essay in which he levels a brutal attack on a black writer who was apparently referred to by some as "Martin Luther Queen," James Baldwin.[44] In contrast to the texts I have been analyzing thus far, this essay is much more explicitly concerned with the *act* or *aim* that is definitional of homosexuality. It also suggests how the figure of the black homosexual is linked—via desire and identification—to those other Others of black nationalism, the white man and the black woman.

While Cleaver's apparent objective in this essay to evaluate the works of a writer he describes as "a fascinating, brilliant talent,"[45] much of it reads like a psychoanalytic case study of a mode of black subjectivity that men like Baldwin exemplify. What Cleaver seems to find of primary value about Baldwin is that his work makes visible a psychic structure that is apparently difficult to detect:

> Self-hatred takes many forms; sometimes it can be detected by no one, not by the keenest observer, not by the self-hater himself, not by his most intimate friends. Ethnic self-hate is even more difficult to detect. *But in American Negroes, this ethnic self-hatred often takes the bizarre form of a racial death-wish, with many and elusive manifestations.* Ironically, it provides much of the impetus behind the motivations of integration. (100–101; my emphasis)

At the most basic level, this "racial death-wish" has two components: the first is a loving and identificatory attitude toward white culture and white people; the second is a hatred of black culture and black people. Given the simple symmetry of this psychic structure as Cleaver describes it, it is not entirely clear why he insists on the difficulty of detecting its presence. (I will have more to say about this momentarily.) But the value of Baldwin's writings—which the essay stresses throughout—would seem to stem from their rendering explicit the twin impulses that constitute the racial death-wish:

> There is in James Baldwin's work the most grueling, agonizing, total hatred of the blacks, particularly of himself, and the most shameful, fanatical, fawning, sycophantic love of the whites that one can find in the writings of any black American writer of note in our time. (99)

Indeed, Cleaver praises Baldwin in *Notes of a Native Son* for being "frank to confess that, in growing into his version of manhood in Harlem, he discovered that, since his African heritage had been wiped out and was not accessible to him, he would appropriate the white man's heritage and make it is own" (100). In making explicit *his* identificatory desire for whites, Baldwin directs attention to the existence in other black intellectuals of the very same desire:

> In this land of dichotomies and disunited opposites, those truly concerned with the resurrection of black Americans have eternally to deal with black intellectuals who have become their own opposites, taking on all of the behavior patterns of their enemy, vices and virtues, in an effort to aspire to alien standards in all respects. The gulf between an audacious, bootlicking Uncle Tom and an intellectual buckdancer is filled only with sophistication and style. On second thought, Uncle Tom comes off much cleaner here because usually he is trying to survive, choosing to pretend to be something other than his true self in order to please the white man and thus receive favors. Whereas the intellectual sycophant does not pretend to be other than what he actually is, but hates what he is and seeks to redefine himself in the image of his white idols. *He becomes a white man in a black body.* A self-willed automated slave, he becomes the white man's most valuable tool in oppressing other blacks. (102–3; my emphasis)

At the psychic level, the kind of black intellectual that Baldwin exemplifies, then, is defined by a kind of racial transvestism: "his behavior patterns," his "vices and virtues" are all modeled on white standards. What Cleaver denounces here is a *psychic* disposition that is characterized by an idolatrous and mimetic desire for whiteness, a traitorous identification with the "alien standards" set by the enemy that reduces one to a "tool" useful for "oppressing other blacks."

Cleaver's critique of black intellectuals follows a radically desublimating trajectory, deploying a series of corporeal metaphors to deflate their aspirations. Even as he characterizes the "intellectual sycophant" as being driven by an impulse "to redefine himself in the image of his white idols," Cleaver calls attention to the limits placed on this impulse by the blackness of the body: unable to become a white man, the intellectual sycophant becomes instead "a white man in a black body." This particular corporeal metaphor identifies an *intrasubjective* structure that is self-enclosed and self-immolating. (It recalls Fanon's "thematization" of the man of color's psyche under colonial racism as riven by an interracial and intrapsychic "division.")

The figure of the "bootlicking Uncle Tom" to whom Cleaver likens the "intellectual buckdancer," however, calls attention to the body in a different way: it suggests a form of *intersubjective* contact toward which the self-loathing black man is oriented—a homosocial act toward which this interracial mimetic desire is inclined. According to Cleaver, the desire to "become(s) a white man in a black body" can take the physical form of a black male body on its knees or perhaps prostrate before the body of a white man. "Bootlicking" constitutes, in other words, the physical expression of the racial death-wish.

But when Cleaver suggests that Uncle Tom actually "comes off cleaner" than "an intellectual buckdancer," he raises the possibility that not all corporeal performances of servility are transparent expressions of a self-debasing black male desire. Apparently some instances of "bootlicking" ought to be read as acts of strategic mimicry: "usually [Uncle Tom] is trying to survive, *choosing to pretend to be something other than his true self* in order to please the white man and thus receive favors." The distinction introduced here between two *modes of racial performance* suggests, moreover, a discrete distinction *between two different models of black manhood*. One kind of black man, exemplified ironically by Uncle Tom, remains insulated from the unmanning effects of whatever humiliating acts of racial self-abasement he is forced to commit in "trying to survive" and thus retains his "true self"; another kind of black man expresses and exposes the essential falsity of his self in the orientation of his mind and body toward white men.

What emerges through this figure of the bootlicking Uncle Tom is an epistemological uncertainty that Cleaver attempts to resolve through a hermeneutic practice that is essentially homophobic in structure. To the problematic I raised earlier—namely, how one can detect the presence of the racial

death-wish in a black subject given its "many and elusive manifestations"—
the solution Cleaver offers involves being able to differentiate between certain black male bodies that are driven by the impulse of "trying to survive"
even as they assume the "bootlicking" posture and those that adopt that position because they are driven by the genocidal impulses of the racial death-
wish. The litmus test for distinguishing between the two involves testing for
the presence of a suicidal identification with a specific manifestation of black
female sexuality (as I will show momentarily); it involves distinguishing
between non-homosexual men who may play Uncle Tom and even lick the
white man's boots without having these behaviors express their "true sel(ves)"
and homosexual men whose sexual receptivity to white men is the transparent signifier of a suicidal and ultimately genocidal death-wish.

The significance of a black homosexuality that takes the white man as its
object for Cleaver is that it represents the ultimate corporeal manifestation
of the racial death-wish that animates all self-loathing black men. If the contradiction that defines this debased racial masculine identity is the impulse
to "become(s) a white man in a black body," then "the black homosexual,"
Cleaver writes,

> *when his twist has a racial nexus*, is an extreme embodiment of this contra-
> diction. The white man has deprived him of his masculinity, castrated him
> in the center of his burning skull, and when he submits to this change and
> takes the white man for his love as well as Big Daddy, he focuses on "white-
> ness" all the love in his pent up soul and turns the razor edge of hatred
> against "blackness"—upon himself, what he is, and all those who look like
> him, remind him of himself. He may even hate the darkness of the night.
> (103; my emphasis)

We should then emend Harper's assertion in order to account for the specific
form of homosexuality that comes to serve in Cleaver's writings as "the primary signifier" for a "failed manhood" that is coextensive with an "insufficient
racial identification" with blackness (50). The homosexual in question is one
whose "twist has a racial nexus," who takes the white man as his sexual object.
Moreover, as Michele Wallace has noted, he is a homosexual who adopts the
passive role in his sexual relations with white men: "If one is to take Cleaver
at his word, the black homosexual is counterrevolutionary (1) because he's
being fucked and (2) because he's being fucked by a white man."[46]

If, as Leo Bersani has argued, the homophobic fascination with gay male sex is animated by a specific fantasy of men experiencing "the suicidal ecstasy of taking their sex like a woman," the version of this scenario Cleaver offers in his writings is colored by a particular racial and sexual history. In order to assert that the black gay man's assumption of the passive and receptive role is the expression of a "suicidal ecstasy," Cleaver constructs a genealogical account of this particular manifestation of homosexual desire. The black man who is fucked by the white man, as Wallace notes, "reduces himself to the status of our black grandmothers who, as everyone knows, were fucked by white men all the time."[47] The significance for Cleaver of the enforced miscegenation that slavery depended upon is that it inaugurated an interracial heterosexuality whose ultimate aim was genocidal. The penetrated and penetrable body of the black woman serves as the privileged object of not only the sexual desires of white men, but also their genocidal impulses as well:

> What has been happening for the past four hundred years is that the white man, through his access to black women, has been pumping his blood and genes into the blacks, has been diluting the blood and genes of the blacks—i.e. has been fulfilling Yacub's plan and accelerating the Negroes' racial death-wish. (102)

Through this allusion to Yacub, the arch-villain in Elijah Muhammad's cosmology who seeks to eradicate the black race through miscegenation, the sexual desire of the white man vis-à-vis black women is rendered genocidal. As Wallace has observed, it is the position of being fucked that is being rendered abhorrent here, and black women are simply reduced to this position: as possessions of white men they are "symbol(s) of defeat," or as possessions of black men they are "spoils of war."[48] Evacuated of agency and desire in Cleaver's account, they are consigned to one of these roles, dependent on the balance of power between black and white men. Black homosexuals "with a racial twist," however, are vilified in much the same terms, as they are mainly reduced by Cleaver to the same position as black women: as sexually receptive objects of white male penetration.

Cleaver asserts the pathological character of a black male sexualized desire for white men by emplotting the violent heterosexual history of slavery in the family narrative defined by Freud as the "negative Oedipus complex." Cleaver's account of the psychogenesis of this racial-sexual perversion neatly parallels this lesser-known variant of the classic psychoanalytic tale of sexual development, in which the male child identifies with and desires the

"wrong" parental figures.[49] Instead of identifying with the paternal figure—
"Big Daddy," the white man—the black homosexual desires him; this desire,
moreover, is framed through an identification with a maternal figure, the
black female slave, and thus takes a feminine, which is to say passive, turn.
And because the black homosexual's desire for the white man is facilitated
through this identification with the sexuality of black women, he will
attempt to provide "Big Daddy" with the same "gift" offered by his mothers
and grandmothers, a miscegenated child:

> It seems that many Negro homosexuals, acquiescing in this racial death-
> wish, are outraged and frustrated because in their sickness they are unable
> to have a baby by a white man. The cross they have to bear is that, already
> bending over and touching their toes for the white man, the fruit of their
> miscegenation is not the little half-white offspring of their dreams but an
> increase in the unwinding of their nerves—though they redouble their
> efforts and intake of the white man's sperm. (102)

Black men who submit to the penetration of white men are, in other words,
courting a white male desire that fuses sexuality and violence, a desire whose
privileged objects have been the bodies of black women. But what the black
homosexual's "intake of the white man's sperm" produces is not a racially
debased offspring, but the very sexual neurosis—"the unwinding of . . .
nerves"—that defines his identity. His impossible desire to make his body
and self whiter—to make them "yellow," as it were—takes shape as a desire
to make his body more "feminine," more maternal. This passive sexual orientation is the signature feature of a black subjectivity whose libidinal structure has been fundamentally shaped by a racist violence that it has lovingly
incorporated, a sexualized violence whose aim is to eradicate the black race
by producing white(ned) offspring. To submit willingly and pleasurably to
the penetration of the white man is to internalize this sexualized genocidal
desire as a racial death-wish.

Here we witness a key set of symbolic substitutions, the codification of a
master trope essential to the negotiation of intraracial division in black
nationalist projects (and also to Asian American cultural nationalism, as I
will suggest momentarily). What I have been attempting to specify are all the
meanings that condense in a cultural nationalist symbolism whereby homosexuality comes to serve as the "primary signifier" of an identity that is
racially inauthentic and inadequately masculine—meanings that exceed its

function as a signifier of gender. The aspect of this homosexual figure that I want to emphasize most here is *the interracial mimetic desire* that is said to be constitutive of it. The formula that Cleaver provides for this disposition—"a white man in a black body"—encapsulates a form of racial subjectivity that recent theorists and critics have tended to characterize as hybrid.[50] The term hybridity expresses a conceptual view of identity that stresses—often in evaluatively neutral, descriptive terms—its necessary racial and cultural impurity: in reference to subjects of color, it suggests the presence "within" them, as it were, of whiteness. As I suggested in my references to Fanon at the outset of this study, this "thematization" of intrapsychic hybridity as "division" functions as a sister trope to emasculation and feminization in suggesting the unmanning effects of racism. In the view of the *nationalist* writers I am examining here, however, the condition of hybridity is often given the pejorative label *assimilationist* or *integrationist*. The traces of whiteness within the black psyche are rendered as markers of *an assimilationist desire—which is to say an interracial mimetic desire—to become white.*

The black man who is defined by this subjective orientation is then rendered as being driven by a homosocial mimetic desire that specifically takes the white man as its object: he wants to "become(s) a white man in a black body." This homosocial assimilationist desire finds what Cleaver terms its "extreme embodiment" in the body of the black homosexual, "already bending over and touching [his] toes for the white man." There is a peculiar twist to the path of identification that is introduced by the homosexual body: for it is only through a corporeal identification with his black mothers and grandmothers that the black gay man gives sexual expression to his mimetic desire for white men. To render explicit the sexual mechanics that are implied here: it is assumed that the black man will serve as the "bottom" in these exchanges, that his desire will take corporeal shape through an identification with a sexually receptive (black) femininity, that he will seek to become the white man by inviting the white man to come into him. If homophobic fantasy tends to associate, as Leo Bersani has argued, the rectum with the grave, homosexual receptivity with death, this linkage is given a "racial twist" in these writings: for the white male desires that are expressed in modern interracial homosexual exchanges are depicted as continuous with a sexualized racist desire that white slave owners expressed by impregnating their female slaves. Insofar as this enforced miscegenation is rendered as genocidal—leading to the gradual eradication of the black race through the dilution of black blood—the black homosexual can be depicted as giving expression to what Cleaver terms a "racial death-wish."

What is condensed in this representation of the homosexual is a set of desires that are depicted as not only contiguous but permeable: an inter-racial homosocial assimilationist desire to become like the white man; an intraracial cross-gender identification with a sexually receptive femininity; a racial death-wish that signals the internalization of a sexualized and geno-cidal racist hatred whose privileged objects have been women of color. It is over and against this model of identity that nationalist rhetoric projects its vision of racial and masculine authenticity. The "authentic" identity that Cleaver and Baraka attempt to identify in their writings is not constructed in a simple binary opposition to white manhood; it is, more precisely, tri-angulated by a hybridized third term: the black man who wishes (at the level of his sexual fantasy) he were female, and who wishes (at the level of racial fantasy) he were white. The hybridity of this vilified figure locates him in a kind of netherworld of race and gender, identifying with figures whose identities he can never wholly claim as his own (the black female slave, the white male slave owner), a neither-nor-ness that seems to locate him in the sexual limbo of "faggotry" and in the racial limbo of a "yellow" liminality.[51]

Asian American Cultural Nationalism: The "Uncle Tom Minority"?

In the sentence above, I have used the word "yellow" advisedly. For as I shift into a brief account of Asian American cultural nationalism, which I will explore at length in later chapters, I want to explore for a moment the cat-achrestic set of meanings that congregate around this term. Yellow, within the African American context, has been used as a term that refers to biracial subjects—those hybrid subjects who possess white blood as well as black; it is also a term that resonates with meaning in U.S. discourses of masculinity, referring to men who exhibit a glaring absence of the qualities of courage and fortitude so essential to traditional conceptions of manhood. Given these two meanings of the term, it would seem that the "inauthentic" man-hood that black nationalist rhetoric denigrates is also, in a sense, a "yellow" manhood. This term points toward the miscegenated body that emblema-

tizes the "perverse" desire for a white(ned) body that purportedly characterizes homosexuals like James Baldwin and the alleged cowardice of integra-
tionists like "roywilkins." But since yellow is also the color that has most
often been used in U.S. racial discourse to refer to "Orientals" (at least to
those of East Asian descent), the question that thus emerges is whether the
first two meanings of "yellow" in black nationalist discourse might shade
over into the third—whether men who are *racially* yellow in the sense of
being Asian might also be perceived as yellow in those other senses, as harboring an idolatrous and indeed sexualized desire for whiteness, and as lacking the qualities of conventional manhood.

By raising this issue I am not suggesting that there is an implicitly anti-
Asian sentiment that subtends black nationalist denunciations of the "inauthentic" form of black manhood exemplified by the homosexual: indeed, no
such sentiment is apparent in the texts I have been citing. Moreover, black
nationalism's Third Worldist outlook and resistance to the war in Vietnam
was predicated on a sense of solidarity with Asians abroad; moreover, the
prominent roles played by Yuri Kochiyama in Malcolm X's Organization for
Afro-American Unity and by Richard Aoki in the Black Panther Party suggest the ways in which black nationalist activists were open to alliances with
Asians in the United States.

I call attention to this potential conflation between these three different
meanings of yellow because, as I will demonstrate below, it occupies a central place in the cultural nationalist polemics of Frank Chin. Chin was and
is the primary spokesperson for a group of male writers who are generally
credited with producing the seminal articulation of Asian American cultural
nationalism. Often referred to as the *Aiiieeeee!* group or the *Aiiieeeee!* editors,
Chin along with Jeffery Paul Chan, Lawson Fusao Inada, and Shawn Wong
edited an influential collection of Asian American writings that was first
published by Howard University Press in 1974. In their preface to this volume, which was entitled *Aiiieeeee!*, Chin and his colleagues announced that
their intent was to refute a vision of Asian America "that reinforces white
racist stereotypes and falls short of the vision Malcolm X and other blacks
had for their 'minority'" (xix). As can be discerned from their evocation of a
political leader who has been described as "a Black Power paradigm—the
archetype, reference point, and spiritual adviser in absentia for a generation
of Afro-American activists,"[52] the *Aiiieeeee!* editors' assumptions concerning

what an adequate cultural nationalist evocation of their minority would be like were significantly shaped by the rhetoric of black nationalism. The allusion to Malcolm X—who was famously eulogized by Ossie Davis as "our manhood, our living, black manhood!"[53]—also hints at the gendered dimensions of this cultural nationalist project; it is symptomatic, moreover, of a rhetorical strategy the *Aiiieeeee!* editors characteristically adopt—they invite their readers to see the Asian American population through black nationalist eyes and to identify those who exhibit the same markers of "inauthenticity" catalogued by writers like Baraka and Cleaver.

The primary object of the *Aiiieeeee!* editors' critical wrath is a group of Asian American writers—mostly female and/or foreign-born—who project a view of Asian Americans that corresponds, in their opinion, to the stereotypes embodied by figures like Charlie Chan and Fu-Manchu. It is against these promoters of a "fake" Asian American cultural identity—one that affirms white racist stereotypes—that Chin and his colleagues pit their exemplars of the "real." The stereotype that the *Aiiieeeee!* editors accuse "fake" Asian American writers of promoting and identifying with in their work is described in explicitly gendered terms. The following passage—which appears in the 1972 essay "Racist Love," coauthored by Frank Chin and Jeffery Paul Chan—makes this quite evident:

> The white stereotype of the Asian is unique in that it is the only racial
> stereotype completely devoid of manhood. Our nobility is that of an effici-
> ent housewife. At our worst we are contemptible because we are womanly,
> effeminate, devoid of all the traditionally masculine qualities of originality,
> daring, physical courage, creativity. We're neither straight talkin' or [sic]
> straight shootin'.[54]

The Asian American subjects they castigate are those whose racial consciousness has apparently been framed through an identification with this "womanly" and "effeminate" stereotype. As King-Kok Cheung has observed, there is a pronounced misogyny in this passage as well as a veiled homophobia: it simply takes for granted that "womanly" qualities are "contemptible"; consequently, it also denigrates "effeminate" men who harbor those qualities.[55] What's only implied in the passage above, however, is rendered explicit in the one below, which is from a later essay:

> It is an article of white liberal American faith today that Chinese men,
> at their best, are effeminate closet queens like Charlie Chan and, at their

worst, are homosexual menaces like Fu-Manchu. No wonder David Henry Hwang's derivative *M. Butterfly* won the Tony for best new play of 1988. The good Chinese man, at his best, is the fulfillment of white male homosexual fantasy, literally kissing white ass. Now Hwang and the stereotype are inextricably one.[56]

The *Aiiieeeee!* editors' characterization of David Henry Hwang (whom they seem to confuse with his dramatic creation, Song Liling, the protagonist of his *M. Butterfly*) resonates with Cleaver's description of the black homosexual, "already bending over and touching [his] toes for the white man." Throughout their writings, the *Aiiieeeee!* editors deploy—as do Cleaver and Baraka—the figure of the homosexual as a privileged signifier for a masculine identity "devoid of all the traditionally masculine values" and thus indicative of a "fake" racial consciousness, wholly defined through an identification with the stereotype.

In later chapters, I explore more fully the misogynistic and homophobic symbolism that structures the rhetoric of (in)authenticity deployed by Chin and his cohort, a rhetoric that derives from the writings of the Black Arts movement. What I want to highlight here, however, is an apparent conundrum that these Asian American writers face as a consequence of this ideological borrowing. For the qualities identified as markers of inauthenticity in black nationalist discourse—markers of a "yellow" manhood, as it were—and which are ascribed to a certain sector of the African American populace, would seem to adhere—on their account, at least—with a particular resiliency to the Asian American population as a whole.

That black nationalist rhetoric might attach the qualities it associates with the "inauthentic" to the Asian American population *in toto* is in fact suggested by the authors of "Racist Love" themselves. In that essay, Chin and Chan describe a political rally held in San Francisco's Chinatown in 1969, during which David Hilliard of the Black Panthers apparently "told the Chinese-Americans they were the 'Uncle Tom minority' and were contributing to holding the blacks back" (74). They also refer to a scene from Richard Wright's autobiography, *Black Boy*, that would seem to anticipate Hilliard's assertion. They introduce this passage in the following way:

> We meet Shorty, an elevator operator in the deep South. Shorty needs
> a quarter for lunch and tells the white man, "I'll do anything for a
> quarter." He offers the white man his ass to kick. The white man kicks,

then throws a quarter on the ground. Shorty picks it up with his teeth, the white man says. Shorty, by white Southern standards, is assimilated and happy. (74)

Chin and Chan then quote directly from Wright's text:

> "I'm going north one of these days," Shorty would say.
> We would all laugh, knowing that Shorty would never leave, that he depended too much upon the whites for the food he ate.
> "What would you do up north?" I would ask Shorty.
> "I'd pass for Chinese," Shorty would say. (qtd. in "Racist Love," 74)

While the authors of "Racist Love" characterize Shorty's "comparison of himself to the Chinese" as "loathsome," neither of them, as David Leiwei Li has observed, "disputes the role Hilliard assigns the Asian American or argues against his misconception that the Asian is part of the institutional infrastructure that subordinates African Americans."[57]

Hilliard's view of the role that Asian Americans occupy within U.S. racial hierarchies—while partially a "misconception," as Li notes—is not exactly an anomalous one. It reflects, as Gary Okihiro has observed, a pervasive U.S. optics of race that is insidiously monochromatic,

> a construct of American society that defines race relations as bipolar—between black and white—and that locates Asians (and American Indians and Latinos) somewhere along the divide between black and white. Asians, thus, are "near-whites" or "just like blacks."[58]

Hilliard's contention that Asians represent the "Uncle Tom minority" does not simply present them as "near-whites," however;[59] neither are they described as "just like blacks." Rather, Asian Americans are presented as being just like *certain* kinds of blacks: those, in particular, who are derided in nationalist discourse as Uncle Toms; those who are driven by a cowardly integrationist politics that expresses an idolatrous desire for whiteness, like Baraka's roywilkins; those who offer up their asses for the white man to kick, like Wright's Shorty, or, to fuck, like Cleaver's Baldwin.

What these examples suggest is a convergence between the figure of the inauthentic in black nationalist rhetorics of identity and the location that Asian Americans occupy in dominant U.S. mapping of race relations. To be an Asian American is to be like an African American who wants to be white—it is to be trapped in the perpetual motion of a failed racial mimesis. The citations of Wright and Hilliard in "Racist Love" suggest that men who are *racially* yellow (i.e., Asian American men) might be perceived as yellow in the other two senses: as harboring an idolatrous mimetic desire for whiteness that can take a homosexual form, and as lacking in "traditional masculine qualities" like "daring" and "physical courage." What's somewhat surprising about the *Aiiieeeee!* editors' assessments of the Asian American population is that they seem to affirm, rather than to deny, the racial analogies drawn by Hilliard and Wright.

In their discussion of the stereotype, for instance, the authors of "Racist Love" give the impression that the "contemptible" judgments of the Asian American population they ascribe to Hilliard and Wright might actually be accurate. Indeed, the clean distinction between the stereotype and reality that the *Aiiieeeee!* editors underscore throughout their writings—the neat binary between "how we are seen" and "how we are" they insist upon—is always turning against itself, even at the grammatical level. In the phrases they use to describe the stereotype, there is a preponderant use of the first person plural "we," which is nearly always coupled with a version of the simple predicate "are *x*." So instead of phrases like "we are seen as womanly, effeminate, etc." we find phrases like "we *are* womanly, effeminate, etc." Their persistent use of the formulation "we are *x*" signals a disturbance of the boundary between the "fake" and the "real": it suggests that the stereotype is not simply a fictive image superimposed upon "us," but it also expresses something of "our" actual experiences and identities. The notion that the stereotype so intimately shapes the identities of Asian Americans is asserted in the following passage from "Racist Love":

> In terms of the utter lack of cultural distinction in America, the destruction of an organic sense of identity, the complete psychological and cultural subjugation of a race of people, the people of Chinese and Japanese ancestry stand out as white racism's only success. (66)

As a "subject minority," Chin and Chan continue, Asian Americans have been "conditioned to reciprocate [white racism] *by becoming the stereotype,* live it, talk it, embrace it, measure group and individual worth in its terms, and believe it" (66–67; my emphasis).

In Chapter 3, I will explore at length Chin's depiction of an Asian

American masculinity that is wholly shaped by an identification with a racist stereotype, a subjectivity that mirrors black nationalist representations of the "homosexuality" as "the primary signifier" for the compromised forms of manhood embodied by men of color who willingly acquiesce to white racism's identificatory dictates. For now, I want simply to indicate that in Chin's account of this "inauthentic" form of Asian American masculinity, he foregrounds the same kind of feminizing mimetic desire that is ascribed by black nationalists to the figure of the black homosexual. In an autobiographical essay entitled "Confessions of a Chinatown Cowboy," Chin asserts that "the most typical Chinaman born in the most typical Chinatown" is "the chameleon Chinaman."[60] Lacking an ethnically distinct ideal of virility of "their own" with which they can identify, Asian American men are left imitating "styles" of masculinity that belong, properly speaking, to men of other races:

> Hungry, all the time hungry, every sense was out whiffing for something rightly ours, chameleons looking for color, trying on tongues and clothes and hairdos, taking everyone elses [sic], with none of our own, and no habitat, our manhood just never came home. Hunger and copycat.[61]

But the "solution" that Chin prescribes for this problematic interracial mimetic desire that threatens to homosexualize Asian American men, as I will also be demonstrating, is not the eradication of this desire, but rather its melancholic intensification via the aesthetic. For in his evocation of the literary domain as a site where Asian American men might resist this racist unmanning, the wholly virile and racially authentic masculinity that he codifies is not only defined by an aggressive and violent mode of homosocial mimesis, it is—at bottom—a virtual copy of the aesthetic subjectivity memorialized in Ellisonian evocations of the African American vernacular.

To arrive at an understanding of the attraction that the cultural nationalist rhetoric of African American writers holds for the *Aiiieeeee!* editors, it is necessary to recognize how the vision of racial and masculine authenticity they appropriate from and share with writers like Cleaver, Baraka, *and* Ellison is framed by a certain conception of *literary* identity. If Asian Americans are perceived within the U.S. racial imaginary as a "womanly" race, and if they also perceive themselves that way, this feminizing view can best be corrected, Chin and his colleagues insist, by fashioning wholly virile and racially distinct forms of manhood within the domain of literature. It is only by forging a *vernacular* vision of Asian American manhood, they insist, that the feminizing and emasculating effects of racism can be combated.

Vernacular Manhood

As I will demonstrate in later chapters, the aesthetic theories codified by Ellison and Chin privilege a subject whose racial and masculine "authenticity" is underwritten by his ostensible link to the vernacular forms of cultural expression that typify working-class communities of color. To cite Harper's characterization of the vernacular pretensions of Black Arts writers, Ellison and Chin claim to be "incorporating into their work the semantics of 'street' discourse, thereby establishing an intellectual practice that was both 'black' enough and 'virile' enough to bear the weight of a stridently nationalist agenda."[62] But as I will be arguing, such vernacular theories—including those articulated in a post-structuralist idiom by Houston Baker, Jr., and Henry Louis Gates, Jr.—rather than highlighting the grammar, syntax, or idioms of "'street' discourse"—privilege instead a certain signifying intent. It is this intent, which is ultimately authorial in nature, that Frank Chin asks us to "hear" in the texts he deems "authentic," works that have purportedly "taken the schizophrenic yakity yak we talk and made it a backtalking, muscular, singing stomping full blooded language loaded with nothing but our truth."[63] It is this intent that Ralph Ellison asks us to hear in the jazz-inflected tradition of cultural performance in which he places his own writing: a tradition that "expresse[s] a yearning to make any- and everything of quality *Negro American*; to appropriate it, possess it, re-create it in our own group and individual images."[64]

This intentionalism is not unique to such ethnonationalist evocations of the vernacular. The distinction that Ellison and Chin make between spoken vernaculars and their literary deployment is, for instance, very much akin to the one that Mikhail Bakhtin posits between the "organic" hybridization of languages that occurs as a consequence of intercultural contact and the "intentional" hybridization of language that is characteristic of novelistic discourse.[65] Robert Young notes that this Bakhtinian distinction foregrounds the agency of the writer: "As with carnival and heteroglossia, it is the organizing intention of the artist that dialogizes hybridity," thereby enabling it to take on a "contestatory" force.[66] But in my analyses I bring into focus how the "contestatory" force—the aesthetic intent—that comprises the essence of the vernacular subjects championed by Ellison and Chin is depicted not only as racially authentic but also as wholly virile. What these writers valorize (as do Baker and Gates) is a *masculine* figure who speaks back from the racial margins, whose linguistic prowess lies in his deft capacity to repeat parodically and subversively the languages that constitute the center, none of which he should be able to claim as properly his own. He is defined by a violent and aggressive capacity to incorporate, appropriate, and mangle whatever linguistic materials enter into his verbal domain.

In order to clarify the masculinity that is ascribed to these aesthetic subjects, it is necessary to bring into sharper focus an aspect of vernacular theories—even those couched in post-structuralist terms—that has been noted by Diana Fuss. In reference to the work of Gates and Baker, Fuss writes that "The key to blackness is not visual but auditory; essentialism is displaced from sight to sound."[67] But the *orality* the vernacular privileges suggests not only its auditory dimension, it also points toward the aggressive *identificatory* impulse to which the vernacular subject gives expression. Implicit in Ellison's rendering of the vernacular subject and much more explicit in Chin's is a certain *alimentary* imagery, which figures the syncretic and appropriative sensibility being championed as the expression of a relentless mimetic hunger. Chin's cultural legacy as a "Chinaman," he insists, is a heroic orality that is essentially appetitive—or, as he puts it in the aptly titled short story, "The Eat and Run Midnight People,"

> being a Chinaman's okay if you love having been outlaw-born and raised to eat and run in your mother country like a virus staying a step ahead of a cure and can live that way, fine. And that is us! Eat and run midnight people, outward bound. . . . we live hunched over, up to our wrists in the dirt sending our fingers underground grubbing after eats. We were the dregs, the bandits, the killers, the get out of town eat and run folks, hungry all the time eating after looking for food. . . . We eat toejam, bugs, leaves, roots, and smut and are always on the move, fingering the ground, on the forage, embalming food in leaves and seeds, on the way, for part of the trip when all we'll have to eat on the way will be mummies, and all the time eating anything that can be torn apart and put in the mouth, looking for new food to make up enough to eat.[68]

Though Ellison's aesthetic writings rely less centrally on this kind of alimentary imagery, he and Chin both lionize a vernacular subject that is a kind of linguistic cannibal, promiscuously devouring whatever languages and discourses that may come their way and making them their own. Implicit, then, in the exempla of literary identity that these writers celebrate is a particular *psychological* disposition: the man who can subversively imitate the voices of other men is one who is driven, at least figuratively, by a violent and cannibalistic mimetic impulse to murder and devour them.

The mode of identification expressed by this mimetic desire is one that Kaja Silverman, drawing on the vocabulary of Max Scheler, has termed "idiopathic."[69] In her study *Male Subjectivity at the Margins*, she describes idiopathic identification as "conform[ing] to an incorporative model, constituting the self at the expense of the other who is in effect 'swallowed.'"[70] She further notes that this form of identification "sustains conventional masculinity."[71] A primary reason why the aesthetic functions in these writers' works as the masculine domain *par excellence* is that it enables them to project a certain view of racialized manhood that is predicated on this virilizing idiopathic identification.

Although Ellison and Chin both present their writings as emerging from the depths of a distinct *minority* tradition, the literary genealogies they trace for themselves include writers of other races. While they stress the distinctiveness of an African American or Asian American cultural sensibility, they also invoke a *hybrid* canon of male artists whose works provide their own with models that they both seek to emulate and supersede. But the African American or Asian American distinctiveness of the sensibilities they champion, however, is to be found in the muscularity with which other cultural forms are absorbed, reworked, and remade. The ethnonationalist aesthetics that these writers champion, in other words, are predicated on a modality of hybridity that emphasizes a highly aggressive and appropriative—an idiopathic—form of identificatory desire, one that is depicted as manifestly virile. The attraction that the literary sphere holds for them, moreover, has to do with the more utopian forms of male homosociality it is believed to engender. As one voice striving to achieve a singular literary identity by struggling against literary antecedents and brethren of all races, the male writer of color perceives himself achieving not only a measure of manhood, but a particular form of homosocial intimacy, one that is expressed through the complexly agonistic interplay of authorial voices rather than through than the potentially "homosexualizing" forms of male-male contact that characterize the prevailing social order.

The hybrid homosocial desire—the interracial mimetic hunger—that lies at the heart of the vernacular subjects canonized by Ellison and Chin is, at bottom, a highly idealized, homophobically sanitized version of the hybrid homosexual desire that white racism attempts, in their view, to engender in men of color. In the literary sphere, the feminizing and passive assimilationist impulse that is characteristic of the "homosexual" posture in which white racism threatens to place men of color is re-presented as a more virile and active kind of mimetic hunger.

Invisible Desires: Homoerotic Racism and Its Homophobic Critique in *Invisible Man*

In asserting a continuity between the works of cultural nationalist writers like Frank Chin and Amiri Baraka and those of Ralph Ellison, this study forwards a view of the author of *Invisible Man* that may seem counterintuitive, at least to some readers. But what I will demonstrate in the following chapters is how intimately linked these writers are in their shared reliance on a set of homophobic figurations for depicting the libidinal structure of racism, and also in their mutual belief in the capacity of literature to transcend the unmanning effects of white racism.

There are, however, many good reasons for perceiving Ellison and a writer like Amiri Baraka as positioned at opposite ends of the ideological spectrum. While Baraka's writings—at least those produced in the sixties—evince an undisguised anger at whites and white culture and espouse a separatist ethos, the interviews and essays by Ellison with which most readers are familiar express a nearly Pollyannaish optimism about the possibilities of American democracy and black life. Moreover, Ellison's views are expressed in a mannered and elegant prose style that seems to float above the often vitriolic rhetoric that cultural nationalist writers tend to deploy in their polemics. It is also true that a very real antagonism emerged between Ellison and black nationalist writers in the late sixties and early seventies, a period when the political and literary reputations of more overtly confrontational writers like Baraka were on the rise, at least within black literary circles, and when much speculation emerged over Ellison's apparent inability to complete a second novel. As Darryl Pinckney has observed, "Black Power nearly buried [Ellison's] reputation as he faced impolite audiences of black students from Harvard to Iowa, and refused to join in the mood of outrage, declining to call himself black instead of Negro."[1] In order to bring into focus how this ideological divide has in fact been overstated, I want first to devote some attention to uncovering how it has been produced.

The tenor of the attacks directed at Ellison by many black writers who were angered by the author's apparent apolitical detachment is conveyed quite vividly by Ernest Kaiser. In an essay included in a 1970 issue of *Black World* devoted to Ellison, Kaiser describes Ellison as "an Establishment writer, an Uncle Tom."[2] In his afterword to the anthology *Black Fire*, Larry Neal faults Ellison for so entirely framing his representation of black life in literary and philosophical terms drawn from high Western culture, citing the irrelevance of such a perspective to the "New Breed" of black Americans:

> The things that concerned Ellison are interesting to read, but contemporary black youth feels another force in the world today. We know who we are, and we are not invisible, at least not to each other. We are not Kafka-esque creatures stumbling through a white light of confusion and absurdity. The light is black (now, get that!) as are most of the meaningful tendencies in the world.[3]

For at least one critic, Ellison's open appropriation of white cultural resources was enough to throw into question his masculinity. In an essay that appeared in the same issue of *Black World* as Kaiser's, Clifford Mason asserts that "[t]he burden that Ellison's genius put on his manhood (and what our racial needs required) was for him to have been a lion *sui generis*, not an acquiescer posing as a tiger. Black literature deserved its own references, its own standards, its own rules."[4] The only black literary manhood worthy of the name, Mason claims, is one that insists on "its own references, its own standards, its own rules." As the many attacks on Ellison make clear, he is perceived as "an ascquiescer posing as a tiger" rather than as "a lion *sui generis*" because of his unapologetic insistence on the *racial hybridity* of his literary identity, on the fundamental influence on his work of writers like Eliot, Faulkner, Hemingway, Malraux, and Dostoyevksy.

Given these criticisms, one might conclude that the literary project to which Ellison devoted his career was irrelevant to the needs of black nationalism—that proponents of a Black Aesthetic would find no suitable materials in Ellison's writings for fashioning the politicized identity, the revolutionary black masculine subjectivity, they heroized. Ellison's own statements during this period, moreover, seem intent on widening rather than narrowing the perceived ideological gap between his own position and that taken by writers like Baraka. But if he came to serve as a whipping boy for many black nationalist writers, he certainly gave as good as he got. Even before Baraka became Baraka—when he was simply LeRoi Jones—he was subjected to Ellison's pointed critique. In a review of Jones's *Blues People* originally published in the *New York Review of Books* in 1964 and included as part of *Shadow and Act*, Ellison wrote: "The tremendous burden of sociology which Jones would place upon this body of music is enough to give even the blues the blues."[5]

In this review, Ellison clearly stakes out an oppositional position to an emergent strand of black intellectual work that he presents Jones's book as epitomizing:

> *Blues People*, like much that is written by Negro Americans at the present moment, takes on an inevitable resonance from the Freedom Movement, but it is itself characterized by a straining for a note of militancy which is, to say the least, distracting. Its introductory mood of scholarly analysis frequently shatters into a dissonance of accusation, and one gets the impression that while Jones wants to perform a crucial task which he feels *someone* should take on—as indeed someone should—he is frustrated by the restraint demanded of the critical pen and would like to pick up a club. (248)

Given that Ellison himself had devoted an entire section of his book of essays, *Shadow and Act*, to the blues as well as jazz, it is fairly clear whom he might be suggesting as that "someone" capable of taking on that "crucial task" of engaging in a serious study of this topic, whose analytical skills would be disciplined enough to honor "the restraint demanded of the critical pen." Several of the essays in *Shadow and Act*—which came out in 1964, the year after Jones's study was published—could easily have been subtitled "Blues People." In one of them, "Richard Wright's Blues," Ellison adopts an essentially sociological approach to the relationship between Southern black life and the blues, an approach he denigrates Jones for taking in his book. There seems to be a kind of narcissism of small differences at play in Ellison's critique of Jones, an aggression at a rival whose affinities are themselves the source of the aggression.

What I would like to suggest here is that the perceived gap between the ideologies espoused by black nationalists and those espoused by Ellison has been greatly exaggerated by the parties themselves. As a corrective to this view, it is worth considering that the anthology in which Addison Gayle, Jr., criticized Ellison as a "literary assimilationist"—*The Black Aesthetic* (1971)— contains ten other references to Ellison, none of which is especially critical. Indeed, Hoyt W. Fuller's essay "Toward a Black Aesthetic" cites Ellison (along with Miles Davis and Cassius Clay, among others) as an exemplar of a "special" black style. Moreover, sandwiched between Clifford Mason's and Ernest Kaiser's essays in the December 1970 issue of *Black World* (which basically label the author of *Invisible Man* an Uncle Tom) is a piece by Larry Neal in which he essentially retracts the charges he leveled at Ellison in the Afterword to *Black Fire*. This essay, "Ellison's Zoot Suit," was subsequently reprinted in *Speaking For You* (1987), an anthology of criticism on Ellison, much of which tends to adopt a reverential attitude toward the author and his works.[6]

Darryl Pinckney's account of the resurrection of Ellison's reputation in black literary critical circles, moreover, suggests that it may have actually been facilitated by the very black nationalists who seemed intent on burying it. He notes that the rise of Afro-American Studies departments—in many ways an institutional legacy of black nationalism—contributed greatly to the privileged status Ellison now enjoys: Ellison's work "benefited mightily from the rediscovery of folklore in Black Studies and he lived long enough to witness the elevation of *Invisible Man* to a sort of Ur-text of blackness." This rehabilitation of the novel's racial authenticity, as Pinckney notes, is clearly connected to a tradition of scholarship that has emphasized its author's connections to black folk culture.[7] Moreover, this burnishing of folkloric credentials has enabled a view of the writer to emerge that presents him—*pace* Clifford Mason—as fully capable of bearing the "burden that [his] genius put on his manhood," of answering "what our racial needs required." "By the time Ellison died in 1994," according to Pinckney, "he was regarded as a cultural treasure, a vindicated father figure for a generation of formerly militant and post-militant black writers who wanted folklore, blues, jazz and black literature to be brainy yet *virile* subjects" (my emphasis). The resurrection of Ellison's reputation has much to do, as I will elaborate more fully in a later chapter, with the way in which his aesthetic writings—like that of many of the Black Arts aestheticians who would seem to have opposed him—premise their conception of racial, masculine, and literary authenticity on a certain, highly romanticized notion of the black working class, who are imagined to be the bearers of a more muscular form of minority culture. A primary reason why this vernacular ideology has proven to be so attractive to both Baraka and Ellison is precisely because it provides the ideological resources for depicting male writers of color as "brainy yet virile subjects," as exemplars of a racially authentic and wholly masculine literary identity.

To suggest that Ellison's literary project was, like that of many Black Arts writers, framed by questions of gender requires retracing the trajectory of his development as a writer in terms different from the ones critics have generally tended to use. The imposing presence of the author's own extensive commentary has influenced most critics to produce what Kerry McSweeney calls "canonical" readings of *Invisible Man*, interpretations that "implicitly or explicitly examine the novel within the frameworks provided by Ellison."[8] Such interpretations of Ellison's novel generally echo the optative sentiments concerning American race relations voiced in the novel's epilogue and eloquently reaffirmed in numerous interviews and essays, thereby deemphasizing the palpable anger at whites (and, in the main, at white *men*) that resounds through the vast bulk of the novel.

One consequence of Ellison's increasingly conservative political stance—his transformation from committed Marxist fellow traveler to anticommunist cold war liberal—is that his later characterizations of his intentions in writing the novel tend to wash out into woolly abstractions and liberal bromides. Take, for instance, the following commentary from his introduction to the thirtieth edition of *Invisible Man*:

> So if the ideal of achieving true political equality eludes us in reality—as it continues to do—there is still available that fictional *vision* of an ideal democracy in which the actual combines with the ideal and gives us representations of a state of things in which the highly placed and the lowly, the black and the white, the northerner and the southerner, the native-born and the immigrant are combined to tell us of transcendent truths and possibilities such as those discovered when Mark Twain set Huck and Jim afloat on the raft.[9]

What becomes easily obscured when readers take up Ellison's invitation to read the novel in these terms is that "true political equality" seems to be as elusive in *his* "fictional vision" as it is in the real world. While he suggests that *Invisible Man* was "fashioned as a raft of hope, perception and entertainment that might help keep us afloat as we tried to negotiate the snags and whirlpools that mark our nation's vacillating course toward and away from the democratic ideal" (xx–xxi), it is simply true that nowhere *in* the novel is a vision of interracial brotherhood comparable to Twain's ever fleshed out.

In light of Leslie Fiedler's radically desublimated reading of Huck and Jim's raft, moreover (a reading of which Ellison was aware and to which he seems to allude in the novel itself), this radically *sublimated* invocation of "classic" American literature's royal couple seems intent on leading the reader to gloss over the intense focus on interracial homoeroticism (insofar as it is emanates from white males, at least) that is nearly omnipresent in *Invisible Man*.[10] For what should be apparent to any reader of Ellison's novel is how deeply embedded it is in a Freudian hermeneutic—how profoundly shaped it is by an interpretive framework that views erotic desire as an essential motive force behind all social interactions. It is this dimension of the novel that I want to explore in this chapter—its carefully crafted and implicitly homophobic depiction of the libidinal motivations of white men who take a putatively altruistic interest in the lives of black men.

In the reading of *Invisible Man* I will put forward, the novel emerges as not unlike a series of case studies in white male psychology—a sustained meditation on the nature of the interest that various *types* of white man have taken at various times in the lives of black men. As it encapsulates several stages of African American history in the movement of its narrative, *Invisible Man* attempts to lay bare the psychological motivations of white men who played a significant role in each of those moments: Southern moderates who, like the townsmen depicted in the novel's first chapter, tolerated and even encouraged the program of black uplift promoted by Booker T. Washington and institutionalized at Tuskegee; Northern liberals who, like the character of Norton, provided indispensable financial support through their philanthropy for these endeavors; the bohemian patrons—allegorized in the novel in the figure of Young Emerson—who supported the Harlem Renaissance; and, finally, white Communists who—like their fictionalized counterparts, the members of the Brotherhood—sought to enlist blacks in their revolutionary struggle against capitalism. I examine the psychological portrait that

Ellison offers of each of these types through the characters he uses to exemplify each of them. I will show how Ellison's inventory of white male "Negrotarians" underscores a psychic uniformity shared by them all—a uniformity that is revealed by the consistency with which they cloak within their benevolent actions an insidious and erotic intent.

What my reading will ultimately disclose in the novel is an underlying homophobic symbolism, one that verges on rendering all of these white male figures psychically indistinguishable. In suggesting that the optics of white male racial vision are fundamentally shaped by homoerotic impulses, Ellison depicts the predatory nature of racist desire as proximate—if not entirely equivalent—to homosexual desire. Latent in *Invisible Man*, in other words, is a version of the homophobic symbolism that links Ellison to the black nationalist writers of the sixties and seventies—a symbolism that renders homosocial racism equivalent to a kind of homosexuality.[11] To demonstrate how close *Invisible Man* comes to making this symbolic equation I will examine an *earlier* version of the novel's pivotal eleventh chapter (in which the narrator is incarcerated in what seems to be a factory hospital). This excised chapter, as I will demonstrate, actually give the novel's representations of white masculinity an added level of aesthetic coherence by making of homosexual desire a disturbingly apt symbol for the desires that racist white men seek to satisfy in their dealings with black men.

I follow my reading of *Invisible Man* with a brief analysis of the work of the prominent sociologist Robert E. Park, whom Ellison credits for provoking his own literary meditations on how whites see, or refuse to see, blacks. I do so for three reasons. First of all, I suggest that Park's perspectives on blackness provide a kind of template for the white vision he submits to psychoanalytic critique in his novel. Secondly, I draw attention to the gendered dimension of Park's racial views—his basic feminization of the Negro—in order to explain the masculinist impetus that animates both the writing of *Invisible Man* and the development of his account of the African American vernacular (which I will examine at length in chapter 2). Finally, by bringing to the fore how Ellison's literary project is shaped by an agonistic relation to Park's sociology, I seek to disclose the *multi*racial dimension of the representational regime he presents himself as writing against—to draw attention to an interracialism that is nowhere visible in *Invisible Man*'s symbolic economy but which structures it nonetheless.

"The Battle Royal": Black Male Bodies and White Male Visual Pleasures

Invisible Man was not, in fact, the first published work of fiction by Ellison to bear that title: it was also used for a short story that appeared in 1947, a piece that reappeared in 1952 as chapter 1 of Ellison's first novel. That this chapter was initially given the same name as the novel conveys the sense that the events it records are somehow prototypical—that they provide a foretaste of the events that will come after. At several pivotal moments in *Invisible Man*, when the narrator comes to the realization that he is being used by a white male figure (or figures) who appeared to be his ally, he experiences a sense of déjà vu. And if these later moments give the sense that it had all happened before, the novel's initial chapter suggests that it happened for the first time in the last few days before his departure for college from the small southern town in which he was raised. What happens there is that the protagonist becomes intimately acquainted with the role that black men are expected to play—the pleasures they are supposed to satisfy—in serving as the objects of the white man's putative benevolence.

At first glance, however, it does seem as if the townsmen who are the invisible man's primary antagonists in the first chapter are different than the white male characters who appear later. There's something crude and overt about the violence they inflict—or rather that they watch being inflicted—on the bodies of black men, and something so obviously sadistic about the enjoyment they take in this violence. Later white male characters are, to be sure, more subtle about the pleasures they derive from their manipulation of the invisible man's actions, pleasures that are more effectively masked beneath a veneer of benign intent, or so highly sublimated that they scarcely appear as pleasures at all. But as my analyses will make clear, the differences that emerge between the white male characters introduced in this first chapter and those introduced later are one of degree rather than of kind.

A crucial point of resemblance between all of the white male characters depicted in the novel is that they all present themselves—and seem to conceive of themselves—as friends of the Negro. Indeed, the narrator's description emphasizes that the men who attend the "smoker"—the bacchanalian gathering that comprises the central event of this chapter—are in fact "the town's leading white citizens" (17): respectable men who enjoy cordial relations with their black neighbors, or, more accurately, with *certain* of their black neighbors—those who, like the narrator and his family, exhibit the properly submissive attitude. Because the invisible man, in particular, fancies himself "a potential Booker T. Washington," and expresses the proper "meekness" in his social interactions, he finds himself "praised by the most lily-white men of the town" (18, 16). This selective generosity is, of course, the reason why he has been invited to the smoker; he is there ostensibly to deliver a repeat performance of his graduation speech, in which he asserted "that humility was the secret, indeed, the very essence of progress" (17). Their munificence also materializes in the unexpected gifts the invisible man receives at the conclusion of the evening's events: a new briefcase and a college scholarship.

As Ellison's harrowing narration quickly makes clear, however, the façade of respectability maintained by the "town's big shots" by light of day requires the repression of a range of primal impulses—impulses that only find release in certain quasi-ritualized practices like the smoker. The entire point of this event, it would seem, is to allow the townsmen an opportunity to indulge a number of sensual impulses that are ordinarily restrained. Some of these are oral—they are "wolfing down the buffet food, drinking beer and whiskey and smoking black cigars" (17)—but mostly, they are visual: for their primary source of entertainment is a series of spectacles—three of them, to be precise—in which the bodies of young black men figure prominently. In the first, a group of black boys from the town (including the narrator) are forced to watch a nude white woman dance; in the second, they are made to fight each other blindfolded in the battle royal; and finally, they are made to scramble after counterfeit coins on an electrified rug. What I want to emphasize in my analyses is the *vicarious* nature of the pleasure that these white men take in these spectacles—that these are purely *voyeuristic* rituals in which enjoyment seems to derive from the watching rather than from the doing.

The desire that the second and third of these spectacles cater to—the battle royal and the scramble after the coins—is straightforwardly sadistic and racist. It is a desire that the invisible man has been aware of even while being praised for his "meekness" by the white townsmen. For he senses that "what they really would have wanted" was that "I should have been sulky and mean" (17). What they wanted, in other words, was an excuse to inflict a disciplining violence upon a young black male who did not know his place. The narrator's "meekness" frustrates this desire for violence, a desire that is voiced during the battle royal when a spectator yells out, referring to the narrator: "I want to get at that ginger-colored nigger. Tear him limb from limb" (21). But while these men seem to refrain from acting out their desire for violence—they do not climb into the ring, for instance—they nonetheless have this desire satisfied by watching. In this regard, the bodies of the black boys serve two distinct though related functions: they serve as the *objects* of physical violence, but also as its *agents*. This distinction suggests that there are two vicissitudes of the scopic desire that the townsmen satisfy in these spectacles, the first deriving from the sight of a black male body convulsed by pain, and the second from the sight of a black male body itself inflicting that pain. The second of these implies that these white men experience an identificatory thrill in watching black male bodies do what they themselves wish to do. It suggests that white men see the black male body as an instrument that enables them to experience vicariously the gratification of a desire that they must refrain from acting out themselves.

These spectacles of violence, moreover, seem imbued with an ambiguous homoeroticism. This effect is partially produced by their temporal placement in the first chapter: for the battle royal and the scramble after the coins follow a prior spectacle that affects how the latter two are read. What Ellison describes first is a classically voyeuristic scenario (a group of white men watching a nude white woman dance) into which is inserted the group of black boys. These boys are positioned between the dancer and the white townsmen as a kind of human scrim—a partially invisible screen of black male bodies—through which the movements of the nude dancer are still visible. Their intermediate positioning suggests that they are being made, on the one hand, to participate in the scopophilia of the townsmen (to look at the white women as the white men do) and, on the other, to function as objects of the townsmen's vision (to be looked at by the white men as the white woman is). The dual role that the black man plays in the other two spectacles—as both vicarious agent and object of white male desire—is given its first manifestation within the triangulated eroticism of this voyeuristic scenario.

As in the battle royal, these white men use the bodies of black men to give vicarious expression to desires that are ordinarily repressed. While these men are clearly aroused by the sight of the nude female dancer, most of them refrain from physically expressing their state of excitation. A reason for their restraint is suggested by the narrator's account of what happens to them when they allow their bodies to give expression to the their arousal. He describes, for instance,

> a certain merchant who followed [the dancer] hungrily, his lips loose and drooling. He was a large man who wore diamond studs in a shirtfront which swelled with the ample paunch underneath, and each time the blonde swayed her undulating hips he ran his hand through the thin hair of his bald head and, with his arms upheld, his posture clumsy like that of an intoxicated panda, wound his belly in a slow and obscene ground. The creature was completely hypnotized. (20)

The body of this white man becomes increasingly grotesque and ridiculous as it becomes sexually excited, as if somehow inadequate to the desires that surge through it. Indeed as more of the white townsmen become excited, try to "sink their beefy fingers in the soft flesh" of the dancer, and chase her around the ballroom, she looks at them with "disgust" (20). Notably, these men are restrained by the rest.

The townsmen apparently find a better way of experiencing their sexual excitation, however, by making use of the black boys' bodies. They force these young black men to play a role similar to the one played, according to Laura Mulvey, by the cinematic male hero.[12] Their black male bodies serve here as a sort of corporeal screen upon which the white men project a more idealized image of their own arousal. For the narrator notes how the men force one boy to keep looking, even as he "began to plead to go home": he was the "largest of the group, wearing dark red fighting trunks much too small to conceal the erection which projected from him" (20). These white men seem to experience their arousal more fully by vicariously sharing in the sexual arousal of these black boys. It is as if they look upon the erect black penis as a kind of prosthetic device that enhances their own sense of sexual pleasure.

In order to function as *identificatory* objects, however, the bodies of these black boys must become a focus of visual interest; and as a result of figuring so prominently in the vision of highly aroused white men, those bodies would seem also to attain the status of *erotic* objects in and of themselves. Indeed Ellison's physical descriptions draw attention to similarities between the black boys and the "magnificent blonde," which suggest that their bodies are being made to play a similar role. In their state of partial and sweaty undress—"We were a small tight group, clustered together, our bare upper bodies touching and shining with anticipatory sweat"—these young men resemble the dancer: "beads of perspiration glisten[ed] like dew around the pink and erected buds of her nipples" (18, 19). This likeness is further suggested by the almost cinematic synchronization that the narrator's description establishes between the movements of the performers' bodies and the scene's diegetic "soundtrack." The body of the young man who tries to hide his erection is presented as moving in response to the same aural agency as the nude dancer: much as she dances in concert to the accompaniment of "[a] clarinet vibrating sensuously" (19), his erection "project[s] from him as though in answer to the insinuating low-registered moaning of the clarinet" (20).

The correspondence between the black boys and the "magnificent blonde" is also suggested by the complicated sense of identification that the narrator experiences as he is forced by the townsmen to look closely at her naked body. While his response is extremely complex—mingling guilt, fear, desire, hatred, and sympathy—I want to focus here on how those elements suggest its fundamentally identificatory quality. These elements are all evident in the following passage:

> I wanted at one and the same time to run from the room, to sink through the floor, or go to her and cover her from my eyes and the eyes of the others with my body; to feel the soft thighs, to caress her and destroy her, to love her and murder her, to hide from her, and yet to stroke where below the small American flag tattooed upon her belly her thighs formed a capital V. (19)

The first impulse recorded here is self-protective: he wishes literally to remove his body from the scene, apparently to shield it from the punishment that his own prohibited sexual desire may bring about, or to cease the looking that elicits his desire. The second impulse—to go to her and cover her with his body—is much more ambiguous. For the gesture he imagines seems partially sexual, an expression of the same desire that leads him to imagine "feel[ing] the soft thighs," caressing, loving, and stroking her. But it also suggests an underlying sympathy—an impulse to "cover her from my eyes and the eyes of others," to shield her from the scopophilic looking in which he is nonetheless participating. This sympathetic desire, moreover, casts a different light on the first impulse recorded here: for his desire to protect her body from the scopic appetites of white men suggests that his own wish to "sink through the floor" expresses a desire to protect his own body from an eroticized white male look. An awareness in the narrator begins to emerge here, in other words, that he and the woman are both being made to play a similar, debasing role: both of them have been made to offer up their bodies for the visual enjoyment of white men.

The narrator's awareness of his identification with the nude white woman also produces a more disturbing response: a "desire to spit upon her," to "destroy her . . . and murder her." For what he seems to see in the body of the nude dancer is a symbolization of his own experience of humiliation, a humiliation that derives from being deprived of control over his own body. For the lack of control he experiences here seems to find an apt and infuriating emblem in the lack that is conventionally ascribed to women—an anatomical "lack" whose usual referent is initialed by the capital "V" he glimpses between the dancer's thighs. The misogyny of the narrator's response, in other words, is produced by his awareness of how the woman's "castration" mirrors back to him his own.

In this scene—which seems to assume a paradigmatic status in the novel—the bodies of the narrator and the other black boys answer to a white male pleasure that is rendered as polymorphously perverse. As a result, the black male body appears to take on a certain semiotic and erotic malleability that appears to disrupt the binary distinctions of active/passive and masculine/feminine. It seems feminine to the extent that it serves as objects of a homoerotic look and of a vicariously inflicted sadistic violence, but in serving as an active agent of violence and in displaying a sexual arousal that renders white male bodies it also seems to assume a heightened masculinity.

In its very malleability, however, this body testifies to the power held over black men by white men, and it is the disappropriation of this power that this scene registers as a kind of castration. Ultimately, the pleasure in which these white men indulge in this scene derives from the sadistic control they exert over black men—what they wish to see mirrored back to them is their unrestricted ability to make the bodies of other men bend to their desires. In his reading of analogous scenes in a number of African American texts, Lee Edelman has suggested that such representations link the "castration" that homosocial forms of antiblack racism engender with "the denial of the black man's agency through his transformation into a material receptacle, the malleable object of the white man's 'will and pleasure.'"[13]

To put this another way, at the heart of the experience of racial humiliation that this chapter records is the emasculation that is effected when control and mastery over one's body is relinquished. To be forced to have the very movement's of one's body dictated by the whims of another man, a white man—this is, at bottom, the essence of the disempowerment that is depicted here through the gendered symbolism invoked by Ellison. It is a form of unmanning that remains in effect even when the actions one's body is made to perform seem unambiguously to signify as masculine. Conversely, it is the absolute control of another man's body—and of black male bodies in particular—that would seem to comprise the essence of this homoerotic white male pleasure.

Norton: Incest, Narcissism, and White Male Philanthropic Desire

It is this libidinally inflected investment in the control over black male bodies that links the townsmen to the next white male character introduced in the novel: Norton, the philanthropist who provides financial support for the college attended by the invisible man. At first glance, this Northerner seems to lack the eroticized interest in blacks so evident in the Southerners Ellison presents in chapter 1. But Norton's psychic investment in the black students is depicted as also having its origins in a repressed erotic desire. For Norton's philanthropic work enables him to satisfy, through the mechanism of sublimation, an incestuous desire for his dead daughter.

The incestuous nature of Norton's paternal passions is suggested most dramatically by the intense fascination with which he listens to Trueblood's blues-toned narrative: the black sharecropper recounts how he inadvertently had sex with his daughter. In his reading of this scene, Houston Baker, Jr., treats Norton's desire as largely symptomatic of underlying impulses that are ultimately economic.[14] This interpretation, however persuasive, tends to render epiphenomenal the more straightforward reason for Norton's interest: Trueblood has violated the taboo against incest and incurred no retribution for it; he has thus successfully acted out a sexual desire that Norton has devoted his life to repressing. Baker makes another observation in passing, which he seems to treat as self-evident, that I wish to explore more fully in my own analysis: he suggests that Norton's desire to assist the black students of the college contains "a carnal undercurrent."[15] The exact nature of this "carnal undercurrent" that motivates Norton's philanthropy is not, however, all that self-evident, though it proves crucial for a full understanding of the psychological motivations Ellison ascribes to this character. To arrive at this understanding, it will be necessary to examine the relationship that Ellison's characterization establishes between the interest Norton took in his dead daughter and the interest he now takes in the lives of the black men whom he views as a "living memorial" to her (43).

While the incestuous quality of Norton's paternal love is suggested most dramatically by the rapt attention he gives to Trueblood's story, it is also implied by the excessive sentimentality with which he describes his deceased daughter to the narrator.

> She was a being more rare, more beautiful, purer, more perfect and more delicate than the wildest dreams of a poet. I could never believe her to be my own flesh and blood. Her beauty was a well-spring of purest water-of-life, and to look upon her was to drink and drink and drink again . . . She was rare, a perfect creation, a work of purest art. A delicate flower that bloomed in the liquid light of the moon. A nature not of this world, a personality like that of some biblical maiden, gracious and queenly. I found it difficult to believe her my own . . . (42; ellipses are Ellison's)

While every sentence in this highly romanticized description is intended to emphasize the chasteness of both Norton's paternal love and its object, many of those same sentences simultaneously engage in the subtle disclosure of the incestuous desire they are desperately trying to repress. For instance, many of Norton's phrases underscore the otherworldly purity and delicacy of his daughter's beauty. But the simile he uses to capture her ethereal nature—he equates her with "a well-spring of purest water-of-life"—renders his own love for her as a desire to "look upon her" and to "drink and drink and drink again." These phrases call to mind the scopically and orally inflected carnal desires of the white townsmen described in the novel's first chapter. Similarly, Norton twice asserts that he found it difficult to believe that she was his daughter, intending to accentuate yet again her otherworldliness and purity. But by establishing such an extreme contrast between himself and his daughter, he implies that his own concerns are more worldly and less pure. Moreover, by simply voicing an uncertainty over her parentage, Norton seems to imagine a condition in which the incest taboo would not hold sway, a condition in which his paternal passions, such as they are, would require no repression.

But repressed they have been: Norton has apparently refrained from directly acting out his incestuous desire. Furthermore, an insurmountable barrier to that desire has been put in place by her death. Norton suggests, however, that he has kept his paternal love alive by finding a substitute object for it in the black students of the college. He tells the narrator that the most "important," "passionate," and "sacred" "reason" for his philanthropy is his desire to "construct a living memorial to my daughter," and thus he views the students as "a monument to her memory" (45, 43). He explains to the invisible man that the bond between them is, therefore, quite personal: "So you see, young man, you are involved in my life quite intimately, even though you've never seen me before. You are bound to a dream and to a beautiful monument" (43). It is also clear from the mixture of agricultural and financial metaphors that Norton uses to describe his relationship to the students of the college that he sees them as substitute objects of his paternal love. Norton reminisces about the time when he first saw the land on which the college was erected: "years ago, when all your beautiful campus was barren ground. There were no trees, no flowers, no fertile farmland" (37). The capital investment he made in the college was intended to make this "barren ground" capable of bearing fruit, to assist in its fertilization. The crop that his investment has yielded are the black students the college produces: Norton tells the narrator that through these students, "I can observe in terms of living personalities to what extent my money, my time and my hopes have been fruitfully invested" (45). What Norton's fertilizing investment has helped to produce—what his investiture of seed money has brought into existence—is a race of surrogate children: a black multitude who owe their existence to him, a crop of "living personalities" through which his own lives on. But since these students are also associated with the "barren ground" that has been rendered so fertile as a result of his skillful husbandry, they would also appear to play the role of substitute wife. Norton's relationship to the students of the college has been modeled, in other words, on his relationship to his daughter—a child whom he wished was his wife, a would-be wife who was also his child.

If this substitution is possible—if the student body of the college can stand in for the body of a dead daughter—then it would seem that Norton is able somehow to achieve some form of gratification through his philanthropic endeavors. But Ellison does not insinuate that Norton experiences a sexual attraction to the black students he assists. Rather, he suggests that the psychic gains that Norton enjoys through his philanthropic work are largely egoic. Norton takes pleasure in the feeling of mastery he experiences through the "first-hand organizing of human life" that his work on behalf of the college entails (42). He also derives a narcissistic pleasure from watching the students become model Washingtonian subjects. For what he sees in them is an endless potential for self-replication: "Through you and your fellow students I become, let us say, three hundred teachers, seven hundred trained mechanics, eight hundred skilled farmers, and so on" (45). In this fantasy of self-reproduction, Norton identifies the form of gratification he seeks through his philanthropy: rather than satisfying his body's carnal urges, he appeases the prodigious demands of his ever-enlarging ego. All of this suggests that the project of uplift allows Norton to play out a narcissistic paternal fantasy in which blacks play an instrumental role—a narcissistic fantasy that has incestuous origins. Norton's work on behalf of the college enables him to see himself as a benevolent father who has successfully sublimated his tabooed desire toward the production of a whole race of surrogate children. But while Ellison presents the racial fantasy that undergirds Norton's philanthropy as lacking a manifest sexual content, it is in fact the "carnal undercurrents" of this fantasy to which his characterization draws attention.

Young Emerson: Homosexuality, Fiedler's Raft, and White Male Philanthropic Desire

Through his depiction of Norton, Ellison levels a broadly Freudian critique of the tradition of white philanthropy that supported Southern black colleges like Tuskegee.[16] In his homophobic description of Young Emerson, the homosexual liberal who describes himself as a modern-day Huck Finn, he criticizes in similar, though more explicitly sexual, terms another generation of white philanthropists: the wealthy patrons who sponsored the Harlem Renaissance. In the essays where he directly addresses that movement, Ellison attacks it as catering to the tastes of wealthy whites who, in the midst of their own sense of alienation and ennui, "sought in the Negro something primitive and exotic."[17] Ellison argues that the relationships of patronage that developed between black artists and white patrons had a fatal effect on the work produced—that the art of the Harlem Renaissance was primarily shaped by the demands of "white faddists" who wished "to indulge their bohemian fancy for things Negroid."[18] The character of Emerson is cast as one of these "white faddists," placed as he is firmly within the milieu of the Harlem Renaissance. Laboring under the oppressive influence of a domineering father, he seems to glimpse a kind of escape in the Harlem nightclub he frequents, a club that provides a "rendezvous for writers, artists and all kinds of celebrities" (185). He enjoys the company of "jazz musicians," and presents himself as wanting only to help those like the invisible man: the would-be "New Negroes" who have recently arrived from the South (188). Even though the invisible man is not an artist, he becomes the would-be object of Emerson's patronage. Through his account of Emerson's underlying motives, Ellison once again suggests that white men who purport to be working in the interests of black men are, in fact, furthering their own— interests that are, in this case, explicitly homosexual.[19]

If Ellison discloses a self-serving paternal narcissism within Norton's ostensible altruism, he seems to present Emerson's desire to help black men as deriving, in contrast, from a more sympathetic identification. As a gay man who has read Freud's psycho-mythological account of primitive sons who gang up and murder an oppressive father (a copy of *Totem and Taboo* sits open on the table in his office), Emerson apparently sees himself and the narrator as brothers of a sort, bonded together in a common struggle against paternal "tyranny" (187). He tells the narrator: "We're both frustrated, understand? Both of us, and I want to help you . . ." (187). He insists

> "I know many things about you—not you personally, but fellows like you.
> Not much, either, but still more than the average. With us, it's still Jim
> and Huck Finn. A number of my friends are jazz musicians, and I've been
> around. I know the conditions under which you live—" (187–88)

But by and large, the distracting emphasis that the narrative places on Emerson's homosexuality works to undermine any sense that this sympathy is genuine. When he admits to the narrator that "all our motives are impure," this comes as no surprise to the reader, for Ellison's stereotypical descriptions of Emerson make clear what this neurotic and effete white man who enjoys the company of black men is after (186).

Ellison's description is replete with literary allusions that leave no doubt as to Emerson's sexual orientation, and that make clear the precise nature of his "fancy for things Negroid." The nightclub "with a truly continental flavor" where he frequently meets his Harlem friends, the Club Calamus, is named after the section of Whitman's *Leaves of Grass* that celebrates the erotic love of man for man. Emerson confesses to the narrator that "my father considers *me* one of the unspeakables," thereby casting himself as a devotee of Oscar Wilde (188). He immediately follows this confession with a second: "I'm Huckleberry, you see" (188). The meaning of this second admission would be particularly clear to scholarly early readers of Ellison's novel, published as it was just four years after Leslie Fiedler's famous and controversial essay, "C'mon Back to the Raft Ag'in Huck Honey!" Emerson sees the Harlem nightclub as a latter-day equivalent of Huck and Jim's raft (or at least Fiedler's version of it): it represents for him a place far away from the oppressive and "sivilizing" influence of a sterile bourgeois culture of Victorian respectability, a wilderness where the love that reigns is, as Fiedler puts it, the "mutual love of *a white man and a colored.*"[20] And if Emerson sees himself as a modern version of Fiedler's Huck, he not only seeks to gain his own sexual freedom in his liaisons with black men, he also wants to imitate his model by freeing the "Nigger Jims" he meets from their bondage.

By revealing to the narrator the contents of the letter he carries, Emerson does emancipate the narrator from his dependence on the figures of paternal authority that have subjugated him: Norton and Bledsoe. But the narrative makes clear that the relationship Emerson himself wishes to form with the invisible man would simply institute other forms of bondage. For Emerson's putative offer of friendship takes the form of an offer of employment. He invites the narrator to serve as his valet: to function not only as a domestic servant, but also as hired companion of his bedroom and closet. Apparently the only qualifications that make the narrator suited for this position are the contours of his body. Ellison notes that Emerson looks at the invisible man with "a strange interest in his eyes," an interest that focuses on his physique (180): "'You have the build [of an athlete],' he said, looking me up and down. 'You'd probably make an excellent runner, a sprinter'" (183). The relationship that Emerson wishes to establish with the narrator is not only homosexual, but also defined fundamentally by the inequality of power that structures the relationship of employer and employee.

This covert desire to place the invisible man in a subordinate role is also suggested by the acquisitive interest that Emerson, as a collector of beautiful exotic objects, takes in the invisible man.[21] For Ellison suggests that by taking the position offered him, the narrator would become simply another exhibit in Emerson's "museum" of an office. Displayed prominently in this room are various objects from all over the world:

There were paintings, bronzes, tapestries, all beautifully arranged. . . .

. . . a teakwood chair with cushions of emerald-green silk . . . a beautiful dwarf tree . . . a lighted case of Chinese design which held delicate-looking statutes of horses and birds, small vases and bowls, each set upon a carved wooden base . . . [and] an aviary of tropical birds set near one of the broad windows. (180–81)

Ellison makes clear that the invisible man is in danger of becoming part of this display by linking him with one of the birds held captive in Emerson's aviary. The narrator watches as a "large bird began a song, drawing my eyes to the throbbing of its bright blue, red and yellow throat. It was startling and I watched the surge and flutter of the birds as their colors flared for an instant like an unfurled oriental fan" (181). This same bird seems to sound a note of warning as Emerson approaches the narrator in advance of his job offer: "I got up, dazed, and started toward the door. He came behind me into the reception room where the birds flamed in the cage, their squawks like screams in a nightmare" (192). To accept Emerson's invitation of employment would be tantamount to becoming, like the caged bird, part of a "museum" devoted to objects that gratify a taste for things exotic. And if the invisible man would come to resemble the bird by accepting this offer, he would also apparently come to resemble, once again, the nude dancer whose gaudy coloring matches that of the bird's iridescent throat: her hair is "yellow," her face "rouged," and her eyes "smeared a cool blue" (19). He would be made to function as the "feminine" object of an erotic, white male visual pleasure.

By presenting Emerson's purportedly benevolent interest in black men as motivated by both a homosexual attraction and an underlying racist impulse, Ellison introduces a latent homophobic logic into his novel. For if the exploitative relationship that Emerson wishes to establish with the narrator is presented as mirroring the exploitative relationships that the other white male characters seek to forge with black men, then his homosexual desire is presented as analogous to the erotic desires that the other white male characters seek to satisfy through their subordination of black men. The erotic motivations of these supposedly benevolent white men, who are revealed as closeted racists, are thereby likened to the libidinal impulses of gay men. But it is important to note that this homophobic logic, while clearly present, does not exert a wholly cohesive force in the novel as it was finally published.

For neither Emerson nor his homosexual desire assume a fully paradigmatic status vis-à-vis the other white male characters and their desires. While he, Norton, and the townsmen are presented in a loose conspiracy to "Keep this Nigger Running," to make the actions of the narrator cater to their desires, they diverge in the kinds of pleasures they seek. Although the interest that Emerson and the townsmen take in black men seems saturated with homo-eroticism, Norton's erotic interest does not centrally focus on the bodies of black men and only manifests itself in a highly attenuated form. Moreover, this sexual element seems missing from the Brotherhood, Ellison's literary representation of the Communist Party. Brother Jack and his cohort are not presented as impelled by any force of libido. Rather, they appear as nearly robotic, devoid of any human emotion at all, driven as they are in their polit-ical machinations by an abstract and dehumanizing logic, by a "scientific" view of history in which black men appear merely as variables to be factored into a calculus of power.

All the white male characters are presented, in other words, as variations on a theme, but none of them emerges from the novel as the definitive artic-ulation of that theme. But in a moment when the narrator reflects upon the similarity of the white men he has known, he imagines the possibility of a figure that could symbolize all of them:

> And now I looked around a corner of my mind and saw Jack and Norton and Emerson *merge into one single white figure*. They were very much the same, each attempting to force his picture of reality upon me and neither giving a hoot in hell for how things looked to me. I was simply a material, a natural resource to be used. I had switched from the arrogant absurdity of Norton and Emerson to that of Jack and the Brotherhood, and it all came out the same. (508; my emphasis)

There is no such "single white figure" that appears in the published version of the novel. The townsmen do take on a kind of paradigmatic status, as I established earlier, but they are rendered in the aggregate, as a collective mass of white men; they are not individuated sufficiently for any one of them to stand in typologically for the other white male characters in the book.

Such a character does appear, however, in an *earlier* version of the novel's eleventh chapter. This white man—invisible in the published work—com-bines features of every other white male character, almost as if he were a kind of composite sketch. Notably, this "single white figure" is depicted as homosexual, and his "impure" interest in the invisible man—which mixes together a sadistic racism and a homosexual desire—is presented as a kind of archetype for the interest that other white men take in black men. The latent homophobic symbolism detectable in the final version of *Invisible Man* manifests itself, then, in a more disturbingly explicit form in Ellison's earlier conception of the novel.[22]

A "Single White Figure"

In 1963, Ellison published a piece that he identified as the novel's original eleventh chapter under the title, "Out of the Hospital and Under the Bar." In this text, Mary Rambo, who is a relatively minor character in the published novel, plays a much more significant role. She is working as a janitor in the factory hospital where the narrator has regained consciousness to find himself confined in an odd womb-like machine. The narrator has no memory of who he is or of how he got there. Mary discovers the invisible man in his state of incarceration and wishes to help free him. But she is put off by what she believes to be the narrator's lack of trust in her: she thinks that his amnesia is only an act. Only when he improvises a tale that explains his predicament, with Mary's prodding assistance, does she come to believe him. What concerns us here is the story he tells. The reason for his incarceration, he explains to Mary, is that he has struck and possibly killed a white man who tried to assault him sexually.

This story, while it has a fictive status within the diegetic world of the novel, takes on a certain allegorical force in relation to the exchanges with white male characters that have been recounted earlier. In the midst of spinning this tale, the narrator finds himself suddenly "gripped by a feeling that I was relating an actual happening, something that had occurred sometime, somewhere, in my past."[23] This sense that the story is partially a reenactment of previous events is further suggested by the narrator's description of the white man who propositions him: this figure combines key features of the other white male characters who have appeared already in the novel. Even within his state of amnesia, the narrator seems to remember (if only unconsciously) certain details from each of his encounters with white men, and apparently draws upon them as he creates this character. He places this encounter in what would seem to be a Southern setting, and thus this invented character's regional identity connects him with the townsmen who orchestrate the battle royal.[24] This invented character's homosexuality suggests that he is also partially derived from Young Emerson. The detail that connects him to Norton, moreover, connects him to each of the other white male characters. For this white man tries to coerce the narrator into succumbing to his sexual advances by demanding: "Now nigger, I want you to stand still while I put this twenty-dollar bill in your pocket" (255). Every white man the narrator has thus far met has made his seemingly altruistic overtures through an offer of money.

Because of the confessional status of this invented narrative, the desires that he imputes to this figure seem to symbolize the white male desires that the narrator has already been asked to satisfy in his earlier exchanges. What this imagined character wants, first of all, is for the invisible man to acknowledge verbally the hierarchy between them. He asks the question, "Look at me, black boy, what kind of man am I?" to which the narrator replies: "You're a white man" (254). He also demands that the invisible man specify his own racial identity:

> "And he said, 'All right, all right, so I'm a white man, and what are you?'"
> "And what you say then, boy?" [Mary] asked.
> "I said, 'I'm colored, sir,' but it seemed it make him very angry. . . . His face changed while I was looking at it fast."
> "Yeah, he wanted you to call yourself a nigger [. . .]" (254)

But the self-naming to which he wishes the invisible man to submit involves an acceptance of a very specific definition of what, exactly, a "nigger" is:

> "[. . .] 'Well he became very angry and said, 'That's right, you're a black, stinking, low-down nigger bastard that's probably got the syph and I'm white and *you're supposed to do whatever I say, understand* . . . ?'"
> (254; my emphasis)

To be the "nigger" for the white man is not only to accept and acknowledge one's racially subordinate status, it is more precisely to relinquish authority over one's body—to allow one's body to do whatever the white man says it should do.

This figure's desire to impose his will upon the actions of the invisible man is presented, however, as merely a means by which he can achieve another end. After the narrator supplies the correct racial answer to the query, "Look at me, black boy, what kind of man am I?" the man quickly demands: "That's right, but what *other* kind of man am I?" (254). The narrator explains to Mary that though he was initially baffled by this question, he quickly came to understand its meaning:

> "I was thinking about trying to run past him, when all at once he jammed his hand in his pocket and brought out a big roll of bills. He said, 'Now nigger, I want you to stand still while I put this twenty-dollar bill in your pocket.' And I looked at him, and saw that the side of his mouth was twitching and his voice was shaky. I had never heard a man's voice sound like that . . ." (255)

Eventually, the invisible man tells Mary, "he reached out and touched me and I swung the bottle at him and ran" (256).

In essence, Ellison suggests here that what leads this imaginary white character—who is both a white man and "that *other* kind of man"—to coerce the invisible man into assuming the subordinate position of "nigger" is ultimately a homosexual desire to use his body as a source of erotic pleasure. Put more generally, this exchange suggests something like the following: *white men seek to subordinate black men because that subordination enables them to use the black male body to gratify an erotic desire that is essentially homosexual.* While the homophobic logic of this assertion is disturbing enough, what's even more disturbing is the cohesive force it exerts as a whole over the initial version of the novel. For this fabricated story is not only shadowed by the narrator's past encounters—it not only mirrors "actual happening[s] . . . that had occurred sometime, somewhere in the past"—it also adumbrates the "happening" that will occur in the future: his seduction into the political machinery of the Brotherhood.

The connection between this imaginary white man and the members of the Brotherhood is suggested by a microscope he carries—a microscope with which he initially threatens to strike the narrator, and which he then offers as part of his payment. The narrator reveals to the reader that he's added this detail by "remembering the instruments pointed at me by the physicians" (253). But as an instrument designed to enhance the vision of scientifically minded men, the microscope links this figure not only to the doctors, but also to the men of the Brotherhood, who will, in subsequent chapters, attempt to bend his actions to their will by opening up to him their "scientific" view of history. This linkage is further suggested by Mary Rambo: "I heard them nurses talking 'bout you. They say they even got one of the psychiatristses[sic] and a socialist or sociologist or something looking at you all the time" (245, 248). Psychiatrist, socialist, or sociologist: they are all about the same to Mary. Moreover, Ellison's chapter as a whole suggests that they all then resemble that *other* "kind" of white man: the racist homosexual conjured up by the narrator in order to explain his predicament. In other words, Ellison asserts that beneath the purportedly "scientific" and benign interest that Brother Jack and his cohort take in the black race is a racist desire that resembles this imaginary white man's desire to have the invisible man assume the subordinate position of "nigger." Moreover, Ellison insinuates another claim, though he never fully fleshes it out: that the members of the Brotherhood seek to impose control over the lives of black men in order to satisfy an erotic desire that remains largely closeted—an invisible desire, we might say—that resembles the homosexual desire of this "single white figure."

The "Lady of the Races": The Sociology of Robert E. Park

For the most part, the attacks that Ellison levels at various types of racially progressive white men in *Invisible Man* are mirrored by the criticisms he offers of their real-life counterparts in his extra-novelistic commentary: in numerous essays and interviews (which I will be addressing in the next chapter), he questions the motivations of the philanthropists who supported Booker T. Washington's regime at Tuskegee, the bohemian patrons who sponsored the Harlem Renaissance, and the white Communist Party functionaries who attempted to mobilize the black working class. One white figure whom Ellison describes as having played a pivotal role in shaping his novelistic vision, however, seems entirely absent from *Invisible Man*: Robert E. Park, the prominent sociologist who was a foundational figure in the so-called "Chicago School."

This absence seems all the more curious given the prominent place that Park's ideas occupy in Ellison's own account of the genesis of *Invisible Man* and in his remembrances of a crucial event that fueled his literary aspirations. In the introduction he wrote for the thirtieth anniversary edition of the novel (1982), Ellison suggested that the process of writing began when he suddenly heard the "ironic, down home voice" of his protagonist and narrator, a voice that "seemed to tease me with allusions to that pseudoscientific sociological concept which held that most Afro-Americans difficulties sprang from our 'high visibility.' "[25] In an interview that was published in *Harper's Magazine*, Ellison described *Invisible Man* as a "novel about a man characterized by what the sociologists term 'high visibility.'"[26] When asked by Arlene Crewdson in 1974 to explain what he had been referring to, he replied with the following:

> Sociologists used to say—for example Park and Burgess published right here in Chicago, you know, which is one of the centers for American sociology—used to say that the great problem of the American Negro is caused because of his high visibility. After all, we have more pigment than most people so if you put us in a crowd you can always pick us out.[27]

Park also assumes a pivotal role in Ellison's account of a seminal event that fueled his literary aspirations more generally. In the introduction to *Shadow and Act* (1964), Ellison describes with some lingering bitterness an incident that had happened three decades earlier, when he was a sophomore at Tuskegee, still nursing aspirations to become a professional musician and composer:

> I had undergone, not too many months before taking the path which led to writing, the humiliation of being taught in a class in sociology at a Negro college (from Park and Burgess, the leading textbook in the field) that Negroes represented the "lady of the races.". . . Well, I had no intention of being bound by any such humiliating definition of my relationship to American literature. (xx)

The view of the Negro that Park promoted, which apparently engendered a profound sense of "humiliation," came to epitomize for Ellison the perspective on black life that he would devote his literary career to combating. This encounter taught Ellison that "nothing could go unchallenged; especially that feverish industry dedicated to telling Negroes who and what they are, and which can usually be counted upon to deprive both humanity and culture of their complexity" (xx).

Despite the patently self-mythologizing impulse that structures these autobiographical fragments, they do nonetheless suggest an enduring intellectual preoccupation on Ellison's part with the prominent sociologist's views. After all, Ellison was still making reference to Park's writings in 1982, some five decades after encountering them, long after he had ceased to be a leading figure in the field. But if what Ellison suggests in these references is at least partially true—that his literary aspirations grew out of a disciplinary quarrel with sociology in general and with the views of Park in particular, and that this antagonism played a significant role in the development of *Invisible Man*'s governing conceit—then the question that emerges is this: where are the traces of this antagonism to be found in the novel itself? For no character appears in *Invisible Man* who typifies "the sociologist" in the same way that Brother Jack does the Communist Party ideologue, or Norton the Northern philanthropist, and so forth.

If we are to take Ellison at his word, however, it is possible to discern traces of Park's legacy in the novel's focus on the "look" of putatively progressive white men as it fixes upon the bodies of black men. What links together all of the white male characters is a particular way of seeing black men—a seeing that is so distracted by race that it renders black men invisible, a seeing that also aligns black men with femininity. A kind of prototype, in other words, for this kind of interracial homosocial look can be found in the two assertions of Park's that Ellison directly references in his essays and interviews: 1) that it is the "high visibility" of racial difference that impedes whites from wholly recognizing the humanity of blacks; and 2), that the Negro is the "lady among the races." In the psychoanalytic reading of white masculinity that he offers in his novel Ellison basically interprets the second of these assertions as a consequence of the first. In *Invisible Man*, when white men look at black men all they seem to see are the "highly visible" marks of racial difference etched upon their bodies. While Park explains this tendency on the part of white Americans—as I will discuss momentarily—as the expression of a supposedly universal human tendency, *Invisible Man* offers a more racial- and gender-specific psychoanalytic reading of this mode of seeing: what Ellison brings into critical focus are the ways in which white *men* look at black *men*, suggesting that the impulses expressed through this looking are, ultimately, of a sadistic and erotic kind. By situating Park's views in a psychoanalytic framework, the second of his assertions—which insists on the femininity of the Negro—is rendered as an effect of the first. Ellison suggests that if white men see the Negro—and the black man in particular—as feminine, this is not a product of the latter's racial temperament, as Park suggests; rather, this "femininity" is a projection of white male desires—it is a reflection of the ultimately erotic and sadistic pleasures that white men take in manipulating the bodies of black men. If white men see the black man as feminine, in other words, this is because they *wish* him to play a role that is traditionally fulfilled, under a racist patriarchy, by white or black women. It is not, then, simply the image of the hypervirile black male codified in the rape mythos— an ideology that would have been embraced by the most overtly racist of white supremacist ideologues—that Ellison subjects to psychoanalytic critique in *Invisible Man*, but the feminizing image of blackness promoted by progressive whites—by, for instance, the eminent sociologist Robert E. Park.[28]

That the figure of Robert E. Park provided a focal point for Ellison's hostility toward the discipline of sociology is apparent from his review of Gunnar Myrdal's *An American Dilemma*. Ellison wrote this essay in 1944, one year before he began composing his first novel. Ellison's critique of Myrdal's work targets the discipline of sociology as a whole: he tends to present sociologists, in George O'Meally's words, as members of an "insidious circle," even a "conspiracy."[29] White social scientists who claim to work on behalf of racial equality, according to Ellison, have actually "used their graphs, charts and other paraphernalia to prove the Negro's biological, psychological, and intellectual and moral inferiority" (305). Exemplary of this tendency is the work of Park, whose racial progressivism Ellison appears to acknowledge,[30] but who maintains a view of the Negro's genetically transmitted racial "temperament" that is so abhorrent it warrants a comparison to "the preachings . . . of Dr. [Joseph] Goebbels" (308).

Traces of Park's legacy also become discernible in *Invisible Man* when we consider his involvement in two of the programs for black uplift that it pillories. Ellison hints at these connections in his introduction to *Shadow and Act*. He identifies "that feverish industry dedicated to telling Negroes who and what they are" as including not only "sociologists," but also Booker T. Washington's so-called "Tuskegee regime" and "an older generation of Negro leaders and writers—those of the so-called 'Negro Renaissance'" (xx). Park (like Norton) provided significant support to both of these institutions.

When Ellison refers to Park, in his review of *An American Dilemma*, as "the man responsible for inflating Tuskegee into a national symbol, and who is sometimes spoken of as the 'power behind Washington's throne'" (307), he is alluding to the work Park did for Washington before embarking on his academic career. Prior to his assuming a faculty position at Chicago at the age of forty-nine, Park served, for roughly a decade, as Washington's press agent and ghost writer. According to Louis R. Harlan, Park not only drafted grant proposals to procure funding for Tuskegee, he also helped bring many of Washington's manuscripts "into more polished and sophisticated condition": he "researched, drafted, or revised most of Washington's writings for publication between 1905 and 1912, including his principle magazine articles and even many of his letters, particularly to foreigners."[31]

Park was also an important figure, according to the historian George M. Fredrickson, for the Harlem Renaissance. According to Fredrickson, Park's highly influential assertions concerning the Negro's racial temperament—the very ones that apparently engendered a feeling of "humiliation" in the young Ellison—helped "set the tone for subsequent appreciation of black cultural achievements," facilitating the "patronizing white encouragement of the 'New Negro' movement and the 'Harlem Renaissance.'"[32] Park's writings helped repopularize a racial doctrine that Fredrickson terms "romantic racialism," which was originally formulated by progressive white intellectuals of the antebellum who were mainly fervent opponents of slavery. While these romantic racialist thinkers "acknowledged that blacks were different than whites and probably always would be," Fredrickson writes, they also "projected an image of the Negro that could be construed as flattering or laudatory in the context of some currently accepted ideals of human behavior and sensibility."[33] The "flattering" image of the Negro disseminated by these nineteenth-century intellectuals, however, tended largely to reaffirm "the 'child' stereotype of the most sentimental school of proslavery paternalists and plantation romancers"; indeed their primary argument against slavery was that "it took unfair advantage of the Negro's innocence and good nature."[34] The Negro, within the stock formulations of romantic racialism, was "singularly childlike, affectionate, docile, and patient."[35] This doctrine enjoyed a resurgence in the early decades of the twentieth century largely because of Park, according to Fredrickson, and it was the reascendence of this ideology that helped pave the way for the Harlem Renaissance.

I want to conclude this chapter with brief analyses of the two contentions of Park to which Ellison makes direct reference: his claims concerning the Negro's "lady"-like "temperament" and his "high visibility." Reexamining the pivotal role that this eminent sociologist's views had in shaping Ellison's aesthetic vision helps to explain its highly masculinist character, which I will be elaborating in the next chapter.[36] For the Negro temperament Park identifies is depicted not only as feminine but also as tending toward a rather limited repertoire of expressive modes. I will also be drawing attention to the *multi*racial context of the cultural conversation in which Park is engaged. While this does not lead us to a hidden Asian American subtext to Ellison's own writings, it does enable us to recognize that he was writing in response to a sociological understanding of race that addressed the "high visibility" of both Japanese Americans and African Americans.

*

Given the eminent status that he enjoyed as a sociologist, it is not entirely surprising that Robert E. Park would be the primary target of many of Ellison's critical remarks concerning this discipline. He was, according to George M. Fredrickson, "widely recognized as the foremost white student of race relations in the period between the World Wars."[37] The vast bulk of the research that Park conducted and supervised during the decades he taught at the University of Chicago and at Fisk University focused sympathetically on the plight of minority groups, a legacy that places him in a comparable position in his field to the one occupied by Franz Boas in anthropology. Indeed, Fred H. Matthews, in his book-length study of the sociologist, asserts that "like Franz Boas, Park was a leading figure in the transition from a 'biological' to a 'cultural' point of view in the study of group conflict."[38] The sociological approach to race relations championed by Park identified white prejudice as the primary factor in determining the subordinate place that blacks and other racial minorities occupied in the U.S. social order. Ellison himself acknowledged, if somewhat begrudgingly, the significance of this work: "The positive contributions of Dr. Park and those men connected with him are well established. American Negroes have benefited greatly from their research; and some of the most brilliant of Negro scholars have been connected with them" (*Shadow*, 307). Ellison also alludes in this essay to the several prominent African American sociologists who received their training under Park: Horace Cayton, St. Clair Drake, and E. Franklin Frazier.

Despite Park's evident racial progressivism, he seemed to maintain a residual belief in the genetic bases of racial difference through much of his intellectual career.[39] Whether he ever fully abandoned this belief is a matter of some debate. At any rate, it was his assertions concerning the Negro's "racial temperament" that seemed to have most provoked Ellison's outrage. Ellison evidently encountered Park's views in an essay that was included in the

Introduction to the Science of Sociology. This textbook—which was widely known as the "Green Bible," according to the historian Henry Yu[40]—was edited by Park and Edward Burgess and first published in 1921. At just over a thousand pages in length, this anthology of writings by a number of influential philosophers and social scientists served as the standard textbook in the field for nearly two decades. Park's commentary on the Negro's racial temperament is found in a piece entitled "Temperament, Tradition, and Nationality," which is drawn from a slightly longer essay he had published in 1918, "Education in Its Relation to the Conflict and Fusion of Cultures." Here I will be considering the original, slightly longer version of this essay, which contains Park's analyses of Negro American folk culture: it is on the basis of these analyses that Park draws his conclusions concerning Negro temperament in particular as well as his more generalized hypotheses concerning the dialectic between the biological and cultural determinants of racial identity, between what he terms "temperament" and "tradition." It is also on the basis of this material that Park identifies a kind of Negro aesthetic.

While Park's focus in this essay is on temperament, the "complex of inherited characteristics, which are racial," he does acknowledge that the "racial will is, to be sure, largely social, that is modified by social experience."[41] But "the history of the American Negro," he argues, provides an invaluable archive for identifying which aspects of the "racial" will are inherited, are a product of temperament. He does so by comparing the folk culture of American blacks with that of European ethnic groups—Italians, Scots, and Finns, in particular. While certain commonalities can be found in the folk songs of each of these groups, he insists that those of blacks are "ruder and more primitive" (275). What Park means by this is the lack of formal complexity and sophistication he finds in the *lyrical* content of this music. He thus concludes that it is not in their words that their racially distinctive character is to be found; rather,

> In Negro folk-songs the music and expression are everything. The words, often striking and suggestive to be sure, represent broken fragments of ideas, thrown up from the depths of the Negroes' consciousness and swept along upon a torrent of wild, weird, and often beautiful melody. (276)

By focusing on melody, Park claims to provide the key for divining essential features of the Negro's racial temperament. He argues that W. E. B. Du Bois was mistaken in referring to spirituals in *The Souls of Black Folk* as "sorrow songs," a label that affirms the erroneous notion that most of them are "in a plaintive minor key" (278). "As a matter of fact," Park contends,

> investigation has shown that actually less than 12 per cent of Negro songs are in a minor key. There are no other folk-songs, with the exception of those of Finland, of which so large a percentage are in the major mood. And this is interesting as indicating the racial temperament of the Negro. It tends to justify the general impression that the Negro is naturally sunny, cheerful, optimistic. (278)[42]

Largely on the basis of this interpretation of these folk-songs, Park offers his own conclusions in the final pages of this essay concerning the constituent elements of the Negro's racial temperament:

> The temperament of the Negro, as I conceive it, consists in a few elementary but distinctive characteristics, determined by physical organizations and transmitted biologically. These characteristics manifest themselves in a genial, sunny, and social disposition, in an interest and attachment to external, physical things rather than to subjective states and objects of introspection, in a disposition for expression rather than enterprise and action. (138–39)

The Negro is, then, genetically predisposed to aesthetic expression, but of an obviously limited kind. The kind of art toward which he will be inclined, given the pressure exerted by the "selective agency" of his temperament, will give expression to his "genial, sunny, and social disposition"; it will apparently be absent of "subjective states and objects of introspection," nor will it convey "enterprise and action." Negro expression will therefore tend to be "in the major mood."

Shortly following the passage cited above is the one that apparently engendered a feeling of "humiliation" in the nineteen-year-old Ellison. In it Park elaborates further the "distinctive[ness]" of the racial characteristics intrinsic to the Negro:

> The Negro is, by natural disposition, neither an intellectual nor an idealist, like the Jew; nor a brooding introspective, like the East Indian; nor a pioneer and frontiersman, like the Anglo-Saxon. He is primarily an artist, loving life for its own sake. His *métier* is expression rather than action. He is, so to speak, the lady among the races. (139)

The two rhetorical strategies Park deploys in this passage seem to work at cross purposes: on the one hand he suggests the existence of a *continuum* of racial types; and on the other he invokes a series of *binary oppositions*, drawing most importantly on the familiar binary of sexual difference. The clash of these rhetorical strategies produces some logical dissonances that Park attempts to resolve by privileging the second: he tends, in other words, to collapse his continuum of racial types into a crude binary. At one level, he simply lists various races and their "elemental characteristics": the intellectual, idealistic Jew; the brooding, introspective East Indian; the pioneering, frontier-loving Anglo Saxon; the artistic, life-loving, and expressive Negro. But at another level, he fractures this continuum by invoking the analogy of sexual difference to set the Negro apart from the other races as "the lady among the races"; at a single semantic stroke, the elemental "characteristics" reflective of the other races are lumped together as masculine, despite the contradictions that emerge from the arbitrary imposition of this sexual binary. For instance, the putatively masculine tendency toward "enterprise and action" that defines the Anglo-Saxon would appear to be equally lacking in the Jew, East Indian, and Negro (given their respective racial traits), yet it is only the Negro that is singled out as "the lady among the races." Similarly, the intellectualism, idealism, and brooding introspection apparent in two of the allegedly masculine races—the Jew and East Indian—would seem to be as foreign to the action-oriented Anglo-Saxon as they apparently are to the Negro; but again, the feminizing label is only affixed to the latter.

One point I would like to make about this passage, which has larger ramifications for my project as a whole, is that it illustrates how a binarized mode of thinking drawn from the putatively natural presupposition of sexual difference abets the construction of a black/white conception of racial difference. By separating out the Negro here as the feminine race, all of the other races are rendered as similar enough to be implicitly categorized together as masculine. A collateral effect of the imposition of this gendered binary is that what we might call the intermediate races here—the Jew and the East Indian—are positioned as more proximate to the Anglo Saxon than to the Negro, are rendered proximate to whiteness. This tension between a conception of racial difference that is grafted onto to the supposedly more self-evident binary of sexual difference and one that depicts a multiplicity of races takes a decidedly different shape in the historical period I examine in the second half of this study, where I address the writings of Frank Chin.

I would also like to emphasize that Park's feminizing account of the Negro's racial temperament—the account that Ellison presents himself as seeking to challenge—carries with it an incipient theory of black aesthetic expression. For the gendered divide that Park's typology establishes between the Negro as "the lady among the races" and the more presumably masculine races suggests an aesthetic divide as well. If, on the one hand, the lady-like Negro is "primarily an artist"—if "his *métier* is expression"—and if, on the other, he is not genetically predisposed to brooding introspection and intellectual idealism (as are the Jew and East Indian, respectively), then it would follow that the art he produces would be rather unidimensional—would simply be the spontaneous expression of the Negro's "genial, sunny and social disposition." Park's writings thus directly link Negro expression and femininity. Given the gendered terms in which this racializing discourse is couched, it seems nearly inevitable that in dedicating his literary career to challenging "that feverish industry dedicated to telling Negroes who and what they," Ellison would be driven by an impulse not only to reverse a view of the Negro as "lady"-like, but also to assert the virility of black aesthetic expression.

It is worth acknowledging, however, that Park's writings on race were progressive for the period. Even his patently patronizing assertions concerning Negro temperament, when seen in the context of the more virulent expressions of nativist xenophobia and racism that were dominant in the United States during the late teens and early twenties, appear relatively benign. Moreover, as Fred H. Matthews puts it, "Park's belief in distinctive 'racial temperaments' was shared by militant Negroes of the early twentieth century, including W. E. B. Du Bois, who stressed the emotional expressive nature of 'the Negro.'"[43] But this biological emphasis is in tension with the emphasis Park places elsewhere in his writings on the *social* determinants of race prejudice. (It is this dimension of his thought in which the concept of "high visibility" appears.) According to Matthews, the more progressive and productive aspect of Park's sociology was contained in his belief that "the basis of [racial] difference was not racial traits as such but people's sensitivity to them."[44] "From this perspective," Matthews continues, "what is important is less the innate qualities of the different racial groups than the terms and stages of their interaction and the attitudes which are produced therein."[45] By developing what Matthews calls an "interactional theory" of race relations, "Park did much to encourage what later became the dominant mode of [sociological] analysis, the study of 'prejudice' among dominant or 'majority' groups."[46] Matthews ultimately concludes that "Park's theory of racial temperament . . . was logically separate from the fresher interactional theories which his students would carry forward," students who included the African American sociologists Charles S. Johnson and E. Franklin Frazier, as well as the first generation of Asian and Asian American sociologists, a group that included figures like Frank Miyamoto and Rose Hum Lee.[47]

That Ellison was as dismissive of this apparently more progressive dimension of Park's writings as he was of the more obviously regressive assertions concerning Negro temperament is discernible from statements I have already cited. In the introduction to the thirtieth edition of *Invisible Man* he refers to this aspect of Park's thought as "pseudoscientific," and he describes "high visibility" as "a phrase as double-dealing and insidious as its more recent oxymoronic cousins, 'benign neglect' and 'reverse discrimination,' both of which translate 'Keep those Negroes running—but in their same old place'" (xv). Ellison's objections center on the ways in which Park's conception of "high visibility" seems to make racial pigmentation itself the determining cause of white racism; this, to a certain extent, holds African Americans themselves—or at least their skins—responsible for the racism to which they are subjected.

Ellison's gloss of Park's "interactional theory" of race relations—"most Afro-American difficulties sprang from our 'high visibility'"—is not entirely accurate. Park's emphasis was not, strictly speaking, on the bodily markers of racial difference so highly visible to the white eye, but on certain "deep-seated, vital, and instinctive impulses" within the white psyche that will inevitably fixate on those bodily markers. While this contention is less "insidious" than Ellison would contend, what is troubling about Park's views is the way in which his assertions concerning the Negro's temperament appear to suggest that blacks lack a putatively universal trait—a tendency toward racial antipathy that is abundantly apparent in the Anglo-Saxon and discernible in the Japanese.

It is likely that Ellison encountered Park's assertions concerning "high visibility" in the same textbook in which he confronted the claim that the Negro was "the lady among the races." Three of Park's contributions to the *Introduction to the Science of Sociology* elaborate his account of race prejudice: "The Assimilation of Races," "Conflict and Race Consciousness," and "Social Contacts and Race Conflict." The first two of these pieces were drawn from a longer essay Park had published in 1913, "Racial Assimilation in Secondary Groups"; the third had originally been published in 1917 as an introduction to Jesse F. Steiner's *The Japanese Invasion*. Interestingly, what Ellison described as "that pseudoscientific sociological concept which held that most Afro-Americans difficulties sprang from our 'high visibility'" originated from a set of arguments that Park developed to address a predicament shared by both Japanese and African Americans. Indeed, the topical point of departure for these pieces is the question of why *both* of these minority populations in particular have been unable to blend into the mainstream of American life.

In these essays, Park posits the existence of a *universal* human tendency toward racial antipathy that has been present in all cultures and societies. When we look beneath the specific racial animosities that mark a given cultural moment, Park insists, we will perceive "deep-seated, vital, and instinctive impulses. Racial antipathies represent the collision of invisible forces, the clash of interests, dimly felt but not yet clearly perceived."[48] Park asserts "the existence in the human mind of a mechanism by which we inevitably and automatically classify every individual being we meet" (625). This natural tendency toward classification leads us to distinguish between *groups* of individuals—to distinguish, most fundamentally, between those whom we know and those whom we do not. While "[p]eoples we know intimately we respect and esteem," Park argues, "[i]n our casual contact with aliens, it is the offensive rather than the pleasing traits that impress us. These impressions accumulate and reinforce natural prejudices" (761). If we acknowledge the existence of a natural aversion to those whom we perceive as "aliens," and a related tendency to be "impress[ed]" by their "offensive rather than [their] pleasing traits," then we are very close to grasping the natural quality of *racial* discrimination in particular. For Park asserts that "[w]here races are distinguished by certain external marks, these furnish a *permanent* physical substratum upon which and around which the irritations and animosities, incidental to all human intercourse, tend to accumulate and so gain strength and volume" (761; my emphasis). And again: "When a race bears an external mark by which every individual member of it can infallibly be identified, that race is by that fact set apart and segregated" (625). Park thus emphasizes the tremendous difficulty that any "alien" group faces as it attempts to assimilate into a larger group. To do so, members of these minorities must overcome racial antipathies that are the expression of "deep-seated, vital, and instinctive impulses."

The successful process of assimilation that European immigrants to the

United States have undergone, Park argues, only attests to the nearly insuperable obstacles faced by minorities whose appearance is more drastically different from that of the majority population. For the only immigrants who have successfully assimilated in the American mainstream—namely those of European descent—have done so through a physical self-refashioning as well as a mental one. Assimilation entails not only a "a more or less complete adoption by the members of the smaller groups of the language, technique, and mores of the larger and more inclusive ones," it also demands the "eras[ure of] the external signs which formerly distinguished the members of one race from those of another" (757). Thus we find that "[i]n America it has become proverbial that a Pole, Lithuanian, or Norwegian cannot be distinguished, in the second generation, from an American born of native parents" (757). Immigrants of European descent are able to overcome the natural racial antipathy to which white Americans—like all human subjects—are prone because they are able to make themselves talk, think, *and* look like white Americans.

The Negro and the Oriental have, in contrast, been unable to assimilate into the mainstream population because they are simply unable to refashion themselves *physically* as American subjects:

> [T]he chief obstacle to the assimilation of the Negro and the Oriental are not mental but physical traits. It is not because the Negro and the Japanese are so differently constituted that they do not assimilate. If they were given an opportunity, the Japanese are quite as capable as the Italians, the Armenians, or the Slavs of acquiring our culture and sharing our national ideals. The trouble is not with the Japanese mind but with the Japanese skin. The Jap is not the right color. (760)

While Michael Omi and Howard Winant have criticized the approach to race relations that Park founded for developing an ethnicity-focused paradigm that "could not appreciate the extent to which racial inequality differed from ethnic inequality,"[49] this emphasis on the high visibility of racial difference as the catalyst for white racist attitudes toward Asians and blacks suggests otherwise.

But while it is possible to see the analytic and political advantages of Park's insistence on the particularity of racist forms of chauvinism, the sense of fatalism conveyed by the rhetorical formulations he uses to elaborate this argument has troubled some of his readers, including Gunnar Myrdal. This fatalism, which verges on *naturalizing* racist antipathy, is apparent in the following passage:[50]

> The fact that the Japanese bears in his features a distinctive racial hallmark, that he wears, so to speak, a racial uniform, classifies him. He cannot become a mere individual, indistinguishable in the cosmopolitan mass of the population, as is true, for example, of the Irish, and, to a lesser extent, of some of the other immigrant races. The Japanese, like the Negro, *is condemned to remain* among us an abstraction, a symbol—and a symbol not merely of his own race but of the Orient and of that vague, ill-defined menace we sometimes refer to as the "yellow peril." (760–61; my emphasis)

If it is true, as Park insists, that there exists in the human mind an ineradicable tendency toward racial antipathy, and if the Japanese, like the Negro "is *condemned* to remain among us an abstraction, a symbol" of alterity, is trapped within his "racial uniform," then it would seem that racism, like the poor, will simply always be with us.

Beyond this fatalism, moreover, there is another problematic aspect of Park's account to which I would like to call attention, which is that the tendency toward racial antipathy he identifies as a universal human trait is unevenly distributed among the various races. While it is on abundant display in the discriminatory practices of white Americans and evident in "the national pride and the national egotism" of Japanese Americans, as I will elaborate below, it seems to be less evident in the Negro. In the brief discussion of the antebellum South he includes in "The Assimilation of Races," Park seems to imply that the Negro slave simply lacked the "deep-seated, vital, and instinctive impulses" that manifest themselves in the putatively universal human tendency to feel antipathetic toward those who wear a "racial uniform" different than one's own.

In his account of American slavery, Park works from the assumption that slave systems are simply one of the natural solutions that human societies have developed to address the problem of racial competition and conflict, providing a mechanism for assimilating an "alien" minority population into the values of the majority culture. Indeed, Park insists that "[s]lavery has been, historically, the *usual* method by which peoples have been incorporated into alien groups" (761; my emphasis). The assimilation of the Negro to the U.S. social order was accomplished most effectively in the case of domestics who worked in the master's house, as it enabled white slave

owners to overcome their natural racial antipathy by drawing the Negro into
the ambit of the family:

> It is difficult to conceive two races farther removed from each other in tem-
> perament and tradition than the Anglo-Saxon and the Negro, and yet the
> Negro in the southern states, particularly where he was adopted into the
> household as a family servant, learned in a comparatively short time the
> manners and customs of his master's family. He very soon possessed himself
> of so much of the language, religion, and the technique of the civilization
> of his master as, in his station, he was fitted or permitted to acquire. Even-
> tually, also, Negro slaves transferred their allegiance to the state of which
> they were only indirectly members, or at least to their masters' families,
> with whom they felt themselves in most things one in sentiment and
> interest. (762)

Despite Matthews's contention that "Park's theory of racial temperament . . .
was logically separate from [his] fresher interactional theories," there is no
reason to believe that the concept of temperament, invoked in the very first
sentence of this paragraph, is being in any way questioned by the sentences
that follow.

Indeed the opening sentence and the contrast it establishes invite the
reader to recall that the Anglo-Saxon is, by temperament, "a pioneer and
frontiersman," which casts his slave-owning endeavors in a rather flattering,
even patriotic light. And if the social role played by the white slave owner
was in keeping with his racial temperament, the same would appear to be
true of the Negro slave. In his earlier essay on temperament, Park had described the Negro not only as "sunny, genial, and social," but also as marked
by a "natural attachment to known familiar objects, places, and persons," as
therefore "pre-adapted to local and personal loyalties" (140). This predispo-
sition toward loyalty, then, made of the Negro an ideal slave; and the system
of slavery provided the Negro with a "vocation" perfectly suited to his racial
temperament.[51] When we thus treat Park's belief in a biologically based racial
temperament as, *pace* Matthews, continuous with his "interactional theory"
of race relations, what becomes evident is the following: that the "lady"-like
temperament ascribed to the Negro presents him as lacking a tendency
toward racial antipathy that is allegedly a universal human propensity, one
that is abundantly apparent in the Anglo-Saxon. In other words, the racialized femininity that the Negro exemplifies is not only defined as the antithe-

sis of the racialized forms of masculinity embodied by the other races, it is
also defined by the absence of a putatively universal human trait—that psychological "mechanism by which we inevitably and automatically classify
every individual being we meet" that can manifest itself as racial antipathy.

To conclude my analysis of Park's account of "deep-seated, vital, and
instinctive impulses" that generate race prejudice, I would like to address the
differences he suggests between the two objects of white discrimination that
are his focus: the Negro and the Oriental. Park generally treats anti-black,
anti-Japanese, and anti-Chinese racism as identical: "Japanese, Chinese, and
Negroes cannot move among us because they bear marks which identify
them as members of their race" (625). Yet he also suggests that "prejudice
against the Japanese . . . is now more pronounced than it is against any other
oriental people" (624). "The reason for this," Park continues, "is that the
Japanese are more aggressive, more disposed to test the sincerity of that statement of the Declaration of Independence which declares that all men are
equally entitled to 'life, liberty, and the pursuit of happiness'" (624). This
aggressiveness on the part of Japanese immigrants, which is expressed by
their willingness to hold the United States accountable to its stated egalitarian values, apparently expresses the resurgence of Japanese national ideals
rather than an embrace of American ones: if "the Japanese is still less disposed than the Negro or the Chinese to submit to the regulations of a caste
system and stay in his place," this is due to the fact that

> [t]he Japanese are an organized and morally efficient nation. They have the
> national pride and the national egotism which rests on the consciousness
> of this efficiency. In fact, it is not too much to say that national egotism,
> if one pleases to call it such, is essential to national efficiency, just as a cer-
> tain irascibility of temper seems to be essential to a good fighter. (624)

Whereas the Negro and the Chinese are apparently willing to acquiesce to
their subordinate and separate positions in racially stratified society, the
"national pride and the national egotism" of the Japanese seemingly make it
more difficult for them to do likewise. While the essential compatibility of the
national ideals of the Japanese with those of the United States has not assisted
in their assimilation (because the "Jap" "bears in his features a distinctive racial
hallmark," because "he wears, so to speak, a racial uniform"), it does suggest
an essential similarity between these two national/racial groups: for if the Japanese possesses "a certain irascibility of temper . . . essential to a good fighter,"

this renders him rather like the masculine Anglo-Saxon, who is, we will recall, a "pioneer and frontiersman."

Evident in this passage is a clash of rhetorical strategies similar to the one that emerged in a passage I examined earlier, in Park's quasi-taxonomical survey of different racial types. Here too, though in a more understated way, an analogic reference to the binary of sexual difference works to underwrite a binarized conceptualization of racial difference. This reductive impulse operates even in those moments when Park seems attentive to the differences of ethnicity that break up the homogeneous category, Oriental. But the distinction Park makes between the Japanese and the Chinese relies upon and seems to reaffirm both binarizing logics: the Japanese, by being rendered similar to the Anglo-Saxon, is positioned as proximate to whiteness and thus implicitly to masculinity; likewise, the Chinese, by being rendered similar to the Negro, is positioned as proximate to blackness and thus implicitly to femininity. In addition, by suggesting that it is the fact that the Japanese is "more aggressive" than the Chinese that makes him "more disposed to test the sincerity of" the ideals enshrined in the Declaration of Independence, a third binary is implied here: in addition to being categorizable as more black or more white, more masculine or more feminine, races can also be distinguished by whether their essential temperaments suit them to being more or less American.

*

In my analyses of the sociological representation of race that Ellison literally presents himself as writing against, I have attempted to underscore the multiplicity of identitarian discourses that converge in it: racial, sexual, ethnic, and national. I have also emphasized the discursive momentum that seems to build up when the analogy of sexual difference is introduced in order to "explain" the nature of racial difference. The binarizing impetus that is released when an account of racial identity is couched in the language of gender seems to colonize, as it were, any other categories of identity introduced into that account. While it is a rather complicated nexus of binaries—action/expression, frontiersman/artist, white/black, Japanese/Chinese, American/non-American—that Park's writings mobilize, they are all rendered analogous, whether explicitly or implicitly, to that of masculine/feminine.

As will become clear in the second half of this book, gender will perform a similar function in binding together the identitarian discourses that converge in the racial representations that Frank Chin presents himself as challenging in his work. But while the interweaving of these various articulations of identity will take a formally similar structure in the period in which Chin writes, there will be some important differences. The most apparent of these differences will be that many of the qualities attributed by the Parkian sociology of the teens and twenties to the "lady"-like Negro Chin will regard as associated with the Asian. By pointing out the continuities and the discontinuities in the racializing discourses that Ellison and Chin confront in their writings I hope to accomplish two things: first, to demonstrate the persistence with which the category of race depends upon that of gender for the articulation of its meaning—in both racist and antiracist representations; second, to show that an analytical methodology that is attentive to the inter-articulation of racial, gendered, and sexual discourses can remain sensitive to the historically variable forms that this inter-articulation of identitarian discourse can take.

I will turn now in the next chapter to a consideration of Ellison's writings on the aesthetic, drawing particular attention to their masculinism—a masculinism that should be seen, I am arguing, as a response to the feminizing view of black expression epitomized by the writings of Robert E. Park. To recognize this masculinism is to perceive Ellison's rhetorical stance as prefiguring the ones adopted by the cultural nationalist writers with which I began this study. The affirmative and more expansive tenor of Ellison's critical pronouncements on black cultural expression are often seen as opposed to the supposedly more reductive and politically dogmatic aesthetic manifestos penned by writers like Amiri Baraka; however, the significant amount of ideological ground these projects actually share becomes apparent when their central and mutual reliance on a rhetoric of masculinity is acknowledged. Ellison, by linking the literary struggle for racial equality with the reclamation of black manhood, establishes an ideological template that will be reworked in the aesthetic theories of later male writers of color. To the nationalist male writers of the sixties and seventies, African American and Asian American, Ellison was, I would argue, a kind of ideological "ancestor," despite the fact that this intellectual genealogy was stridently disavowed by both parties.

TWO

Bluesprints for Negro Manhood:
Ellison and the Vernacular

> I don't deny that . . . sociological formulations are drawn from life, but I do deny
> that they define the complexity of Harlem. . . . Which is by no means to deny
> the ruggedness of life there, nor the hardship, the poverty, the sordidness, the
> filth. But there is something else in Harlem, something subjective, willfully, and
> complexly and compellingly human. It is that "something else" which makes for
> our strength, which makes for our endurance and our promise. This is the proper
> subject for the Negro American writer. Hell, he doesn't have to spend all the
> tedious time required to write novels simply to repeat what the sociologists and
> certain white intellectuals are broadcasting like a zoo full of parrots—and getting
> much more money for it than most Negro writers will ever see. If he does this,
> he'll not only go begging, but worse, he'll lie to his people, discourage their inter-
> est in literature, and emasculate his own talent.
>
> —*Ralph Ellison*[1]

At the very least, what can be gleaned from my analyses in the previous chapter and from statements like the one above is the pivotal function Ralph
Ellison assigned to sociology in shaping his literary project. Ellison's writings
on black cultural production function as a kind of reverse discourse: by
claiming "folklore, blues, jazz and black literature to be brainy yet *virile* subjects," as Darryl Pinckney puts it, Ellison sought to invert the view of black
expression promoted by Robert E. Park and other sociologists.[2] I will be looking in some detail in the concluding section of this chapter at the culmina-
tion of his aesthetic theories: the celebratory account he offers of the African
American vernacular tradition in his collection of essays *Shadow and Act*, in
which he engages in a near point-by-point rebuttal of Park's various assertions
concerning the Negro's creative proclivities. If Park insisted that expression
came naturally to the Negro, that it was simply a product of his genetically
transmitted racial temperament, Ellison maintained that "authentic" black

writers—like jazz players and bluesmen—only achieved mastery over the craft through an arduously achieved sense of discipline and an exacting study of prior aesthetic styles. If Park heard the "naturally sunny, cheerful, [and] optimistic" personality of the Negro expressed in folk songs and spirituals, Ellison attuned his ear instead to the blues, which give expressive form to a "tragicomic" sensibility that exemplified the particular contributions made by the Negro to American culture. If Park presented the Negro as the "lady among the races" in contrast to the Anglo-Saxon pioneer, Ellison countered with a view of jazz musicians and other black artists as "frontiersmen."

In drawing out the oppositional stance that Ellison adopts toward sociology in general and Park's views in particular my intent is not to reduce his literary project to a disciplinary quarrel with the views of one social scientist, however influential. It is, rather, to underscore the central function that this agonistic relationship to other purportedly "inauthentic" representations of black life performs in Ellison's conception of the aesthetic. This agonistic stance comprises, I want to suggest, the modernist core of Ellison's beliefs— beliefs that have been shared by a range of male writers of color—about how and why the literary domain functions as the site of resistance *par excellence* to a racism whose injurious effects are imagined through a gendered and sexualized symbolic vocabulary.

The term "sociological" is a highly resonant one in Ellison's writings: of the handful of adjectives that he affixes to those representations of the Negro he finds objectionable, "sociological" seems to be a particular favorite. Nearly every example he provides in his nonfictional writings of a representation of black life that needs to be corrected seems to bear the traces, in some way, of the sociological. This much is evident in his characterizations of the figure who is most regularly thought of as challenging his preeminence in the canon of African American male writers, Richard Wright. While Ellison will just as often refer to him as socialist rather than sociological, as ideologically constrained more by his membership in the Communist Party than by the fundamental influence on his work of the "Chicago School," it is not difficult to establish that many of the critical volleys he directs at "sociology-minded" writers also have Wright as their implicit target. After all, Wright plainly acknowledged his intellectual debt to sociology in his foreword to Horace Cayton's and St. Clair Drake's study of Chicago's South Side, *Black Metropolis*; he also drew heavily on this research in constructing his own documentary account of the Great Migration, *12 Million Black Voices*.[3]

Ellison's well-known criticisms of Wright indicate that the binary distinction he makes between "authentic" and "inauthentic" representations of blackness does not neatly coincide with a division between black- and white-authored texts. When he identifies particular members of "that feverish industry dedicated to telling Negroes who and what they are, and which can usually be counted upon to deprive both humanity and culture of their complexity,"[4] these figures are not always white. Indeed, as the epigraph to this chapter suggests, it often seems that what Ellison finds most distasteful are the *black* writers who "repeat what the sociologists and certain white intellectuals are broadcasting like a zoo full of parrots." Particularly salient for the purposes of my study is the linkage this passage makes between the passive repetition of demeaning white representations and an emasculated aesthetic sensibility. Black literary representations that merely parrot white "sociological formulations" are depicted as indicative of a racial "inauthenticity" figured as racial betrayal ("he'll lie to his people") and of an aesthetic "inauthenticity" that is figured as an abdication of manhood ("he'll . . . emasculate his own talent"). Discernible here is a version of the gendered rhetoric of inauthentication that is more forcefully articulated by writers like Amiri Baraka and Eldridge Cleaver. Indeed, I hope to suggest in this chapter that the gendered and sexualized symbolism that black nationalist writers deployed in the late sixties and early seventies in order to distinguish between the "authentic" and "inauthentic" may have been partially derived from a similar symbolic structure that was deployed by Ellison, first to distinguish his literary project from that of the Harlem Renaissance writers and then to separate himself from Richard Wright. In each of these moments, the black male writer's rhetorical need to claim the authenticity of his own literary project seems to require the invalidation (often in gendered or sexualized terms) of a prior model of black literary production.

A version of the masculinist binary that Phillip Brian Harper has located in the black nationalist rhetoric of authenticity, in other words, can be found in Ellison's assertions concerning the nature of black cultural expression. This dimension of his literary project is apparent in the premium he places on an aggressively mimetic form of homosocial desire as the primary psychic impulse animating all "authentic" literary production. Literary identity for Ellison is, at bottom, an intensely virile affair—it is fundamentally experienced as a kind of Bloomian agon, predicated as it is on the incorporation, imitation, and supercession of rivals. I will attempt in this chapter to map the ideological determinants that shaped Ellison's conception of the aesthetic, but in so doing I want also to insist on the psychic needs that this particular conception of the literary fulfills. I want to consider the *fantasmatic* quality of Ellison's insistence on viewing literature as "A Very Stern Discipline."[5]

This agonistic dimension of Ellison's aesthetic theory will likely be most familiar to readers from the vernacular theory he elaborates in *Shadow and Act*: from his commentary on the relationship of the novelist's craft to jazz and the blues, and, more specifically, from his celebrations of the "jam sessions" that are so central to the mythos surrounding these musical forms. In several of the essays he included in this volume, Ellison, by depicting his literary identity as being modeled on jazz and the blues, claims to occupy an organic relationship to the black working class. The strenuousness with which Ellison trumpeted this affiliation between his writing and the essential spirit of jazz and the blues was matched by the vigor with which he attempted to distinguish himself from Richard Wright. For, as most readers of Ellison also know, he rather consistently distinguished his view of writing from that of Wright's, never missing an opportunity (from about 1960 onward) to insinuate that the work of his former mentor and close friend was compromised by its ideological allegiances to sociology and Marxism. What is clearly being staged and also mystified in these aspersions, which are *calculatedly* casual, is the intense sense of rivalry that came to define his relationship to Wright. That a passionate homosocial rivalry of this kind is absolutely fundamental to the development of an authentic and individualized sense of literary voice is, in fact, theorized by Ellison in his writings on the vernacular; it also speaks to the centrality of a certain aestheticized version of male homosocial desire in the more recent vernacular theories of Houston Baker, Jr., and Henry Louis Gates, Jr.

I will begin this chapter, however, by bringing into focus the agonistic structure at the heart of Ellison's *first* formalized account of what black writing should be—one that preceded his rivalry with Wright. As the work of Michel Fabre has made clear, in the years before he began writing *Invisible Man* Ellison saw himself not as an adversary of Wright's, but rather as a devoted protégé.[6] Indeed, the primary "Other" against which Ellison projected his initial vision of black literary authenticity was that cultural movement for which Robert E. Park served (according to George Fredrickson and George Hutchinson) as a kind of ideological nursemaid—the Harlem Renaissance.[7]

Hating the Renaissance: "The Fruits of That Foul Soil"

In the final chapter of his study *The Black Image in the White Mind*, George Fredrickson suggests that the image of the New Negro promoted by advocates of the Harlem Renaissance bore a significant resemblance to the stereotype of the Old Negro that it was intended to replace. "The New Negro," according to Fredrickson, "as perceived by many whites, was simply the old romantic conception of the Negro covered with a patina of the cultural primitivism and exoticism fashionable in the '20s."[8] It is Park's description of the Negro as "the lady among the races" that instantiates for Fredrickson this resurgent romantic racialist view; and since the eminent sociologist "would come to be recognized as the foremost white student of race relations in the period between the World Wars," his patronizing view of the Negro's racial temperament "set the tone for subsequent appreciation of black cultural achievements."[9]

Given Ellison's antagonism to both Park and the Harlem Renaissance, it is somewhat surprising that he makes no direct mention in his nonfictional writings of this connection. The disdain with which Ellison regarded the movement, however, is clear not only from his depiction of its milieu in the ninth chapter of *Invisible Man* (which I examined in Chapter 1), but also in the first pieces of literary criticism he ever published: reviews and essays that appeared in the late thirties and early forties in socialist periodicals like *The New Masses*. The account of the Renaissance that Ellison offers in these pieces is virtually identical to the one that had been presented by Richard Wright in his 1937 literary manifesto, "Blueprint for Negro Writing." Indeed, there is much in these essays to confirm Michel Fabre's assertion that Ellison felt "a good deal of loyalty to Wright's controversial principles" during the crucial decade before he began writing *Invisible Man*, much more than he would later tend to admit.[10] One thing he shared with Wright was the extremely dim view he took of the black literary works that were produced during the twenties.

At the heart of Wright's and Ellison's critical perspective on the Harlem Renaissance is a governing assumption about the nature of the interracial relationships that sustained the movement, relationships that were often ones of patronage. The dominant view has tended to be that the inequities of power between the black and white figures at the heart of the Renaissance had a corrosive effect on the art that was produced. More recently, cultural critics Ann Douglas, George Hutchinson, and Ross Posnock have tried to offer more positive readings of the forms of interracialism characteristic of this cultural movement.[11] They have suggested that this highly critical view of interracialism reflects a residual black nationalist bias that has tended to frame most studies. Rather than trying to settle the issue of whether the interracialism of the Renaissance was generally equitable or exploitative—which is the issue that largely divides the recent treatments from the earlier ones—I would like to explore how it is that Ellison and Wright distinguish between disabling and enabling forms of interracialism. For Ellison and Wright, the question was not whether interracialism *in toto* was good or bad—both recognized that, in order to attain the forms of cultural and literary power they sought, a significant amount of interracial interaction was both necessary and desirable. But Ellison and Wright saw in the patronage that was an indelible part of the Harlem Renaissance a clear example of disabling interracialism.

In other words, the "inauthenticity" of the typical New Negro artist, as Ellison and Wright depict him, has everything to do with a basic orientation toward whiteness, an orientation that tended toward abjection and hapless mimicry and that was also clearly demarcated in class terms. This much is clear from the following passage, from Ellison's review of Hughes's *The Big Sea*, in which he heralded the arrival of a new nationalistic and potentially revolutionary spirit among working-class Negroes of the twenties:

> It happened that those who gave artistic expression to this new spirit were of the Negro middle class, or, at least, were under the sway of its ideology . . . these writers sought to wed the passive philosophy of the Negro middle class to the militant racial protest of the Negro masses. Thus, since the black masses had evolved no writers of their own, the energy of a whole people became perverted to the ends of a class which had grown conscious of itself through the economic alliances it had made when it supported the war. This expression was further perverted through the bohemian influences of white faddists whom the war had destroyed spiritually, and who sought in the Negro something primitive and exotic; many writers were supported by their patronage.[12]

The reason why Negro writing in this period was so susceptible to being "perverted through the bohemian influences of white faddists," Ellison suggests, has everything to do with the fact that it was largely an expression of "the shallow, imitative culture of the educated middle class Negro" (22). Not only did this writing, expressive of black bourgeois values, espouse a "passive philosophy," it produced a writing that was "apologetic in tone," "timid of theme, and for the most part technically backward."

Ellison is basically echoing here assertions that Wright had made four years earlier in his "Blueprint for Negro Writing." In this essay, Wright paints the culture of middle-class blacks in a most unflattering light, describing it as "parasitic and mannered";[13] he characterizes its literary products as

> prim and decorous ambassadors who went a-begging to white America. They entered the Court of American Public Opinion dressed in the knee-pants of servility, curtsying to show that the Negro was not inferior, that he was human, and that he had a life comparable to that of other people. For the most part these artistic ambassadors were received as though they were French poodles who do clever tricks. (394)

Referring more pointedly to the products of the New Negro Renaissance, Wright describes them as "the fruits of that foul soil which was the result of a liaison between inferiority-complexed Negro 'geniuses' and burnt-out white Bohemians with money" (395). Given the ideological debt that both Wright and Ellison openly acknowledge to modernist aestheticians like Eliot and Hemingway, it is not surprising to find that the Other against which they define the authenticity of art is a tradition of writing they depict as inanely bourgeois. While the Negro middle-class culture that flourished during the Renaissance is not explicitly identified in these essays with *femininity* per se, it is linked with a form of interracialism that is presented as enfeebling—as, indeed, emasculating.

In speaking of "the fruits of that foul soil which was the result of a liaison between inferiority-complexed Negro 'geniuses' and burnt-out white Bohemians with money" Wright is alluding to the sexual legacy of the Negro Renaissance—a dimension of it that became for many black writers, including Wright and Ellison, the apt symbol of its shortcomings. It is not difficult to see how the desire of a white patroness like Charlotte Mason for the writers she sponsored to produce an image of blackness catering to *her* expectations might have been perceived as analogous to the sexual desires of white Bohemians seeking an erotic taste of the exotic in Harlem nightclubs and rent parties. Wright's choice of phrase, "the fruits of that foul soil," also makes reference to what might justifiably be called the great "open secret" of the Harlem Renaissance.[14] Ann Douglas's monumental *Terrible Honesty: Mongrel Manhattan in the 1920s* is arguably the first study to address directly and explicitly an aspect of this cultural movement that has generally been acknowledged only through innuendo: namely, that "most of the best-known black male writers on the New York scene were homosexual."[15] By Douglas's count, this group includes most of the major male writers of the Renaissance: Langston Hughes, Countee Cullen, Wallace Thurman, Alain Locke, and Claude McKay; it also includes "minor talents" like Richard Bruce Nugent and Harold Jackman.[16] According to Eric Garber, Harlem in the twenties was not only home to a thriving "homosexual subculture" that was "uniquely Afro-American in substance," it was also a place where white homosexual men found "social acceptance," a sense of "identification," and a "feeling of kinship."[17] The white male figure who was the most influential proponent of Harlem's artists, Carl Van Vechten, was part of this group.

Phillip Brian Harper has suggested that it was this "widely acknowledged though generally only coyly acknowledged" aspect of the Harlem Renaissance that writers of the Black Arts Movement were responding to in their criticisms of it.[18] If the homosexuality of figures like Cullen and Locke—which symbolized their "inadequately developed black consciousness" and a concomitant "failed masculinity"[19]—proved an embarrassment to black male writers of the sixties and seventies, as Harper suggests, then the same seems to have been true for Wright and Ellison writing decades earlier.

In none of his critical remarks concerning the Renaissance, however, does Ellison explicitly allude to this dimension of the Renaissance. The only reference of this kind to be found in his published writings is in the ninth chapter of *Invisible Man* (which I examined in the previous chapter). What is implied in Ellison's depiction of Young Emerson—the neurotic decadent and devotee of Oscar Wilde whose homosexuality seems to allegorize the "bohemian fancies for things Negroid" that wealthy whites sought to indulge during the Renaissance through their sponsorship of black artists— is that the offer of employment he extends to the invisible man has been extended before, and that other black men have been quite willing to accept that offer. What this scene conjures, in other words, beyond the edges of what it actually depicts is a spectral figure of another kind. Although the reader is spared the experience of meeting such a character, the narrative does seem to imply the existence of young black men who would, unlike the invisible man, be happy to play "Nigger Jim" to would-be "Hucks" like

Young Emerson. What this scene suggests but never fleshes out, in other words, is another kind of invisible man—the black "faggot" stigmatized by his sexualized desire for white men. Hovering in the space between the ninth chapter of *Invisible Man*, "Recent Negro Fiction," and "Blueprint for Negro Writing," in other words, is an incipient version of the homophobic symbolism that Cleaver and other black male writers of the sixties and seventies would use to invalidate their rivals. All of these writers vilify a sexualized mimetic desire that is oriented both toward white men and the values of an enervating bourgeois order.

The Writer as Proletarian Hero: A Marxian Blueprint for Negro Writing

If the ideological embrace of white middle-class norms (and the sexual embrace of white men) produced a writing that was "shallow" and "imitative," as Wright and Ellison suggest, then a more authentic black literary tradition can only emerge, they argue, through developing an organic connection to the black working masses. In examining the "blueprint" for a more authentic Negro writing that both writers elaborate, I want to show that the shift in *class* allegiance they advocate does not involve a repudiation either of mimetic desire or of interracialism, but rather a refiguring of them.

Both Wright and Ellison describe the ideal relationship that the Negro writer ought to adopt to the culture of the working masses as involving a complex mimetic interplay: on the one hand, he needs to develop within himself a folk consciousness that is already possessed by working-class Negroes and that is already developing into a revolutionary proletarian consciousness; on the other, he must prefigure in his own individual psyche a revolutionary transformation of consciousness that must be reproduced in the psyches of each member of the black working class. From the first point of view, the writer is seen as a figure who must emulate an already existing model of consciousness immanent to the "folk"; from another, the writer is a kind of Mosaic or vanguardist figure, helping to lead the "folk" toward the higher form of consciousness necessary for revolutionary change.

In "Recent Negro Fiction," Wright describes this interplay in relation to a burgeoning race or "nationalist" consciousness. The Negro writer, insists Wright, must engage with "Negro folklore," which expresses a "collective sense of Negro life in America" imbued with nationalist implications (397). Negro writers must reckon with the nationalist spirit of black folk culture, in order not to encourage but to change and transcend it, "*possess* and *understand* it" (398). The only way the black writer will be able to achieve this is through "a Marxist conception of reality" (399) that can reveal the limitations and dangers of nationalism. A Marxist perspective not only clarifies that nationalist aims are ultimately "unrealizable within the framework of capitalist America" (398), but also offers "the maximum degree of freedom in thought and feeling [that] can be gained for the Negro writer" (399). As necessary as Marxism is to the Negro writer, however, it is "but the starting point. No theory of life can take the place of life" (399). What supplements Marxism is a particularity of vision that can only be attained through a disciplined training in the craft of writing, one that derives from a careful reading of a broad range of writers:

> Eliot, Stein, Joyce, Proust, Hemingway, and Anderson; Gorky, Barbusse, Nexo and Jack London no less than the folklore of the Negro himself should form the heritage of the Negro Writer. Every iota of gain in human thought and sensibility should be ready grist for his mill, no matter how far-fetched they may seem in their immediate implications. (399)

The writer is to serve, then, as a kind of crucible into which the nationalist sensibility expressed in Negro folk culture is poured. And through an ideological alchemy that fuses together modernism and Marxism, he will be able to forge a Negro writing capable of molding the nationalist consciousness of working-class blacks into a properly revolutionary consciousness.

The Negro writer, Wright insists,

> is being called upon to do no less than create values by which his race is to struggle, live and die.
>   By his ability to fuse and make articulate the experiences of men, because his writing possesses the potential cunning to steal into the inmost recesses of the human heart, because he can create the myths and symbols that inspire a faith in life, he may expect either to be consigned to oblivion, or to be recognized for the valued agent he is. (399)

While this passage places the Negro writer at the very vanguard of the black working classes, exemplifying and prefiguring in his own work a revolutionary form of consciousness that he will help to disseminate through his writings across the Negro population, the passages I have examined earlier suggest a different relationship of mimesis, and an alternate temporality. In them Wright insists that the writer must follow and emulate the masses: in order to "possess" and "understand" the nationalist terms in which they make sense of their experiences, he must leave himself open to that "body of folklore, living and powerful," through which "the Negro achieved his most indigenous and complete expression."

Further complicating this doubly mimetic relationship to black working folk is the suggestion that it is only achievable through substantive forms of *interracial* contact. Negro writers must not simply study the work of white writers like Eliot, Stein, Joyce, Proust, Hemingway, and Anderson, they must also interact with progressive white writers. Though Wright's essay begins by underscoring the debilitating effects on Negro art of one version of interracialism (i.e., the patronage of the Harlem Renaissance), it concludes with a section entitled "The Necessity for Collective Work," which emphasizes the need for contact between the races: "The Negro writers' lack of thorough integration with the American scene, their lack of a clear realization among themselves of their possible role, have bred generation after generation of embittered and defeated literati" (402). Wright stresses the inadequate access to resources that black writers face as a result of segregation and asserts that this situation only intensifies the most regressive nationalist tendencies. This predicament can only be rectified, Wright insists, by an *intensification* of interracial solidarity:

> The ideological unity of Negro writers and the alliance of that unity with all the progressive ideas of our day is the primary prerequisite for collective work. On the shoulders of white writers and Negro writers alike rest [*sic*] the responsibility of ending this mistrust and isolation. (402)

If the Negro writer requires unimpeded access to American civilization in order to meet the demands of the revolutionary role he is being called upon to play, as Wright insists, this can only be achieved by encouraging interracial and collective work. Interracialism *per se* is not the problem, then, but rather the forms of interracialism that flourished under the Renaissance.

Nearly all of Wright's claims about the ideals to which black writing ought to aspire are echoed and amplified by Ellison. Indeed, the only significant ways in which his "Recent Negro Fiction" goes beyond Wright's "Blueprint for Negro Writing" is the specific mention it makes of writers who exemplify both the regressive and progressive directions that black writing could take. Ellison thus identifies Zora Neale Hurston and Arna Bontemps as clinging to the obsolete concerns of the Renaissance, while he commends Langston Hughes and Richard Wright in precisely the terms laid out in "Blueprint for Negro Writing": for their connection to working-class Negroes, which is apparent from their use of folklore and their commitment to Marxism; and for their awareness of the aesthetic techniques of modernist writers such as Joyce, Stein, Anderson, and Hemingway.[20] An important reason for the unusual aesthetic success of Hughes and Wright is that they "*experienced freedom of* association with advanced white writers" (25). In contrast to the more debilitating forms of interracialism characteristic of the Renaissance, the interracial association experienced by Wright and Hughes was fruitful because it afforded them access to that cultural resource so important to all writers, but "controlled" in the United States "on the basis of color"—"the possession of Western culture" (25).

In order to substantiate more fully the progressive effects of such interracial contact, Ellison draws from Wright's biography, placing particular emphasis on his experience in the Chicago John Reed Club. The effects of this experience were, Ellison insists, wholly transformative, enabling Wright to develop "disciplines which were impossible within the relaxed, semipeasant environs of American Negro life" and indeed amounting to "attainment of a new sensibility, of a rebirth" (25). Throughout "Recent Negro Fiction," Ellison makes use of Wright's life in this way, as entirely exemplary. Indeed, this essay is a virtual hagiography: it canonizes Wright for living out in his own life and works the narrative of poetic development outlined in "Blueprint." The hyperbole in Wright's descriptions of the Negro writer's responsibilities ("to fuse and make articulate the experiences of men," to "create the myths and symbols that inspire a faith in life") is matched by Ellison's. As the following passage makes clear, Ellison's prose is hard at work in this essay, seeking to develop the appropriate imagery for conveying the Negro writer's revolutionary role—a role for which writers of the twenties were entirely inadequate:

> The grinding impact of the depression upon the aroused Negro people was transforming its folk consciousness into a working class awareness. Negro communities sprouted picket lines, and shouted slogans showing an awareness of the connection between world events and Negro lives. And the

writer who had stood aloof from the people, confining himself to transmitting the small, thin, compromising voice of the black middle class, found himself drowned out in the mighty protesting roar of the black masses. And when the writer attempted to transmit this new sound it was as though he had encountered a strange language; it cracked the crude mechanism of his prose. Yet the speech patterns of this new language had long been present in Negro life, recorded in the crystallized protest of American Negro folklore. It was only that now this protest was receiving intensification and amplification as a result of the folk Negro's reaction to mechanized capitalist suffering: the pressure was bursting the shell of the Negro people's folk consciousness. (23)

While the extended conceit that Ellison elaborates here strains a bit, it is one that renders writing akin to a technology of aural reproduction and transmission. The writer is a figure who should seek to "transmit" "the mighty protesting roar of the black masses"—to act like a kind of radio tranceiver, capturing, amplifying, and broadcasting the "protest" of the black masses. In order to fulfill that function, the writer will require the "mechanism" of a prose less "crude" than that which was used by writers of the Harlem Renaissance. He will need to develop "prose mediums capable of dealing with the complexities of the society in which its new consciousness struggled to be born": these "prose mediums" will have to draw from the experimentalism of modernist writing as well as from black vernacular traditions (23).

Richard Wright emerges from "Recent Negro Fiction" as the only Negro writer who has thus far shown himself capable of shouldering this revolutionary burden of representation. In *Native Son*, Ellison continues,

> we have *the first* philosophical novel by an American Negro. This work possesses an artistry, penetration of thought, and sheer emotional power that places it into the front rank of American fiction. Indeed, except for its characters and subject matter, *it seems hardly identifiable with previous Negro fiction.* (22; my emphasis)

While Wright's accomplishments are initially described as "the continuation of the fictional trend started by Hughes," the passage above presents him as having superseded his predecessor. By emphasizing the "first-ness" of Wright's novelistic accomplishment, Ellison suggests that it is possible for a talented writer to resume an earlier literary trend and yet to produce work that appears to have no precedent—that "seems hardly identifiable with previous Negro fiction." Later in the essay, Ellison similarly suggests that Wright's novel,

> examined against past Negro fiction, represents the take-off in a leap which promises to carry over a whole tradition, and marks the merging of the imaginative depiction of American Negro life into the broad stream of American literature. For the Negro writer it has suggested a path which he might follow to reach maturity, clarifying and increasing his social responsibility. (25)

A fully developed literary maturity entails not only exceeding the accomplishments of the figure whose path one followed, but also producing a work that appears to have no precedent at all. Implicit here even in 1941 is an agonistic and competitive model of black cultural production and writing that Ellison would continue to codify and elaborate through his nonfictional writings over the next quarter-century: a model of literary identity that is predicated on the erasure of prior models of emulation and that presents itself precisely as a model that later writers "might follow to reach maturity."

That Ellison, in the years before he began composing *Invisible Man*, perceived Wright as precisely such a model is evident from sources other than "Recent Negro Fiction." Ellison's letters to Wright from the late thirties to mid-forties, a correspondence that has been brought to light by Michel Fabre, intimate that his regard for the more advanced writer was imbued with an intensely mimetic homosocial desire. In drawing attention to this aspect of Ellison's relationship to Wright, my intent is not to "queer" it, to disclose a hitherto closeted erotic dimension of it. It is to suggest, however, that Ellison's adamant refusal later in his career to acknowledge any dimension of their relationship that might resemble an Oedipal rivalry has everything to do with suppressing the intensely mimetic aspects of it that are so palpable in "Recent Negro Fiction" and in the correspondence that Fabre examines.

In his analysis of this correspondence, Fabre's main purpose is to suggest that Ellison was, in those crucial years shortly before he began writing his novel, much closer to Wright than he tended later to admit: politically, aesthetically, and emotionally. The two were both deeply critical of the Communist Party USA for its support of the war effort, the discipline it attempted to exert on its intellectuals and writers, and its inability to contend with the specific issues confronting American Negroes. In the letters

Fabre cites in order to detail the deep sense of political and aesthetic affinity that the two men shared, what also comes across quite powerfully is the deeply identificatory nature of the bond as it was apparently experienced by Ellison.

The letter in which the intensity of this bond is most palpable is one Ellison wrote some three months after "Recent Negro Fiction" appeared (November 3, 1941). Given that Ellison would later stress the differences between his own Southwestern upbringing and Wright's Southern one, it is striking that he here describes them both as coming North "from the same region." In the following passage, Ellison describes the revelatory effect that reading Wright's documentary account of the Great Migration, *12 Million Black Voices*, has had on him:

> I have known for a long time that you have suffered many things which I know, and that the truths which you have learned are Negro truths. (That's one reason I have always been amazed by those who distrust you.) . . . Of this, however, I am now sure more than ever; that you and I are brothers. Back when I first knew you, remember, I often speculated as to what it was that made the difference between us and the others who shot up from the same region. . . . I think it is because this past which filters through your book has always been tender and alive and aching within us. We are the ones with no comforting amnesia of childhood, and for whom the trauma of passing from the country to the city of destruction brought no anesthesia of consciousness, but left our nerves peeled and quivering. We are not the numbed but the seething. God! It makes you want to write and write and write, or murder. Like most of us, I am shy of my naked personal emotions, they are too deep. Yet one gets strength when he shares his deepest thoughts and emotions with his brother. And certainly you could have found no better way to share your experience with the rest of us.[21]

What links Wright and Ellison is not only the shared experience of racism and poverty (apparently of a specifically Southern variety), but also the fact that they are endowed with a capacity—because they are writers—to remember the painful details of this experience.

Other passages echo this point, that Wright's prose has the effect of making its black readers acknowledge and re-experience in its most jagged forms a shared sense of pain. The emotional identification with injury engendered by Wright's prose apparently arouses in its reader a desire for a kind of retributive violence: it makes Ellison "want to write and write and write, or murder."[22] The most revolutionary function of Wright's writing is its capacity to incite a transformative anger, to function as a kind of "weapon more subtle than a machine-gun, more effective than a fighter-plane. It is like Joe Louis knocking their best men silly in his precise, impassive, alert Negro way."[23] Indeed, the fraternal metaphors that abound in this letter are often martial, apparent evidence of their mutual reading of André Malraux; it is clear that Ellison saw himself and Wright as brothers-in-arms, as members of a "virile fraternity" engaged in a war against racism:

> *12 Million Black Voices* calls for exaltation—and direct action. My emotional drives are intensified and reorganized in such a manner that the only relieving action would be one through which all our shames and wrongs would be wiped out in blood. But this is not all. After reading your history . . . , I was convinced that we people of emotion shall land the most telling strokes, the destructive-creative blows in the struggle. And we shall do it with books like this![24]

While passages like this one suggest that Ellison saw himself and Wright as brothers-in-arms—imply, in other words, a certain egalitarian quality to their bond—others acknowledge the hierarchy between them. If Wright had laid out for the Negro writer "the path which he might follow to reach maturity," Ellison was quite willing to acknowledge his debt directly: "It gives me something to build upon, my work is made easier, my audience brought a bit closer. I'm a better man for having read it."[25]

"Richard Wright's Blues": A Modernist Bluesprint for Negro Writing

Fabre's analyses of this correspondence indicate how unalloyed Ellison's loyalty to Wright still was in the mid-forties, just before he began composing *Invisible Man*.[26] He plainly saw Wright as championing a kind of writing that he wanted to emulate. Fabre also finds in Ellison's specific praise of Wright's capacity to engender a shared sense of pain in his black readers a provisional formulation of the blues aesthetic with which he would identify the author of *Black Boy* in 1945. Four years after "Recent Negro Fiction" appeared, Ellison would publish "Richard Wright's Blues" in *The Antioch Review*. While at least one critic—Joseph Skerett, Jr.—has seen this essay as marking a kind of "break" from Wright, as interweaving into its praise elements of criticism, Fabre's analyses invite a different reading.[27] If "Richard Wright's Blues" does indeed record a break, the one it seems to commemorate is Ellison's and Wright's mutual departure from the Communist Party. It is among the first of Ellison's reviews to appear in a nonsocialist periodical, and it was published in 1945, a year after Wright had publicly announced his resignation from the Party in the pages of *The Atlantic Monthly*, in the essay "I Tried to Be a Communist." Read in this context, what is remarkable about Ellison's lyrical tribute to *Black Boy* is that he constructed a largely new aesthetic framework—one absent of Marxian references—in which to valorize Wright.

At the heart of the blues, as Ellison famously defined them in this essay, is the immediacy of its depiction of emotional pain, something that he had identified in his earlier letters to Wright as essential to the Negro aesthetic he himself hoped to follow:

> The blues is an impulse to keep the painful details and episodes of a brutal experience alive in one's aching consciousness, to finger its jagged grain, and to transcend it, not by the consolation of philosophy but by squeezing from it a near-tragic, near-comic lyricism. As a form, the blues is an autobiographical chronicle of personal tragedy expressed lyrically.[28]
> . . . like a blues sung by such an artist as Bessie Smith, [Wright's] lyrical prose evokes the paradoxical, almost surreal image of a black boy singing lustily as he probes his own grievous wound. (79)

It was toward this justifiably famous definition that Ellison was inexorably moving, according to Fabre, when he described the Southern past that "filters through" *12 Million Black Voices* as one that "has always been tender and alive and aching within us," as a "trauma" that "left our nerves peeled and quivering."

But while Ellison once again links Wright's aesthetic authenticity to his use of folk culture, the black folk of "Richard Wright's Blues" are no longer the heroic proletarian subjects who will foment historical changes on a revolutionary scale. Instead they are Southern peasants, scarred by the Jim Crow system under which they live. Physically and emotionally brutalized by the violence of white racism, they respond with what Ellison terms "homeopathic dose[s] of violence," which they turn inward, at both fugitive individualists like Wright and at wayward individualistic impulses in their own psyches (86). The oscillating mimetic interplay between the "authentic"

Negro writer and the masses, each amplifying the revolutionary impulses in the other, is replaced here by a far more antagonistic and violent relationship. In the analysis Ellison offers of Wright's depiction of the affective ties that hold together the Southern Negro community—ties in which love is infused with the most casual and omnipresent brutality—he replaces the Marxian vocabulary of his earlier essay with a Freudian one. If Southern Negroes are depicted in "Recent Negro Fiction" as ushering in the revolution through their spatial movement from the countryside to the cities, their temporal movement from feudalism to modernity, their ideological movement from a "folk" consciousness to a proletarian one—if they are depicted in the previous essay as *the* privileged subjects of historical change—they are depicted here as psychically and historically frozen in a state of arrested development.

The most salient aspect of Negro folk practices is for Ellison their putatively "physical" or "erotic" character: "Negro music and dances are frenziedly erotic; Negro religious ceremonies violently ecstatic; Negro speech strongly rhythmical and weighted with image and gesture" (88). What these "physical" or "erotic" forms of expression represent are the "channelization" of an individuating intellectual energy that would, in a freer society, find expression through language, through properly intellectual work. In order to substantiate this point, Ellison refers to "the rapidity of Negro intellectual growth in the North" (88):

> In the North energies are released and given *intellectual* channelization—
> energies which in most Negroes in the South have been forced to take
> either a *physical* form, or, as with potentially intellectual types like Wright,
> to be expressed as nervous tension, anxiety, and hysteria. Which is nothing
> mysterious. The human organism responds to environmental stimuli
> by converting them into either physical and/or intellectual energy. And
> what is called hysteria is called suppressed intellectual energy expressed
> physically. (88)

The Southern Negro is, then, a kind of hysteric: he speaks through his body not because he naturally inclines toward physicality, but because he is laying claim to the only medium available for giving expression to those intellectual impulses that in a more emancipated social order might be expressed through, say, literature.

Ellison runs some serious ideological risks in his use of this Freudian conception of hysteria to anatomize the forms of subjectivity possible under a repressive social order. At times he comes close to pathologizing African Americans. But his stated intent in elaborating through psychoanalysis the view of the Negro contained in *Black Boy* is to dismantle perspectives on the Negro that view the physicality and eroticism of his folk culture as expressions of racial temperament—romantic racialist views not unlike those championed by Parkian sociology. Ellison in fact identifies two white ways of seeing the Negro that *Black Boy* challenges. The first he labels "pastoral," and in elaborating the second, Ellison echoes his earlier critiques of the white patronage that sustained the Renaissance. Wright's book frustrates the

> attitude . . . which leads whites to misjudge Negro passion, looking upon it as they do, out of the turgidity of their own frustrated yearning for emotional warmth, their capacity for sensation having been constricted by the impersonal mechanized relationships typical of bourgeois society. The Negro is idealized into a symbol of sensation, of unhampered social and sexual relationships. And when *Black Boy* questions their illusion they are thwarted much in the manner of the occidental who, after observing the erotic character of a primitive dance, "shacks up" with a native woman—only to discover that from possessing the hair-trigger sexual responses of a Stork Club "babe," she is relatively phlegmatic. (86–87)

The "physical" or "erotic" aspects of Negro expression that white enthusiasts (whom Ellison interestingly refers to here as "occidentals") misread as essentially racial are, in fact, the expressions of a complex psychic response—a product of the human need for intellectual expression bumping up against the oppressive constraints of a social order that denies access to the appropriate mechanisms (literacy, education, and so on) for satisfying that need.

The significance of the blues singer as Ellison renders him in this essay, then, is that he reproduces something of the violent corporeality of this hysteric posture in his aesthetic posture. If ordinarily the Southern Negro's body becomes freighted with meanings it cannot adequately bear, then what is extraordinary about the body of the blues singer is precisely the *sound* that it makes. For while his singing is *of* his body, it is not equivalent to it; and in that subtle relay between body and breath, between singer and song, he is able to mirror, distill, but also transpose to another register altogether the form of cultural expression characteristic of his community. What the singing of the blues seems to open up in the singer is a kind of alterity, a temporal gap between the one who was victimized by "a brutal experience" and the one who is able *through the act of narration* to confront and transcend it. Implicit in this celebratory account of the blues singer is a disjuncture between the body that bears a "grievous wound" and the bluesman who "sing[s] lustily as he probes" it.

Despite the intense lyricism that Ellison brings to bear in his tribute to Wright as bluesman, critics like Joseph Skerrett, Jr., have been tempted to read a certain ambivalence into it. This apparent ambivalence can be seen to manifest itself in at least two ways. Firstly, there is the somewhat confusing and confused gender imagery through which the figure of the bluesman is described. For instance, by associating Wright's narrative voice with the body of a black *boy* singing lustily or with the figure of Bessie Smith, Ellison seems to suggests a certain incompleteness to this figure, encoded as immaturity and femininity. (Ellison does not, in other words, evoke here a Robert Johnson or a Jimmy Rushing.) Moreover, the figure of the "grievous wound" carries with it intimations of castration. If Ellison was seeking to project a vision of black expressivity that would counter the less-than-wholly-masculine terms conferred by the romantic racialism of Parkian sociology and the Harlem Renaissance, this image seems an odd choice, given its ambiguously gendered character. Secondly, there is the way in which Ellison's review makes Wright's intellectualism proximate to hysteria. If Wright's writing is related to the hysterical mode of expression typically produced in response to the violence of the South, then his writings might also be compared to "the violent gesturing of a man who attempts to express a complicated concept with a limited vocabulary," whose "thwarted ideational energy is converted into unsatisfactory pantomime," and whose "words are burdened with meanings they cannot convey."

Such a reading of "Richard Wright's Blues"—as containing a veiled critique of the figure it seems to lionize—is abetted by the context in which most readers come across it: as part of *Shadow and Act*, a volume of essays containing several criticisms of Wright's work. In "The World and the Jug," for instance, Ellison famously suggests that it was Ernest Hemingway rather than Wright whom he regarded in his formative years as a literary "ancestor." Wright, as a rough contemporary, was more like a "relative." Hemingway's influence was greater not only because he came first, temporally speaking, but also because he was "a greater artist than Wright."[29] Claiming that he derived his aesthetic by studying modernists like Hemingway, Ellison insinuates that he diverged from Wright, who derived his models elsewhere—from Marxism and sociology. These comments obscure the fact that his 1945 tribute to Wright mobilizes a modernist conception of literary identity that had been codified by Hemingway himself. Ellison casts Wright, in other words, in the very image of that figure who was "the true father-as-artist of so many of us who came to writing during the thirties" (141).

The elements of Ellison's depiction of Wright that seem to imbue him with a sense of incompleteness take on an entirely different meaning when they are seen as embodiments of certain by-now clichéd figures derived from Hemingway's writings. For instance, the intimations of castration in the figure of the bluesman "singing lustily as he probes his own grievous wound" suggest an analogy to the figure of Jake Barnes, whom Ellison describes elsewhere as follows: "Jake Barnes survives, precisely because Jake Barnes is the writer of *The Sun Also Rises*. Ball-less, humiliated, malicious, even masochistic, he still has a steady eye upon it all and has the most eloquent ability to convey the texture of the experience."[30] Ellison's discussion of the bluesman's technique also mirrors the relationship to language advocated by Hemingway. The blues are able to "transcend" "the painful details and episodes of a brutal experience" by keeping it "alive" through representation, but also by "*squeezing* from it a near-tragic, near-comic *lyricism*." The emphasis on lyricism underscores the implacable discipline imposed on the bluesman by the constraints of his form. Twelve bars, no more, no less, with fairly strict rules of repetition—it is by "squeezing" his "autobiographical chronicle of personal tragedy" into this lyric form that the bluesman is able to transcend it. This radical distilling of language required by the blues bears some relation to the aesthetic of understatement and omission so valued by Hemingway.[31]

It is not, however, just the compression of language that Ellison prizes about the blues, it is also the particular attitude toward tragic experience that they express. It is a capacity to glean the "near-tragic, near-comic" significance of brutalizing events, to sing lustily about one's suffering that Ellison prizes here; and it is not unlike the sentiment he often finds Hemingway's writings infused by. In 1964 he explains that one reason he claimed Hemingway as a literary "ancestor" was because his writing "was imbued with a spirit beyond the tragic with which I could feel at home, for it was very close to the feeling of the blues, which are, perhaps, as close as Americans can come to expressing the spirit of tragedy."[32] Grace under pressure is not an inapt formulation for the qualities that Ellison finds in the bluesman, and thus in the figure of Wright himself.

The final two pages of "Richard Wright's Blues" contain two other direct references to Hemingway. First of all, Ellison uses the figure of the matador to describe Wright's agonistic relationship to Western culture (and here again Ellison is recasting an earlier argument that had been rendered in Marxian terms in "Recent Negro Fiction"):

> Wright is pointing out what should be obvious (especially to his Marxist critics) that Negro sensibility is socially and historically conditioned; that Western culture must be won, confronted like the animal in a Spanish bullfight, dominated by the red shawl of codified experience and brought heaving to its knees. (93)

Secondly, in a more convoluted conceit, Ellison compares Wright's attempt to delineate the distorted and wounded forms of humanity in the Southern Negro with a quail hunter's attempt to distinguish his quarry "from the brown and yellow leaves of a Mississippi thicket" (93). Rendering the Negro's humanity is as difficult a task of discernment, Ellison writes, but Wright had a certain advantage in this regard:

> Having himself been in the position of the quail—to expand the metaphor— Wright's wounds have told him both the question and the answer which every successful hunter must discover for himself: "Where would I hide if *I* were a wounded quail?" But perhaps that requires more sympathy with one's quarry than most hunters possess. Certainly it requires such a sensitivity to the shifting guises of *humanity under pressure* as to allow them to identify themselves with the human content, whatever its outer form . . . (94)

Here Ellison not only identifies Wright's aesthetic as having been shaped by Hemingway's aesthetic, but he also presents it as exceeding its model in one particular way. If Hemingway is like "most hunters" in that he can identify his difficult-to-see prey, Wright possesses something that sets him apart: a capacity for sympathetic identification, "a sensitivity to the shifting guises of *humanity under pressure.*" This phrase evokes Hemingway's aesthetic of "grace under pressure" while simultaneously suggesting an element lacking in it, an element that is, by contrast, apparent in Wright's writings: a capacity to identify with the wounded forms of humanity produced by the pressures of Southern racism.

Inauthenticating Wright

Ellison's well-known criticisms of Wright began to appear around 1960, the year of Wright's death. From that point forward, Ellison's interviews and essays tend to include statements underscoring the distinctions between his relationship to literature and that of Wright's and denying the older writer's influence. In the following I want to examine Ellison's account of their relationship as it began to solidify in this period, when the two writers were increasingly seen to embody opposing conceptions of black writing. The interviews and essays I will be analyzing make clear how wholeheartedly Ellison encouraged the perception of an aesthetic divide between himself and Wright. In these pieces, most of which were included in *Shadow and Act*, Ellison presents his writing as being driven by allegiances to the "ordinary" American Negro, to the vernacular traditions of jazz and the blues, and, above all, to the discipline of writing; in contrast, he depicts Wright's literary output as having been compromised by various *ideological* allegiances—to Marxism, to sociology, to existentialism. In examining the rhetoric of inauthentication that Ellison marshals against Wright, I will show how it redeploys and reconfigures certain arguments that both writers had directed against the writing of the Harlem Renaissance.

It was in the course of defending himself against the criticisms leveled at him by Irving Howe in his 1963 essay "Black Boys and Native Sons" that Ellison issued his most disparaging comments regarding Wright: "How awful that Wright found the facile answers of Marxism before he learned to use literature as a means for discovering the forms of American Negro humanity" (120). According to Ellison, Wright's immersion in Marxism not only resulted in the diminishment of his aesthetic capacities, it also effected a kind of racial self-alienation within the writer himself. If his parroting of "the facile answers of Marxism" led him to "dissociate himself from the complexity of his background," this suggests that his internalization of Marxism cut him off from certain aspects of his own black self—the links to Negroness within his very psyche. To demonstrate Wright's disconnection from the mainstream of black life, Ellison makes the following observation, which is quite remarkable given the praise he had given in his 1945 review of *Black Boy*: "if you think Wright knew anything about the blues, listen to a 'blues' he composed with Paul Robeson singing, a *most* unfortunate collaboration!" (140).

In a 1960 interview, Ellison tells Harold Isaacs that Wright "has a passion for ideology and is fascinated by power"; this concern with world politics has led him to "cut his ties to American Negroes."[33] Ellison's criticisms are not usually so narrowly focused on Wright as they are in this interview: more typically, he will cite Wright's ideological biases as exemplary of a "sociological" approach to writing taken by a number of black and white writers. One effect of this rhetorical strategy is that Ellison's criticisms come off as, if not reluctant, offhanded, even nonchalant. By cultivating this studiously un-ruffled critical attitude toward Wright, Ellison plays down any suggestion of an Oedipal dimension to their relationship—he denies any need to, as it were, kill the father. This rhetorical strategy enables Ellison to target and neutralize the one male writer who might be seen as challenging his pre-eminence in black letters; it also allows him to evoke a whole strain of Negro writing that is likewise marred by sociological allegiances. In much the same way that Ellison and Wright in the thirties and forties required the negative example of the Harlem Renaissance to limn the features of the black writing they hoped to produce, Ellison in the sixties needed to conjure forth a tradition of "sociological" writing to contrast with his own, more "authentic" sense of literary craft. "People who want to write sociology," Ellison re-marked of Wright in his interview with Isaacs, "should not write a novel."[34]

The rhetorical strategy I have outlined above—in which a critique of the "sociological" encompasses both a contemporaneous generation of "militant" black writers and Richard Wright—is very much on display in the 1967 interview entitled "A Very Stern Discipline." In this conversation, the primary object of Ellison's criticism is a certain tendency toward the sociological that seems to afflict the work of most recent Negro writers. Though it is easy for Negro writers, Ellison suggests, to rely on the sociological, the more difficult yet richer challenge is to maintain (as he himself has done) one's allegiance to the "very stern discipline" of literature. The mise-en-scène of this interview, which is described in a prefatory paragraph, reinforces this sense of a divide in black letters; it also makes clear that the piece as a whole will privilege the Ellisonian model. The headnote establishes Ellison's credentials as an elder statesman of African American letters: he is identified as the author of a "memorable first novel," "the recipient of the 1952 National Book Award," and one of "the front rank of American writers" (109). He is being interviewed by "three young Negro writers," all of whom are male: Steve Cannon, Lennox Raphael, and James Thompson (109). This scenario casts the interviewers as representatives of a contemporary generation of black male writers who are being exhorted by their literary "father" to emulate his example. Ellison's pronouncements have the feel of Mosaic exhortations, as if he were calling upon the younger members of his tribe to renounce the false god of sociology for the true god of literature. "What is missing today," Ellison announces,

> is a corps of artists and intellectuals who would evaluate Negro American experience *from the inside*, and out of a broad knowledge of how people of other cultures live, deal with experience, and give experience to their experience. We do too little of this. Rather we depend on outsiders—mainly sociologists—to interpret our lives for us. (129)

Black writers who parrot the findings of sociology will tend to evaluate black experience from an outsider's perspective. Such writers will invariably focus on the question, "'How do we fit into the sociological terminology? Gunnar Myrdal said this experience means thus and so. And Dr. Kenneth Clark, or Dr. E. Franklin Frazier, says the same thing . . .' And we try to fit our experience into their concepts" (129–30).

Through his recurrent use of the first person plural in these statements, Ellison seems to suggest that he himself has also been tempted to write from this sociological point of view. But he also insists that he has resisted that temptation out of a recognition that it would result in an elitist disidentification from blackness:

> Well, whenever I hear a Negro intellectual describing Negro life and personality with a catalogue of negative definitions, my first question is, how did you escape, is it that you were born exceptional and superior? If I cannot look at the most brutalized Negro on the street, even when he irritates me and makes me want to bash his head in because he's goofing off, I must still say within myself, "Well, that's you too, Ellison." And I'm not talking about guilt, but of an identification that goes beyond race. (130)

Ellison's use of "we" suggests that he is criticizing a general trend—a temptation, really—that authentic writers must resist. But it is also clear that the prototype he has in mind for the kind of black writer who writes from the perspective of sociology is Richard Wright, whom he describes in "The World and the Jug" as subscribing to "the ideological proposition that what whites think of the Negro's reality is more important than what Negroes themselves know it to be" (114).

Ellison's criticisms of this sociological tendency have, moreover, a gendered and sexual dimension. In "A Very Stern Discipline," the specific sociological findings that he mentions are those of the Moynihan Report, which had been released two years earlier, in 1965:

> If a Negro writer is going to listen to sociologists—as too many of us do—who tell us that Negro life is thus-and-so in keeping with certain sociological theories, he is in trouble because he will have abandoned his task before he begins. If he accepts the clichés to the effect that the Negro family is usually a broken family, that it is matriarchal in form and that the mother dominates and castrates the males, if he believes that Negro males are having all of these alleged troubles with their sexuality, or that Harlem is a "Negro ghetto"—which means to paraphrase one of our writers, "piss in the halls and blood on the stairs"—well, he'll never see the people of whom he wishes to write. (109–10)

The black writer who affirms such a sociological view—one that seemingly calls into question the masculinity of black men—risks, then, the diminishment of his own aesthetic acuity: "He'll never learn to use his own eyes and his own heart, and he'll never master the art of fiction." In order to convey the lapse of aesthetic vision that will result from this allegiance to sociology, Ellison conjures the following image:

> Hell, he [the Negro writer] doesn't have to spend all the tedious time required to write novels simply to repeat what the sociologists and certain white intellectuals are broadcasting like a zoo full of parrots—*and* getting much more money for it than most Negro writers will ever see. If he does this he'll not only go begging, but worse, he'll lie to his people, discourage their interest in literature, and emasculate his own talent. (110)

Discernible in this figure is a linkage between literary inauthenticity, racial inauthenticity, a compromised masculinity, and a passive mimicry of white intellectual models. The distinction that Ellison establishes here between his own work and that of more recent "'angry' Negro writers" rests on the assumption that inauthentic forms of black writing will passively mimic the findings of sociologists while authentic forms will challenge them.

I want to specify what it is about the view of the Negro promoted by sociology that Ellison identifies as particularly problematic. In "A Very Stern Discipline" it is a pathologizing of the Negro as wholly brutalized that Ellison objects to, that he links with the kind of sociological perspective put forward in the Moynihan Report. Given the explicitly *gendered* nature of the findings of the Moynihan Report—which emphasized the emasculation of black males by their own culture—it is not entirely surprising that Ellison would depict the Negro writer who affirms its perspective as "emasculat[ing] his own talent."

Enclosed within the gendered terms that frame Ellison's account of the "sociological," however, are also questions of desire—and, specifically, of white racialist desire. In "The World and the Jug," Ellison generalizes from the specific sins of misinterpretation that he finds Howe guilty of and elaborates a kind of template for white racialist desire—a template that can be discerned in the findings of all "sociology-oriented critics" (108). What turns out to be most problematic about the view of the Negro presented by sociology and affirmed by certain sociologically inclined writers (e.g., Wright) is that it caters to certain "private Freudian fantasies"—that the Negro as depicted in sociology simply serves as "a territory for infantile self-expression." The literary self-emasculation that Ellison ascribes to the Negro writer who parrots the findings of sociology is thus linked to a particular orientation to white racial desire—it involves what Ellison had several decades earlier described as "indulg[ing] white bohemian fancies for things Negroid." It is also involved with a passively mimetic orientation to white culture, a tendency that Ellison had early identified in the writings of the Harlem Renaissance.

Southwestern Jazz and the Vernacular Subject

What should be clear by now is the way in which the rhetoric of inauthentication that Ellison marshaled against Wright in the sixties echoes the rhetoric that both he and Wright had deployed in their Marxian critiques of the Harlem Renaissance. Vilified in either case is a passively imitative relationship to white culture, a literature that is "shallow" and "imitative" and that caters to the racialist fantasies of a white readership. What has changed about this rhetoric of inauthentication, however, is that it is no longer rooted in a Marxian vocabulary of class: while Wright's loyalty to sociology is depicted as alienating him from most black Americans, this posture is not presented as indicative of a bourgeois sensibility. Nonetheless, Ellison still retains in his writings of the sixties a belief that it is the working-class—the "folk"—who are the bearers of the most authentic and muscular form of black culture. He simply offers a different account of the Negro folk culture that should provide the foundation for an "authentic" Negro writing. Ellison identifies the folk sensibility informing his work in regionalist terms—as deriving not from the South but from the Southwest.

The texts that most critics have treated as comprising Ellison's aesthetic theory are the essays and interviews collected in *Shadow and Act*. In them, Ellison details the features of what he identifies as a specifically Southwestern black vernacular tradition. This tradition—which is exemplified by the music of figures like Jimmy Rushing and Charlie Christian—is presented as having had a wholly formative effect not only on Ellison's approach to literature, but also on his sense of national, racial, and masculine identity. While the vernacular sensibility that Ellison codifies and celebrates in these writings is situated in a specific geography, it is also presented as thoroughly in the American grain, as expressive of a national sensibility. It is a sensibility that rejects both black and white notions of racial purity and celebrates instead the mongrelized character of all American identities. In their open embrace of racial hybridity and cultural eclecticism, Ellison's aesthetic ideologies as outlined in this period have been perceived by several critics as transcending the identitarian rhetoric in which his ideological rivals of the sixties are more self-evidently enmeshed. But Ellison's explicit and unambiguous rejection of a crassly biological essentialism does not necessarily amount to a rejection of essentialism *tout court*. As Diana Fuss has observed of the work of two more recent vernacular theorists—Henry Louis Gates, Jr., and Houston Baker, Jr.—essentialism can inhere in things other than bodies:

> What we see in the work of both Gates and Baker is a romanticization
> of the vernacular. As their detractors have been all too quick to point out,
> each of these critics speaks *about* the black vernacular but rarely can they
> be said to speak in it (in the same way that some feminist critics can be said
> to speak about but not in *écriture féminine*). A powerful *dream* of the ver-
> nacular motivates the work of these two Afro-Americanists, perhaps be-
> cause, for the professionalized literary critic, the vernacular has already
> become irrevocably lost. What makes the vernacular (the language of "the
> folk") so powerful a theme in the work of both Gates and Baker is precisely
> the fact that it operates as a phantasm, a hallucination of lost origins. It is
> in the quest to recover, reinscribe, and revalorize the black vernacular that
> essentialism inheres in the work of two otherwise anti-essentialist theorists.
> The key to blackness is not visual but *auditory*; essentialism is displaced
> from sight to sound.[35]

To a significant extent, the vernacular criticism that Gates and Baker both promoted in the eighties had been anticipated two decades before by Ellison, and Fuss's observations concerning the "powerful *dream* of the vernacular" that animates their criticism can be extended backward.

Fuss suggests a certain psychic motivation to these critics' claims to a vernacular critical practice. What is "powerful" about the "*dream* of the vernacular" is the compensatory fantasy about class it helps to sustain. By becoming professional intellectuals, Gates, Baker, and Ellison have all essentially entered the middle class; but by seeking to imbue their own work with the aura of the vernacular, they suggest a connection between their intellectual labors and labors of a more literal kind.

Moreover, as Martin J. Favor has recently observed, the privileging of the vernacular in Gates's and Baker's writings—as well as in the work of W. E. B. Du Bois and Alain Locke—attests to the persistence and power of

> theories of African American culture and literary representation that had at their foundation the valorization of some notion of the African American folk. The rift between "true" and "false," folk and bourgeoisie existed, too. Uniqueness lies in difference, and difference is best represented by a particular class stratum. Class becomes a primary marker of racial difference; to be truly different, one must be authentically folk.[36]

By insisting that their writing is fundamentally shaped by an allegiance to a folk aesthetic, vernacular theorists attempt to legitimate themselves as spokesmen for ordinary black folk—for working-class African Americans who have always been presumed to embody "authentic" blackness. Finally, we should also recall Phillip Brian Harper's observation that the performance of working-class identity in Black Arts writings through the "incorporation" of "the semantics of 'street' discourse" involves the performance of a masculine identity—that verbal facility often serves as "proof of one's conventional masculinity . . . when it is demonstrated specifically through the use of the vernacular."[37] As I will suggest, embedded in Ellison's vernacular theory is likewise a deep concern with the issue of manhood.

One issue that complicates the claims put forward by Ellison is that he, much like Baker and Gates, "speaks *about* the black vernacular but rarely can [he] be said to speak in it."[38] All three of these writers display an ostentatious fluency in the prevailing idioms of high Western literary criticism even as they insist that their criticism is continuous with and an extension of the vernacular tradition it treats—that the vernacular is not simply being described but also embodied by their work. Given the relative absence in their prose of linguistic markers that would more directly and obviously give expression to a vernacular sensibility, how, exactly, is this sensibility to be discerned? How are readers to know that a given piece of criticism is rendered in the vernacular if its syntax, idiom, and grammar are all in Received Standard English?

As Fuss has noted, "the key to blackness" in the work of Gates and Baker "is not visual but *auditory*." The vernacular sensibility that they claim to be describing and expressing in their writings is one that is indexed to what they claim is a certain *sound* that can be heard in their criticism: "A blues text may thus announce itself by the onomatopoeia of the train's whistle sounded on the indrawn breath of a harmonica or a train's bell tinkled on the high keys of an upright piano."[39] However eloquent and evocative this description of the blues sound may be, it is difficult to discern how readers are supposed to "hear" the same sound in Baker's prose itself—unless, of course, we simply accede to the author's claims about his *intent* to produce a blues-toned criticism. Indeed, as I will be arguing, *intent*, or perhaps *attitude*, is the thing that readers are ultimately supposed to "hear" in this mode of vernacular criticism. In other words, the claims that all of these vernacular theorists— Gates, Baker, and Ellison—make about the *sound* of the blues or jazz discernible in certain writings are, at bottom, assertions of a certain *intentionality*—an artistic agency—that they impute to the figures they privilege. What they are able to "perform" in their criticism is not, then, the *sound* of the blues or jazz, but rather the *intent to evoke that sound*. The key to discerning the blackness they specify as authentic is not literally auditory, but metaphorically so. What the auditory stands in for ultimately is a quite specific rendering of aesthetic agency—an agency that is predicated on a violent and aggressively appropriative mode of cultural production.

For instance, in *Modernism and the Harlem Renaissance*, Baker purports to offer "a sui generis definition of *modern Afro-American sound* as a function of a specifically Afro-American discursive practice."[40] But the discernment of this sound depends on a certain parsing of aesthetic intent:

> I suggest that the analysis of discursive strategies that I designate "the mastery of form" and "the deformation of mastery" produces more accurate and culturally enriching interpretations of the *sound* and *soundings* of Afro-

American modernism than do traditional methods. Out of personal reflection, then, comes a set of formulations on expressive modernism and the meaning of speaking (or *sounding*) "modern" in Afro-America.[41]

What "mastery of form" designates in Baker's analyses is the strategy adopted by trickster figures like Booker T. Washington: "The mastery of form conceals, disguises, floats like a trickster butterfly in order to sting like a bee." In contrast, "the deformation of mastery" involves extravagant displays, such as those put on by gorillas seeking to indicate their territory:

> Rather than concealing or disguising in the manner of the *cryptic* mask (a colorful mastery of codes), the phaneric mask is meant to advertise. It distinguishes rather than conceals. It secures territorial advantage and heightens a group's survival possibilities.
>
> The gorilla's deformation is made possible by his superior knowledge of the landscape and the loud assertion of possession that he makes. It is, of course, the latter—the "hoots" of assurance that remain incomprehensible to intruders—that produce a notion (in the intruder's mind and vocabulary) of "deformity." An "alien" *sound* gives birth to notions of the indigenous— say Africans, or Afro-Americans—as *deformed.*[42]

Gates's corollary to the gorilla/guerilla warfare that Baker's vernacular subjects engage in is, of course, the practice of "signifying":

> The ironic reversal of a received racist image of the black as simianlike, the Signifying Monkey—he who dwells at the margins of discourse, ever punning, ever troping, ever embodying the ambiguities of language—is our trope for repetition and revision, indeed, is our trope of chiasmus itself, repeating and simultaneously reversing in one deft, discursive act.[43]

Baker and Gates both valorize an implicitly masculine figure, who speaks back from the racial margins, whose linguistic prowess lies in his deft capacity to repeat parodically and subversively—to ape—the languages that constitute the center, none of which he should be able to claim as properly his own. Despite Gates's insistence that "signifying is not a gender-specific rhetorical game," the agency he ascribes to the vernacular practices he celebrates is nonetheless masculine.[44] What is being prized, ultimately, is a violent and aggressive capacity to incorporate, appropriate, and mangle whatever linguistic materials enter into one's verbal domain—a combative psychological disposition. What is being put on extravagant display in the practices that Baker describes as "mastery of form" and "deformation of mastery" and later as the blues is, at bottom, a kind of virility.

The sense that Gates's signifying involves a form of masculine aesthetic combat is quite apparent in his discussion of black literary history, a discussion in which Ellison figures prominently as "our Great Signifier."[45] While Gates sees Ellison as deploying several different aspects of "signifying" in his writings, he gives special attention to his rivalry with Wright. He sketches the outlines of a reading of *Invisible Man* that suggests how "Ellison in his fictions signifies upon Wright by parodying Wright's literary structures through repetition and difference."[46] This "signifying" on the work of an eminent literary predecessor Gates defines as "critical signification" or "formal signifying," and it constitutes his "metaphor for [black] literary history."[47] In his delineation of a twentieth-century black literary tradition (which includes only one female writer, Zora Neale Hurston), each writer gains a place by critically or formally signifying on the works of those who have come earlier. The vernacular *sound*, then, that Baker and Gates celebrate in their writings has less to do with the ways in which a given text onomatopoetically evokes "the train's whistle sounded on the indrawn breath of a harmonica or a train's bell tinkled on the high keys of an upright piano" than it does with agonistic aesthetic agency that the critics claim to "hear." Ellison can be regarded as "our great Signifier" (Gates's formulation) or as the author of a "Blues Book Most Excellent" (Baker's) not because of how his prose "sounds" but because of the *intent* that is presumed to give his writing its vernacular shape. The vernacular is, at its core, the sound of an aggressive and virile mimesis whose essential blackness is simply assumed. As such the authentic vernacular subject can sound like anyone at all while remaining true to his racial self.

The contestatory paradigm that Gates elaborates through his account of "critical signification" or "formal signifying"—the Bloomian agon through which black writers contest and supersede their predecessors—is apparent in many of Ellison's writings on jazz and the blues. While Gates will cite the African diaspora as the geographical "origin" for the promiscuous and polymorphous capacity for mimesis he celebrates, Ellison will identify the American Southwest—the frontier itself—as the geography giving shape to the jazz sensibility he champions and claims to exemplify. Ellison's account of this jazz subjectivity is detailed in a group of essays that comprise the middle section of *Shadow and Act*. Gathered together under the subtitle "Sound and the Mainstream," all of these pieces were written after the publication of *Invisible Man*. It is clear that his treatment of this musical tradition is also partly an attempt to identify the features of his own literary project, and to emphasize its vernacular underpinnings. In recalling the jazzmen he knew growing up in Oklahoma, he presents them as embodying a redemptive and affirming attitude toward life that is expressed by an intense and disciplined devotion to one's craft.

Anticipating Baker's arguments concerning "mastery of form" and "deformation of mastery" that characterize the best black artists, Ellison celebrates the musicians he knew growing up in Oklahoma for their absolute "technical mastery of their instruments" (189). Whether he is discussing Charlie Christian's relationship to his guitar, Jimmy Rushing's relationship to his voice, Louis Armstrong's to his trumpet, or Charlie Parker's to his saxophone, he emphasizes how each of these musicians possesses a full understanding of "the fundamentals of his instrument . . . the intonations, the mute work, manipulation of timbre" (208). Rebutting any notion that this musical fluency might have come "naturally" (e.g., Park's assertion about the Negro's expressive "temperament"), Ellison insists that it is a product of disciplined study. The jazzmen Ellison champions have, for the most part, received at least some classical training in the use of their instrument (as Ellison did as a trumpeter); they have also schooled themselves in "the traditional techniques of jazz" (208). This technical mastery cannot be gained in artistic isolation, however, for it can only be fully achieved within the context of playing in a jazz ensemble—through "the give and take, the subtle rhythmical shaping and blending of idea, tone and imagination demanded of group improvisation" (189). The "jam session" in particular serves as "the jazzman's true academy" (208). It is only by playing with other musicians who are the acknowledged masters of their instruments that the jazz player develops his own technique to the fullest.

But the jazzman, in order to reach maturity, must undergo a period of "apprenticeship," which is followed by a series of "ordeals" through which he attempts to develop his own individual improvisatory style; these culminate in an "initiation ceremon[y]" in which he must "achieve, in short, his self-determined identity" (208–9). The identity that the jazzman creates for himself is not, however, entirely "self-determined," for it only comes through an agonistic struggle with other players whose style one attempts to supersede. There is, Ellison insists, a "ceaseless warfare for mastery and recognition" waged in these jam sessions, which is most vividly dramatized in "the 'cutting session,' or contest of improvisational skill and physical endurance between two or more musicians" (208). This competitive element cuts to the heart of what Ellison terms "a cruel contradiction implicit in the art form itself. For true jazz is an art of individual assertion within and against the group. Each true jazz moment . . . springs from a contest in which each artist challenges all the rest" (234). This battle to assert one's individual identity is also a grab for immortality. Since each individual style is developed through an appropriative mimesis and transcendence of existing styles, the "original ideas" of even "the most brilliant of jazzman . . . enter the public domain almost as rapidly as they are conceived, to be quickly absorbed into the thought and technique of their fellows" (233–34). To claim his "self-determined identity" as a true jazz musician, a player must earn the recognition of "his fellow musicians, [and] especially [of] the acknowledged masters" (209). But obscurity and defeat are ever-present dangers that the jazz musician necessarily confronts: "even the greatest [of jazz musicians] can never rest on past accomplishments, for, as with the fast guns of the old West, there is always someone waiting in a jam session to blow him literally, not only down, but into shame and discouragement" (209).

The black aesthetic identity that Ellison champions through these figures—an identity whose gendered quality is evident in this passage—is animated by an intensely competitive will, by an impulse to assert one's individuality through an agonistic struggle with one's peers, to imitate, appropriate and supersede all "the acknowledged masters" of one's craft. Its masculinist and homosocial character is apparent from the analogy he makes to Western gunfighters in the passage above, and also from his assertion that in gaining an "acceptance of his ability" from his fellow musicians, the jazzman also attains "his recognition of manhood" (209).

Of the various jazzmen Ellison celebrates in *Shadow and Act*, the ones who take pride of place are those who share his Southwestern background. Oklahoma City, Ellison's birthplace, is basically presented as the birthplace of modern jazz. Of the various Southwestern jazz musicians Ellison recalls, however, it is probably Jimmy Rushing who stands out most boldly. Rushing, a legendarily rotund singer who achieved a measure of fame during the fifties and sixties as a performer with the Count Basie orchestra, is the only musician whom Ellison acknowledges by name in the introduction to *Shadow and Act*. Ellison describes Rushing as a childhood hero and specifically credits him for "help[ing] to keep my sense of my Oklahoma background—especially the jazz—so vividly alive" (xxiii). *Shadow and Act* also contains an essay entitled "Remembering Jimmy," a glowing tribute originally published in 1958. Placed alongside "Richard Wright's Blues," all of these essays elaborate a distinction between the Southern blues tradition and the Southwestern one. They emphasize a regionalist distinction between the blues aesthetic Ellison had ascribed to Wright in 1945 and the more capacious and experimental blues *and* jazz aesthetic that apparently shaped his own writings.

These two different blues traditions do seem to share, however, a tendency toward understatement and a proximity to the corporeal—what Ellison describes in "Remembering Jimmy" as "their ability to imply far more than they state outright and their capacity to make the details of sex convey meanings which touch upon the metaphysical" (245). But while the compression required by the Southern blues is likened to a kind of hysteria—to "the violent gesturing of a man who attempts to express a complicated concept with a limited vocabulary"—the emphasis in Ellison's account of Rushing is placed on the transcendence of generic limits, on the Oklahoma singer's ability to "always find poetry in the limits of the Negro vocabulary" (245). Rushing's technical mastery evinces itself in a linguistic dexterity that has emerged out of a productive "tension between the traditional folk pronunciation and his training in school" (245). Ellison singles out as one of the most crucial aspects of his art

> the imposition of a romantic lyricism upon the blues tradition . . . a lyricism that is *not of the Deep South, but of the Southwest*: a romanticism native to the frontier, imposed upon the violent rawness of a part of the notion which only thirteen years before Rushing's birth was still Indian territory. Thus there is an optimism in it which echoes the spirit of those Negroes who, like Rushing's father, had come to Oklahoma in search of a more human way of life. (245; my emphasis)

The essential mood of the blues as sung by a Southwestern artist like Rushing, whose father (like Ellison's) apparently came West to settle the frontier, is imbued with this romantic lyricism.

Whereas the Southern blues voice of Richard Wright is one that renders audible the sound of a body in pain, Rushing's Southwestern blues aesthetic seems to express the sound of a body in flight. Its ever-upward soar offers an aural image for the tenaciously optimistic sensibility that characterizes, Ellison claims, the black culture of Oklahoma City: Rushing's voice "evoked the festive spirit" of his community, "his song the singing essence of its joy" (242). While blacks in Oklahoma City were well aware of the limits imposed by segregation, they always sought to transcend those limits. What "sounded in Rushing's voice" was the attitude of this community, which "coupled" a recognition of "the rock-bottom sense of reality" to a "sense of the possibility of rising above it" (242).

In his elaboration of the regional sensibility that finds expression in Rushing's voice, which he offers in the introduction to *Shadow and Act*, Ellison sounds quite a bit like a Van Wyck Brooks or Edward Sapir.[48] Like those earlier cultural nationalists, Ellison finds in the particular values of this community an attitude that is prototypically American—one that has been intimately shaped by the geography of the American frontier:

> One thing is certain, ours was a chaotic community, still characterized by frontier attitudes and by that strange mixture of the naïve and sophisticated, the benign and malignant, which makes the American past so puzzling and its present so confusing; that mixture which often affords the minds of the young who grow up in the far provinces such wide and unstructured latitude, and which encourages the individual's imagination—up to the moment "reality" closes in upon him—to range widely and, sometimes, even to soar. (xiii)

The "effects" of this frontier sensibility can be heard not only in the upward soar of Rushing's voice, but more generally

> in the southwestern jazz of the thirties, that joint creation of artistically free and exuberantly creative adventurers, of artists who had stumbled upon the freedom lying within the restrictions of their musical tradition as within the limitations of their social background, and who in their own unconscious way have set an example for any Americans, Negro or white, who would find themselves in their arts. (xiv)

This regional sensibility expresses itself in "a freer, more complex and driving form of jazz" than that which emerged—like Wright's writings—out of the rural South (xiv); by implication, a writing that is similarly shaped by this attitude (like Ellison's, for instance) would likewise be more consonant with the spirit of American nationalism (xiv).

The contrast between the blues aesthetic that Wright's work embodies and that exemplified by Rushing and Ellison also emerges through the emphasis that is placed on the communal nature of Southwestern jazz. The opening image of "Remembering Jimmy" celebrates the agonistic interplay between Rushing's singing and the voices of the other instruments. What sounds in his voice is "the stress of singing above a twelve-piece band." While the voice of Wright's bluesman is rendered in solo, Rushing's is captured by Ellison's prose as "now soaring high above the trumpets and trombones, now skimming the froth of reeds and rhythm." This opening also draws attention to the interplay between Rushing's voice and his audience—in this case a group of young boys including Ellison—who in becoming avid listeners are prodded into performances of their own. In a later passage in "Remembering Jimmy," Ellison elaborates a more detailed description of this particular audience. Rushing's music not only encouraged individualized visions of freedom in Ellison and his friends, it transformed them into active members of a polyvocal community of sound:

> When we were still too young to attend night dances, but yet old enough to gather beneath the corner street lamp on summer evenings, anyone might halt the conversation to exclaim "Listen, they're raising hell down at Slaughter's Hall," and we'd turn our heads westward to hear Jimmy's voice soar up the hill and down, as pure and as miraculously unhindered by distance and earthbound things as is the body in youthful dreams of flying.
>
> "Now that's the Right Reverend Jimmy Rushing preaching now, man," someone would say. And rising to the cue another would answer, "Yeah, and that's old Elder 'Hot Lips' signifying along with him; urging him on, man." And, keeping it building, "Huh, but though you can't hear him out thus far, Ole Deacon Big-un [the late Walter Page] is up there patting his foot and slapping on his big belly [the bass viol] to keep those fools in line." And we might go on to name all the members of the band as though they were the Biblical four-and-twenty elders, while laughing at the impious wit of applying church titles to a form of music which all the preachers assured us was the devil's potent tool. (243)

In listening to the music being produced by Rushing's ensemble, Ellison and his friends do not simply talk about it, they become, in a sense, part of it. They do not simply take in the music as a topic of conversation; they allow that music to structure the very form of conversation itself, to shape the very structure of community that is formed. For this music has the effect of making its listeners talk in a way that echoes the call-and-response polyvocality of the music itself. To talk about the way in which "Hot Lips" Paige's horn is "signifying along with" "the Right Reverend Jimmy Rushing['s] preaching," Ellison and his friends must engage in some signifying of their own. In describing each of the voices they hear, their voices themselves become part of the ensemble of sound, echoing the phrasing of the music through their collective critical interplay. This intimately aural interaction is presented here not as an impediment to individuality, but as its enabling context: for Ellison and his young friends exhort each other to ever more creative displays of "impious wit," and to enjoy the laughter that comes from feeling like one has claimed possession of "the devil's potent tool."

What is being celebrated in Ellison's evocation of this theater of listening is a virilizing form of male homosocial intimacy. Rushing's performance engenders in the listening boys a kind of mimetic desire. Their aural intercourse is the acting out of an identification that is occasioned by the collective participation in an aesthetic experience. These ritualized moments of aesthetic enjoyment engender an identification with a certain style of manhood that is itself mimetic, that is based on the imitation and incorporation of other men.

The same sensibility—the far-ranging eclecticism, the acquisitive incorporation of myriad musical styles and traditions—that led these musicians to concoct "a freer, more complex and driving form of jazz," manifested itself as well, Ellison insists, in a particular attitude toward masculine identity that he and his boyhood friends attempted to approximate. To be a black boy growing up on the Oklahoman frontier, Ellison suggests, was always to be "exploring an idea of human versatility and possibility which went against the barbs or over palings of almost every fence which those who controlled social and political power had erected to restrict our roles in the life of the country" (xiv). This "idea of human versatility and possibility," Ellison specifies elsewhere in this introduction, was "the concept of Renaissance man" (xiii). It was a concept that drove them to "master(ing) ourselves and everything in sight as though no such thing as racial discrimination existed" (7). "Spurring us on in our controlled and benign madness," Ellison continues, "was the voracious reading of which most of us were guilty and the vicarious identification and empathetic adventuring which it encouraged" (xv). In the books they read, Ellison and his friends (many of whom were fatherless, he notes) "were seeking examples, patterns to live by," and so they created "father and mother substitutes," "fabricated [their] own heroes and ideals catch-as-catch can, and with an outrageous sense of freedom" (xv). They found exemplary figures in a variety of guises and races, figures that— as both "archetypes" and "projections"—were "neither white nor black, Christian or Jewish, but representative of certain desirable essences, of skills and powers physical, aesthetic and moral" (xvi). They extracted features and attributes from one figure and combined them with others through a process that Ellison likens to that of editing film (xvi).

The range of models that Ellison and his friends felt entitled, indeed obligated, to imitate attests to the hybridity and, indeed, the cosmopolitanism of this Negro American version of the Renaissance man ideal. The gendered aspect of this hybrid ideal is quite evident:

> We felt, among ourselves at least, that we were supposed to do anything and everything which other boys did, and do it better. Not defensively, because we were ordered to do so; nor because it was held in the society at large that we were naturally, as Negroes, limited—but because we demanded it of ourselves. *Because to measure up to our own standards was the only way of affirming our notion of manhood.* (xvii; my emphasis)

The Ellisonian ideal of Renaissance man is a model of black manhood that eschews a narrowly essentialist ethno-nationalism, that is promiscuous in its identifications and appropriations of models from other races and cultures and extravagantly avows those borrowings. The polymorphously multiracial nature of this ideal seems devoid of any potentially regressive ideas about racial purity; its gendered aspect seems, moreover, relatively benign when compared, for instance, to the relentless masculinism of a writer like Amiri Baraka or Eldridge Cleaver. But while the gender ideology that underwrites Ellison's aesthetic writings of the sixties may well be kinder and gentler, as it were, than the one underwriting those of the black nationalists, the preoccupation with masculinity and racial authenticity is present nonetheless.

That Ellison is intent on imbuing this vernacular subjectivity with a "Negro" nationalist as well as an American nationalist quality is evident in the following passage: "Not only were we to prepare but we were to perform—not with mere competence but with an almost reckless verve; with, may we say (without evoking the quaint and questionable notion of *negri-*

tude), Negro American style?" (xvi–xvii). Ellison insists that whatever forms of cultural expression African Americans "appropriate," "possess" and "re-create" in their "own group and individual images," that as long as they do so with "reckless verve," they will inject those forms with an indelible sense of "Negro American style." Ellison goes on to list some of the cultural realms in which he and his friends glimpsed manifestations of this racially distinct style and the male exemplars of it:

> And we recognized and were proud of our group's own style wherever we discerned it—in jazzmen and prize fighters, ballplayers and tap dancers; in gesture, inflection, intonation, timbre and phrasing. Indeed, in all those nuances of expression and attitude which reveal a culture. (xvii)

What Ellison insists that he and his boyhood friends could detect in these various performances of Negro American style—what he insists they could "hear," in a sense—was something very much like the "sound" of the blues that Baker claims to hear in the black texts he prizes. What registers as black is the sound of a specific intent that is said to signify manhood—one that Ellison describes as "a yearning to make any- and everything of quality *Negro American*; to appropriate it, possess it, re-create it in our own group and individual images"; one that Baker describes as "mastery of form" and "deformation of mastery."

Coda

Put broadly, what this book as a whole grapples with is the question of how and why the literary domain has come to be understood by male writers of color across the twentieth century as providing access to an exhilarating free-dom from the constraints of racism. It has also engaged with the gendered and sexualized quality of the rhetoric that is used, on the one hand, to underscore white racism's most debilitating effects and, on the other, to flesh out the aesthetic sphere's utopian promise. My readings of Ellison's works have attempted to challenge the assumption that they somehow rise above the identitarian embroilments that more explicitly shape the works of other writers of color. Ellison's carefully orchestrated self-presentation tends not only toward a kind of elitism, as some critics have noted, but it also encour-ages the perception of an utter originality, as if he had somehow escaped the petty political squabbles, the sectarian warfare in which many of his less celebrated literary brethren have been involved. I have tried in these chapters to work against this erasure, to detail the intimate ways in which his pretensions to universality have been pressured by the same torsion of ideological forces that have shaped the works of other, less-well-regarded writers. My intent has been to demonstrate the ways in which his literary project is as deeply shaped by questions of racial authenticity, homosocial desire, and manhood as that of writers—like Amiri Baraka or Frank Chin, for instance—whose engagement with such issues is more explicit.

THREE

The Legacy of Fu-Manchu:
Orientalist Desire and the Figure
of the Asian "Homosexual"

In the second half of this study I turn to a writer, Frank Chin, who is much less well known than the one I have been discussing in the first half. For that reason I should begin by offering, for the sake of those readers unfamiliar with his writings, a brief biography in order to indicate his significance in Asian American literary studies. Frank Chin is a fifth-generation Chinese American who was born on February 25, 1940, in Berkeley, California. Most of his childhood was spent in Oakland's Chinatown, where a good portion of his work is set. He attended the University of California, at Berkeley and at Santa Barbara, and he also participated in the Program in Creative Writing at the University of Iowa. Chin has been a tireless and influential promoter of Asian American literature throughout his adult life, though his vision of it has often been criticized for its exclusionary tendencies. As I mentioned in my introductory chapter, Chin co-edited—along with Jeffery Paul Chan, Lawson Fusao Inada, and Shawn Wong—*Aiiieeeee!*, an influential collection of Asian American writings that was first published by Howard University Press in 1974; he functioned as a kind of ideological spokesperson for the editors, authoring several manifesto-like essays for the original and subsequent versions of this collection, which stakes out the parameters of an "authentic" tradition of Asian American writing.[1] He has written two plays, *The Chickencoop Chinaman* (1972) and *The Year of the Dragon* (1974). His collection of short stories, *The Chinaman Pacific & Frisco R.R. Co.* (1988), received the National Book Award. He has also published two novels, *Donald Duk* (1991) and *Gunga Din Highway* (1994), and a collection of creative nonfiction, *Bulletproof*

Buddhists and Other Essays (1998). He has also written comic books, produced documentaries, and worked as a script consultant in Hollywood. He has taught college courses in Asian American literature and helped establish the Asian American Theatre Workshop in San Francisco.

Although he is widely regarded as a pioneering figure in Asian American letters and is a fairly prolific writer, the notoriety Chin enjoys in mainstream literary circles stems less from his literary output than from the rather vitriolic criticisms he has steadily leveled over the years at better-known writers: Maxine Hong Kingston, Amy Tan, and David Henry Hwang, in particular. Even among current Asian Americanist scholars, most of whom recognize his importance, Chin tends to be regarded as a kind of anachronism—as a writer whose early polemics and literary manifestos were crucial to the initial articulation of an Asian American sensibility, but whose dogged loyalty to an overly narrow strain of cultural nationalism has, to a large extent, consigned him to the dustbin of literary history. Indeed, critical treatments of Chin's writings have tended to center on the polemical pieces he has written over the last two or three decades, several of which I discussed briefly in my introductory chapter. The earliest of these are the prefatory essays to *Aiiieeeee!* (1974). A second set of similar essays was written in 1991, and they accompany both the Mentor reissue of the original *Aiiieeeee!* and a second anthology that was published that year entitled *The Big Aiiieeeee!* Much of Chin's reputation is tied to the positions he and his colleagues take in these and other related essays. I will be examining these essays in some detail in this chapter, paying particular attention to the ways in which they rework the gendered and sexualized symbolism codified in the African American male tradition that I discussed in earlier chapters.

As I will demonstrate, this tradition, which links together writers like Baraka and Ellison, also plays a primary structuring role in Chin's works: it shapes the ways in which he writes about the psychological structure of Asian American male subjectivity as it is injuriously shaped by U.S. ideologies of race, gender, and sexuality and about the capacity of literature to undo that damage. As such, the polemics of Chin and his colleagues are driven by an impulse to project a literary image of what might be termed Yellow Power. Because of their masculinist stance, Chin and the other *Aiiieeeee!* editors have come under steady attack from feminist and other critics since the publication of their influential anthology. However, many scholars—and even those who are deeply critical of their misogyny—have also found Chin's polemics to be quite productive for their own work. It is probably self-evident that my own study finds his writings to be of significant critical value, though it too will focus on what is problematic in them.

I focus in this chapter on the gendered and sexualized rhetoric that Chin relies on to describe the psychological damage that white racism threatens to inflict on Asian American men, a rhetoric that has been inherited most directly from black nationalism. What Chin consistently attacks as embodiments of the most debased and debilitating forms of Asian American male identity are figures he reads as homosexual—figures who allegedly harbor a sexualized form of *assimilationist* desire that mirrors the desires imputed to the homosexual of color by black nationalist writers like Baraka and Cleaver. In the next chapter, I will turn to his dramatic, fictional, and autobiographical writings to consider the reasons why his protagonists tend to be characterized not by an *absence* of an intense interracial homosocial desire, but rather by its overwhelming *presence*: a desire vis-à-vis black and white men that palpates with aggression and violence, with identification and love; a desire that mingles masochism with its putative opposite; a desire that is essentially *melancholic* in nature. In Chapter 5, which explores Chin's reflections on the idea of a "yellow" vernacular, I will demonstrate how a putatively virilizing form of this intense homosocial desire is rendered by him as the quintessential expression of racially and culturally authentic forms of Asian American manhood.

In establishing the tie that binds Frank Chin to his black literary "ancestors" (to invoke an Ellisonian turn of phrase), my intent is not to reduce him to a mere shadow, a paler imitation. It is, rather, to acknowledge that the dominant language for thinking about race in our culture is one that has been established, by and large, to address the place of African Americans. Recognizing that this legacy shapes the works produced by Asian American writers should not lead us to assume that they are merely copying an "original" whose unquestioned "authenticity" suggests the "inauthenticity" of all imitations. (Moreover, as I established in Chapter 2, the vernacular aesthetic tradition canonized by writers like Ellison, Baker, and Gates is not opposed to imitation; rather, it makes of imitation the stuff of black cultural life.) An honest acknowledgment of this legacy should lead us to grapple with—as Chin's writings indeed force us to do—a certain sense of racial "belatedness" that frames the attempts of Asian American writers to write themselves into a literary landscape largely shaded in black and white. In tracing this influence, however, my point is not to expose Chin as a kind of failure, nor is it to present this borrowing as inherently inappropriate; rather, my intent is to show how Chin's rendering of the "impossible" position in which Asian writers are placed by the dominance of a black model becomes the basis for an Asian American literary tradition that is likewise predicated on a highly masculinist interracial agonism. So if Chin's literary project is one of repetition (and are there any that are not?), it involves a repetition with a difference. In order to attend to that difference, I will also be examining the torsions that necessarily structure Asian American attempts to rework a model that was produced to fit the needs of African American men—torsions that stem not only from the distinctive racial histories that shape the lives of African Americans and Asian Americans, respectively, but also from the different constructions of racialized masculinity that are a key effect of these histories.

This chapter will begin with an analysis of the polemical writings of Chin that comprise a kind of counterpart to Ralph Ellison's criticisms of the liberal sociology inaugurated by Robert E. Park. If Ellison's novel, as he often suggests in his commentary, is parasitic upon the sociological view of the Negro it is intended to undermine—if it seeks to expose the vision of sociology through a corrosive re-presentation of it—then Chin's writings are similarly dependent on the racial view they hope to overturn. Indeed, an analogue to the Parkian view of the Negro "as the lady among the races" can be found in—and is, in fact, central to—the stereotypes of the Asian that Chin presents himself as seeking to inauthenticate.

As I sketch out several of Chin's key claims, I will also be suggesting how they have tended to be affirmed and even elaborated by subsequent Asian American intellectuals. I do so because I believe it is crucial to acknowledge the debt that current Asian American literary and cultural critics owe to the legacy of Frank Chin. Several of his axiomatic formulations have fundamentally shaped the critical lexicon of Asian American Studies. I will be exploring and expanding upon three of these claims in my own study: 1) anti-Asian racism has a gendered, and generally feminizing, dimension to it; 2) it relies on the ascription of certain ostensibly positive traits to Asians as a race, all of which depict them as members of a "model minority"; and 3) U.S. popular culture functions as the preeminent site for the dissemination of injurious Asian stereotypes.

While such assertions are still widely in circulation in the field, scholars have tended almost to disavow the generative force of Chin's polemics, associated as they are with what has come to be seen as a historically important but no longer relevant paradigm for the study of Asian American culture and identity. This tendency is further explicable in light of the misogynistic and homophobic rhetoric in which Chin couches such claims—an aspect of his writings that my own study will make abundantly clear. However, I believe that it is important for scholars whose work depends upon such claims—even as they seek to rework them—to recognize that they are nonetheless heirs (however ambivalent) to axioms that were given their most powerful early articulation by Frank Chin. To acknowledge and even to honor (if somewhat perversely) that legacy while simultaneously confronting the misogyny and homophobia that are absolutely integral to it may be a tricky thing to do, but it is what I intend this study to achieve—to gain some sort of analytic purchase on how and why it is that the things most useful and even moving about Chin's writings are inextricably linked with what is most hateful.

The Feminization Thesis and the Model Minority Myth: Charlie Chan

> In conjunction with the relative absence of Chinese wives and family among immigrant "bachelor" communities and because of the concentration of Chinese men in "feminized" forms of work—such as laundry, restaurants, and other service-sector jobs—Chinese male immigrants could be said to occupy, before 1940, a "feminized" position in relation to white male citizens and, after 1940, a "masculinity" whose racialization is the material trace of the history of this "gendering."
>
> —Lisa Lowe[2]

> Chinese American men . . . have been confronted with a history of inequality and painful "emasculation." The fact that ninety percent of early Chinese immigrants were male, combined with anti-miscegenation laws and laws prohibiting Chinese laborers' wives from entering the U.S., forced these immigrants to congregate in the bachelor communities of various Chinatowns, unable to father a subsequent generation. While many built railroads, mined gold, and cultivated plantations, their strenuous activities and contributions were better known to the American public as restaurant cooks, laundry workers, and waiters, jobs traditionally considered "women's work."
>
> —King-Kok Cheung[3]

While the two influential critics of Asian American literature cited above, Lisa Lowe and King-Kok Cheung, substantiate their claims above with a degree of nuance and a careful sense of historical contextualization absent in his, they are nonetheless recirculating the terms of a critical discourse that begins, in a sense, with Frank Chin. This legacy also shapes the work of David L. Eng, whose psychoanalytic book-length study, *Racial Castration: Managing Masculinity in Asian America*, "analyzes the various ways in which the Asian American male is both materially and psychically feminized within the context of a larger U.S. cultural imaginary."[4] The writings of these critics suggest the generative impact of Chin's axiomatic assertions concerning the unmanning effects of white racism on the Asian American population as a whole and on Asian American men in particular. What might be termed Chin's "feminization thesis" is crystallized in the following statement, which is arguably the most widely cited selection from his oeuvre:

> The white stereotype of the Asian is unique in that it is the only racial stereotype completely devoid of manhood. Our nobility is that of an efficient housewife. At our worst we are contemptible because we are womanly, effeminate, devoid of all the traditionally masculine qualities of originality, daring, physical courage, creativity. We're neither straight talkin' or [sic] straight shootin'.[5]

If Chin's account of the stereotype takes on a certain resonance within the context of my study, this stems from its seeming echo of Robert E. Park's contentions concerning the racial temperament of the "lady"-like Negro. For it would appear that the stereotype of the Asian—at least as Chin describes it—is endowed with a racial femininity comparable to that which Park saw as essential to the Negro.

The misogyny with which Chin describes this feminizing view of the Asian is clear. As Cheung points out, Chin and his colleagues "seem . . . to be buttressing patriarchy by invoking gender stereotypes, by disparaging domestic efficiency as 'feminine,' and by slotting desireable traits such as originality, daring, physical courage, and creativity under the rubric of masculinity."[6] She does acknowledge, in the passage I have cited above, that this "feminization thesis" has its basis in historical fact. But she nonetheless points out that this rhetoric displays "a sexist preference for stereotypes that imply predatory violence against women to 'effeminate' ones."[7] Cheung is referring here to a lament that often turns up in Chin's writings—which I will be examining in these chapters—concerning the absence in U.S. racial discourse of an image of the Asian man that projects a threatening masculinity comparable to that projected by stereotypical depictions of black, red, or brown men. I will offer a more elaborate account of this sense of racial and masculine envy below, and I will also explore his depiction of the character of Fu-Manchu, a figure generated out of early twentieth-century fears about the Yellow Peril that would seem to embody the kind of racial and sexual menace that Chin wishes were projected onto Asian men. I begin my study of Chin, however, by fleshing out his claim that the particularity of U.S. Orientalism lies in the emphasis it places on stereotypes that ascribe a non-threatening racial femininity to Asians: "The white stereotype of the Asian is unique in that it is the only racial stereotype completely devoid of manhood."

The image of the Asian that he presents himself as seeking to challenge has its origins, Chin often claims, in the worldview of the Christian missionaries who saw the Chinese (and then other Asians) as harboring (like the Negroes Park described) an innate sense of humility and docility—traits that rendered them model subjects of conversion. In the passage below, he ventriloquizes the sentiments this missionary discourse ascribes to the Chinese:

> We are meek, timid, passive, industrious. We have the patience of Job.
> We are humble. A race without sinful manhood, born to mortify our
> flesh. Religion has been used to subjugate the blacks, chicanos, and Indians
> along with guns and whips. The difference between these groups and the
> Chinese was that the Christians, taking Chinese hospitality for timidity
> and docility, weren't afraid of us as they were of other races. They loved
> us, protected us. Love conquered.[8]

At times, as he asserts the pervasiveness of this Orientalism across the whole of Western civilization, his writings can seem a parody of a strain of cultural criticism deriving from the work of Edward Said or resemble the rantings of conspiracy-minded protagonists from the fiction of Don DeLillo or Thomas Pynchon. In the following, Chin suggests that the entire history of Western culture and Christianity can be seen as culminating in "the Christian science fiction of the good Chinese":

> The thrust of Western thought and civilization has been toward industrial
> control of the individual—from the Greek philosophers of the "Golden
> Age" and the Romans, to the absolute moral and social hierarchies of the
> dim lights of the Dark Ages, to Castiglione, Machiavelli, Kant, to Goethe's
> scientific philosophy, to Hegel; all lead, with precision and singleminded

high-handedness, to the industrial identity as a mass of consumer products whose moral goods are counted in dollars and cents. Both the organization of assembly line industry and advertising, which created consumerism, were designed, measured, and engineered by "social scientists," the primitives of anthropology and sociology, in the 1920s and thirties. These decades were characterized by movies, comic strips, and other mass media, all reflecting the myth of the China missionary and the Christian science fiction of the good Chinese—odd, wonderful, effeminate, smart as a whip, cunning, devious, inscrutable—the image of failed white manhood gone moldy and repulsive.[9]

While the connection Chin alludes to here between Christian missionaries and social scientists is something he alleges rather than substantiates, it is a link that has been established and examined by a recent and more disciplined scholar of "the Oriental Problem," Henry Yu, in his study *Thinking Orientals: Migration, Contact, and Exoticism in Modern America*. In this book, Yu identifies Progressive Protestant missionaries in the early twentieth century as providing the initial ideological framework through which Asians were understood by liberal Americans. He also argues, however, that a second group of white men—sociologists of the Chicago School who worked under the tutelage of Robert E. Park—quickly superseded the missionaries as they drew from them in framing the terms in which Asian Americans were seen by liberal Americans and also in which they saw themselves. On this point, Yu is echoed by David Palumbo-Liu, who finds in Park's writings an early instantiation of the view of the "Asian/American" that helped solidify the national and racial self-image of the United States in the early part of the twentieth century.[10]

In the passage above, Chin identifies the twenties and thirties as crucial decades in the emergence and codification of the feminizing stereotype he presents himself as seeking to combat. The nexus of institutions he presents as crucial to the dissemination of this stereotype in this period is very much akin to the "feverish industry" that Ellison depicted as conspiring to produce a demeaning image of the Negro. But if Ellison's primary object of critique was Park's sociology, as I argued in my previous chapter, Chin's critical ire is directed more forcefully at the mass culture that emerged in this period. Anticipating the focus on popular representations in the work of such scholars as Elaine Kim and Robert Lee, Chin suggests that the culture industry played a vital role in this watershed moment, codifying and popularizing what he terms "the Christian science fiction of the good Chinese."[11] This emphasis on the mass media is apparent from such statements as the following:

> The period from the late twenties through the thirties that spawned Charlie Chan, Fu-Manchu, and Leong Gor Yun also produced a rash of popular songs, Charlestons, and fox trots about "China boys" being stranded in America without their women. Such a song was "So Long Oolong (How Long You Gonna Be Gone)," that tells of a girl, "Ming Toy," pining for her sweetheart, "Oolong" stranded in America. . . . Also, a series of popular novels and movies, involving passive Chinese men, worshiping white women and being afraid to touch them, appeared in *Son of the Gods*, *East is West*, and the Fu-Manchu and Charlie Chan series.[12]

Chin's most developed account of the anti-Asian stereotype is contained in an essay entitled "Racist Love" (1972), which he coauthored with Jeffery Paul Chan. Significant portions of this piece were later worked into the various prefatory essays to the *Aiiieeeee!* anthology. Critic Patricia P. Chu finds in this essay "a forerunner of the current 'model minority' paradigm, which depicts Asian Americans as exemplary minorities because they achieve success without demanding fundamental changes in American society."[13] Chin and Chan identify what is particular to the Asian stereotype by comparing it to the stereotypes ascribed to other races: namely, blacks, Chicanos, and Indians. "The difference between these groups" and the Chinese, they write,

> was that the Christians, taking Chinese hospitality for timidity and docility, weren't afraid of us as they were of other races. They loved us, protected us. Love conquered.
>
> It's well-known that the cloying overwhelming love of a protective, coddling mother produces an emotionally stunted, dependent child. This is the Christian love, the bigoted love that has imprisoned the Chinese-American sensibility. (69)

The timidity, docility, and childishness that the paternalistic white racial imaginary ascribed to Asians, they suggest, also produced an image of the Asian man as feminine: as "womanly, effeminate, devoid of all the traditionally masculine qualities of originality, daring, physical courage, creativity" (68). According to Chin, this view of the Asian man as a privileged object of racist love—as a subject endowed with a childlike docility, an absence of racial antipathy toward whites, and, above all, an absence of "traditionally masculine qualities"—is exemplified by the figure of "Charlie Chan, the Chinese detective, who first appears in 'The House Without a Key' walking with 'the light dainty step of a woman.'"[14] This character, invented by author Earl Derr Biggers, is also described by Chin as a "fat, inscrutable, flowery but flub-tongued effeminate little detective."[15]

King-kok Cheung has suggested that a certain homophobia can be "detect[ed]" in Chin's account of this feminizing stereotype. This homophobia, however, is not simply detectable; rather, as I will be arguing, it is palpable and central. It is, moreover, intimately bound up with the misogyny: for by disparaging the feminine, these passages denigrate not only women but also those men who are in some way "feminine." In his descriptions of the feminizing stereotype that Charlie Chan epitomizes, Chin tends to reiterate the commonplace homophobic logic that equates effeminacy with homosexuality, that makes the "faggot" the privileged signifier of failed manhood. If white racism invites Asian men to be seen as "neither straight talkin' or [sic] straight shootin,'" this then also encourages them to be seen as lacking the most defining quality of normative masculinity, straightness itself. In his introduction to *The Big Aiiieeeee!* (1991), he states explicitly what he implied in his earlier characterization of Biggers's fictional creation: "it is an article of white liberal American faith today that Chinese men, at their best, are effeminate closet queens like Charlie Chan."[16]

While Chin's statements about the figure of Charlie Chan are rather notorious, they basically repeat the insinuation that because this character is effeminate, he is, more or less, gay. A less tendentious analysis of Biggers's fictional creation is offered by Jachinson Chan in the third chapter of his study *Chinese American Masculinities: From Fu Manchu to Bruce Lee*.[17] Generally affirming Chin's contentions concerning the gendered terms in which this character is depicted, J. Chan examines the differences between Biggers's literary creation and the historical figure upon which he was based: Chang Apana, a Chinese American detective in Hawaii who was famous not only for his criminological acumen, but also for his fearlessness and facility with a horsewhip. These more conventionally masculine qualities that the real Apana exemplified, as J. Chan points out, are notably missing in the imaginary Charlie Chan, thus giving credence to Chin's claim that the racist effect of such fictions was to impute an absence of masculinity to Asian men. But unlike Chin, J. Chan does not detect in Biggers's character any sense of homosexuality; rather, he sees Charlie Chan as "non-sexualized" in a way that undermines the sexual agency usually associated with virility. In short, Charlie Chan is reduced to an emasculated breeder. Charlie Chan's model of masculinity links asexuality with a stereotypical cultural stoicism that promotes a submissive male identity that is content in spite of systemic racial discriminations. (53)

If, as I have been suggesting, the general interchangeability of "sissy" and "faggot" in Chin's writings suggests a semantic sloppiness to the homophobic discourse he marshals in them, there is nonetheless something more interesting at play in his insistence on the "homosexuality" of the images of Asian masculinity that circulate in the wider culture. To understand what is at stake in his persistent claims of a linkage between Asian masculinity and homosexuality, it is necessary to turn to his account of the figure who would seem to epitomize a racial view that is the very opposite of the one crystallized in the character of Charlie Chan. I now turn to an analysis of the other avatar of stereotypical Asian identity that Chin persistently rails against in his polemical writings, the villainous Dr. Fu-Manchu.

The Homosexualization Thesis and the Yellow Peril: Fu-Manchu

It has come to be widely acknowledged that racial images tend to be paired, that "the most negative stereotype," as Sander Gilman puts it, "always has an overtly positive counterweight."[18] In reference to Asian Americans, this duality manifests itself in the sometimes oscillating and sometimes coincident depiction of Asians as, on the one hand, the model minority and, on the other, the Yellow Peril. In Chin's work, this duality is linked with the figures of Charlie Chan and Fu-Manchu. Popularized during the twenties and thirties, Chan and Fu constitute an Asian version of that historically contemporaneous duality between the Parkian view of the Negro as "the lady among the races" and the myth of the black male rapist promoted by white supremacists. The evil Dr. Fu-Manchu was a fictional character invented by the British author Sax Rohmer. Fu was the central villain in a series of novels and films that were popular on both sides of the Atlantic in this period. The two protagonists of Rohmer's fiction are the heroic Nayland Smith and his sidekick, Dr. Petrie, who also serves as narrator. They and their allies work ceaselessly to thwart the diabolical plots of Fu, the malevolent and preternaturally brilliant figure who leads a shadowy and insidious Oriental conspiracy whose intent is world domination. In their allusions to this character in "Racist Love," Chin and Chan seem, at times, to suggest that Fu-Manchu functions as the Asian counterpart to such figures of racial menace as the "hostile black stud," Geronimo, and General Santa Ana.

But before I address how Chin defines the racialized sexualized masculinity Fu embodies, I want briefly to summarize how this masculinity has been described by other commentators. Elaine Kim describes Fu as "completely asexual."[19] Robert Lee terms Fu's sexuality "ambiguous," because it "combines a masochistic vulnerability marked as feminine and a sadistic aggressiveness marked as masculine."[20] In noting this gendered duality, Lee is echoing Jachinson Chan, who asserts that while Fu appears to embody "a hegemonic masculinity," insofar as "he clearly seeks hegemony and he uses his power to dominate other men, regardless of race or nationality," this masculinity is partially undermined, as Fu "does not have any sexual attributes and he does not exhibit any sexual needs."[21] The evil doctor's thirst for power—which connotes virility on one level—is thus depicted as so overwhelming that it effectively calls into question his manhood on another level: "He is only interested in European women when he wants to engender a superior breed of children. Dr. Fu-Manchu is represented as a desexualized breeder who rapes women in order to procreate."[22] Chan ultimately concludes that Rohmer's depiction of Fu carries "contradictory sexual overtones."[23]

By pointing out the ambiguity or contradiction of Fu's sexuality—indeed, the inscrutability of it—Lee and J. Chan are highlighting its basically nonnormative quality. In so doing, they are following the lead established by Chin in his writings on the stereotypes inscribed in such figures. They part company from him, however, in scrupulously avoiding the homophobia that frames his description of the Fu stereotype. This avoidance is eminently understandable. But what gets lost in this translation from a homophobic idiom to one that is, admittedly, more queer-friendly, is something more than the acknowledgment of a critical debt. What gets lost, more importantly, is an opportunity to engage with and to understand the immense rhetorical power of the kind of homophobic discourse that Chin marshals—a discourse that possesses a considerable capacity to provide psychically compelling explanations of how racism produces its injurious effects. And it is the rhetorical power of this homophobic symbolism that I want now to examine. In the following, I intend to illuminate the cannibalistic power of the homophobic epithet in Chin's polemics: its capacity to swallow whole an entire range of non-masculine signifiers, and its ability to provide narrative coherence to the range of injurious psychic experiences to which Asian Americans are subjected as a result of racism.

In Chin's account of the stereotype, homosexuality functions as the privileged signifier of a masculine lack that must be ascribed to the Asian male if he is to serve as the ideal object of "racist love." As a result of the exceptionalism that structures his account of anti-Asian forms of racism, he insists that even those depictions that explicitly depict the Asian male as a phobic object—like the Fu fictions—also impute to him a "homosexuality." From Chin's perspective, the apparent opposition between the figures of Charlie Chan and Fu-Manchu is, in the end, illusory: "The differences between the evil Dr. Fu-Manchu and the good detective Charlie Chan of the Honolulu Police Department," Chin insists, "are superficial."[24] In essence, Chin collapses Fu and Chan by insisting that both—along with all Asian male figures who embody a feminine stereotype—are gay. In the passage below, which is taken from the 1991 introduction to *The Big Aiiieeeee!*, the centrality of this conflation to the conception of anti-Asian stereotyping promoted by Chin and his colleagues is quite apparent:

> It is an article of white liberal American faith today that Chinese men,
> at their best, are effeminate closet queens like Charlie Chan and, at their
> worst, are homosexual menaces like Fu-Manchu. . . . The good Chinese
> man, at his best, is the fulfillment of white male homosexual fantasy,
> literally kissing white ass.[25]

While a distinction is half-heartedly posited here between Chan and Fu—"at their best" versus "at their worst," "effeminate close queens" versus "homosexual menaces"—it is clear that this distinction is, in Chin's view, academic. Whatever distance might appear to open up between these two figures—between the Asian male as model minority and as Yellow Peril—is immediately closed by the homosexuality that appears to draw them together.

In such passages, it is clear that the "homosexuality" being invoked is mainly a vicious misnomer. This is evident from the odd dislocations in Chin's assertion that the "good Chinese man" expresses his "homosexuality" by "literally kissing white ass." While the ass may be the part of the male body usually associated with gay sex, its invocation in this context seems to have little to do with sexual pleasure per se: to want to kiss ass suggests less a desire for sexual gratification than it does a willingness to grovel, to humiliate and subordinate oneself to another man. In reducing the ideology of racism to "white male homosexual fantasy," moreover, Chin makes a rhetorical gesture that recalls the opening of Amiri Baraka's essay "American Sexual Reference: Black Male": "Most American white men are trained to be fags." If the white man's desire vis-à-vis the yellow man is, to use their formulation, a desire to have his ass kissed, this is undoubtedly the expression of a racist desire to have one's racial and masculine superiority affirmed: it does not necessarily express, however, a sexual hunger for another man's touch.

The pattern of this homophobic symbolism should seem, by now, rather familiar, as I have been examining it throughout this study. It is mainly being used here to underscore the "perversity" of the racialized masculinities that white racism seeks to gender. But despite its crude reiteration here, what is illuminating about it is the attention it draws to questions of desire—to the issue of what men of color are invited to want, how they want it, and how these desires are shaped by the desires of other men. To understand how this symbolism—drawn from the black writers who were, in my view, Chin's models—functions, I want to turn to a somewhat more developed account of this allegedly "homosexual" stereotype, which is found in an *autobiographical* essay entitled "Confessions of the Chinatown Cowboy."

In "Confessions," which was published the same year as "Racist Love" but which he authored alone, Chin fleshes out more fully his vision of the "gay" yellow man as object of racist love. He explains that "unlike the white stereotype of the evil black stud, Indian rapist, Mexican macho, the evil of the evil Dr. Fu-Manchu was not [hetero]sexual, but homosexual," and provides a brief sketch of the desires given expression in cinematic representations of this figure.[26] Chin describes how Fu usually appears in these texts:

> Dr. Fu, a man wearing a long dress, batting his eyelashes, surrounded by muscular black servants in loin cloths, and with his bad habit of caressingly touching white men on the leg, wrist and face with his long fingernails is not so much a threat as he is a frivolous offense to white manhood. (66)

Fu's homosexuality is apparently suggested in these films by the repertoire of swishy gestures his body performs. The gayness of Fu's gestures are thrown into relief, it is worth noting, by the apparent stillness of the "muscular black servants in loin cloths" who surround him. Of these gestures the most significant for Chin is Fu's "bad habit of caressingly touching" the man he apparently desires—the white hero, "All-Joe American" (66).[27]

Fu's desire, Chin insinuates, is a sexual desire for white men. But in describing "the sexual 'evil' offered by Fu-Manchu to the white race," he focuses primarily on the desires of the white man: Fu's alleged gayness answers to "the white male fantasy of white balls being irresistible" (66). Indeed both Chan and Fu, Chin writes, are "visions of the same mythic being, brewed up in the subconscious regions of the white [male] Christian's racial wetdream" (66). "The good Chinese man" is gay, apparently, because that is what the white man wants him to be—because, it *seems* to be implied, the white man himself is gay. Chin's imagery mirrors Baraka's in "American Sexual Reference: Black Male" and Fanon's in the sixth chapter of *Black Skins, White Masks*; and, for that matter, it mirrors Ellison's in *Invisible Man*. In outlining the libidinal forces that shape the male racist gaze as it glances upon the Asian man, Chin attempts to "out" the racist white male as a kind of homosexual. Indeed the white male subject Chin describes does seem marked by a kind of femininity, at least in the structure of his desire. For if All-Joe American wants mainly to feel "irresistible," his would seem to be a quintessentially "feminine" desire—a desire to be desired, to want to be an *object* rather than a *subject* of desire.[28] What white men really desire, apparently, is to *be desired* by yellow men.

The fact that he wants to be scoped and indeed to be wanted by other men is, according to Chin, no cause for concern to All-Joe American: Fu is merely "a frivolous offense to white manhood." The suggestion that straight white men are profoundly untroubled by a homosexual desire directed toward them—that they indeed welcome this desire—seems a strange assertion, especially considering the widespread homophobic panic that ensues any time gay men insist on their visible inclusion in such bastions of straight male homosociality as, say, the armed forces. The more typical straight male response to homosexuality is evoked by Leo Bersani in the passage below, which glosses the outrage voiced by heterosexual men in the military during the nineties in response to the proposed lifting of the ban against openly gay recruits:

> The *New York Times* reported on April 3, 1993, that a radar instructor who chose not to fly with an openly gay sailor, Keith Meinhold, feared that Meinhold's "presence in the cockpit would distract him from his responsibilities." The instructor "compared his 'shock' at learning there was a gay

sailor in his midst to a woman discovering a 'man in the ladies' restroom.'"
Note the curious scatological transsexualism in our radar instructor's (let
us hope momentary) identification of his cockpit with a ladies' restroom.
In this strange scenario, the potential gay attacker becomes the male
intruder on female privacy, and the "original" straight man is metamor-
phosed, through another man's imagined sexual attention, into the
offended, harassed, or even violated woman.[29]

There is a vast difference in the level of homophobia given expression by the
actors in the scenario depicted by Bersani and in the one staged by Chin. We
might consider whether this difference has something to do with the fact
that Bersani is describing an exchange that is racially unmarked—and therefore, we might presume, all-white—while Chin is describing one that is
interracial. In fact this difference, this *racial* difference, seems to make all the
difference in the world.

To understand why the allegedly homosexual Fu "is not so much a threat
as he is a frivolous offense to white manhood," it is necessary to examine the
contrast Chin draws between this figure and the other stereotypical male
figures of racial menace he cites in "Confessions": "the evil black stud, Indian
rapist, [and] Mexican macho" (66). "Instead of threatening white goddess
blond bigtits with sexual assault," Chin writes, "Dr. Fu swishes in to threaten
the All-Joe American with his beautiful nymphomaniac daughter" (66).
What the image of the darker-skinned rapist represents in white racist fantasy is pretty obvious: his violent, overpotent masculinity and heterosexuality reflect any number of racial and sexual anxieties.[30] Racist fantasies concerning this figure—if they are stripped down to their bodily particulars—
assume that if a black/brown/red penis forcefully penetrates a white vagina,
all sorts of apocalyptic consequences will follow. In contrast, the thing that
Fu does not do in this scenario, and thus the thing he cannot be, is related
to the thing he does not appear to have. For if the black/brown/red rapist
expresses his threatening heterosexuality and manhood with the appropriate
organ, Fu expresses his "homosexuality" with something else altogether: he
"swishes in to threaten the All-Joe American *with his beautiful nymphomaniac daughter*" (66; my emphasis). *It is through the body of his daughter*, Chin
tells us, that Fu enacts his desire, as if the potential penetration of her body
by All-Joe American would somehow enact the fulfillment of her father's
erotic wishes. Chin's insistence on Fu's homosexuality essentially erases the

daughter's heterosexual desire by overwriting it as the displaced expression of her father's. The image of a yellow female body is made to function as the expression of a yellow male "homosexual" desire.

And if Fu's desire only finds form within the body of a woman, that particular corporeal habitation would then seem to color and shape—to gender—his desire. Fu does not, apparently, wish to do to other men what men are supposed to do to women: he does not harbor the active, masculine, and penetrative homosexual desire usually imputed to the gay sexual predator, the desire to make the straight man take the woman's place. Rather, since his desire requires the mediation of his daughter's body, it takes on a feminine, penetrable shape—his is apparently a passive desire to assume the yellow woman's place, to be used by the white man as she is. The interracial homosexual desire that the yellow man harbors, Chin implies here, involves an *identification* with the position of the yellow woman. It is, in other words, a desire to be fucked by the white man.[31]

What subtends Chin's depiction of Fu as homosexual is a racialized homophobic fantasy about gay sex the contours of which I outlined in the introduction to this study, in my discussion of Eldridge Cleaver's essay "Notes of a Native Son." In Cleaver's view, the desire for white men harbored by black homosexuals like Baldwin takes its corporeal shape through an identification with black women: they enact the impossible fantasy of wanting to "become(s) a white man in a black body" by allowing white men to come into their black bodies—by "bending over and touching their toes for the white man." In denigrating the black homosexual that Baldwin typifies, Cleaver insists that such men are driven by identification with black women, with those "grandmothers" whose sexual availability to white men was ensured by the institutionalized practices of slavery. Fu's homosexuality on Chin's account—like Baldwin's in Cleaver's—is apparently shaped by an *intra*racial and cross-gender identification.

As I pointed out in my introductory chapter, this identification with women of color is connected in Cleaver's essay, paradoxically, with another form of mimetic desire that follows a different track. For this identification with black femininity enables the expression of an interracial homosexual desire for white men that also has an identificatory component. For the racially perverse desire that black intellectuals like Baldwin are accused of harboring is a desire to "become a white man in a black man's body"— a desire to become white. In translating this contention into the Asian

American context, Chin suggests that Fu's desire (one that renders white men "irresistible," which can lead to "the bad habit of caressingly touching white men on the leg, wrist and face") is an assimilationist desire.

In essence, the homosexual desire that stereotypical figures like Fu and Chan are alleged to harbor is depicted in Chin's writings as a sexualized manifestation of a racially perverse desire that Asian Americans are encouraged by white racism to harbor. In "Confessions," Chin writes: "The movies were our teachers. In no uncertain terms they taught Americans that we were lovable for being a race of sissies, cowed by women, and not black with all our hearts, living to accommodate the white man" (66). The fact that Hollywood films always cast white actors in the role of Charlie Chan makes evident the whiteness at the heart of the model minority identity that Asians are encouraged to strive for:

> Hollywood on high sacrificed three white men, gave us their sons Warner Oland, Sidney Toler and Roland Winters, Charlie Chans I, II, and II, cast in the image of the most perfect Chinese so that we might liken ourselves unto him, and be guided along the true path toward assimilation. (66)

What is clearly being vilified here—and vilified as "homosexual"—is an assimilationist orientation toward white masculinity, an orientation that the mainstream cinema encourages. These films attempt to instill in the Asian male subject a desire to become, as it were, a white man in a yellow body.

I have thus far been stressing the similarities between the homophobic symbolism that structures Chin's writings and the one that shapes the black nationalist tradition. But if my reading of Chin has made clear how successful this translation is, it is not my claim that it is also seamless. For we must also confront certain key differences that emerge in Chin's reworking of this homophobic symbolism.

In the black and white scenarios that Baraka, Cleaver, and Ellison describe, the assimilationist desire to which the black homosexual gives carnal expression has its counterpart in the interracial mimetic desire of the white male racist. The beatnik, as he is described by Baraka, and Young Emerson, as he is depicted by Ellison, both harbor—along with a sexualized attraction to black men—an identificatory desire for the vibrant culture that blackness signifies, and the manhood that black male bodies symbolize. The "perversity" of the white male racist desire such writers hope to expose stems from its fusion of the homosexual and the mimetic. Baraka's Superspade and the townsmen in chapter 1 of Ellison's *Invisible Man* tend to affirm—as does Norman Mailer's White Negro—the assertions that Fanon makes in chapter 6 of *Black Skin, White Masks* concerning the white man's orientation toward the black man: namely, that the Negrophobic white man is, at bottom, both a Negrophile and a homosexual.

The "homosexuality" of All-Joe American as it is expressed vis-à-vis Asian men, at least, takes a quite different form. In the scenario that Chin labels the "white [male] Christian's racial wetdream," what the white man sees in the yellow man is not an *object* of desire and identification, but rather a kind of *subject*—one who returns to the white man an image of himself as "irresistible." And this has much to do with the nonthreatening nature of the "homosexuality" Fu signifies. To put this another way, if the black man's body provides a mirror to the white man of what he desires and wishes he were, it then also threatens to expose to him what he does not have and cannot be; this threat thus generates a reactive rage. In contrast, the yellow male body—and the desire it houses—would only seem to mirror back to the white man what he already knows he is and has.

In the end, what fuels Chin's outrage—what leads him essentially to call the white man a "faggot"—is not the *presence* of homosexual desire for the yellow man in "the white Christian's racial wetdream" but rather its *absence*. What throws the yellow man's lack of racialized manhood into relief is the white man's lack of a phobically charged sexual desire for him. Fanon's analyses of white racial fantasies lead him to conclude that for the white man the Negro *is* a penis—that the black man signifies for the white man all the masculine plenitude he feels himself to lack; Ellison's analyses of white male racial psychology lead to similar conclusions. In contrast, what Chin sees in the popular texts that would seem to depict white male racial fantasy is not an analogous sexual desire for the yellow man but rather a relative indifference. Fu is apparently "not so much a threat as he is a frivolous offense to white manhood" because he does not signify for the white man a terrifying phallic manhood worthy of desire or emulation. There are, as it were, no White Orientals here.

The thing that Chin laments, then, is not exactly that Asian men are the objects of racist love, but that they are not the objects of the right kind of racist love—the right kind being that which black male writers like Ellison find so galling. The predicament that Chin identifies here through his homophobic representations is, ironically, one that has also been identified—

though in an entirely different political context, and for entirely different ends—by the gay Asian Canadian filmmaker Richard Fung. In contrast to the penis that the black man simply *is* in the white racist imaginary, according to Fanon, "the Asian man is defined," Fung writes, "by a striking absence down there."[32] In his essay "Looking for My Penis," Fung does in fact locate a substantial archive of sexualized images of Asian men in gay porn; but the yellow men he finds—like Chin's version of Fu—are mainly identified with penetrability rather than penetration.

This Asian male inadequacy is not something that Chin plays down; indeed, it is something he rather obsessively plays up. Put in less inflammatory terms, all he is trying to point out is something many subsequent critics of "the model minority myth" have also noted: that Asian Americans tend to get valued by whites insofar as they attempt to assimilate into the mainstream values of white culture and avoid emulating the example provided by African Americans and other, more "angry" minority groups. But by deploying the homophobic and misogynistic symbolic vocabulary of black nationalist writings and directing it toward Asian Americans themselves, he genders both his own locutionary position and that of his Asian American male audience. He engages in a kind of rhetorical blackmail in order to assert something like the following: *if we yellow men court the racist love of white men by trying to be like them (and thereby affirm their "irresistibility"), we will not only lack the kind of threatening masculinity that men of other races possess in abundance, we will essentially become faggots.*

The Color of Smoke: Rereading Fu-Manchu

In the paragraphs above, I have been adumbrating the concerns that will be central to the next two chapters of this study. As I will make clear, Chin's literary specialty—the dimension of the Asian American experience he writes most movingly, if disturbingly, about—is the self-loathing, the masochism, and the melancholy that define an Asian American masculinity fundamentally shaped by the injurious constructions of race and masculinity that prevail in our culture. To understand the complexity and power of Chin's vision, it is necessary to engage with the psychic insights he is able to offer—and not *despite* his use of the homophobic symbolism he draws from the black tradition, but rather *through* it.

But before I continue with my study of Chin, I want to end this chapter by putting Chin's assertions concerning popular representations of Asian masculinity to productive use. I do so, however, by taking the homophobic rhetoric in which they are couched as a critical point of departure. I want to consider the possibility that Chin may have, as it were, stumbled onto something in his claim that Fu-Manchu is depicted as a "homosexual menace." It is not my intent in the following to offer an authoritative or comprehensive "queer" reading of the multitudinous cinematic, televisual, and novelistic depictions of Fu. Rather I want to situate Rohmer's fictions in a set of roughly contemporaneous discursive contexts that might explicate more fully the somewhat inscrutable racialized sexuality they ascribe to Chinese men—a sexuality that Chin homophobically and reductively reads as *homo*sexuality, and that Jachinson Chan and Robert Lee read, somewhat unsatisfactorily, as "ambiguous" or "contradictory." My focus here is *The Insidious Dr. Fu-Manchu* (1913), the first novel in Sax Rohmer's series.

My agenda here is also, in part, historicist. Thus far, I have mainly been interested in what the Fu fictions meant to Frank Chin writing in the seventies; my readings, therefore, have been readings of his readings. But both Chin and Ellison identify the twenties as a watershed moment, not only in the construction of the racial ideologies they both seek to challenge, but also in the emergence of the two culture industries that helped popularize those ideologies: that of the mass media and that of the social sciences. Rohmer's writings, like Park's, achieved the height of their popularity during this period, and they occupy a place in Chin's project comparable to the one assumed by sociology in Ellison's—as the exemplification of an influential and "inauthentic" representation of minority identity that must be overturned for a more "authentic" ethnonationalist tradition to emerge. My reading of *The Insidious Dr. Fu-Manchu* is intended, as well, to suggest a more expansive and comparative view of how racial ideologies of the twenties were constructed—of how blackness and Asianness were shaped not only in relation to whiteness, but also in relation to each other—and also of how the discourse of racial difference was written in a language of gender and sexuality.

In my reading of *The Insidious Dr. Fu-Manchu*, I focus on the "queerness" the novel ascribes to its eponymous villain. I do so by situating this novel in relation to two contemporaneous discursive contexts. The first of these is a public health discourse that developed in response to the perceived threats

posed by large-scale Chinese immigration in the early decades of the twentieth century to the Anglo-American West—a discourse that linked Orientals
with various forms of contagion that threatened the sexual health of whites
who might come into intimate contact with them. The second discursive
context concerns the figure of Oscar Wilde, whose advocacy of a decorative
Orientalist aesthetic became the marker of both racial and his sexual alterity. I will also show how this particular figuration of the Orientalist Wilde—
as an emblem of a dissident sexual and racial identity—circulates in a number of African American literary writings as well: in texts authored by two
gay male writers of the Harlem Renaissance—Bruce Nugent and Wallace
Thurman—and also in Ellison's *Invisible Man*.

As transatlantic texts that traveled well from one side of the Atlantic to
the other, the Fu fictions suggest the easy translatability of British anxieties
about the emergence of Chinese immigrant populations in urban centers
like London to an American context—their popularity in the United States,
in other words, suggests the existence of a parallel set of anxieties that centered on the Chinatowns that emerged in cities like San Francisco. Fu's secret
headquarters is hidden in London's Chinatown, a detail suggesting that the
threat posed to the West by the Yellow Peril is a domestic and urban concern
as well as a matter of foreign policy. Robert Lee observes that the Chinatown
in which Fu sets up shop and the Orient it metonymically stands in for are
both depicted in rather generic terms that "collapse(s) national histories into
an ahistorical cultural category of Oriental Otherness."[33] Fu's "Chineseness,"
Lee writes, "is only a marker of his generalized Oriental alienness. Chinatown, long familiar to American readers as a den of vice and moral corrup-
tion, is less distinctively Chinese than Oriental."[34] While this is an undoubtedly accurate appraisal of the novel, Nayan Shah's study of the cultural
politics of public health as it pertained to Chinese immigrants in San Francisco suggests that there were more specific sexualized racial anxieties (or
racialized sexual ones) engendered by the emergence of Chinatown communities in the United States—anxieties generated by particular cultural
practices. Of the practices Shah describes (which include the emergence of
"bachelor" communities, and of domestic arrangements that did not mirror
white bourgeois norms), two figure prominently in the first Fu novel: female
prostitution and the opium trade. The cultural anxieties Shah notes at a local
level—in the writings and policy decisions of San Francisco area politicians,
missionaries, and physicians—mirror the ones that the Fu fictions provoke

and manage. These anxieties revolve around the threat to white bourgeois domesticity constituted by the presence of sexually active Asian women and by opium dens. The dangers that Chinese prostitutes were perceived as posing to respectable married white men, according to Shah, included not only syphilis, but also an exposure to a range of "perverse" sexual practices including sodomy, genital mutilation, and bestiality.[35] Likewise, the generally all-male context of the opium den was depicted as facilitating the experience of "perverse social relations, ambiguous sexuality, and queer domesticity."[36]

In his study of Rohmer's fictions, J. Chan notes the central role played by versions of both of these figures: the dangerous and sexually desirable Oriental woman (who may or may not be under Fu's control), and the opium den and the drug trade more generally. In the first novel in the series, *The Insidious Dr. Fu-Manchu*, the ambiguously Oriental character of Karamaneh plays a pivotal role. Though she provides crucial assistance to the white heroes as they work to thwart Fu's nefarious plans, and though she eventually becomes Dr. Petrie's loyal wife in a later novel, her initial appearance—and the overpowering white male desire it elicits—presents her exotic sexuality as a threat to white male fortitude and something that must be domesticated. In chapter 4, Dr. Petrie confesses to the reader the conflicting and overpowering nature of the desires she instills in him:

> It is with some shame that I confess how her charm enveloped me like a magic cloud. . . . Her clothes or her hair exhaled a faint perfume. Like all Fu-Manchu's servants, she was perfectly chosen for her peculiar duties. Her beauty was wholly intoxicating. . . .
>
> At that moment I honestly would have given half of my worldly possessions to have been spared the decision which I knew I must come to. After all, what proof had I that she was a willing accomplice of Dr. Fu-Manchu? Furthermore, she was an Oriental, and her code must necessarily be different from mine. Irreconcilable as the thing may be with Western ideas, Nayland Smith had really told me that he believed the girl to be a slave.[37]

The threat posed by Karamaneh and other enigmatic Oriental women in the series is defused as they switch allegiances and come to substitute a white male master for a yellow one. As J. Chan points out, "Eastern women" in these novels "are represented as slaves who are, in turn, 'naturally' attracted to Western men"; reference is generally made to "natural or social laws to prove that the only purpose for women is to love their men."[38]

Opium, J. Chan also points out, plays a pivotal role in the first Fu novel as well: it "is the main drug which destroys life, while Dr. Fu-Manchu's 'elixir vitae' allows him to escape death and old age."[39] The centrality of this drug to popular imaginings of China and the Chinese, J. Chan argues, derived from the historical context of British imperial endeavors in China. British control was solidified, after all, through the two opium wars—wars that provoked fierce debates both in England and in the United States. The emergence of opium dens in Western metropoles like London and San Francisco, moreover, localized wider racial and sexual anxieties, which are apparent in the public health discourse Nayan Shah examines in *Contagious Divides*. A significant source of these anxieties was the ritualized socialized practices that accompanied the act of smoking opium:

> The common method of smoking opium encouraged a special intimacy. The bunks could accommodate a pair of opium smokers who would lie facing each other with their heads resting upon blocks of wood or tin cans. Between them would be a lamp and a pipe with a sixteen-inch bamboo stem connected to a ceramic bowl. The preparation for smoking opium was elaborate and required instruction. The smoker dipped a needle into a container of prepared opium and then held the needle above the lamp's flame, where the opium bubbled and swelled to several times its original size. Once it was properly "cooked," the opium was transferred to the pipe's bowl, where it was rolled into a small "pill." This pill was tilted and held over the flame, and the smoker drew in the fumes.[40]

It was not just the physical nature of this interracial homosocial intimacy that troubled local politicians and reformers, according to Shah, but also that "the dens permitted mingling without regard for the social distinction of either class or race, creating the fraternity and egalitarianism of vice that undermined the republic of virtue and status distinctions."[41]

A visit to an opium den comes at a crucial moment in *The Insidious Dr. Fu-Manchu*, as it occasions the first contact between the white heroes and their yellow nemesis. Dr. Petrie's horrified description of this experience, during which he and Nayland are disguised as addicts, is replete with the same kinds of images that permeate the medical and public policy discourse examined by Shah in his study:

> The next moment I found myself in an atmosphere which was literally poisonous. It was all but unbreathable, being loaded with opium fumes. Never

before had I experienced anything like it. Every breath was an effort. A tin oil-lamp on a box in the middle of the floor dimly illuminated the horrible place, about the walls of which ten or twelve bunks were ranged and all of them occupied. Most of the occupants were lying motionless, but one or two were squatting in their bunks noisily sucking at the little metal pipes. These had not yet attained to the opium-smoker's Nirvana. . . .

Yan performed a curious little shrug, rather of the back than of the shoulders, and shuffled to the box which bore the smoky lamp. Holding a needle in the flame, he dipped it, when red-hot, into an old cocoa tin, and withdrew it with a bead of opium adhering to the end. Slowly roasting this over the lamp, he dropped it into the bowl of the metal pipe which he held ready, where it burned with a spirituous blue flame.

"Pass it over," said Smith huskily, and rose on his knees with the assumed eagerness of a slave to the drug.

Yan handed him the pipe, which he promptly put to his lips, and prepared another for me.

"Whatever you do, don't inhale any," came Smith's whispered injunction.

It was with a sense of nausea greater even than that occasioned by the disgusting atmosphere of the den that I took the pipe and pretended to smoke. Taking my cue from my friend, I allowed my head gradually to sink lower and lower, until, within a few minutes, I sprawled sideways on the floor, Smith lying close beside me. . . .

The smoky lamp in the middle of the place afforded scant illumination, serving only to indicate sprawling shapes—here an extended hand, brown or yellow, there a sketchy, corpse-like face; whilst from all about rose obscene sighings and murmurings in far-away voices—an uncanny, animal chorus. It was like a glimpse of the Inferno seen by some Chinese Dante. (33)

Petrie's nausea is most specifically provoked by his having to put his lips over the very same pipe as Yan, the Chinese proprietor of the establishment, and the revulsion he expresses was shared by American social critics of the opium den. Shah cites the report of Dr. H. H. Kane, who was concerned about the "'loathsome contagion' that could be passed unwittingly from one smoker to the next . . . detail[ing] several instances of unsuspecting smokers contracting syphilis from the pipe, including a 'respectable young man' who contracted a 'syphilitic chancre of the lip'."[42]

Clearly operant in these phobic depictions of sharing the pipe is a racist *and* homophobic revulsion at the physical intimacy—at the literal mixing of bodily fluids—involved. Also presented as horrifying is the contagious pleasure that smoking generates, one that draws men together in a delirious intimacy, eliciting from them "obscene sighings and murmurings." The novel later discloses Fu's own proclivities for this particular pleasure, a disclosure that occurs when Dr. Petrie fixes his medical gaze on the evil doctor's mouth. Petrie recalls how he noticed, when seeing Fu's evil smile, "his teeth, small and evenly separated, but discolored in a way that was familiar to me. I studied his eyes with a new professional interest, which even the extremity of our danger could not wholly banish" (84). Petrie deduces from these details that Fu has an appetite for opium—something that the evil doctor soon confirms. This is a somewhat surprising revelation because Fu does not seem to indulge in hedonistic activities of any other kind.[43] His only pleasure comes, it would seem, through a practice that is everywhere else described in the novel as involving sordid homosocial intimacy.

Petrie is drawn to Fu's mouth not simply because of the teeth that give away his addiction, but also because of the uncannily perfect English that emerges from it. To the narrator this fluency seems somehow to throw into relief Fu's malignancy:

> I had never supposed, prior to meeting Dr. Fu-Manchu, that so intense a force of malignancy could radiate—from any human being. He spoke. His English was perfect, though at times his words were oddly chosen; his delivery alternately was guttural and sibilant. (84)

As Elaine Kim has observed of villainous figures like Fu, they depart from the more typical linguistic stereotype of the Asian in that they do not—as Charlie Chan does, for instance—speak a comical broken English. Instead, villains like Fu speak English, Kim writes, "with a flowery, almost unnatural fluency that [is] humorous or sinister."[44]

Fu's "flowery, almost unnatural fluency" in English is hinted at by another bodily detail. Nayland Smith's first physical description of Fu—which is offered in the second chapter of the novel, many pages before his actual appearance—notes a certain bard-like aspect of his physiognomy:

> "Imagine a person, tall, lean and feline, high-shouldered, *with a brow like Shakespeare* and a face like Satan, a close-shaven skull, and long, magnetic eyes of the true cat-green. Invest him with all the cruel cunning of an entire Eastern race, accumulated in one giant intellect, with all the resources of science past and present, with all the resources, if you will, of a wealthy

government—which, however, already has denied all knowledge of his existence. Imagine that awful being, and you have a mental picture of Dr. Fu-Manchu, the yellow peril incarnate in one man." (13)

Similar to the way in which "his teeth, small and evenly separated, but discolored" intimate his opium use, his Shakespearean brow seems to foreshadow the fact that, when the reader meets him, Fu will display an uncanny fluency in the King's English. Indeed, the evil doctor's preternatural eloquence seems all the more apparent in the context of certain momentary lapses in Doctor Petrie's own narrative command:

> How can I paint the individual who now stood before us—perhaps the greatest genius of all times? (84)

> He came forward with *an indescribable gait*, cat-like yet awkward, carrying his high shoulders almost hunched. . . . [His eyes] possessed an iridescence which hitherto I had supposed possible only in the eye of the cat—and the film intermittently clouded their brightness—*but I can speak of them no more*. (84; my emphasis)

> He was not as other men. The dread that he inspired in all with whom he came in contact, the terrors which he controlled and hurled at whomsoever cumbered his path, rendered him an object supremely sinister. *I despair of conveying to those who may read this account any but the coldest conception of the man's evil power*. (109)

In the twentieth chapter, Petrie similarly apologizes: "It is beyond my powers to convey the sense of the uncanny which the episode created," referring to a moment when the protagonists hear Fu's disembodied voice eerily declare, seemingly out of nowhere: "Another victory for China, Mr. Nayland Smith!" (137).

There are two obvious explanations for Rohmer's persistent use of this rhetorical device. First of all, statements like the ones above comprise his rather banal attempts to make use of the figure of the sublime—they record Petrie's momentary terror and loss of selfhood in the face of an evil and intellect so monumental and overpowering as to temporarily dam the flow of turgid prose that, for the rest of the narrative, flows so easily from his pen. Indeed, such statements are always followed by a lengthy description of what Petrie claims he is unable to describe—a description that usually piles on adjective after adjective detailing the inscrutability and enormity of Fu's evil and intellect. The second reason for these occasional lapses in the narrator's power, as becomes obvious in later chapters, is that they are intended to whet the reader's appetite for a sequel.[45] This much is clear from the following excerpt from the final chapter.

> I come to the close of my chronicle, and feel that I betray a trust—the trust of my reader. For having limned in the colors at my command the fiendish Chinese doctor, I am unable to conclude my task as I should desire, unable, with any consciousness of finality, to write Finis to the end of my narrative.
>
> It seems to me sometimes that my pen is but temporarily idle—that I have but dealt with a single phase of a movement having a hundred phases. One sequel I hope for, and against all the promptings of logic and Western bias. If my hope shall be realized I cannot, at this time, pretend to state.
>
> The future, 'mid its many secrets, holds this precious one from me. (192)

Another effect of these kinds of phrases, finally, is to reaffirm the irreducible difference to the West of the Eastern sensibility that Fu epitomizes—to comment yet again on the Orient's fabled inscrutability.

This rhetorical device that is insistently used throughout this 1913 novel to convey an evil that it cannot quite name but whose shadowy presence is everywhere bears some resemblance—though I believe it to be a coincidental one—to another trope in currency around the same time that was used to indicate another kind of unnameable yet pervasive "evil." In pointing out this similarity, it is not my argument that the trope of the unspeakable in reference to homosexuality—the conceit describing homosexuality as the love that dare not speak its name—is somehow explicitly *encoded*, to borrow the Birmingham school's terminology, in Rohmer's novel. I am suggesting, however, that its coincidental convergence with the rhetorical device used to describe "Fu-Manchu, whom I had never seen, but whose name stood for horrors indefinable!" may provide the basis for the kind of racialized "queer" reading Chin claims to perform but does not—a historically contextualizing decoding practice, as it were, that suggests how the Fu fictions might catalyze the discursive crossing of an Orientalism that views the East as inscrutable and of a homophobia that views homosexuality as the love that dare not speak its name.[46]

In many ways, however, producing a "queer" reading of this text seems an endeavor that is both anachronistic and redundant. Most contemporary readers will find *The Insidious Dr. Fu-Manchu* a deliciously campy text, and it is not difficult to imagine the role of the novel's villain being played by a drag queen—an ersatz Bette Davis in yellowface, if you will. Such a reading of Fu is greatly facilitated by the lavish and excessive detail with which the narrative describes his sumptuous and enormous apartment:

> It was an apartment of such size that its dimensions filled me with a kind of awe such as I never had known: the awe of walled vastness. Its immense extent produced a sensation of sound. Its hugeness had a distinct NOTE.
>
> Tapestries covered the four walls. There was no door visible. These tapestries were magnificently figured with golden dragons; and as the serpentine bodies gleamed and shimmered in the increasing radiance, each dragon, I thought, intertwined its glittering coils more closely with those of another. The carpet was of such richness that I stood knee-deep in its pile. And this, too, was fashioned all over with golden dragons; and they seemed to glide about amid the shadows of the design—stealthily.
>
> At the farther end of the hall—for hall it was—a huge table with dragons' legs stood solitary amid the luxuriance of the carpet. It bore scintillating globes, and tubes that held living organisms, and books of a size and in such bindings as I never had imagined, with instruments of a type unknown to Western science—a heterogeneous litter quite indescribable, which overflowed on to the floor, forming an amazing oasis in a dragon-haunted desert of carpet. A lamp hung above this table, suspended by golden chains from the ceiling—which was so lofty that, following the chains upward, my gaze lost itself in the purple shadows above.
>
> In a chair piled high with dragon-covered cushions a man sat behind this table. The light from the swinging lamp fell fully upon one side of his face, as he leaned forward amid the jumble of weird objects, and left the other side in purplish shadow. From a plain brass bowl upon the corner of the huge table smoke writhed aloft and at times partially obscured that dreadful face.
>
> From the instant that my eyes were drawn to the table and to the man who sat there, neither the incredible extent of the room, nor the nightmare fashion of its mural decorations, could reclaim my attention. I had eyes only for him.
>
> For it was Dr. Fu-Manchu! (80–81)

Fu's decorative tastes, which are on extravagant display in his apartment, and also his taste for opium invite a comparison with another roughly contemporaneous figure, one whose name was also eponymous for a kind of unnameable villainy and whose abodes were also replete with exotic decorative objects from the Orient: Oscar Wilde. Indeed, the context provided by Wilde—and, more specifically, the readings of his work and celebrity offered by Eve Kosofsky Sedgwick and Curtis Marez—make a synchronic "queer" reading of the crossings of Orientalist and sexual discourses in the Fu texts seem not just plausible but even inevitable. Indeed, Rohmer's portrayal of Fu resonates with certain *racializing* depictions of Wilde that were disseminated by some of his English and American detractors.

In her essay "Wilde, Nietzsche and the Sentimental Relations of the Male Body," Eve Sedgwick finds in *Dorian Gray* evidence of a "gay-affirming and gay-occluding orientalism," arguing more specifically that its depictions of drug addiction are displaced representations of the "secret vice" of homosexuality. This assertion works to align Fu with this Oriental(ist) "queer"-ness. Even more pertinent here are the analyses that Curtis Marez offers in his essay "The Other Addict: Reflections on Colonialism and Oscar Wilde's Opium Smoke Screen," which concerns itself with the "aggressive re-racializ[ation] of Wilde" that his American and English critics engaged in. In their attacks, these critics fixed upon his advocacy of Oriental art as evidence that "as an Irishman Wilde was as primitive as the exotic objects he celebrated."[47] Wilde's advocacy, via the Aesthetic Movement, of "non-Western ornamentation"— and especially of the use of decorative objects from the Orient—was used by his detractors to, as it were, put him in his racial place, and was cited as evidence of Wilde's own racialized alterity as an Irish primitive to the Anglo-American West.[48]

Marez substantiates this claim by examining a number of caricatures published in numerous U.S. and English periodicals in the late 1890s that depicted Wilde variously as a "'simian' Irishman," as "a minstrel-like character" who was clearly supposed to be black, as a Native American, and as a "Chinaman."[49] The last set of caricatures, which depict Wilde as Chinese, also made reference to his taste for Chinese opium.[50] Marez concludes that these "cartoons demonstrate the simultaneous autonomy and interdependence of sex, gender, and race" in the late nineteenth-century Anglo-American imaginary.[51] These representations also demonstrate how the categories of the primitive and the pervert were seen at the turn of the century as eminently comparable if not wholly interchangeable. They foreshadow the thesis codified by Freud in his *Three Essays on Sexuality* that rendered largely identical the mental lives of savages and those of sexual deviants.

The examples provided by Marez in his study along with Sedgwick's identification of a "gay-affirming and gay-occluding *orientalism*" around the figure of Wilde suggest that a particularly vibrant connection emerged in the popular imaginary linking homosexuality and decorative tastes favoring exotic objects of the East.[52] It is in this context that I would like to revisit a particular scene in *Invisible Man*, one that suggests the persistence of this semiotic link into the 1940s: the ninth chapter, which records the encounter between the protagonist and Young Emerson. For the knowing reader, the first clue provided to this would-be benefactor's "impure" motives is some of the decorative objects displayed in his office (186), which to the narrator resembles a "museum" (180):

> There were paintings, bronzes, tapestries, all beautifully arranged. . . .
>   . . . a teakwood chair with cushions of emerald-green silk . . . a beautiful dwarf tree . . . a lighted case of Chinese design which held delicate-looking statues of horses and birds, small vases and bowls, each set upon a carved wooden base . . . an aviary of tropical birds [was] set near one of the broad windows . . . their colors flared for an instant like an unfurled oriental fan. (180–81)

These details, especially in light of Marez's analyses, seem to confirm other references that are made in this chapter concerning Young Emerson's Wildean pretensions, which include the following admission: "I'm afraid my father considers *me* one of the unspeakables" (188).

In a chapter as replete with "queer" literary allusions as this one (Twain's *Huckleberry Finn*, or at least Leslie Fiedler's notorious reading of it, and Walt Whitman's Calumus poems are evoked), it is one particular Orientalist detail that makes evident its allusion to the interracial homosexual milieu of the Harlem Renaissance: as the narrator enters the room, he notes the location in which Young Emerson had previously been sitting when he spies "on a table that held a beautiful dwarf tree . . . smoke rising from a cigarette rising in a jade ash tray" (180).

This last phrase is clearly an allusion to the central image that holds together the short piece of experimental writing generally regarded as the first piece of published African American fiction expressing an openly homosexual sensibility: Richard Bruce Nugent's "Smoke, Lilies and Jade." Nugent's piece was included in *FIRE!!*, the short-lived magazine (only one issue was ever produced) that was released to much controversy in 1927, at the height of the Harlem Renaissance. "Smoke, Lilies and Jade" is a stream-of-consciousness narrative (though it is told in the third person) recounting the exploits and meditations of Alex, an artist thoroughly devoted to the Wildean ideals of dissipation and decadence, who langorously describes his desire for both Melva, his black fiancée, and Beauty, a white male lover. According to David Levering Lewis, "Alex is largely Nugent himself, and Beauty a composite of [Rudolph] Valentino, Miguel Covarrubias, Harold Jackman, nameless Narcissi of the Village, and the Hughes with whom the author once walked back and forth all night." Nugent's piece ends, in Lewis's words,

> in a montage of pederasty and androgyny, Beauty metamorphosing into Melva. . . . and Melva into beauty and prose dissolving into pointillistic soft pornography while Alex, stoned, hears the Hall Johnson Choir singing "Fy-ah, Lawd" in a Harlem church.[53]

A motif that repeats throughout Nugent's story, a recurrent imagistic echo that holds together its fragmentary and elliptical narrative, is the following phrase and its various permutations (the ellipses are all Nugent's):

> And he had an ivory holder inlaid with red jade and green . . . funny how the smoke seemed to climb up that ray of sunlight[54]

> . . . maybe it was wrong to think thoughts like these . . . but they were nice and pleasant and comfortable . . . when one was smoking a cigarette through an ivory holder . . . inlaid with red jade and green (101)

> soon the moon would rise and then he would clothe the silver moon in blue smoke garments . . . truly smoke was like imagination (102)

> . . . in truth it was fine to be young and hungry and an artist . . . to blow blue smoke from an ivory holder (103)

> . . . oh the joy of being an artist and of blowing blue smoke thru an ivory holder inlaid with red jade and green (104)

Though the substance Alex is smoking here may be marijuana—or even possibly tobacco—rather than opium, that it is meant to establish a link to Wilde is made quite clear in the following passage: "was it Wilde who had said . . . a cigarette is the most perfect pleasure because it leaves one unsatisfied" (102).

The final African American literary reference I want to cite that renders visible a linkage between the Orient and homosexuality via the figure of Wilde—a linkage that resonates with Rohmer's fictions—is the conclusion of

Wallace Thurman's novel *Infants of the Spring*. Thurman was—along with Langston Hughes, Zora Neale Hurston, Aaron Douglas, and Nugent—one of the editors of *FIRE!!* He was also a frequent habitué of the boarding-house on 137th Street where many of the group associated with *FIRE!!* lived and threw extravagant parties—a house that came to be known as "Niggeratti Manor." Thurman's novel, written in 1932, is essentially a roman à clef of the Harlem Renaissance, and nearly all of its important figures are roundly pilloried in it.[55] One key event—which happens near the end of the novel and which signals the impending demise of the movement—is Paul Arbian's eviction from Niggeratti Manor and his move to the gay enclave of Christopher Street in Greenwich Village. (Arbian is regarded by most readers as Bruce Nugent's fictional counterpart—Nathan Huggins describes him as "a decadent and one of the few truly talented characters in the novel.")[56] But it is in the novel's climactic final scene that Thurman sought, in Huggins's words, "to bury the renaissance once and for all," providing it with a "symbolic end."[57]

In the novel's final chapter, Raymond Taylor (Thurman's own fictional stand-in) receives the news that Paul has committed suicide. Upon arriving at Paul's new apartment, Raymond is ushered into the bathroom, where he finds the body. Paul has staged his suicide carefully, timing it so that his death would be discovered during a party that was planned for that night. Raymond confronts what the narrator calls "the gruesome yet fascinating spectacle" of Paul's corpse and surmises the following:

> Paul had evidently come home before the end of the party. On arriving,
> he had locked himself in the bathroom, donned a crimson mandarin robe,
> wrapped his head in a batik scarf of his own designing, hung a group of his
> spirit portraits on the dingy calcimined wall, and carpeted the floor with
> sheets of paper detached from the notebook in which he had been writing
> his novel. He had then, it seemed, placed scented joss-sticks in the four
> corners of his room, lit them, climbed into the bathtub, turned on the
> water, then slashed his wrists with a highly ornamented Chinese dirk.
> When they found him, the bathtub had overflowed, and Paul lay crumpled
> at the bottom, a colorful, inanimate corpse in a crimson streaked tub. (283)

Paul's intent in staging this elaborate suicide had been to ensure that his first novel would be a success, as he had provided it with the most extravagant publicity possible. These plans are thwarted because of the bathwater that has soaked the pages of his manuscript, causing the ink to run and rendering the words unintelligible. The only traces of Paul's novel that remain are the title sheet which reads,

Wu Sing: The Geisha Man (283),

and the dedication page:

To
Huysman's Des Esseintes and Oscar Wilde's Oscar Wilde
Ecstatic Spirits with whom I Cohabit
And whose golden spores of decadent pollen
I shall broadcast and fertilize
It is written
Paul Arbian

In his treatment of Thurman's novel, Nathan Huggins summarizes this concluding scene in some detail and writes: "Wallace Thurman [thus] buried the Harlem Renaissance—or Niggeratti Manor—with Paul Arbian. One might say, the manner was appropriately exotic and decadent."[58] Huggins finds in this climactic scene of *Infants of the Spring* confirmation of the flaws that basically doomed the Harlem Renaissance from the start: the ways in which the cultural output in that movement was compromised by a white patronage that overvalued "exotic and decadent" depictions of the Negro. In noting the "appropriate[ness]" of Arbian's suicide, however, Huggins treats the meaning of the Orientalist signifiers that saturate this final scene as self-evident—as simple markers of exoticism and decadence. Assuming that the meaning of these Orientalist signifiers is as transparent as Huggins suggests lends further credence to (and also extends the historical reach of) the claims that Sedgwick and Marez make about the racial and sexual meanings that hovered around the figure of Wilde.

The fact that Huggins apparently felt no need to comment on the racial meanings of the Orientalist signifiers in Thurman's novel is symptomatic of nearly all the scholarship that examines the racial and cultural politics of the twenties and thirties—the period that both Chin and Ellison identify as a crucial one for popularizing the exotic images of racial alterity that they would seek to challenge in their writings. The existing scholarship on the Harlem Renaissance—including recent studies like George Hutchinson's, Ann Douglas's, and William J. Maxwell's, whose explicit focus is interracialism—restricts its focus entirely to black-white issues, thereby rendering invisible the other racial projects characteristic of the United States in this period. A similar exceptionalism but of a different shade is evident in the work of Asian Americanist scholars.[59]

Recent studies by Robert Lee, David Palumbo-Liu, and Henry Yu that address the place of Asian Americans in the race politics of this period do not substantially engage with the issue of how Asian/white relations were structured in relationship to black/white relations, let alone explore the possible crossing of Asian and black concerns. (Ironically, it is a cultural critic whose skepticism concerning ethnic studies approaches is quite apparent, Walter Benn Michaels, who has come closest to illuminating the polychromatic nature of the literary race politics that prevailed in the United States during these decades in his study, *Our America*.)[60] By pointing out this tendency, I am not trying to claim that my own project does what these others do not— that it offers a more, as it were, polychromatic and exhaustive account of the racial and literary politics of this period. I am suggesting, however, that many of the texts I have been examining here indicate the need for such a study to emerge.[61]

To return more narrowly to the matter at hand, however, which is the literary project that Chin attempts to inaugurate through his own writings: his rejection of Fu also expresses a rejection of the Orientalist aesthetic in which Rohmer's fictions are steeped—an aesthetic for which the flamboyant Wilde was a highly visible advocate and which therefore became, as Sedgwick's and Marez's analyses suggest, a marker of homosexual identity. As the depiction of the evil doctor's sumptuously decorated apartment makes clear, the Fu novel invites its readers to indulge their desire for objects of the exotic East in much the same way that Wilde's *The Picture of Dorian Gray* enjoins its readers to identify with the pleasures its protagonist takes in Oriental decorative objects and in opium. This association of an Orientalist aesthetic with homosexuality persists and seems wholly codified in the later African American texts that I have alluded to: for Nugent, Thurman, and Ellison, a Wildean aesthetic preference for Oriental objets d'art seems to serve transparently as an emblem of "queer" identity.

This convergence of exoticizing and sexual discourses may explain not only Chin's inability to embrace Fu as a signifier of racialized sexual menace, but also his vehement rejection (in his early polemics, at least) of any interpretation of Chinese American texts that would connect them back to an ancient and timeless Orient:

> An American-born Asian, writing from the world as Asian American who does not reverberate to gongs struck hundreds of years ago or *snuggle into the doughy clutches of an America hot to coddle something ching chong*, is looked upon as a freak, an imitator, a liar. The myth is that Asian Americans have maintained some cultural integrity as Asians, that there is some strange continuity between the great high culture of a China that hasn't existed for five hundred years and the American-born Asian.[62]

In Chapter 5, I will explore more fully the tradition of "fake" Asian American writing that Chin derides, consisting of texts that "snuggle into the doughy clutches of an America hot to coddle something ching chong." The white appetite for these Orientalist images of China (of "the great high culture of a China that hasn't existed for five hundred years") has been whetted—Chin argues—by texts like the Fu-Manchu and Charlie Chan fictions. In contrast, the Asian American literature Chin advocates (in his early writings) will sever the kind of connection between Asian immigrants and the ancient and timeless Orient that Rohmer's fictions posit as a given.

In the next chapter, I will show that Chin's intense *dis*identification with the Orientalist aesthetic to which the figure of Fu is linked coincides with an identification at another level—at the level of desire. Indeed, a version of the kind of homoerotic intimacy that *The Insidious Dr. Fu-Manchu* depicts with a kind of racialized and homophobic horror Chin will in fact lyrically celebrate, even as he gives expression to a racialized and homophobic terror of his own.

"Shells of the Dead": The Melancholy of Masculine Desire

Readily apparent in the fictional and dramatic works that comprise Frank Chin's literary corpus is a kind of obsessive-compulsive quality. Ever again, like a terrier furiously working a bone, he seems always to return to a single story—trying each time to get it right or, perhaps, to let it go. This narrative focuses on the plight of an Asian American male protagonist—usually a frustrated artist—who is struggling against a social order that attempts to box him into an identity that he experiences as racially inauthentic and emasculating. In response, he seeks an ideal of racialized manhood with which to identify, an ideal that usually assumes a paternal shape; this paternal longing fixes upon certain white and black male figures and is frustrated; eventually, and often tenuously, the protagonist comes to recognize the racial inappropriateness of the paternal models he has chosen and seems to find instead a yellow father figure. Patricia P. Chu has argued that this narrative, which she terms "the author-hero myth,"[1] derives its basic elements from the patriarchal tradition of "classic" American literary studies presided over by figures like Leslie Fiedler and Lionel Trilling—the tradition Nina Baym subjected to feminist critique in her influential essay "Melodramas of Beset Manhood." While Chu's rendering of this narrative offers a useful account of its literary genealogy, which helps to stitch its concern with Asian American masculinity to a wider cultural fabric, my intent in this chapter is to bring into focus the psychic longings, the thwarted desires, and the ambivalent identifications that structure it—to throw into relief the *melancholic* shape of the story that Chin tells over and again.

My analyses will center on two texts: an autobiographical sketch entitled "Riding the Rails with Chickencoop Slim" and *The Chickencoop Chinaman*, his first play. Both are narratives of thwarted love and frustrated grief. The desire they memorialize is a deeply homoerotic one, shot through with a strongly identificatory element. It fixes upon images of masculinity that are the province of other races—black and white avatars, in other words, of racialized manhood. What I will show is how this homoerotic interracial fascination in Chin's writings is both symptomatic of the feminized form that yellow masculinity assumes in a black and white world, and is also foundational—in its melancholic reworking—to the more virile form of Asian American manhood he comes to endorse, and that he also claims to exemplify.

The "myth" that Chin's writings compulsively recount—which Chu describes as "the most insistent and influential story told about the struggles of Asian American males for authorship" (64)—is articulated most starkly in his polemical essays, many of which were coauthored with the other *Aiiieeeee!* editors. In these pieces Chin and his colleagues attempt to vindicate a group of "authentic" Asian American writers—mostly male figures like Louis Chu and John Okada—who languished in obscurity while the works of a "damned mob of scribbling women"—in this case Jade Snow Wong, Amy Tan, and Maxine Hong Kingston—enjoyed an unmerited acclaim. Like a Trilling or a Fiedler lionizing Hawthorne at the expense of Stowe, Chin seeks in his essays to give these male authors the prominence they deserve.[2] I will explore these polemics in more detail in the next chapter, but the *patriarchal* nature of the claim they make is fairly clear: for the "authenticity" of Asian American literature in the present to be acknowledged, a past tradition of yellow literary "fathers" must be rendered visible.

In her treatment of this canon-building project, Chu emphasizes the adversarial, even Oedipal, relation that Chin and his colleagues adopt toward two sets of inauthentic "cultural fathers": "first, the white creators of the detested Asian stereotypes and, second, their alleged Asian or Asian American counterparts, from Pardee Lowe to Amy Tan" (71). By "slay[ing]" these false fathers, according to Chu, the *Aiiieeeee!* editors seek to "creat[e] a descent line of [their] own," presenting themselves as the patriarchs of a more authentic Asian American literary tradition (71). While this account does convey how issues of literary paternity comprise a major concern of the *Aiiieeeee!* editors, it does not fully engage with the *filial* posture that Chin and his colleagues adopt toward an earlier generation of "authentic" Asian

American writers. Evident in their championing of writers like Louis Chu and John Okada is not so much a desire to *be* literary "fathers," but rather a desire to *have* them.

The intensity of Chin's desire for Asian American literary "ancestors" is very much apparent in his afterword to the 1976 edition of John Okada's *No-No Boy*. (The *Aiiieeeee!* editors were instrumental in convincing the University of Washington Press to reissue this 1957 novel, which had long been out of print.) In this brief essay, Chin explains why discovering Okada's novel was such a significant event for him:

> What if there were no whites in American literary history. There is no Melville, no Mark Twain, no Kay Boyle, no Gertrude Stein, no Tom Robbins, not even a Rod McKuen. A white American writer would feel edgy if all the books ever written in America were by blacks, browns, reds, yellows, and all whites had ever published were cookbooks full of recipes for apple pie and fried chicken.
>
> That's what I grew up with. . . .
>
> . . . For me, the discovery of John's 1957 novel was like a white writer feeling gloomy and alone in a literary history, discovering Mark Twain. *No-No Boy* proved I wasn't the only yellow writer in yellow history. The book was so good it freed me to be trivial.[3]

Okada, along with Carlos Bulosan, Louis Chu, and Toshio Mori, were among the select group of early writers that Chin identified in the seventies as providing an authentically Asian American literary genealogy for the current generation. As critics have noted, Chin began in the early nineties to sketch out an even more far-reaching (though equally selective) *Asian* tradition of yellow literary "fathers." This revised heroic canon was comprised mainly of certain Chinese myths that were popularized in texts like *Three Kingdoms, Journey to the West*, and *Water Margin*.[4]

In his polemical writings, Chin presents this filial desire for powerful Asian and Asian American father figures as being satisfied by the discovery and promotion of literary predecessors. But in his fictional and dramatic works, he tends to focus not on the satisfaction of this desire, but rather on its frustration. Chin's creative works do not, by and large, feature happy endings in which the Asian American male protagonist finds and comes to embrace the yellow paternal figure he has been seeking all along. One reason why Chin's literary writings have been viewed by critics with some interest and also some frustration is precisely because they seem to be in significant tension with the polemics they are so clearly intended to affirm.

The earliest critic to call attention to this tension, Elaine Kim, does so with some exasperation. While she allows that Chin's apparent aim—"creating protagonists who can overcome the devastating effects of racism on Chinese American men"—may be a valid one, she is somewhat perplexed that the male protagonists in his plays and early fiction are "alienated adolescents, incapacitated by the sense of their own impotence."[5] Rather than projecting a powerful and whole sense of manhood, his works depict "the Asian American male . . . as a victim of his community, his family, and women in general" (189). The attitude he takes toward his characters is, according to Kim, one of "basic contempt," and he "leaves the reader with the impression of futility and bored misanthropy" (189). What Kim is mainly objecting to in Chin's writings is their predominant tone and mood, the affect in which they are drenched: alienation, impotence, contempt, and self-contempt. Michael Soo Hoo echoes Kim's appraisal in his review of *The Chinaman Pacific and Frisco R. R. Co.*, a collection of short fiction that reworks much of the material used in the two plays: "Throughout the eight stories, Chin presents the condition of Chinese America in an uncompromising state of decay, masochistically prolonged, and involving empty, hollow shells of people."[6] Hoo describes one such piece, "The Chinatown Kid," as "like all the stories in the book . . . a tale of horrific isolation and self-contempt."[7] The affective materials out of which Chin builds his fictional worlds are simply unsuitable, in Kim's judgment, for his stated goal of projecting a viable Asian American manhood through literature.

It is not simply the mood of Chin's early works, however, that signals for Kim their failure: it is also that their central narratives do not achieve the kind of closure toward which his essays gesture. Exemplary of this failure, according to Kim, is Chin's first play, *The Chickencoop Chinaman*. "The play contains a series of lessons for Chinese Americans," she writes, and among the most central of these is "that Asian American culture can be found neither by imitating whites nor by imitating Blacks" (186). These lessons are dramatized through the frustration of the male protagonist's idolatrous relationship to two paternal figures, one black and the other white. But while the play works to underscore the racial inappropriateness of these figures as objects of an Asian American filial desire, it fails, in Kim's view, to deliver on its implied promise of an appropriate paternal substitute: there are "vague references to a 'Chinatown Kid' who used to frequent boxing matches and whose name no one can remember," but this figure never arrives on stage (186). When Tam Lum, the protagonist, first appears,

> speak[ing] aggressively and with wit, it seems that he will be the new Chinese American man. But the play ends with Tam, "like a mad elephant, blowing his nose in the dark," chopping green onions with a Chinese cleaver. . . . He has . . . rejected the myth that Asians could be like Blacks, but he has as yet found nothing to replace the stereotypes and false directions. There are no new mythical heroes; the Chinatown kid is not his father but a nameless dishwasher who was afraid of old white ladies peeking at him through keyholes. (187)

Ultimately, Kim concludes that in *The Chickencoop Chinaman*, "instead of building a new manhood and a new culture . . . through his imaginative writing, Chin creates an overriding sense of the utter futility of the male protagonist's efforts to redefine himself" (186). The play concludes with the spectacle of "the Asian American male protagonist squirming helplessly, pinpointed by his own verbal barbs" (187).

Kim's frustration with *The Chickencoop Chinaman* stems from its apparent failure to fulfill the promise that it seems to hold out: that its protagonist will redeem his manhood by finding a racially appropriate father figure with which to identify. What Tam comes to embrace instead is a kind of masochism. But what Kim reads as a failure of aesthetic nerve other critics regard as evidence that Chin's creative output is more complex and nuanced than his polemics. Chu sees Chin's two plays as "richer than his critical account" partly because of the more incisive focus they bring to certain psychic issues: "they record how the negative effects of white racism may be internalized and how the battle described as external in the Chin essays may become an interior, intrasubjective struggle."[8] Similarly, Sau-ling Wong finds value in how Chin's creative texts explore the "gut-churning libidinal forces" that tie Chinese Americans ambivalently to their individual and collective histories.[9]

I am in general agreement with Wong and Chu's appraisals: for what I find most useful about Chin's literary writings is directly tied to the insights they enable into the psychic as it is shaped in relation to the social—or, to put it more precisely, how certain psychological narratives come to occupy in them a privileged interpretive force in giving meaning to the social. The particular elements of Chin's mapping of the Asian American male psyche that are the most illuminating, moreover, are those that Kim finds most troubling: they revolve around his concern with alienation, impotence, and self-contempt. Where I will part company with Kim's interpretation of the central narratives that preoccupy Chin's creative works is in her assumption that the *masochism* in which they are saturated is somehow in tension with the ideal of Asian American *masculinity* he promotes. Indeed, I will show in this chapter that what passes for manhood in Chin involves the fervent embrace of a racialized self-loathing that resembles the obsessive self-reproaches that are, in a certain Freudian narrative, characteristic of *melancholic* subjects. In so doing, I will offer an account of the central myth that Chin's writings ceaselessly reenact that is different from the one that Patricia Chu has offered: while the story he tells again and again in his fiction, drama, autobiographical sketches, and even in his one published poem is indeed a "melodrama of beset manhood," it is also—and perhaps more centrally—a narrative of frustrated grief that is also a narrative of frustrated love; it is, in other words, a narrative structured by melancholia.

C'mon Back to the Train Ag'in, Frank Honey!

In order to bring into focus the melancholic shape of the narrative that recurs throughout much of Chin's literary writings, I want to turn to a brief autobiographical sketch entitled "Riding the Rails with Chickencoop Slim," which was first published in 1976, two years after the appearance of *Aiiieeeee!* In light of the homophobia that frames his polemical critiques of stereotypical representations that define Asian men as homosexual, what is quite astonishing about "Riding the Rails" is the extent to which Chin seems to "confess" his own interracial homoerotic proclivities. This essay recounts a period when he worked as a brakeman for the Southern Pacific Railroad: he was evidently "the first Chinese brakeman the Southern Pacific ever hired."[10] "Riding the Rails" is explicitly an elegiac text: in it he pays loving homage to the man he was ("BRAKEMAN! That's the person I remember being, the one I enjoy remembering on the railroad, the image I love") and to the white men he worked with ("the men, my teachers, the good and bad men, old timers, brakemen and switchmen, enginemen whose kind will soon be extinct") (84, 80). As it turns out, the man he was—especially in the texture of his desires—bears no small resemblance to the allegedly homosexual figure of Fu-Manchu. A crucial difference emerges, however, between the desire he imputes to the stereotype of Fu and the interracial homoerotic desire he avows as his own. Chin suggests that the interracial mimetic desire he indulges in his loving exchanges with his white coworkers engenders in him a heightened sense of his own masculinity—he postulates, in other words, a form of interracial or assimilationist desire that is virilizing rather than feminizing. Moreover, the eroticism he celebrates is one that he attempts to distinguish from the sexual. It is "consummated" in highly eroticized moments of intersubjective commingling that are depicted as carnal in a virtual rather than literal sense.

It is the elegiac narrative frame of "Riding the Rails," I will be arguing, that seems to inoculate Chin's authorial persona from the homoeroticism his writing celebrates: as the homosocial pleasures so extravagantly on display in this text would appear to be contained temporally, would seem to be part and parcel of the man Chin *was* and is no longer. To a certain extent, then, "Riding the Rails" operates as a narrative of *mourning*: the psychic work it accomplishes is that of letting go of a love object that has proven to be inadequate—of coming to grips with object loss. As recent theorists who have revisited Freud's writings on mourning and melancholia have pointed out, however, this binary between a normative and successful form of grief and its more pathological and obsessive counterpart is in many ways an untenable one.[11] Indeed, as I will show, the grief to which "Riding the Rails" gives expression seems as much thwarted as it is resolved—this text is as melancholic as it is mournful. The story Chin tells in this autobiographical piece—like the one Freud recounts in "Mourning and Melancholia"—describes how an apparent letting go can function simultaneously as a hanging on.

*

At the heart of Chin's account of railway life is a highly lyrical celebration of the moment in which one feels the massive machinery of the train shudder into motion. To be moved by the train, as Chin makes clear in the following passage, is to experience a particular corporeal pleasure:

> You're moving. Being moved. The sound of the slack being taken up car by car, steel joint by steel joint, is heard crashing at your back; the crash and

tug of the first car and each afterward is echoed in the muscles of your back, a sudden blossoming of a dark heat up your back and fading into the muscles of your shoulder and neck, more lightly again, and a hundred times again. (86)

What's rendered here as pleasurable by Chin's imagery is the "touch" of this man-like train: the travel of the train's power through gargantuan lengths of serpentine metal, and its eventual "blossoming" into the body. The homo-erotic quality of this depiction is further emphasized by the repeated references to the back as the site where this exchange of energy take place, and its emphasis on the direction from which this energy arrives. Indeed this account tends to read *almost* as if it were a paean to gay sex, to the joys of being rectally stimulated. But while Chin imbues this passages with an intense *eroticism*, he also suggests that the pleasure it depicts is not quite sexual. The "man" to which he is coupled here is, after all, not human, but rather an anthropomorphized technological object. Moreover, while the highly aestheticized imagery used here tends to romanticize and eroticize the contact between man and man-like machine, it also tends to evaporate the literally sexual aspect of the act to which it seems to refer: the passage suggests and yet refrains from specifically alluding to an anal erotics.

The homoerotic intimacy Chin enjoys with the train engenders, more-over, a secondary form of intimacy between *actual* men. For this eroticized (though not quite sexual) travel of energy from train to man is not a solitary pleasure. Rather, it is shared with the other men in the cab (who are all white):

The loudness of the four engines increases and we sit down heavily into the gathering density of sound, the rising pitch of vibrations and concussive sounds that reach right through the flesh and clutch the heart and deeper into the valves of the heart, the lips of the valve. Through the floor, into our bones, comes the bone brightening sound of the wheels. (86)

To move and be moved by the train, Chin tells us, is to hear the train's "dark heat" as "concussive sounds," and also to feel that aural energy as a kind of physical presence, a "gathering *density* of sound" capable of "reach[ing] right through the flesh" and "clutch[ing] into the valves of the heart, the lips of the valve" that is apparently palpable enough for the men to "sit down heavily into." The rhythmic power of the train's "thrusting tons" is given a tactile, material, and even erotic sensuousness here—indeed, it is rendered as a corporeally intrusive force, capable of something like a penetration—and this despite the fact there is no literally sexual moment of contact.

Furthermore, as the men within the cab experience together the "touch" of the train—as the "dark heat" of the train "reaches" equally into their innards—they coalesce grammatically into something like one body: thus it is "*we* [who] sit down into the gathering density of sound" to feel the "clutch" of "the bone brightening sound" within "*the* flesh," "*the* heart," and in "*our* bones." This breakdown of subjective distinction apparently also engenders a breakdown of *racial* distinction, as the following passage suggests:

> "Caboose to Engine 2509, highball!" comes over the radio. "Highball, 2509," the *Chiquita Banana hurdy gurdy* hoghead [Murphy] says, and you become familiar with new voices of motion in your flesh. Our bodies are speed-fluent now; they've been overtaken by, found out by, the dark untranslatable intelligence of violence and speed. (86; my emphasis)

The strange adjectival mass—"Chiquita Banana hurdy gurdy"—used here to describe Murphy refers (we only find out later) to the straw hat he wears and to his resembling an organ grinder when he operates the train's machinery. The presence of these unexplained modifiers, however, seems to raise the question of Murphy's ethnic and racial identity—is he perhaps Latino or Italian?—only to render it irrelevant. Though he is, in the end, Irish, what difference does it make, Chin's description asks us to ponder, when the individual identities of all the men in the cab have been subsumed by that subjective, corporeal, and grammatical mass, "our bodies"?

The allure that the moment of speed holds for Chin stems from the eroticized intimacy it engenders between men of different races, the profound homosocial bond the workers form through their communal engagement in an almost mythically heroic act of labor. As the men within the cab work together to control the larger masculine force of the train, and as they are pleasurably "overtaken by . . . the dark untranslatable intelligence of violence and speed," they become indistinguishable: the matter of race is dissolved into the universalizing, rhythmic thumping of a massive engine. What Chin attempts here is to prise open a boundary—however delicate and unstable—between the homoerotic and the homosexual, to imagine a figurative "coupling up" of male "bodies" that resembles and is yet somehow different from the more literal coming together of male bodies that occurs in gay sex. He offers here a model of interracial, homoerotic intimacy that is distinct from the "homosexual" relationship depicted in the "white Christian's racial wet-dream." He suggests here, in other words, a similarity but also a crucial difference between his own libidinal relation to white men and the "homosexual" desire he derides as Fu's. This difference stems partially from the way in which the eroticism of this male-male "contact," while it verges on the threshold of the sexual, never crosses over into it. But secondly, Fu's desire, as we have seen, involves an identification with the feminine—it is given corporeal form in the figure of his daughter; in contrast, Chin's desire, as we shall see, involves an identification of a different order altogether.

As the men within the cab become wedded to each other and to the train's machinery, they not only achieve a kind of communion, but also a kind of transubstantiation. Chin follows his description of the pleasurable travel of the energy into his own body—the "blossoming" of the train's "dark heat" up his back—with the following sentence: "I feel I'm growing large, that my bones and muscles are overwhelming with size and strength" (86). Chin suggests here that this "contact" with the massive machinery of train enables him to appropriate some of its immensity in his own person. And as his body fantasmatically "overwhelm[s] with size and strength," so too does his ego:

> In every engine I rode there was the possibility that I would become the intelligence of its thrusting tons. As I walked out onto the tracks, I would alert myself for the sight of the engine. And I'd say, "Hey, look at me! I'm going to get in that thing and make it do what I want. I'm going to make that thing go!" That was a fact. And that made me more than just a hundred and thirty pound Chinese boy claiming the rails laid by his ancestors. I was above history. *I was too big* for the name of a little man, Frank Chin. No, sir. I was a *thing*: BRAKEMAN! That's the person I remember being, the one I enjoy remembering on the railroad, the image I love. (83–84; my emphasis)

In becoming the "intelligence" that controls that masculine "thing," the train and its "thrusting tons," Chin too becomes "a thing: BRAKEMAN!" He is no longer a "boy," "a little man," but a masculine subject "too big" to be reduced to the markers of his racial identity: the small size of his Chinese body, the historical legacy of his ancestor's labors, and his name. He sees himself as being made over into the image of the man-like "thing" he controls; he *identifies with* the train. Thus each man within the cab—as he is "overtaken" by the train's energy and fused with his companions—is presumably, like Chin, transformed into a masculine "thing."

The train, then, plays a key role in the bond that emerges between the workers. It functions as an eroticized object of mutual identification that enables the brotherhood of the rails to function as a kind of Edenic homosocial horde. The train stands in roughly the same relation to all of the men within the cab: it signifies an image of supreme virility with which all of them identify as they are "overtaken" by it, and which amalgamates them into a single homosocial corpus. Described here is a triangulated structure of identification that engenders an eroticized bond between men of different races. Chin's vision of the social group thus bears some resemblance to Freud's account of it in *Group Psychology and the Analysis of the Ego*. The masculine image of the train (and also of "John Wayne," as we shall soon discover) functions much as the image of the leader in Freud's account. The *"primary social group,"* as Freud defines it, *"is a number of individuals who have put one and the same object in the place of their ego ideal and have consequently identified themselves with one another in their ego."*[12] In fulfilling the function of ego ideal, the technological status of the train is crucial. For its superhuman massiveness renders it ultimately unattainable as an identificatory ideal, and thus tends to override any differences between the men who strive to emulate it:[13]

> When I was a brakeman, I weighed a hundred and thirty pounds, and using the fireman's lift I could maybe carry my own weight a little ways. My weight combined with the hoghead's [engineer's] would come to less than five hundred pounds. And out there somewhere, black, hot, alive, waiting for use, part beast, part machine, was an iron horse, a three hundred and sixty ton three thousand horsepower locomotive. Me and the hoghead were expected to climb inside that thing and become its intelligence, attach our lives to it, and make it go. ("Riding," 83)

Through a kind of corporeal mathematics, Chin emphasizes how the sheer size of the train works to render negligible any bodily distinctions between himself and the white engineer: the disparity between his 130 pounds and his companion's 370 is rendered more or less moot when compared to the 360 tons of the train.

To place this in a slightly different context, Chin appropriates in "Chickencoop Slim" a masculine iconography that has been codified in certain texts of "classic" American literature. His portrayal of the homosocial world of the railroad calls to mind, for instance, the multiracial crew of Melville's *Pequod*: it is a vision of a universalizing and eroticized brotherhood that is achieved through communal participation in an act of labor. Through much of this memoir, Chin engages in a full-throated celebration of this homosocial "utopian" vision. It is this aspect of the myth enshrined in the canon of "classic" American literature—the interracial homosocial romance identified by D. H. Lawrence and Leslie Fiedler as central to works like *Moby-Dick* and *Huck Finn*—that remains unexamined in Patricia Chu's reading. But while Chin makes evident here and in other texts his investment in this iconography—in what Robyn Wiegman has termed the "canonical architecture" of the "classic" American literary tradition[14]—he also gives a quite different account of interracial bonding than that which appears in works by white male authors like Twain: he offers, as it were, a view from the other end of the raft. Even as Chin voices his own desire for the moments of homoerotic connectedness that come in the moment of travel, he also intimates (almost in the same breath) that, for the man of color, this desire will always be thwarted. For that larger manhood—which binds the men together as they identify with it—is not only symbolized by the massive machinery of the train, it is also given a human name:

> No matter how many times you've gone out, how many engines and crummies you've ridden, you get the call, get your orders, are told the train is yours, you pick up your gear, your lantern, and step outside into a low, flat world of heavy and steel, and again, as it was the very first time, it's like *John Wayne* stepping outside and turning a commonplace outdoor scene into the West, his West. You take possession. (82; my emphasis)

Chin reveals here that the masculine entity that occupies the apex of that triangulated structure of identification and desire is not simply a suprahuman, supraracial technological thing, but also a white man produced by the technology of Hollywood. The image of manhood that the men all try to emulate consists, in fact, of *two* images superimposed upon one another: the masculinized machinery of the train, and the iconic figure of the cowboy that has been manufactured by the cinematic machinery of the Western. To see oneself as a "railroader" is to see oneself, Chin tells us, as "*the steel and iron version* of John Wayne, Gary Cooper" (86; my emphasis).[15]

What begins to trouble this homosocial paradise is the reemergence of the

thing that it had appeared to cast out, to transcend: the racial difference
between Chin and his white coworkers. For while Chin makes clear that he
sees in Murphy and the rest of his white coworkers a family resemblance to
that archetypical figure of American manhood, John Wayne, the "mythic
Westerner," he also reveals that the reverse of this is not true. For when Chin
looks at himself through the eyes of Murphy, the white engineer, he sees a
different body, a bodily difference:

> Now and then a strange smile, a look in his [Murphy's] eyes, gives him
> away. His relationship with these engines, like the mythic Westerner's
> relationship with the perfect machinery of his guns, is promiscuous.
>   "You're Chinese, huh?" he says. "I thought you were an Indian in that
> hat." (85)

Murphy sees in Chin not another myself—not another incarnation of "John
Wayne"—but simply an *other*, a man of color, an "Indian." With this "look,"
the equalizing potential of the identificatory bond is shattered: of the two
men, only the white engineer is liable to be mistaken for—to mistake himself for—the hero of a John Ford film. Because of the difference that race
makes, Murphy is able to flesh out his mimetic relation to "the mythic westerner" in a way that Chin cannot, no matter what hat he wears.

Moreover, this passage reveals that Murphy not only enjoys a privileged
relation to the image of "John Wayne," he also exerts a much greater authority over the machinery of the train. For if the engineer is to the train as the
gunslinger is to his guns—as Chin's analogy suggests—then it is Murphy
alone who functions as the train's governing "intelligence." This particular
distribution of power is also alluded to in the following:

> In his Chiquita the Banana straw hat, and his hands playing between the
> handles of the throttle, the reverser, the brakes, the air valve, speaking in
> melodies and rhythms more than words, he [Murphy] seems a lot less than
> a man controlling a finely honed, ugly set of machines, seems doing some-
> thing gentler than operating a catastrophe. There should be a little spider
> monkey with a fez blinking on his shoulder. There should be the sound of
> plump-noted innocuous hurdy gurdy music answering the motion of his
> hands. (85)

While this "racialization" of the Irish Murphy still works to comic effect,
seemingly underscoring the irrelevance of ethnic identity to the moment of
speed, Chin's elaboration of this conceit makes evident that it is the engineer

who functions as the train's governing "intelligence." Murphy *alone* exerts his calm mastery over the machinery of the train. And if he is likened to an organ grinder operating his hurdy gurdy, Chin is implicitly likened to the monkey he imagines "blinking" on Murphy's shoulders. He comes to resemble a little man-like creature who dances in time to the rhythm of a technology he does not control.

This admission on Chin's part, that Murphy in fact controls the train's "thrusting tons," puts the text's celebration of the homoerotic pleasure of locomotion in a rather interesting light. The experience Chin eroticizes involves an opening up of his identity and his body to the "dark heat" of the engine as it "crashes," "clutches," and "reaches" into his innards. If the agency that controls the machinery of the train turns out to be Murphy, then the homoerotic "contact" he has celebrated is, in the end, not so different from the "homosexual" contact for which Fu apparently hungers. To be "overtaken by" the physical energy of the train—to have one's body rendered so pleasurably "speed-fluent" by it—is, by Chin's tacit admission, to have been "overtaken by" the white man who ultimately controls it, Murphy.

And in that white man's eyes, let us remember, Chin has glimpsed a certain "look" that verifies not only a racial but also a "sexual" truth. Murphy's relationship with the engine, Chin tells us, recapitulates the "mythic Westerner's relationship with the perfect machinery of his guns," which is "promiscuous." This curious choice of adjective emphasizes the quantitative, which is to say genocidal, dimension of the racist violence with which the figure of the gunslinger is associated: he kills often and indiscriminately. The term "promiscuous" also insinuates a sexual dimension to this violence. If the Indian represents for the Cowboy an object of both murderous and sexual desires, then what does Chin represent to Murphy? Chin suggests something like the following: *if he, the white man, looks at me and sees an Indian, then he wants to destroy me as he did the Indian; and if he wants to kill me, this also means (somehow) that he desires me sexually; and, finally, if the train constitutes the modern equivalent of the gunslinger's weaponry, it is through the train that he will violate my body and murder me.*

We discover here again Chin's homophobic tendency to define any scenario anatomizing the racial and masculine subordination of the yellow man to the white as a "homosexual" scenario. Murphy's comment—"You're Chinese, huh . . . I thought you were an Indian in that hat"—reveals that his acknowledgment of racial difference also expresses a racist disdain. But while his "look" might well betray, to put it crudely, a desire to fuck over the man of color, it doesn't necessarily suggest—as Chin intimates—a desire to fuck him. Murphy does seem to recapitulate some of the western gunslinger's historical racism, but Chin suggests that he also resembles the homophobe's fantasmatic vision of the "promiscuous" and sexually predatory gay man, who wishes to do to straight men what straight men do to women.

*

Chin is not content, however, merely to show how even his own desire for white men might lead him into a scenario that looks rather homosexual. He also raises the homophobic ante by including in his memoir two set pieces—parables for reading—that assert that to be mingled so pleasurably with the train and the white man who controls it is to face death. In the first, which comes very near the beginning of the memoir, he recounts to us what he calls "the Universal Brakeman's Story," a narrative that warns of the deadly fate that awaits anyone who takes his love of trains too seriously (80). This is the preamble to the "first and best" variant of this story as it was told to Chin (80):

> "I was brakin' for, why it musta been the I.C., yeah. Sure, it was the Illinois
> Central and there was this little fella, a switchman, Shannon his name
> was, tough little bastard, made out of chicken gizzards and spit. Well I'll
> be damned he don't go and get himself *coupled up, I mean, coupled up* . . ."
> (81; my emphasis)

The narrator of this story tells Chin how "just for a leetle momentito as the couplings come apart you could see him, how he was, pinched you know. God he died sudden! Like a dam breaking. Blood!" (81). In light of the "couplings" we've been examining thus far, this cautionary tale—in its emphatic repetition of the phrase, "coupled up, I mean, coupled up"—seems to issue a warning against the very pleasures the essay has also celebrated: the pleasurable and intimate "contact" between man and man-like train, and between yellow and white man. To be so "coupled up" to that gigantic masculine "thing," the train, and to the white man who in fact marshals its dark power, is to face the possibility of a gruesome death.

If Shannon's tale implies the danger of interracial male-male contact, this message is conveyed more explicitly later on in the essay, in the "history lessons" Chin's mother passed down to him. Immediately following the passage in which he becomes aware of the significance of Murphy's "look," Chin recounts his mother's opinion of her son's proletarian exploits—she sees them as all too reminiscent of his forefathers':

> There'll be no legends or stories or songs about a Chinese brakeman on the SP line. It's very satisfying to my mother because she sees my extraordinarily unsung railroad career as being somehow very Chinese. Like the Chinese who chipped roadbeds out of solid granite at the rate of six inches a day, I achieved anonymity. (85)

The history that she sees embodied in the railroad does not tell of heroic yellow men hand in hand with heroic white men in carving out a virgin wilderness. What this history tells us instead, she suggests in the following passage, is that:

> She believes everything she says, the story about the Chinese being dynamited by the Irishmen. Every day or so the air violently bloomed the arms and legs of Chinese to make the Irishmen laugh. (85)

To be coupled up with the white man on his terrain, this mother's fable warns, *is to face the utter destruction of your own body*. The inevitable reintrusion of racial difference in the bond between himself and his white engineer threatens to resurrect the racist violence that was directed by Murphy's Irish ancestors at Chin's, the "coolies" who built the railroad.

Through this history and through the story of Shannon, Chin issues a homophobic warning against his own interracial homoerotic desire: having confessed his desire for those pleasurable and erotic (though not quite sexual) moments of subjective commingling that the thrill of motion engenders, he depicts that desire as potentially fatal, as leading ultimately to dismemberment and death. To become so tethered to the white man in loving bonds of labor, as Chin himself has, is to risk becoming not only a "homosexual" yellow man, but also a dead one.

Melancholic Manhood

Apparent, then, in "Chickencoop Slim" is a certain fatalism present in most of Chin's creative works. By putting his own libidinal investment in white men and the manhood they embody on extravagant display in this text—by making evident an underlying similarity between his desire and Fu's—Chin asserts that the ideological structure of white racism exerts a determining force that is nearly total: he suggests that, since many of the images representing manhood in our culture are white, an orientation toward those images and the men who approximate them that is not just loving but also erotic is literally inescapable, even for him. Thus his fervent loathing for Fu also expresses a kind of homophobic self-loathing: what he sees and hates in Fu—an eroticized desire for the white man—is something he sees and hates in himself. Moreover, Chin asserts not only the irresistible force of desire— the inability of the yellow man to cease being drawn to that image of manhood that our culture has defined *as* "irresistible"—but also the immovability, the intransigence, of racial difference—the brute social fact that men like Murphy will always look upon a man like Chin and see an "Indian." He dramatizes in his memoir the intensity of his own desire for an intensely homoerotic interracial bonding only to underscore the inevitability that such a desire will be disappointed. He recounts, in other words, something like a story of unrequited love.

What does one do, then, when one's love is not returned, when one looks through the eyes of a lover/friend and sees oneself not as an object of identificatory love, another myself, but as something other, an object of racist disdain? Chin's answer: one gets angry; one hungers for vengeance; one begins to hate that man one also loves. One strives, in other words, to "get over it," to assert the inadequacy of the object to one's love for it, to mark that object's loss and to mourn it. And this, as we shall now see, is the work that Chin does in recollecting his days on the railroad—it is the work of writing, and also the work of mourning. For as a memoir, "Chickencoop Slim" presents itself as literally memorializing his former relation to the white men who were his companions. Thus the essay appears also to mark the passing of the man Chin used to be—a man who was, in the confusion of his desires, rather Fu-like. This temporal and subjective irony is indeed accentuated by the brief précis with which the essay opens—"A *former* brakeman, *now* a playwright, returns to the freights for one last run" (80; my emphasis)—and through the ironic self-naming in the title, which likewise suggests an inequation between the author, "Frank Chin," and his autobiographical protagonist, "Chickencoop Slim."

In order to trace more precisely the trajectory of Chin's desire as he transforms himself from brakeman to playwright, I will turn now to those works of Freud's that offer, I believe, a surprisingly parallel narrative of subject development, of how subjectivity itself is formed in relation to a thwarted object-choice. Freud's thought is also quite apposite to Chin's in its confused and confusing conception of desire. For Freud's works enact, as Mikkel Borch-Jacobsen has made abundantly clear, a futile struggle to keep desire and identification apart: at the heart of the Freudian subject, there is no real distinction between those two impulses.[16] We have already seen in Chin's relation to his white coworkers an intermingling of the erotic and the identificatory. The white man is for Chin the object of *an eroticized, loving identification*, and thus resembles the object with which Freud's "Mourning and Melancholia" begins. In that essay, Freud describes the proto-melancholic object as *simultaneously* "anaclitic"—an object of properly sexual desire, someone that the subject would like to "have"—and narcissistic—an object of identification, someone the subject would like to "be." This murky muddling together of desire and identification offers a fair description of Chin's relation to his white coworkers: he identifies with them, and his identification is saturated with a kind of loving eroticism. The libidinal component of Chin's desire is, however, rendered by him as not quite sexual (not quite a desire to "have" the object), but instead as a desire for an eroticized connectedness (something like a desire to "be with" the object). But if there is some difference between the *sexualized* identificatory tie to the object that Freud describes in "Mourning and Melancholia" and the *eroticized* identificatory tie Chin describes in "Chickencoop Slim," what's significant here is a continuity: both writers not only underscore the importance of the libidinal component of (homo)social bonds, but they also describe a similar psychic response in the subject to the rupturing of such bonds, to object-loss.[17]

In Freud's narrative, when the object is lost to a proto-melancholic subject—either through the object's death, or through "all those situations of [the subject's] being wounded, hurt, neglected, out of favour, or disappointed [by or with the object]"[18]—he is particularly unwilling or unable to transfer his libido to a new object. Instead his "free libido [is] withdrawn into the ego and not directed to another object. It [does] not find application there, however, in any one of several ways, but serve[s] simply to establish an identification of the ego with the abandoned object" (170). Two interrelated processes are involved here: 1) the turning back of libido from the object to the subject, or the transformation of object-libido into narcissistic libido—*the subject loves himself as he once loved the object*; and 2) the identification of the ego with the lost object—*the subject becomes like the lost object*.

What was loved in the lost object was already an idealized image of the self, and so it is relatively easy for an aspect of the self to stand in for that lost object through the intensification of an identificatory impulse that was already present to begin with. Thus the subject's love for the object is not eradicated; but instead of being directed toward a person in the world, that love is turned back toward the altered ego, which has been made over in the image of and can now take the place of that lost object.[19] What was once an *intersubjective social relation* has become an *intrapsychic structure*.

Bearing all of this in mind, let us now examine Chin's characterization of the "present" state of his identity in a long passage that comes near the end of the essay:

> In the vastness of speed, you become roomy enough to accept the knowledge that the railroader you believed in, the steel and iron version of John Wayne, Gary Cooper, Westerner you were and still are is no good. The independent, self-reliant, walk-tall common sense, personal-experience-favoring good man doing what a man has to do who built the railroad and made it work a hundred years ago, who led civilization and learned only from his mistakes and shot straight and dealt square, the iron rider, the Marlboro man in this part of the Twentieth century as a real man is racist, bigoted, politically and socially prejudiced against all reform and book learning and finds it difficult to acknowledge the existence of a world beyond the railroad and his home.
>
> The men I worked with in California, with rare exceptions, were just that. Though I didn't think so then, I couldn't then. I guess I became a little like them, in order to survive. I took on their style, accepted their nicknames, maintained an inner stupidity I believed was manly nobility. I'd lie to protect it, give a conductor so drunk he couldn't get on the caboose by himself an arm and my word. And I know that this is my last trip ever as just this man. (86–87)

From the perspective of the man he is now, the writer, Chin looks back upon his former identity and freely avows the "assimilationist" desire that had driven him to the railroad: as a brakeman, he had not only tried to emulate the white cowboy heroes of Hollywood Westerns and cigarette ads, but had also sought to imitate, on a day-to-day level, the masculine styles of the white men who were his companions, men like Murphy.

The present Chin, however, has apparently not entirely repudiated his loving identification with images of white manhood: for his realization that "the

Marlboro man in this part of the Twentieth century as a real man is racist, big-
oted, politically and socially prejudiced" does not lead Chin to renounce that
identification, but rather to "accept the knowledge that the railroader you
believed in, the steel and iron version of John Wayne, Gary Cooper,
Westerner you were *and still are* is no good" (my emphasis). Despite his substitution of the second person pronoun for the first, Chin tells us here that he
still retains something of his former self—that his mimetic relation to the *ideal*
of white manhood embodied by "John Wayne," in fact, persists, though it is
charged with a certain ambivalence that we will explore momentarily. What
has changed, however, is his relation to men like Murphy: he now forswears
a homosocial relation to "the Marlboro Man" as "a real man." In this light, we
should recall that his memoir warns specifically against—through his mother's
"history lesson" and Shannon's tale—the pleasures of interracial "coupling."
Chin has renounced, in other words, those pleasurable and eroticized
moments of *contact* with the white man, but not his mimetic desire *per se*.

What Freud's account helps us to understand is how the present Chin's
persistent identification with "the steel and iron version of John Wayne, Gary
Cooper, Westerner" enables him to forgo the very homosocial contact he
eroticizes as pleasurable. While the moment of Murphy's "look" has signaled
for Chin the frustration of his desire, the white man's loss as an erotic object,
this has not resulted in the cessation of his desire. For by continuing to identify himself with "John Wayne," Chin can sublimate the erotic desire he formerly felt for men like Murphy into a narcissistic self-love (which was there
from the beginning). He can renounce the highly eroticized *contact* with the
white man that railway work requires—can sustain object-loss—because,
insofar as he has come to resemble the ideal of white manhood all of the railway workers aspired to, he has in a sense made of himself a compensatory
love-object, a substitute for the man who was desired, and in whose image he
has been fashioned: "I was a thing: BRAKEMAN! That's the person I
remember being, the one I enjoy remembering on the railroad, *the image I
love*" (83–84; my emphasis). He substitutes for an *inter*psychic homosocial
relation to the white man as a "real man" an *intra*psychic narcissistic relation
to an idealized image of white manhood that he houses within himself. Chin
can continue to love the heroic (white) railroader as an ideal that he himself
now embodies, that has been memorialized within him. The mechanism of
identification thus enables Chin's love for the white man to remain alive.

Freud tells us, however, that "identification, in fact, is ambivalent from the very first; it can turn into an expression of tenderness as easily as into a wish for someone's removal."[20] It can express simultaneously, in a classically Freudian paradox, both love and hate. The aggressive aspect of identification is structurally related to the process upon which it is psychically modeled. Identification involves an "introjection" of the object, "a setting up of the object inside the ego," a process of internalization that signals "a kind of regression to the mechanism of the oral phase."[21] The desire to become the other—identification—as it is described in *Group Psychology*, is intimately bound up with a sadistic and aggressive desire to eat and destroy him:

> It [identification] behaves like a derivative of the first, *oral* phase of the organization of the libido, in which the object that we long for and prize is assimilated by eating and is in that way *annihilated as such*. The cannibal, as we know, has remained at this standpoint; he has *a devouring affection for his enemies* and only devours people of whom he is fond.[22]

The identificatory relation toward an object fuses together "affection" for the object and a desire that the object be "annihilated as such."

In a passage that comes near the opening of "Riding the Rails," we find that woven through Chin's elegiac praise of his former coworkers are traces of precisely such murderous intent: "More interesting to me are the men, my teachers, the good and bad men, old timers brakemen and switchmen, enginemen *whose kind will soon be extinct*" (80; my emphasis). What's curious about this sentence is its matter-of-fact positioning of these white men on the doorstep of extinction, its prophetic certainty—and this in a text that makes no mention of the historical and material conditions that might bring about their imminent demise: the shift from the railways to the roadways and airways as the dominant means of transporting goods, for instance. Without such an explanation, the reader is left to wonder if this sentence, in relaying a historical truth, is also expressing a fantasy of revenge.

A bit later we find something that looks quite a bit like such a fantasy in Chin's description of how veteran engineers answer the call of nature during their work: the older engineers, instead of using the toilets within the engines, would simply urinate out the door of the moving train. Chin recounts how once, while watching one of these men relieve himself in this manner, he

> wondered how many bodies of engineers, heads bent down and to the right, the tips of the index fingers and thumbs of both hands light-hoisting a penis, have been found by the side of the tracks, near barnyards or

anywhere for that matter. It was so easy to see him displaced by sunlight and a complete view of the passing country.

But should he go. Should his clinging to the classic old way of an engineer having no time to mess around with toilets on the engine be his undoing, and he be gone, doing what a man has gotta do, I would be alone. (83)

In each of these passages, which seem to dramatize a homicidal fantasy, we also find a curious suspension: though these men will "soon be extinct," their expected demise remains imminent; though it is "easy" for Chin to imagine them "displaced by sunlight and a complete view of the passing country," they remain poised in the doorway in the moment before their fatal fall. What Chin lingers upon is the experience of anticipation: the looking forward to a murderous consummation that nonetheless remains in a state of deferral. A moment is frozen, in which sadistic intent achieves an almost crystalline temporal purity. What better way to keep a murderous hatred alive, to keep it inviolate and chaste, than to memorialize the instant immediately anterior to its consummation: a moment in which the hated object remains forever courting a mortal blow, one forever captured in the movement of its furious descent.

There is, however, another reason for this suspension, this need to hold in abeyance the unleashing of murderous violence. For if Chin has, through identification, become the compensatory object of his thwarted love, it is also true that he has come to resemble the lost object who was and is also an object of sadistic hatred. To kill the other is also to kill the self that has been made over in its image. Chin's concluding image neatly dramatizes this predicament. He closes by presenting himself, aptly enough, as part of another interracial male couple:

I turn to a student brakeman named Hughes, who is just completing his first student trip. He's wearing Murphy's overalls. I say, "You know, Hughes, you can't be too safe on the railroad, especially when you're pulling pins or tying air or anything around the wheels and couplings. Why, I remember a guy who got himself coupled up. That's right. He was a brakeman, see . . ." (89; ellipses are Chin's)

In these concluding lines of his memoir, Chin seems to offer "proof" that his love for men like Murphy has been superseded by hate. Having identified himself so thoroughly with them, he is literally able to step into their shoes: he has become one of them, and as a sign of his transformation he begins to recount the narrative that "every man who's ever turned a wheel or pulled a pin has his own version of," "the Universal Brakeman Story"(80). Further-more, this mimetic transformation is linked here with an implicitly aggres-sive attitude toward the men whom he formerly loved: Hughes, garbed as he is in Murphy's overalls, appears as a proxy for the man whom Chin has lit-erally replaced through identification. And to that figure, in the guise of evincing an affectionate concern, Chin tells a tale whose outcome is bodily dismemberment and death, a tale that seems to express, by now, less a warn-ing that a sadistic fantasy.

The key facet of this final image, however, is the figure of Hughes and what he represents. For while he clearly stands in for Murphy, he just as eas-ily stands in for Chin: though he wears Murphy's overalls, he, like Chin, is a brakeman. The figure toward which Chin directs his hatred is neither purely an image of self nor of other, but rather an image that mingles both. Chin's aggression toward the white man follows here a circuitous route: it fixes upon an object that deflects a portion of it back toward himself. A loathing of an other with which one has identified begins to look quite a bit like a self-loathing. And if the psychic dynamic that begins to emerge from this melancholic narrative seems masochistic, let us turn one final time to Freud's account, which suggests the proximity of melancholic identification to that form of masochism he would later term moral.

According to Freud, an insistent and excessive expression of "dissatisfac-tion with the self on moral grounds is far the most outstanding feature" of melancholia ("Mourning," 169); this self-hatred is, at bottom, the displaced expression of a hatred directed at the lost object, the one who was loved and hated and has now gone away:

> If one listens patiently to the many and various self-accusations of the
> melancholia, one cannot in the end avoid the impression that often the
> most violent of them are hardly at all applicable to the patient himself,
> but that with insignificant modifications they do fit someone else, some
> person whom the patient loves, has loved or ought to love. This conjecture
> is confirmed every time one examines the facts. So we get the key to the
> clinical picture—by perceiving that the self-reproaches are reproaches against
> a loved object which have been shifted on to the patient's own ego. (169)

The melancholic, in other words, expresses his sadistic hatred of the lost object by berating the portion of the self that has been made over in its image, through a kind of masochism. For the altered ego not only serves as the surrogate object for the subject's libidinal desire, it also bears the brunt of his aggressive impulses as well. The melancholic regression into narcissism, having installed the loved *and* hated lost object within the ego, determines the ultimately masochistic route through which a sadistic hatred of the lost-object is expressed. The melancholic, according to Freud, is only able to batter the object of his loving hatred by battering that altered portion of the ego that has been made over in its image:

> If the [melancholic's] object-love, which cannot be given up, takes refuge in narcissistic identification, while the object itself is abandoned, then hate is expended upon this new substitute-object [the altered ego], railing at it, depreciating it, making it suffer and deriving sadistic gratification from its suffering. The self-torments of melancholiacs, which are without doubt pleasurable, signify, just like the corresponding phenomenon in the obsessional neurosis, a gratification of sadistic tendencies and of hate, both of which relate to an object and in this way have both been turned round upon the self. (172)

Insofar as Chin maintains his own libidinal and identificatory desires by coming to resemble their object—the white man—he serves as the substitute object not only for his love for the white man, but also for his hatred of them as well. And thus his wrath and anger at the white men with whom he was so intimately coupled find expression in a kind of self-contempt. He has become the very thing he both loves and hates.

*

The reading I have thus far been offering of "Riding the Rails with Chickencoop Slim" has focused on its depiction of an interracial mimetic desire that has as its primary object a certain ideal of *white* manhood enshrined in American popular culture. Chin perceives his coworkers like Murphy (and they apparently perceive themselves) as embodying "the steel and iron version of John Wayne." I have also suggested that this monumental masculinity finds its supraracial and suprahuman incarnation in the machinery of the train itself. It is the pleasurable experience of having one's body rendered "speed-fluent" by the energy of the train as it "blossoms" into his backside that gives Chin the feeling of having become "a thing: BRAKEMAN!"—an entity "too big for the name of a little man, Frank Chin." It is also the sensuous sensation of both "moving" and of "being moved" that catalyzes the apparently supraracial intersubjective "coupling up" that this text so lyrically celebrates, even as it underscores its transiency and its danger. The technological "thing"-ness of the train, I have been asserting, is symptomatic of the "utopian" dimension of Chin's homoerotic imaginings, bespeaking his desire for a form of male bonding that could somehow transcend race.

Given Chin's explicit and at times abject adoration of the images of black manhood that both racist and black nationalist discourses promote, however, it is also possible to see his depiction of the train in a quite different light. The pleasurable travel of the train's energy into his own body Chin depicts as "a sudden blossoming of a *dark* heat up your back and fading into the muscles of your shoulder and neck, more lightly again, and a hundred times again" (86; my emphasis); the engine over whose "thrusting tons" Chin and his coworkers exert their communal mastery is described as "*black*, hot, alive, waiting for use, part beast, part machine, . . . an iron horse, a three hundred and sixty ton three thousand horsepower locomotive" (83).

From the emphasis that Chin's descriptions place on the *blackness* of the gargantuan, masculine train, it is possible to discern a secondary narrative of desire and loss—one that pivots around an *African American* masculine ideal. Indeed, I want now to argue that both black and white men function in this text—and in nearly all of Chin's writings—as melancholic objects. As commentators like Judith Butler and Anne Cheng have noted, the distinction that Freud makes between a normative mourning and a pathological melancholia seems to break down, especially in later works like *The Ego and the Id* and *Group Psychology and the Ego*, in which the latter form of grief seems to comprise the very psychic process through which the ego is formed and maintained. If the ego as it finally emerges from Freud's writings takes shape as the precipitate of various lost objects, it very much resembles the form of subjectivity that Tam Lum—the protagonist of Chin's first play, *The Chickencoop Chinaman*—embodies: he is likened at one point to "those little vulnerable sea animals born with no shells of their own so he puts on the shells of the dead."[23] For melancholia in Chin's writings—as it is in Freud's—is not defined by a singular object of frustrated desire and grief; nor does it revolve around a punctual moment of loss. The narrative that appears to be secondary in "Riding the Rails"—one that revolves around the *blackness* of the masculinity embodied by the "thrusting tons" of the train—emerges front and center in another of Chin's melancholic fictions, *The Chickencoop*

Chinaman. Though that text also features an Asian American male protagonist who is drawn to the white masculine ideal exemplified by "the mythic Westerner," the plot focuses more centrally on his attempts to come to terms with the loss of a *black* masculine ideal. I turn now to the intertwined narratives of frustrated grief that comprise this drama.

"Shells of the Dead": The Chickencoop Chinaman

The Chickencoop Chinaman, as Patricia Chu has noted, "is structured primarily around the theme of the Chinese American hero's search for a father, more broadly, for a positive male cultural identity."[24] Tam Lum, the protagonist of this play, is presented as a kind of orphan whose filial impulses are directed toward "white and black heroes"; the most prominent of these is Ovaltine Jack Dancer, a black ex-boxer who once held the title of world champion.[25] Tam is a documentary filmmaker, and the project he is working on is a life history of Ovaltine. Tam's function as a kind of exemplary culture hero would seem to have a dual aspect: he mirrors the degraded condition of Asian American masculinity in a racial landscape that is wholly shaded in black and white, and he also prefigures the "authentic" form of racial and masculine identity that Asian men ought to adopt if they are to emerge from the shadows cast by black and white men. Within the terms of the melancholic narrative that gives the play its dramatic structure, then, Tam must learn to work through the fixation with "white and black heroes" that initially defines his identity—to mark their loss to him as appropriate love objects and move on.

The fixation with white masculinity that Chin works over at length in "Riding the Rails" comprises a relatively minor aspect of *The Chickencoop Chinaman*. The play offers no real counterpart to a figure like Murphy, no actual white man who incites a complex mixture of love, hate, and identi194

tification in the Asian American male protagonist. Instead, the ideal of "the mythic Westerner" is embodied by the Lone Ranger, who is described in the stage notes as "a legendary white racist with the funk of the West smouldering in his blood. In his senility, he still loves racistly, blesses racistly, shoots straight and is cuckoo with the notion that white folks are not white folks but just plain folks."[26] Very little drama is provoked by Tam's relationship to this character and thus to the ideal of white masculinity he represents. Indeed, this figure appears only once, in a dream sequence that comes early in the second act. This scene opens with a monologue in which Tam recounts his childhood belief that the Lone Ranger was Chinese American. The Lone Ranger then appears to the adult Tam in a surreal vision and is revealed to be an old white man, addled by drugs and senility, literally propped up by his faithful sidekick, Tonto. He spouts various racist clichés and shoots Tam in the hand, leading him to conclude: "The masked man . . . I knew him better when I never knew him at all. The Lone Ranger ain't no Chinaman, children" (38). This relatively brief treatment suggests that the adult Tam, by the time the play opens, has already worked through his childhood fixation with the figure of the "mythic Westerner."

The fixation that Tam has much more difficulty coming to terms with concerns another boyhood hero, Ovaltine. Tam's fascination with black culture in general and with the figure of Ovaltine in particular is shared by Kenji, an old friend who assists him in completing his documentary on the ex-boxing champ. Tam's orientation toward blackness is evident from the focus of his film and from his frequent use of mannerisms and phrases that are coded in the play as African American. Kenji, whose childhood nickname was "BlackJap," also uses black slang; he lives in a black neighborhood in Pittsburgh called Oakland, and the walls of his apartment are "covered with posters of black country, blues and jazz musicians" (9).

Early in the play, Tam tells Kenji that his documentary will "turn on two things, man, double action, right? that title defense against Claude Dupree he did in his forties. His greatest fight, right? One. And Two how his daddy, Charley Popcorn, made him be that kind of fighter" (14). The drama focuses on the obstacles that eventually prevent Tam from making the kind of film he initially envisions. In so doing, it puts into question his profound fascination with black men, which is apparent from the documentary's subject, in two different ways. It suggests that an Asian American masculine subjectivity shaped around an intense identification with black cultural forms will take on a kind of queer coloring; it also questions the validity of an Asian American aesthetic project that takes African American culture and history as its central subject.

The character of Lee, who is described in the stage notes as a "possible Eurasian or Chinese American passing for white" (3), articulates these criticisms most forcefully. She is immediately suspicious of Tam's choice of documentary subject, assuming that it has an exploitative dimension to it. She tells Kenji at one point: "I hate people making it on the backs of black people" (19). She is also appalled by the regularity with which Tam and Kenji adopt black slang and mannerisms. She sees their appropriation of African American culture as demeaning, as expressing a racial self-hatred. Her disgust leads her to voice the following withering appraisal of Tam:

> He's the worst kind. He knows he's no kind of man. Look at him, he's like those little vulnerable sea animals born with no shells of their own so he puts on shells of the dead. You hear him when he talks? He's talking in so many goddamn dialects and accents all mixed up at the same time, cracking wisecracks, lots of oh yeah, wisecracks, you might think he was a nightclub comic. (24)

Lee's comments not only suggest the melancholic character of Tam's appropriation of black and also white cultural idioms ("he puts on shells of the dead"), but they also equate this imitative idolatry with a lack of masculinity ("he's no kind of man").

Tam's documentary and the rather abject and idolatrous relationship to black masculinity it expresses are also called into question by some rather juvenile bits of homophobic humor that are sprinkled throughout the play. While these scenes never imply that either Tam or Kenji is gay, they do insinuate that their obvious fascination with blackness might be perceived as rather queer—particularly from the perspective of African American men.

There is, for instance, the scene in which Tam and Kenji first meet Charley Popcorn, which takes place in the lobby of the adult movie theater he runs. When Popcorn spots the two men "star[ing] into the auditorium and look[ing] slowly from one end of the screen to the other, gaping," he yells out to them: "Hey, you two queers, sit down and hold hands, and don't bother the perverts willya?" (38, 39). While this hail is presented as based on a misrecognition and also as a kind of joke, it is significant that they are the first words that the play's sole black character utters, and that they are directed at the two Asian American male protagonists. Popcorn's epithet evokes a certain anxiety on the part of the Asian American men concerning how they might be regarded by African American men, even in an environment as heterosexual as a porn palace.

Later in this scene, Popcorn discovers that Tam is Chinese, after assuming he was black from their phone conversation. Popcorn suddenly remembers "a cute little song about Chinese" and starts to sing it:

MY LITTLE HONG KONG DREAM GIRL
IN EVERY DREAM YOU SEEM, GIRL,
TWO ALMOND EYES ARE SMILING
AND MY POOR HEART IS WHIRLING
LIKE A BIG SAIL ROUND MY PIGTAIL (41; capitalized in the original)

Popcorn's responses suggest that he somehow associates Asianness and thus Tam and Kenji with queerness and/or an exotic femininity. Appalled by the older black man's associations, Tam quickly launches into an anecdote that is clearly intended to emphasize the profound sense of intimacy that he and Kenji shared with Ovaltine, the man they think is Popcorn's son—an anecdote that is also intended to emphasize their mutual masculinity and their racial solidarity:

> TAM (*fumbling*): Uh, yeah, as I was saying, I . . . we took Ovaltine for a ride, went out riding with Ovaltine when he was back in Oakland, uh California, where, you know, before we'd seen the Dupree fight? . . . and, we all got out of the short, the car, and under the stars, we stood next to the car, and on the road, you know, pissed all together into the bushes . . . (*Chuckles.* POPCORN *doesn't react* . . . TAM *and* KENJI *exchange looks.*) We were just kids then, but since then we say . . . it was the greatest . . . saw the Dancer come back and know out Dupree in the 11th in Oakland, I guess he was our hero . . . He had fond memories of pissing on the, I mean, off the roadside with you . . .
>
> POPCORN: What?
>
> TAM: I guess that was the greatest piss we ever took in our lives, right Kenji?
>
> KENJI: Yeah, it was a dynamite piss, Mr. Popcorn.
>
> POPCORN: Why you talkin to me about pissin in bushes for? (41; ellipses are Chin's)

Popcorn is understandably baffled by the meaning of this story of collective urination. His confusion calls attention to a certain naïveté on Tam's part, his belief that this anecdote would effortlessly communicate a sense of homosocial and interracial solidarity.

An apparently unintended message that this anecdote might communicate, however, is suggested by Popcorn's earlier hail: "Hey, you two queers." Moreover, an earlier scene in the play has already raised the possibility that telling one black man about how meaningful it was to have once urinated with a black man might put one's heterosexuality into question. The two protagonists' story about "the greatest piss we ever took in our lives" first appears in a dialogue between Kenji and Lee. In his telling of it, however, Kenji (unlike Tam) expresses a clear awareness that it might be construed as having a homosexual rather than homosocial meaning:

> KENJI: Okay. When we were in college, we kidnapped Ovaltine. I mean, Tam did. Tricked him out of his hotel room, and we took him driving out of Oakland and all stood by the car pissing in the bushes. And I remembered I'd been to New Orleans and, you know, stuck over on the colored side. And I had to piss, and didn't know which way to go. And this black dishwasher there *saw my plight* so to speak, and took me out to the can and we took places at urinals right next to each other. I thought that was pretty friendly. And I wanted to tell Ovaltine, you know, but Ovaltine being black might not understand a yellow man, standing next to him, pissing in the bushes, talking about the last memorable time he went pissing with a black man . . . (20; italics and ellipses are Chin's)

Like a series of Chinese boxes, each story about "pissing with a black man" contains within it another story recounting an earlier incident of "pissing with a black man." The original incident occurred during Kenji's travels in the segregated South. Needing to choose whether to identify himself as colored or white, he was assisted by a black dishwasher. By being invited to and then choosing to stand side by side, as it were, with a black man, Kenji apparently experienced a moment of interracial homosocial solidarity that ran in both directions. By relieving themselves together he and the black dishwasher enjoyed a moment of mutual recognition as colored men, one "that was pretty friendly." It is this sense of interracial homosocial solidarity that Kenji apparently *wanted* to communicate to Ovaltine upon initially meeting him. But he refrained from telling this story out of a certain anxiety that, as he explains to Lee, "Ovaltine being black might not understand a yellow man, standing next to him, pissing in the bushes, talking about the last memorable time he went pissing with a black man." Kenji is aware that his expression of past and present racial solidarity might sound like a homosexual "come on"— his is a homophobic anxiety about generating homophobia in another man.

The anxiety that this play registers, then, concerns the homosexual meaning that might be ascribed to the idolatrous and imitative orientation toward black men that defines the play's two male protagonists. In its depiction of Kenji's relationship to Lee, the play suggests that such an orientation to black men must be left behind for Asian male subjects to assume a heteronormative identity. The play concludes with Kenji deciding to claim the child that Lee is pregnant with as his own, though he is unsure as to whether he is the father. His decision to accept the adult responsibilities of patriarchal manhood seems to signal that he has finally gotten over the boyhood fixation on black culture that has impeded his ability to pursue a stable relationship with Lee.

But in its depiction of its main protagonist, Tam, this play questions both the non-normative *sexual* identity that results from his fixation on Ovaltine and also the *aesthetic* identity that emerges from the adoption of an abject and idolatrous relationship to black culture. In this latter context, the story that Tam repeats—of "pissin in the bushes with a black man"—functions as an allegory for the artistic project he is attempting to complete. The anecdote and the documentary are both narrative expressions of an Asian American man's rather abject and adoring regard of the black men he wishes to stand beside. The interracial fascination that Tam must "get over," then, consists of a homoerotic identificatory attachment to black masculinity and also an aesthetic attachment to black male subjects—an investment in the grand historical narratives that are the "proper" legacy, the play suggests, of black men, of black artists.

What throws Tam into existential crisis are certain revelations by Popcorn that make it impossible for him complete the film he had originally envisioned—to tell the story he wanted to tell. These revelations are: first, that Ovaltine is not Popcorn's son; and second, that the stories Ovaltine has built around his "father" are lies. In the following exchange, Tam recites various elements of Ovaltine's biography as they were told to him, and Popcorn proceeds to expose them as fabrications:

> TAM: [. . .] I saw you as a bigger man, man, the way Ovaltine talked about watchin you strip off your shirt, and wash up out of a pan, outside the house. And how his eyes popped out when he was a kid, at your mighty back rippling with muscles!
> POPCORN: Me?
> TAM: And the whiplash scars, how they made him cry, and how that made him sure, he'll be a fighter, a fighter down from his soul!
> POPCORN: Whiplash never touched *my* back! You're sleepin, young man. Dreamin!

TAM: All right. This is the sheet on you. You're Charley Popcorn,
   Ovaltine Jack Dancer's father.

POPCORN: Huh?

TAM: . . . uh let me finish. Ovaltine when he was a little boy in
   Mississippi beat up on a white boy, and you told him you all
   would have to leave that part of the country, and then you told
   him about the welts on your back, and getting whipped. You and
   the family packed up in a car and Ovaltine remembers you and
   him pissin by the roadside next to the car with the ladies hiding
   their eyes. You taught him "psychology" by telling him, no matter
   how bad he ever got beat, or however he got beat, to always smile,
   stand up and say, loud "I did enjoy the fight so very much."

POPCORN: Where you hear all this shit, Mr. Lum?

TAM: From his book, from his mouth, from his aunt, from his
   wife . . .

POPCORN: He wrote it in a BOOK??

TAM: Why, what's wrong?

POPCORN: I ain't nobody's father, especially his'n. I never been to
   Mississippi, or done none of that.

TAM: You gotta be his father. (47–48)

In order to confirm that the stories Tam has been told are lies, Popcorn lifts
his shirt and exposes his back: "You see any kind of whip marks? Tell me,
now, you see any kind of whiplash or dogbite on me? . . . Ovaltine done
bullshit you and the whole world, son. If you come all the way here to see
Ovaltine's daddy, ha, you come for nothing! Ha! That Ovaltine, just can't
leave go of me" (48–49).

Tam's insistence in the face of Popcorn's revelations—"You gotta be his
father"—makes clear that it is not only Ovaltine, however, who can't seem to
"leave go of" this paternal myth. The play offers a rather complex explanation for the intensity of Tam's investment in the paternal narrative that
Ovaltine had spun out. At one level, Tam's resistance to Popcorn's disclosures
is professional in nature—it is that of a documentary filmmaker whose angle
on his subject has been ruined: the story he wanted to emphasize was of
"how his [Ovaltine's] daddy, Charley Popcorn, made him be that kind of
fighter" (14). But Tam has more personal reasons for wanting Popcorn to be
Ovaltine's father, reasons that illuminate his own vexed relationship to the
idea of paternity. For it is clear that Tam, who is presented as a kind of
orphan, has taken Ovaltine as a surrogate father—as a paternal ideal who

embodies a kind of racialized masculinity that Tam wishes to claim as his own. But his intense psychic investment in *Popcorn*'s paternity suggests something a bit more complicated—that in order for Ovaltine to function as a powerful paternal ideal, it is necessary for him to have had the particular experiences of *being fathered* that he has claimed. To be the kind of father Tam wants, in other words, Ovaltine must also be a certain kind of *son*, one who was made by a certain kind of father.

The aura surrounding the father Ovaltine essentially made up—the Popcorn of his memoir—derived from his placement in an African American historical narrative of racist trauma and racial triumph that has deservedly assumed a monumental place in the history of the American nation. This fabricated Popcorn, this fictitious father, had been scarred—physically if not emotionally—by the violence of the segregated South, and had emerged from that experience with his manhood fully intact. Tam's psychic investment in Ovaltine is partly due, then, to the way in which the boxer's fictive autobiography so intimately connects him to a grander historical narrative recounting "The Great Migration" of poor blacks from the segregated South northward (and also, in this case, westward) and to freedom. What Tam came to believe as he listened with credulity to Ovaltine's lies was that he had found an "authentic" African American story to tell.

Popcorn reveals Ovaltine's fictions for what they were: "Man, you shoulda knowed from those stories, that they was dreams! They was lies! All made up. Bullshit!" (50). These disclosures shatter Tam's idolatry of Ovaltine. Even more shattering, however, is Popcorn's explanation of Ovaltine's motivations in generating this myth:

> Those dreams he dreamed, that's not me. That wasn't ever us, even when we were pardners. I always favored him and won't say a word to harm him ever. Let's just say when he started winning, and white people with money and ranches . . . You can't blame anybody if they don't want to live in a room and sometime in the back of an old station wagon no more. But you understand, prizefighting is a business, you gotta be a businessman, you see to be a good prizefighter. (49)

Popcorn believes that Ovaltine first created this paternal legend in order to enhance his desirability as a commodity, to better market his career as a black prizefighter. When Tam begins to insists to Popcorn that Ovaltine "needs you to be his father, can't ya see?" (50), the reply he receives is: "Oh, you are a slick businessman. I see why Ovaltine favors you all right. So he needs a father for this show about him" (50).

Popcorn's revelations also suggest that Ovaltine's entrepreneurial skills are also what give primary shape to his storytelling. His genius as a storyteller and also as an autobiographer stems from his keen awareness of what his audience's expectations are—an awareness that is very much that of "a slick businessman." There are, other words, shades of Houston Baker, Jr.'s, Trueblood in Chin's Ovaltine: it would seem that the stories this boxer has told to his two Asian American fans cater as much to their desires as the narrative that Ellison's sharecropper has told to white men like Norton caters to theirs. Ovaltine has sold Tam and Kenji on a version of his life story that he knew would further the sense of identification he had already engendered in them. How else to explain the fact that Ovaltine's narrative includes a detail about he and his "father" "pissin by the roadside next to the car with the ladies hiding their eyes"? Popcorn's revisionist account of Ovaltine's life suggests that the awkward anecdote Tam had used to express his admiration for and his desire to stand side by side with his black hero had become mere grist for the mill—had simply been absorbed into one of the boxer's manipulative and self-promoting stories.

Within the terms of the narrative of thwarted desire that *The Chickencoop Chinaman* elaborates, then, it is ultimately Popcorn's revelations more than any homophobic injunction that render the object of Tam's identificatory desires inadequate to them. The heroic black man and the heroic black father who made him both turn out to be illusory ideals; Tam's inability to come to terms fully with their inadequacy manifests itself through the bitter, self-lacerating outbursts that comprise much of his dialogue for the remainder of the play. Whatever anger is generated by Tam's recognition of how he had been manipulated by Ovaltine—of how inadequate the object of his affections has been to them—he directs for the remainder of the play at the other Asian American characters. Mainly, however, he directs it at himself. As Elaine Kim has suggested, Tam fails ever to emerge fully from the self-loathing in which he stews through much of the play.

To render Kim's reading more precise, however, it is necessary to recognize that Tam's masochism is directly linked to the attachment he still harbors for the artistic project that he has been producing—an attachment that he is still in the process of working through as the play ends. In the final scene, Tam reveals what his plans for the documentary now are:

TAM: [. . .] I'm not going to dig up the Dancer, mock his birth, make
a fool of him just to make a name for myself. That's the way it is
with us Chinaman cooks! Dat's the code of the kitchen, children.
Anybody hungry (*Rises to go to the kitchen.*)
POPCORN: What about the movie, Mr. Lum?
TAM: There won't be a word of fathers in it, Mr. Popcorn. You'll be
part of a straight, professional, fight film. (63)

Tam partially acknowledges here that Ovaltine's revelations have instilled in
him a resentment and anger at the object of his attachment, emotions that
could be channeled into a documentary that would "dig up the Dancer,
mock his birth, make a fool of him." But the fact that he refuses to make such
a film suggests that he retains a significant level of psychic investment in
Ovaltine, even if he has been disabused of his naïve idolization. The artwork
he will produce will be shorn of its creator's more personal investments—it
will be "a straight, professional, fight film"—but it will not be a hatchet job.

In order to trace where that personal investment may be relocated by the
end of the play, it is necessary to identify the nature of what that investment
was. For the personal significance to Tam of the paternal narrative that
Popcorn was supposed to have fleshed out was directly tied to an intimately
familial audience he hoped that his documentary would reach: his children.
Tam is not only a less-than-successful artist at the play's outset, he is also a
less-than-successful father, estranged from his two children, who now live
with his white ex-wife, Barbara, and her new husband, a white man who is
also a writer. In an early conversation with Lee, Tam says of his children,
Jonah and Sarah, "they've already forgotten me. They got a new, ambitious,
successful, go-for-bucks, superior white daddy" (27). "This guy they're calling 'daddy,'" Tam elaborates, "I hear he's even a better writer than me" (27).
His hopes for the documentary—and particularly for the paternal narrative
it was to foreground—were that it would somehow give expression to his
love as a father to his children:

TAM: My kids might see it some day, and . . . And they'll see . . .
LEE: You see, Tam? You can't turn your back on them. You don't mean
it when you say you want them to forget you.
TAM: I mean it. I mean, in case, they don't forget. I should leave them
something . . . I should have done some THING. One thing I've
done alone, with all my heart. A gift. Not revenge. (27)

The film that Tam hoped to show his children would have had at its center a father he himself wanted to but could not be. But since this story has turned out to be—in Popcorn's terms, "dreams," "lies," and "bullshit"—the paternal impulses that impelled his artistic endeavors would seem to have been entirely frustrated. Hence the masochistic self-loathing that reverberates through Tam's dialogue through much of the play is directly connected to a sense of both aesthetic and paternal inadequacy. It stems from the recognition that the model of art that his documentary exemplifies—an Asian American artwork that features as its protagonist an African American man—cannot serve as an appropriate or effective vehicle for expressing the paternal impulse that impels Tam.

In the play's concluding monologue, however (and this is something Elaine Kim partially obscures in her account), Tam does adumbrate the features of a *different* kind of artwork that would center on Asian Americans, and more effectively address the "children" he imagines as his ideal audience. The very final image of *The Chickencoop Chinaman* is of Tam, standing alone in the kitchen, lit by a spotlight, and directly addressing the audience. The rhetorical contract that structures this closing monologue is suggested by its opening lines: "Ride with me . . . Everything comes sniffin at you in the kitchen sooner or later, *children*, grandmaw used to say. In the kitchen. Always in the kitchen" (65; my emphasis).[27] He then recounts another boyhood experience of being regaled by a mythical story of the American West— one that centered not on the Lone Ranger but on Tam's great-grandfather:

> My grandmaw told me, children, how when she was left alone to roll cigars all by herself, in the Old West when Chinamans was the only electricity and all the thunder in the mountains . . . in them awful old days of few mothers, few fathers, and rare songs . . . she used to leave a light on in the next room, and listen. And talking to us—This is true!—sometimes she heard a train. A Chinaman borne, high stepping Iron Moonhunter, liftin eagles with its breath! "Listen!" she'd say.
> And we'd listen in the kitchen.
> She was on the air.
> The house she said was like when her father came back from the granite face and was put in the next room, broken and frostbit on every finger and toe of him and his ears and nose, from the granite face, by Chinamans, nobodies' fathers, all night long running stolen horses, yelling for speech, for my grandmaw's ma. That's the truth!

Ya hear that cry?

From China Camp, Jacksonville, Westport, Placerville, a gallop and grandmaw's pa coming home.

And he died there, in the light of the next room comfortable, comforting a little girl rolling counterfeit Spanish cigars.

Now and then, I feel them old days children, the way I feel the prowl of the dogs in the night and the bugs in the leaves and the thunder in the Sierra Nevadas however far they are. The way my grandmother had an ear for trains. Listen, children, I gotta go. Ride Buck Buck Bagaw with me . . . Listen in the kitchen for the Chickencoop Chinaman slowin on home. [*Curtain*] (65–66)

By concluding *The Chickencoop Chinaman* with this speech, Chin suggests that Tam has been able to locate an appropriate object of paternal and aesthetic attachment by remembering the legend his grandmother passed on, a legend that memorializes his own great-grandfather as well as the host of Chinese immigrant laborers who, under dangerous and exploitative conditions, helped construct the transcontinental railroad. The scars of an illusory mythical father—Popcorn—are replaced by the scars of a "real" mythical great-grandfather, who "came back from the granite face and was put in the next room, broken and frostbit on every finger and toe of him and his ears and nose." Tam's narrative outburst is intended to leave the reader with the promise of more to come. It would seem that a space has now been cleared for a more "authentic" art to emerge, one that finds in the historical past an *Asian American* narrative of racist exploitation and racial redemption that can be justifiably placed alongside the one in which Ovaltine had fictively situated his own life history.

If Tam seems to glimpse in this closing monologue the direction that his art should now take, this suggests that he has begun to transform himself from the man he was at the beginning of the play. He is described in the character notes that precede the play itself as "A multi-tongued word magician *losing his way to the spell* who trips to Pittsburgh to conjure with his childhood friend and research a figure in his documentary movie" (3; my emphasis). The "spell" he has been under is presumably the one that had been cast by Ovaltine. Having been disenchanted of his idolatry by Popcorn, Tam has found a more suitable object to memorialize in his work: he has not only found the proper "father" to mourn, but has also identified the appropriate racial history to bring into the domain of aesthetic representation—that of his "coolie" ancestors.

To put this another way, Tam's final speech outlines a kind of blueprint for Asian American writing, one that is fleshed out in more detail in his polemical works: this writing should have as its subject Asian Americans; it should bring to light the history of racial marginalization to which Asian Americans have been subjected and record those male heroic figures who were able to resist and transcend this marginalization; it should, moreover, make use of the oral forms of storytelling that Asian American subjects use (as Tam's "grandmaw" does) to keep their culture alive. Given the rather seamless fit between the aesthetic that Tam describes and, to a certain extent, performs in this closing monologue and the aesthetic that Chin promotes, it is easy to see this character as a stand-in for the author, ventriloquizing his creator's promise of things to come. Tam seems to be describing, in other words, the kind of art that he himself—within the diegetic world of the play, anyway—has not produced but that Chin presumably will one day.

It is not entirely clear, however, that that day has ever really arrived. To date, Chin has completed only a single substantial literary work that unambiguously follows the formula schematized at the end of *The Chickencoop Chinaman*, namely, his 1991 novel *Donald Duk*.[28] This work records the coming of age of its eponymous protagonist, whose embarrassment over his name is symptomatic of the more generalized shame he feels about his Chinese heritage. With the help of a magically able father—who is a phenomenal storyteller and cook—and his white friend, Arnold, Donald learns to love his ethnic self: he becomes familiar through his father's stories with Chinese heroic myths; he discovers that his own ancestors helped build the railroad; and he thus finally gets over his apparently unhealthy attachment to the figure of Fred Astaire. The flatness of this work leads Sau-ling Wong to devote just a single paragraph to it in her discussion of Chin's literary treatment of the railroad legend:

> [In *Donald Duk*] didactic intent has taken over: despite employing a potentially unruly dream mechanism in this narrative, his evocation of the Chinese pioneers' life has become dissociated from gut-churning libidinal forces, sanitized to a point not explainable fully by the juvenility of the central intelligence, Donald, and his eminently edifiable white friend Arnold. It is as if, after struggling for years with raw and impossible contradictions, Chin has decided to settle for a defanged version of Chinese American history and the simple warm glow of ethnic pride.[29]

With the exception of this novel, which seems to have been expressly written for a young adult audience, the rest of Chin's literary output has tended to be steeped in the masochistic self-contempt that commentators like Elaine Kim and Michael Soo Hoo have noted.[30]

*

One reason why the seemingly straightforward formula for an "authentic" Asian American writing that Chin outlines in the closing monologue to *The Chickencoop Chinaman* might lead to a masochistic aesthetic becomes apparent when we confront certain aspects of the Iron Moonhunter myth—the legend that Tam "remembers" and that presumably provides a model for the art that he is now ready to produce. This putatively authentic Chinese American legend concerns a "phantom engine said to take the [Chinese] railroad men home toward the coast, reversing the direction of their deepening bondage."[31] In contrast to the *fabricated* African American legend with which Tam is enthralled through much of the play, the Iron Moonhunter myth is presented not only as true, but also as providing a racially appropriate subject and model for Tam's own creative aspirations. This legend, and the oral tradition in which it is embedded ("grandmaw used to say"), would seem to provide Chinese American writers like Tam and Chin with a vernacular of their own—a yellow analogue to black folktales, spirituals, jazz, and the blues. But there are several issues that prevent this legend from fully supporting the rhetorical weight with which it is freighted.

First of all, as Sau-ling Wong has suggested, "There seems to be a good possibility that Frank Chin invented the Iron Moonhunter legend."[32] Wong reaches this conclusion after a fruitless search for archival materials that would lend credence to the suggestion in *The Chickencoop Chinaman* that this was an actual folktale told by Chinese immigrants. The fabricated quality of this myth reveals that Tam in his concluding monologue has actually come to bear a remarkable resemblance to his boyhood hero—both falsify a familial connection to a heroic racial past of mythical proportions. This is another way in which Tam resembles the protagonist of Chin's memoir: both cling melancholically to the men they loved, the men they wanted to be, the men they now know are "no good."

Secondly, the claim that the play seems to make about the racial and ethnic *distinctiveness* of the legend it "remembers" seems to be undermined by the very imagery in which that legend is draped. In making the railroad the locus and origin of a Chinese American vernacular tradition, Chin evokes a historical experience that is rendered as the unique legacy of his ethnic group. The labor that his "coolie" forefathers put into the building of the transcontinental railroad, in Wong's words, "stands as a visible testament to one of the most vital contributions made by [Chinese Americans] to the building of this nation."[33] But as Wong points out, the theme of locomotion celebrated in Chin's writings derives its rhetorical power from a highly canonical and white literary tradition exemplified by texts like Twain's *Huckleberry Finn*, Melville's *Moby-Dick*, and Whitman's "Songs of the Open Road": "What Chin offers is not so much a critique of existing hegemonic discourse on mobility, with its barely disguised violence and expansionist agenda, as an inversion of it to vindicate hitherto marginalized groups."[34] His "inversion" of a canonical white literary iconography that privileges mobility is thus also a repetition; the symbolic terrain in which he attempts to locate a particularly Asian American vernacular has already been mapped, worked over, and mined to death by the most canonical of white writers.

Moreover, if we consider once again the *blackness* of the train as it is rendered in "Riding the Rails," we confront the fact that railroad imagery has long been central to many African American accounts of the vernacular as well. In his 1945 tribute to Richard Wright, for instance, Ralph Ellison had asked his readers to hear in *Black Boy* the "blues-tempered echoes of railroad trains, the names of Southern towns and cities, estrangements, fights and flights, deaths and disappointments."[35] Two figures that are central to Houston Baker, Jr.'s, "blues criticism," as Diana Fuss has observed, "are the railway roundhouse and the crossing sign;"[36] she further notes that "Baker pictures himself as a blues singer riding the freight trains of vernacular tradition and continually switching tracks at the critical crossroads."[37] In this light, Tam's embrace of the Iron Moonhunter myth at the end of *The Chickencoop Chinaman* suggests that he ends up pretty much where he began: in thrall to an African American ideal of black cultural identity. The railroad legend he passes off as distinctively Chinese American turn out to be—like Ovaltine's paternal mythology—"dreams," "lies," and "bullshit"; moreover, it is a fabrication that seems to have been patterned after an African American "original."

Tam, therefore, remains at the conclusion of *The Chickencoop Chinaman* pretty much who he was in the opening—a subject fundamentally shaped by his melancholic identification with black and white masculine ideals he can never fully approximate. Or, as Lee puts it, "He knows he's no kind of man.

Look at him, he's like those little vulnerable sea animals born with no shells of their own so he puts on shells of the dead."

From Melancholia to Masochism to Manhood

What Chin confronts in the melancholic narratives I have been examining in this chapter is the predicament of being yellow and male, of being formed as a masculine subject, in a culture in which nearly all of the dominant images of phallic masculinity are black and white. In order to underscore the libidinal character of the identificatory relationship to these ideals of racialized manhood that Asian American men are thus encouraged to adopt, Chin relies on the symbolic vocabulary provided by homophobic conceptions of homosexuality. White racism thus threatens to make "faggots" of us all insofar as we come to harbor—as he himself acknowledges that he does— a mimetic desire for black and white forms of masculinity. The way out of this psychic predicament, as Chin charts it in these melancholic narratives, is, rather, a different way of staying in. It is less a matter of letting go of this erotic and identificatory attraction to images of black and white masculinity than it is a different way—a melancholic and masochistic way—of hanging on.

Implicit in the melancholic resolution that Chin provides to these narratives is the endorsement of a certain heightened form of racial self-loathing. In "Racist Love," Chin and Chan describe the Asian American population as living in a state of "*euphemized* self-contempt." This suggestive phrase implies that in order for Asian Americans to resist their construction as the privileged objects of racist love, they must de-euphemize, as it were, this self-contempt—to allow themselves to feel more fully a self-hatred that has in a sense been there all along.

Indeed, "Riding the Rails" suggests how a hatred of the self might function as the circuitous expression of a hatred whose proper objects are the hated white other in whose image "our" own subjectivities have been shaped. For if the very shape of our American male identities expresses our ineradicable and loving identification with those white men, real or imaginary, whom our culture has taught us to see as "irresistible" but whom our experiences have also taught us to hate, then, Chin suggests, *so be it*; but then let that identification also express our undying hatred for them. For as we take their identities into our own—as we thus copy and emulate them—let them know that this signals our emancipation from any social bond to them. We no longer need their "touch"; we crave no longer a social bond to them because we possess, after all, our own assimilated identities that bear their traces. We have taken them into us, and need them no longer as "real" men. We make of our assimilated identities memorials to our frustrated love, but also deposit upon them the abundance of our hatred for them. I thus hate you by hating the me I have become in your image; and though I pay the price of hating myself in direct proportion to the degree that I hate you, I am willing to do so for the release of aggression it enables me. And this, ultimately, is the gesture at the heart of the Asian American manhood Chin champions. It is to hate with a passion and with a vengeance the assimilated identity that is one's own.

Thus the protagonist of "Chickencoop Slim"—Frank Chin, the writer— has produced a body of work the most visceral affective component of which is a relentless masochism. To invoke once again Elaine Kim's observations concerning the dominant tenor of his creative output, "Chin creates an over- riding sense of the utter futility of the male protagonist's efforts to redefine himself"; his characters are "alienated adolescents, incapacitated by the sense of their own impotence."[38] He "accepts his oppressors' definition of 'mas- culinity,'" in other words, and then produces a series of male characters who berate themselves for their inability to live up to that definition. What Chin tends to offer up in his writings are literary self-portraits of an Asian Ameri- can masculinity in ruins, of men who seem only to hate themselves for their inability to be men.

A comparable, though aesthetically inflected, masochism emerges from *The Chickencoop Chinaman*. Although that play insists that the Asian American artist will never be able to stand shoulder to shoulder, as it were, with his African American brothers if his attitude toward them is one of fawning adulation, it also seems to suggest the impossibility of finding another model for an authentic minority tradition. Where the narrative tends, then, is toward a masochistic repetition of the predicament in which Tam finds himself at the opening of the play—that of having no non-white ideal of racialized masculinity to claim as his own other than those that are associated with African American culture. If Asian American men are thus consigned to "faking blackness," as Kenji puts it, then the message that the ending of *The Chickencoop Chinaman* seems to convey is that they should at least fully acknowledge and embrace the self-hatred that is expressed in their abject relationship to black culture.

But within this masochism that so palpably infuses his work, Chin finds something—I believe—that he experiences as "redemptive." He finds something in these literary exercises of self-flagellation that gives him, in other words, the illusion of virility, that enables him to feel like a "man." He finds in this virulent masochism an equally virulent sadism, and the masculine subject who brings himself into being through writing is ultimately a sadist to the same degree that he is a masochist.[39] For the moral condemnation he heaps upon myriad objects throughout his writings is not only directed at himself (for he shows himself to resemble the things he castigates), it is also always directed at another, at those loathed objects with which he nonetheless identifies: the "fake" Asian American, the "homosexual," the "feminine," the white man—and even, to a certain extent, the black man. The masculine "redemption" Chin finds within masochism is located, paradoxically, in the sadistic violence of the self-inflicted blow, in the insistent battering of the self that is always a battering of another. Through this incessant recirculation of fury and wrath, what Chin seeks to lay his hands upon is the thing that most defines manhood in our culture: a "promiscuous" violence.

FIVE

The Fantasy of a Yellow Vernacular: Mimetic Hunger and the "Chameleon Chinaman"

Frank Chin's literary works, as I established in the previous chapter, derive much of their affective power from the ways in which they attempt to make a masochistic and melancholic attachment to black and white men the signature feature of both "inauthentic" and "authentic" modes of Asian American male identity. To be an Asian American man, in Chin's account, is to hunger for the kinds of racialized masculinity that men of other races embody without effort. In this final chapter, I return to Chin's essays in order to illuminate how such issues of interracial homosociality frame his conception of the distinctive qualities that comprise an "authentic" minority tradition. As I will make clear in this chapter, his writings on literature are shaped by a profound sense of competition and envy—indeed, of "belatedness"— vis-à-vis other minority cultures. What Chin's aesthetic writings help us to engage with, in other words, are the particular forms of invisibility that Asian American writers confront as they attempt to write themselves into a literary landscape shaded primarily in black and white. It is that liminal space between the black and white literary traditions that Chin illuminates in his writing, and the palpable frustration that propels much of it brings to light the specific obstacles that structure that positioning. It is from this perspective of frustration that the compensatory and even transcendent promise of the aesthetic for men of color can perhaps best be sighted, shrouded in all its fantasmatic allure.

A vivid sense of the dilemma that Chin's writings help us to understand is conveyed in a 1976 essay that I mentioned briefly in my introduction to this study. In this piece, he recounts the trying experience of being asked to speak to the concerns of Asian American writers at the national convention of the Modern Language Association. The other members of this panel were Karl Shapiro, Ishmael Reed, and Thomas Sanchez, whom he describes as "well-known much-acclaimed writers, and poets," who apparently wrote from minority traditions that had, in Chin's view, become recognized parts of U.S. national culture:

> I'm sure that everyone there had read Ralph Ellison's *The Invisible Man* and Richard Wright's *Black Boy*, and had heard of Martin Luther King, Jr., Langston Hughes, George Washington Carver, Leroi Jones, Eldridge Cleaver, and Thurgood Marshall. I'm sure everyone there had read something . . . at least a page . . . of a Vine Deloria work and Dee Brown's *Bury My Heart at Wounded Knee* and knew there was a lot about Indians they didn't know. I'm sure everyone there had read several works by Jews, like me . . . even not seeking Jewish works out I fall into a book by a Jew, even avoiding Saul Bellow and Philip Roth, who writes fine and I don't really avoid. I read *Call It Sleep* by another Jew and like it. Great book. (13)

Whereas Jewish, Native American, and, above all, African American writers can count on readers to possess at least some degree of knowledge of their cultural traditions and history, Asian American writers, according to Chin, face a greater burden. They must address a pervasive ignorance concerning their experiences before their concerns as *writers* can even be voiced:

> Before I could talk about our literature, I had to explain our sensibility. Before I could explain our sensibility I had to acquaint them with our history. Before I could acquaint them with our history I had to dispel the stereotypes they carried in their system like antibodies to the yellow truth. Before I could dispel the stereotype I had to convince them they held stereotypes about yellows. I didn't like working for free trying to do the impossible only to make a fool out of myself again. (14)

The dilemma that Chin depicts here is not so dissimilar from the one that current Asian Americanists—writers *and* critics—face as they too address wider audiences. Despite the emergence since 1976 of a wealth of literary works and critical studies that have attempted in various ways to dispel this cultural ignorance, the singular burden of representation that Chin describes is one that Asian American intellectuals still find themselves negotiating in their work.

The pressure to historicize that shapes nearly all Asian Americanist literary and cultural criticism is partly a response to this burden. Nearly all scholarly studies of Asian American literature thus begin by sketching out a specifically Asian American cultural history—a history that begins with the influx of Chinese immigrant labor in the nineteenth century, tracks the legislative and judicial exclusions that have impeded the access of various Asian groups to full U.S. citizenship, examines the impact of Asian immigrant labor, takes up the internment of Japanese Americans in World War II, explores the impact of various U.S. imperial endeavors in Asia on immigration patterns, and concludes with the increasingly heterogeneous and transnational quality of the Asian population in the United States in the wake of the immigration reforms of 1965. While the most influential recent critical studies—Lisa Lowe's *Immigrant Acts* is exemplary in this regard—have placed this history in the contexts of globalization and U.S. imperialism and have also insisted on the centrality of Asian Americans to the construction of U.S. national identity, the monochromatic focus of this work has mirrored that of most African Americanist scholarship. Critics have tended to argue for—either explicitly or implicitly—a kind of Asian American exceptionalism.

The implicit mantra of much Asian American scholarship is that it is necessary to think *outside* the monochromatic terms that box in U.S. understandings of race—terms that tend, it is true, toward the erasure of those liminal racialized groups that are not in any simple way reducible to the binary of black and white. To a significant degree, my project also insists on the specificity of the problematics and pressures that shape the literary articulation of Asian American identity. But what I intend this study to question is an assumption that cultural assertions of Asian American particularity must necessarily be attempts to transcend the constraints of the black/white binary. In fact, literary assertions of a distinctly Asian American sensibility such as Chin's do not necessarily seek to conjure forth a "yellow" space discretely separated from a black one and a white one. Indeed his account of an "authentic" Asian American cultural identity is defined by a rabid embrace of racial impurity—by an aggressively parasitic and putatively virile orientation toward cultural styles that "belong" to men of other races. What Chin ultimately prizes, as I will be arguing here, is a kind of vernacular subject that bears no small resemblance to the ones championed by Ellison, Baker, and Gates—that is a kind of bluesman in yellowface, as it were, whose aesthetic manhood will be indexed by his capacity to ape the styles of other men and make them his own.

Like the African American writers whose works I examined in the first part of this study, Chin perceives literature as the preeminent domain in which an "authentic" and wholly virile vision of minority identity can be projected. For Chin inherits from writers like Ellison an aesthetic ideology that conceives of writing not only as a racially redemptive cultural practice, but also as one that enables resistance to racism's most emasculating effects. The tradition he reworks as his own is structured by a gendered and sexualized symbolic vocabulary that identifies as racism's most pernicious threat the potential emasculation, feminization, and homosexualization of the man of color. It is a tradition that finds an antidote for the "perverse" forms of interracial homosocial desire that racism threatens to engender in the more salutary forms of desire that the literary domain demands. The aggressive modalities of reading and writing that this aesthetic ideology privileges enable the expression of forms of male homosocial desire that are agonistic, mimetic, and violent. What thus passes for manhood in the writings of Frank Chin, in other words, is a kind of vernacular subjectivity whose formal resemblances to the one prized by Ellison (as well as Baker and Gates) are stunning.

The emphasis Chin places on the vernacular, which echoes that of the African American literary theories I have been examining, is evident in the following passages:

> [The task of the minority writer is] to legitimate the language, style, and syntax of his people's experience, to codify the experiences common to his people into symbols, clichés, linguistic mannerisms, and a sense of humor that emerges from an organic familiarity with the experience.[1]
>
> John Okada [the Japanese American author of the 1957 novel *No-No Boy*] writes from an oral tradition he hears all the time, and talks his writing onto the page.[2]

Discernible here is the claim, one that should be familiar by now, that a defining feature of "authentic" Asian American literary texts is their use of the vernacular. This assertion indicates the ideological debt Chin owes to the various blueprints for black writing that I examined in the first half of this study. Like Ralph Ellison, he conceptualizes the minority writer's primary task to be one of mirroring and giving literary shape to the forms of cultural expression that are organic to working-class communities of color. The novelist John Okada's use of the vernacular is interpreted as bespeaking "an organic familiarity" with the Japanese American community he depicts; his intent is "to legitimate the language, style, and syntax of his people's experience." Chin also insists—as I will suggest later—that the literary posture necessary for the production of this vernacular mode of writing can only emerge through an agonistic struggle with other writers, a struggle that is conceived of in highly masculinist terms. The more historically proximate African American resource that frames Chin's elaborations of the Asian American literary "real" is the black nationalism of the late sixties and early seventies. Chin reiterates the assumption held by Black Arts writers that a properly revolutionary literature must use the language spoken by "the people." They advocate a kind of writing (to reformulate Harper's phrase) that is both "yellow" enough and "'virile' enough to bear the weight of a stridently nationalist agenda."[3]

A second claim also crops up persistently in Chin's writings on the aesthetic, however, a claim that would seem to undermine the first:

> Our condition is more delicate than that of the blacks because, unlike the blacks, we have neither an articulated, organic sense of our American identity nor the verbal confidence and self-esteem to talk one up from our experience. As a people, we are pre-verbal,—afraid of language as the instrument through which the monster takes possession of us. For us American-born, both the Asian languages and the English language are foreign. We are a people without a native tongue.[4]

For it is difficult to square his insistence that the writer should, following Okada's example, write "from an oral tradition he hears all the time" with his contention that "We are a people without a native tongue," that "we are pre-verbal." The very thing that would authenticate the literary tradition he seeks to identify—a distinct Asian American vernacular—is something that he also claims does not exist. Given this seemingly debilitating logical contradiction, the aesthetic Chin promotes seems to be a self-immolating one. It might be ventured that the apparent incoherence of Chin's aesthetic posture derives from his attempt to force a set of black nationalist arguments into a cultural context that is inappropriate to them. My intent in this chapter is, however, to demonstrate the internal coherence of the vernacular theory subtending Chin's cultural nationalist aesthetic. This coherence only becomes discernible, however, if we recognize that his conception of the vernacular ultimately has less to do with the idioms, grammar, and syntax of "'street' discourse" than it does with the expression of a particular *attitude* toward language use itself—an appropriative, violent, and disfiguring attitude that Chin imagines to be the signature feature of those authorial subjects who, like Chu and Okada, allegedly give literary shape to Asian American vernacular forms of linguistic expression.

The lucidity of Chin's vernacular theory, in other words, only becomes apparent when we recognize its *formal* resemblance to that of writers like Ellison, Baker, and Gates—an unmistakable family resemblance in the notion of *aesthetic* subjectivity that lies at the heart of the vernacular traditions these writers celebrate. For in its outlines the vernacular subject that Chin heroizes, as I will be arguing, is virtually identical to the blues and jazz subjects lionized by Ellison and Baker, and the signifying subject celebrated by Gates. The essential vernacular subject for all of these writers is a mimetic subject, whose appropriating, cannibalizing, and aping of other men's languages is depicted as the authentic expression of a black or yellow soul.

"The Chameleon Chinaman": Mimesis as the Absence of Manhood

In order to identify the parameters of the Asian American vernacular sensibility that Chin heroizes in his aesthetic writings, it is necessary to begin by examining the space that would seem to mark its absence. For Chin finds the raw materials for assembling a yellow "signifying" tradition in the very site in which they would seem to be most nonexistent—in the "actual" linguistic practices of "typical" Asian American subjects. In fleshing out his claim that Asian Americans have no "native tongue," he identifies a certain relationship to language as characteristic of that community. This linguistic orientation—which is essentially imitative—is what Asian Americans apparently possess in lieu of a vernacular.

Chin will often evoke the linguistic absence that plagues Asian Americans by contrasting it with the monumental presence in American culture of black and also Chicano vernaculars. "We have no street tongue to flaunt and strut," Chin laments, "the way the blacks and Chicanos do. They have a positive, self-defined linguistic identity that can be offended and wronged. We don't" ("Backtalk," 557). And in *Aiiieeeee!* Chin and his colleagues assert:

> Blacks and Chicanos often write in unconventional English. Their particular vernacular is recognized as being their own legitimate mother tongue. Only Asian Americans are driven out of their tongues and expected to be at home in a language they never use and a culture they encounter only in books written in English. (32)

The ramifications of this linguistic lack are, in Chin's terms—which are always gendered—quite dire. In "Racist Love" he writes:

> The deprivation of language in a verbal society like this, for the Chinese-American, has contributed to (1) the lack of a recognized Chinese American cultural integrity (at the most native-born Chinese-Americans are "Americanized Chinese") and (2) the lack of a recognized style of manhood.[5]

Why the existence of a "recognized style of manhood" is so tightly linked in Chin's writings to the existence of a vernacular has much to do with the influence of black nationalism. As Phillip Brian Harper and Robyn Wiegman have noted, the revolutionary subject this cultural movement attempted to inaugurate was imaged in both physical and discursive terms: it was housed in a hypersexual, physically powerful masculine body, and it spoke in the language of "the street." (We might also recall that Ellison, in his review of *Black Boy*, identified the power of Wright's blues-toned narrative as emanating from its proximity to the black male body, evoking the image of a "black boy singing lustily as he probed his own grievous wound.")

Since the image of Black Macho that subtended Black Arts projected both a linguistic and a corporeal style, Chin's lamentations over the absence of a comparable image of Yellow Macho locate this lack in both of these domains: language and the body. In his essay "Confessions of the Chinatown Cowboy," Chin states this association quite crudely: "deep down in the cultural subconscious, there's a link between tongue and balls that makes us sick."[6] If Asian Americans are perceived as lacking "their own legitimate mother tongue," Chin suggests, Asian American *men* will be perceived as lacking "a recognized style of manhood." The male body becomes in Chin's writings, then, a terrain of signification in and of itself, an expressive medium interpretable through the same racial and gendered protocols as spoken language. It is worth recalling in this context Chin's cataloguing in

"Racist Love" of the various stereotypes that accrue to different races. The abundance of cultural images that ascribe a threatening heterosexuality to blacks and Mexicans—the "hostile black stud" and Santa Ana, for instance— calls attention to the way in which the "homosexual" Fu-Manchu fails to conjure a comparable sense of peril. Within the symbolic economy Chin describes, each of these threatening male stereotypes corresponds with a recognized style of racialized manhood. Unable to embody a manhood comparable to that conferred by the stereotype of the "hostile black stud" and having "no street tongue to flaunt and strut the way the blacks and Chicanos do," Asian American men would appear to occupy an impossible position.

Bearing in mind that Chin's polemics seek to "de-euphemize" the "self-contempt" in which Asian Americans are unknowingly steeped, we can see that his aim here is to instill in his yellow male readers a horrified recognition of the impoverished state of their linguistic and masculine identities— to engender in them the intensified sense of self-loathing that is the primary psychic state his literary works depict. As I argued in the previous chapter, the masochism that characterizes his most effective fictional and dramatic works is in fact a key component of the racialized masculinity he privileges. The melancholia that structures a piece like *The Chickencoop Chinaman*, therefore, is also very much operant in Chin's aesthetic essays. His polemics seek to engender a melancholic longing for the vernacular—to make his yellow readers mourn the loss of a "street tongue" and of "a recognized style of manhood" that has (he also tells them) never existed.

When Chin adopts a more explicitly autobiographical stance in his essays, as he does in the aptly titled "Confessions of the Chinatown Cowboy," he reveals how intimately his own psyche has been shaped by the rather mournful predicament he describes. In the following passage, he recounts an anecdote about growing up in Oakland, California, that recalls one of Kenji's speeches in *The Chickencoop Chinaman*:

> "Why can't you boys, you Negroes and Mexicans," the visiting cop said, all creases, jingling metals and hair on his knuckles, setting every Chinaman boy of us up for an afternoon of fights, "stay out of trouble like the Chinese? Mind your folks? Study hard? Obey the laws?" And there we Chinamen were, in Lincoln Elementary School, Oakland California, in a world where manliness counts for everything, surrounded by bad blacks and bad Mexican kids who were still into writing their names into their skin with nails dipped in ink. They had a walk, a way of wearing their pants on the

brink of disaster, a tongue, a kingdom of manly style everyone respected. Everyone knew what they called you because you had to, to survive in the yard. There we were. There I was, hair held up high and back with Tuxedo wax, edges of hair by my ears turned down and shaped into fake sideburns and spitcurls, toothpick in my mouth, pants low, belt buckle on my hip, and black and white basketball shoes, suddenly stripped and shaved bare by this cop, exposed for copping another man's flash, imitating this from the blacks, that from the Mexicans, something from whites, with no manly style of my own unless it was Charlie Chan swish Fu Manchu. (89–90)

In the multiracial culture he describes, in which none of the acknowledged models of racialized masculinity are yellow, the only way for an Asian American male to pass as masculine is to engage in a kind of interracial performative mimesis. Yellow manhood is presented here as a signifying practice—as something one communicates through the repetition of stylized bodily gestures that belong, properly speaking, to men of other races. Chin suggests the assimilability of these markers of racialized masculinity in his physical self-description: "hair held up high and back with Tuxedo wax, edges of hair by my ears turned down and shaped into fake sideburns and spitcurls, toothpick in my mouth, pants low, belt buckle on my hip, and black and white basketball shoes." But while he thus brings into view the performativity—the iterability—of the masculinity he had attempted to copy as a boy, his anecdote is intended not to expose the tenuousness of racialized constructions of gender; his point, rather, is to underscore how a gendering binary works to affirm the difference between those races that signify a "troubl[ing]" and thus "authentic" racialized manhood and those that do not.

The policeman's hail, as Chin recounts it, forced him to experience the racial difference between his body and those of the other boys as comparable to a sexual one. The cop addresses the "Negroes and Mexicans" in such a way that imposes a binary distinction between those racial groups and "the Chinese." To possess a male body marked as Chinese is, in the eyes of the law, to stay out of trouble, mind one's folks, study hard, and obey the laws. To possess a brown or black one is to do the opposite. It is also to be the only legitimate subjects of the "kingdom of manly style" that reigns in the schoolyard. The masculinity that the black and brown boys effortlessly perform, as it turns out, does not function as a modal, free-floating repertoire of gender codes that anyone can freely appropriate and copy. Rather, it is the special province of those boys who "writ[e] their names into their skin"—whose black and brown skins already spell trouble. Chin's sense of being "suddenly stripped and shaved bare by this cop" mirrors the horror and recognition experienced by the little girl in the stock Freudian narrative who discovers her "castrated" state; like her, the boyhood Chin confronts the radical alterity of his body at the very moment he also realizes its embodiment of lack. The masculinity the other boys have written into their skins is one that Chin can only imitate. When he is exposed as a copy by the cop, his manhood suddenly seems as fake as the sideburns he has sculpted out of hair too straight to be black. He is not only apprehended for his acts of racial theft but also identified as a repeat offender: "for copping another man's flash, imitating this from the blacks, that from the Mexicans, something from whites." The boyhood Chin learns that to be seen as a little imitation man is to be seen as no man at all.

The significance of this anecdote is not simply the centrality of *lack* to Chin's depiction of the degraded state to which Asian American masculinity has been reduced; it is, moreover, the way in which that lack is linked with a kind of defective or failed *mimesis*—with a certain impoverished modality of assimilation. What Asian American subjects possess in lieu of a linguistic and corporeal style of their own is this feeble propensity for imitation. Elsewhere in "Confessions," Chin generalizes from the pattern he identifies in his boyhood self to assert that "the most typical Chinaman born in the most typical Chinatown" is "the chameleon Chinaman" (78). He cites as an example of this "chameleon Chinaman" a friend from childhood who now runs a grocery store in Chinatown: "My friend, born here, the American dream come true, a little business, last year's Pontiac, talks that fine English, sounds like Chicago on the phone, no pigtail and the walk, part Okie sashay, part black strut . . ." (78). This "copping [of] another man's flash" is symptomatic of a mimetic hunger that structures the psyche of all subjects who grow up yellow in a black and white world. To grow up in Chinatown, according to Chin, is to be

> Hungry, all the time hungry, every sense was out whiffing for something rightly ours, chameleons looking for color, trying on tongues and clothes and hairdos, taking everyone else's, with none of our own, and no habitat, our manhood just never came home. Hunger and copycat. (68–69)

In "Backtalk," Chin suggests that "Hunger and copycat" not only describes the corporeal and linguistic vernacular of Chinatown, it is also indicative of a more pervasive Asian American cultural style:

The tongue-tying notion that everything out of your mouth is mimickry [sic] and ventriloquism has been built into our psychology in our seven generations here. And if our basic means of expression is mimickry and ventriloquism, then our art and culture is mimickry and ventriloquism too. Such is our self-contempt. (557)

This mimetic disposition is something that Chin depicts as having been installed in nearly all Asian American subjects by white racism. It is a psychic effect produced by the experience of always being perceived as a "handicapped native," who is

> neither black nor white in a black and white world. In his native American culture he has no recognized style of manhood, in a culture where a manly style is a prerequisite to respectability and notice. [. . .] In his use of language, voice inflection, accent, walk, manner of dress, and combing his hair, the handicapped native steeps himself in self-contempt for being "quick to learn . . . and imitative." At worst, he's a counterfeit begging currency. At best he's an "Americanized Chinese," someone who's been given a treatment to make him less foreign. ("Racist Love," 72; ellipses in brackets are mine)

Chin's tendency to deploy a homophobic symbolism to emphasize the perversity of the nonmasculine condition to which Asian American subjects have been reduced emerges in a particular figure that he uses at times to symbolize this predicament. As Chin fleshes out the "mimickry and ventriloquism" that defines Asian American expression, art, and culture, he gives to this linguistic disposition a a homuncular specificity, a virtual (corpo)reality:

> We don't read, we memorize. *Like ventriloquists' dummies*, we are the tools of other men's languages. Strange words organize our experience and make us the realities, the embodiments, of words we don't understand. Language should be a tool for organizing experience and reality, not vice-versa. ("Backtalk," 557; my emphasis)

> Without a language of his own, [the Asian American] no longer is a man but *a ventriloquist's dummy* at worst and at best a parrot. ("Racist Love," 77; my emphasis)

To be seen as a subject who only imitates speech is to be associated with a particular kind of "body"—one whose resemblance to a "queer" body can be readily seen. For let us consider what a ventriloquist's dummy looks like. We might imagine an artificially constructed man-like thing that appears to speak but whose words are actually spoken by a "real" man, a man whose body the dummy's has been fabricated to resemble and upon whose lap he sits. And when we watch this little imitation man and listen to his imitation speech, we know that the tongue within his mouth, metaphorically speaking, is not his own.

"The Chameleon Chinaman," Part II: Masculine Mimesis

The liberatory potential of literature as Chin depicts it does not derive from its being located in a domain that is somehow free from the interracial mimetic desire that racism instills in Asian American subjects. Rather, the promise of redemption that he locates in the aesthetic stems from its potential to catalyze a different way of perceiving, depicting, and experiencing that mimetic desire. The literary affords an epistemological standpoint from which the "hunger" driving the "chameleon Chinaman" can be imagined as the expression of an aggressive, violent, and wholly virile agency. Literature—or at least those specific texts that he and the other *Aiiieeeee!* editors attempt to canonize—provides such a "corrective" view of Asian American language use:

> Asian American writers—John Okada, Louis Chu, Lawson Inada, Toshio Mori, Hisaye Yamamoto . . . forty years of writing have taken the schizophrenic yakity yak we talk and made it a backtalking, muscular, singing stomping full blooded language loaded with nothing but our truth. No college course in American lit acknowledges them. Whites prefer to call us nuts, and ask us to put up the proof of a uniquely non-Asian, non-white Asian American sensibility, as if there's none.
> There's plenty. ("Backtalk," 557; ellipses are Chin's)

Chin implies here that it is the translation of "the schizophrenic yakity yak we talk" into a written form that resignifies it as "a backtalking, muscular, singing stomping full blooded language loaded with nothing but our truth." The key to this transformation lies, however, in the adoption of a certain interpretive framework—of a specifically *literary* hermeneutic. In the readings that Chin provides of the writers he heroizes, he models an interpretive mode that rewrites ventriloquism and mimicry as the expression of aesthetic intent. The authors he champions are distinguished not simply by their use of the vernacular but by a certain aesthetic mastery that has less to do with, say, originality than it does with a certain Bakhtinian way of shaping and amalgamating pre-existing discourses and languages—with a certain command over the various *mimetic* aspects of literary representation.

Louis Chu's 1961 novel *Eat a Bowl of Tea*, for example, is valorized by Chin for its faithful depiction of the spoken language used by Chinese immigrants: "The manner and ritual of address and repartee is authentic Chinatown. Chu translates idioms from the Sze Yup dialect, and the effect of such expressions on his Chinese American readers is delight and recognition" (*Aiiieeeee!*, 16). In his appraisal of John Okada's 1957 novel, *No-No Boy*, Chin makes a similar claim:

> The book makes a narrative style of the Japanese American talk, gives the talk the status of a language, makes it work and styles it, deftly and crudely, and uses it to bring the unglamorous but more commonly lived aspects of Japanese American experience into the celebration of life. The style and structure of the book alone suggest the Japanese American way of life of a specific period in history. (*Aiiieeeee!*, 26)

The characters that Okada depicts in *No-No Boy* are primarily second-generation Japanese Americans—*Nisei*—who speak an American English that is exceedingly colloquial, relentlessly slangy. It is a vernacular, in other words, that does not seem explicitly marked by any particular ethnic content. This much is apparent from a brief passage from *No-No Boy* that Chin cites directly in *Aiiieeeee!* in order to validate his claim that "John Okada writes from an oral tradition he hears all the time, and talks his writing onto the page" (25). The quote in discussion is as follows: "a bunch of Negroes were horsing around raucously in front of a pool parlor" (qtd. in *Aiiieeeee!*, 25). Chin's gloss of Okada's prose runs as follows:

> Okada changes voices and characters inside his sentences, running off free but shaping all the time. . . . There is a quick-change act here among "horsing around" and "raucously" and "pool parlor." The style itself is an expression of the multivoiced schizophrenia of the Japanese American *compressed* into an organic whole. It's crazy, but it's not madness. (25; my emphasis)

The shifts in "voice" and "character" that Chin claims to see in Okada's sentences apparently express "the multivoiced schizophrenia of the Japanese American." But Okada doesn't merely ventriloquize the amalgam of lan-

guages that Asian Americans speak—"the schizophrenic yakity yak we talk";
he actively "compresse(s)" it "into an organic whole."

While passages like these seem to be making ontological claims about the
existence of an Asian American vernacular, they are in fact establishing an
epistemic standpoint from which "the Chameleon Chinaman" can be seen—
or, rather, heard—as *actively and aesthetically* shaping, compressing, and,
indeed, disfiguring the languages he "imitates." Chin attempts to ascribe to
writers like Chu and Okada the kind of aesthetic agency that traditional literary protocols accord to "great" novelists. Instead of regarding Okada as a
ventriloquist's dummy, we are to see him as "writ[ing] strong in a language
that comes from home . . . from an oral tradition he hears all the time, and
talk[ing] his writing onto the page" (25). This assertion—that Okada is able
to orchestrate so masterfully the multiplicity of voices he hears in the culture
around him because he is a great writer and that is what great writers do—is
no less tautological than the one subtending Bakhtin's description of the discursive control exerted by novelists: "The prose artist elevates the social heteroglossia surrounding objects into an image that has finished contours, an
image completely shot through with dialogized overtones; he creates artisti-
cally calculated nuances on all the fundamental voices and tones of this heteroglossia."[7] The "sound" that Chin exhorts his readers to hear in the prose
of Chu or Okada echoes that which is potentially audible in *Invisible Man*,
the novel that Houston Baker, Jr., terms a "Blues Book Most Excellent."
What Chin asks his readers to do as he guides them through a prose that
appears unmarked by any dint of ethnicity is to *listen* for the sound of a certain masterful, literary intent. The emphasis that he places on the aural and
oral dimension of this writing confirms the rhetorical power gained by
asserting a given text's vernacular credentials: for the sound of the vernacular is, at bottom, the sound of a particular aesthetic agency, one that is imagined as racially authentic and that is propelled by a certain aggression.

The "deformation of mastery," "the phaneric display," the semiotic
guerilla/gorilla warfare that Baker claims to detect in the works of the Harlem
Renaissance is, in a sense, the expression of a racial antipathy toward white
America that has taken linguistic form: the resentment or anger that being
subjected to white racism has produced in the subjects of color can be seen as
finding aesthetic expression through the mastery and deformation of "white"
linguistic and literary forms.[8] Chin discerns a similarly racially aggressive
agency in works like *Eat a Bowl of Tea* and *No-No Boy*. "Chu's portrayal of

Chinatown," he writes, "is an irritating one for white audiences"; it "holds the white reader at a distance" because it is free of the exoticism that such readers have come to expect from literary works set in that locale (*Aiiieeeee!*, 16). That Chu's intention is to thus "irritat[e]" and "distance" white readers is also presumably evident in the language his characters speak, which "is offendingly neither English nor the idealized conception that whites have of a 'Chinaman's tongue'" (16). This hostility toward a white reading public is apparently discernible in Okada's prose as well: the rapid-fire shifts in diction, "the voice changes" that typify his writing are apparently intended to "grate against the white tradition of tonal uniformity and character consistency" (25).

When Chin discusses in more detail the kind of writing that white readers might find "irritating" or "distanc[ing]," he does identify certain linguistic tendencies with which Asian Americans have tended to be associated: bad grammar, indecipherable accents, broken English. The propensity of white readers to interpret stylistic idiosyncrasies on the part of individual Asian American writers as evidence of a less-than-thorough command of English is exemplified for Chin by William Saroyan. Saroyan wrote an introductory essay to Toshio Mori's *Yokohama, California* (1949)—a collection of loosely connected short stories modeled on Sherwood Anderson's *Winesburg, Ohio*—in which praise is intermingled with condescension:

> Of the thousands of unpublished writers in America there are probably no more than three who cannot write better English than Toshio Mori. His stories are full of grammatical errors. His use of English, especially when he is most eager to say something very good, is very bad. Any high school teacher of English would flunk him in grammar and punctuation. (qtd. in *Aiiieeeee!*, 23)

Okada's *No-No Boy*, according to Chin, was ignored by critics and reviewers because they were likewise "embarrassed by Okada's use of language and punctuation" (23).

Chin's intent in these polemics is to draw out the racial condescension that frames how white Americans view Asian American language use in general and how they thus perceive the literature produced by Asian American writers in particular. Any deviation from standard English on the part of Asian American subjects, even among those born and raised in the United States, tends to be perceived as the atavistic eruption of an inassimilable Asianness. Chang-rae Lee's novel *Native Speaker* is also concerned with this predicament. In the following passage, Lee's narrator describes the anxieties that shape how he perceives the English that he and his interlocutor, another Korean American man, both speak:

> We joked a little more, I thought like regular American men, faking, dipping, juking. I found myself listening to us. For despite how well he spoke, how perfectly he moved through the sounds of his words, I kept listening for the errant tone, the flag, the minor mistake that would tell of his original race. . . . When I was young, I'd look in the mirror and address it, as if daring the boy there; I would say something dead and normal, like, "pleased to make your acquaintance," and I could barely convince myself that it was I who was talking.[9]

The anxiety that Lee describes is the linguistic effect of being perpetually perceived as a native speaker in training—or, in Chin's terms, as a "handicapped native," as an American subject whose nativity will always be perceived as a kind of masquerade. The ramifications of this for the writer of fiction are clear enough: any deviation from standard usage will likely be discerned not as the expression of literary creativity but as "the errant tone, the flag, the minor mistake that would tell of his original race." Chin's advocacy is intended to make his readers grant Asian American writers the same kind of creative license as white and black writers—to make them regard the "broken English" spoken by Asian Americans as valid forms of cultural expression rather than evidence of a perpetual foreignness or of an innate linguistic inferiority. He seeks to raise the possibility that Asian Americans as "a new folk in a strange land" might in fact "develop new language out of old words" (*Aiiieeeee!*, 22). To see the prose of a Toshio Mori, a Louis Chu, or a John Okada not as "broken English," but rather as the expression of a creative impulse to *break* English and make it anew, will result, Chin hopes, in an altered view of Asian American language use more generally. If a logic, an order, an intentionality and agency can be seen as shaping these literary representations, then Asian Americans might come to perceive the English they speak not as mangled but as a "new language" that has been "developed . . . out of old words."

But as they ever are in Chin's writings, the illuminating elements of his polemics are encased in a rhetoric that is highly problematic. What is troubling about Chin's assertions becomes apparent in the gendered terms through which he defines the linguistic sensibility he wishes to celebrate as "ours." At times, he resorts to a virulent misogyny in order to evoke the aggression he wants his readers to hear in the language he celebrates. In "Confessions of a Chinatown Cowboy," for instance, Chin models the altered view of Asian American signifying practices he wishes to promote by describing the language of Mr. Mah, a Chinese language teacher he knew growing up, as a "real Chinatown buck buck bagaw, an angry quick-tripping tongue promiscuously raping all the languages we knew, raping them of sense."[10] The essay "Racist Love" closes with a diatribe directed against an unnamed white female editor. This editor had apparently written to Jeffery Paul Chan, asking him to make a couple of grammatical corrections to his short story "Auntie Tsia Lays Dying," which was to be published in an anthology entitled *Asian-American Authors* (1972).[11] Her request, which is cited directly in the text, reads as follows:

> We are . . . distressed about using the word *lays* instead of *lies* in the title of your story and in a sentence near the end of the story. You see, if teachers or students using the book come upon a word usage that they think is incorrect, they write to the author or to us asking what dictionary or other source authorizes it. (qtd. in "Racist Love," 79)

Chin and Chan's response:

> Great white bitch goddess priestess of the sacred white mouth and dumb broad ventriloquist whose lips don't move fine and doesn't know us China-mans mean to reverse the charges with our writing. The object of our writing is no different from that of any other writer. We mean to inject our sensibility into the culture and make it work there. That means we are the teachers. People should ask what dictionary or other sources authorize what we say, how we talk. That's a part of learning how to read. She is illiterate, so self-righteously illiterate, I'm going to write about her. (79)

Even when it not expressed in such openly misogynistic terms, the masculinist quality of the vernacular sensibility Chin champions is quite apparent. The "backtalking, muscular, singing stomping full blooded language loaded with nothing but our truth" is a vernacular that is animated by a highly masculine aggression.

In an essay entitled "Afterward," Chin offers some glimpses into how his own training as a writer—even when it came from racially condescending white male teachers—helped shape his sense of the destructive impulses that animate the process of writing. Apparently referring to his experiences at the Iowa Writers' Workshop, Chin recounts how his teachers—Thomas Gunn, Philip Roth, Jackson Burgess, and Marvin Mudrick—responded to his creative efforts with both praise and condescension. During his time there, Chin realized that "the English I was writing as mine wasn't English to anybody else in the English business."[12] Indeed, he was sometimes treated as a non-native speaker, struggling with an English language that was not his own: "Years ago when Thom Gunn looked up from what I thought were the best poems ever written and asked me if I had trouble with the language, I blanked out, gave up poetry and laughed at the memory" (15). But apparently not all of the responses he received from these teachers troubled Chin: "I didn't worry about being misunderstood, cuz everyone seemed to be able to read me without losing their mind or my sense" (16). Indeed, Roth and Mudrick *were* apparently encouraging to him, though in a somewhat odd way. They were willing to see in his writing a creatively destructive agency even if they were unsure whether his English was really English: "Philip Roth said he liked my novel but wondered if I had to destroy the English language to write it"; "Marvin Mudrick told me I'd invented a new language for a new experience" (15–16).

These exchanges occurred before he met the Asian American writers with whom he would edit the *Aiiieeeee!* anthology and before they "discovered" together the works of Louis Chu, John Okada, and others—a time when "the only references I had were my instincts, and common sense that refused to believe stereotypes and racist renditions of my people that were never remotely confirmed by anything my people did" (16). But even then, Chin insists, he possessed a firm conviction that to develop his identity as a writer (to devote himself to the "stern discipline" of literature, as Ellison might put it) he would have to engage in agonistic struggle with those figures—apparently all male—who possessed a literary power he wished to supersede: "My models were men whose voice and language had a commanding presence and set me off to cap them or make something I sensed just out of their word power" (16).

But after discovering the language in which Chu and Okada wrote, Chin found that

> I wasn't likening myself to everybody I was reading about. Everybody I was reading about was likening themselves to me. I read Chu and Okada with an arrogance, and authority that was emotional, inarguable and prejudiced

toward white notions of quality writing. I discovered the destroyed English language I wrote naturally, Philip Roth had mentioned, a new language for new experience Marvin Mudrick and Jack Burgess see as my invention, in the books by dead men. There were depths and resonances and significant quick touches and flicks of words taking me into recognition effects so rhythmic and total, I knew their writing had me as no other ever had. (16)

We should recognize here a significant difference between Chin's account of his literary motivations and Ellison's. While Ellison seeks to write himself out of the shadow of certain literary "ancestors" that might be perceived as rivals—Richard Wright, most prominently—Chin welcomes his "discovery" of a comparable set of Oedipal figures. Chin relishes the opportunity to conjure forth the kind of rivals Ellison goes to great lengths to pretend he never had. He evokes a primal horde of literary ancestors that would enable him to present his own writings as emerging out of the depths of a tradition.

The literary "fathers" that Chin constructs out of figures like Chu and Okada play the same competitive role as the one Ellison denies to Wright: to provide the "son" with models to emulate and exceed. Like the white writers who were Chin's initial exemplars, Chu and Okada are "men whose voice and language had a commanding presence and set me off to cap them or make something I sensed just out of their word power." Hence his reverence for these earlier authors takes the form of "an arrogance, and authority." The "depths and resonances," the "recognition effects so rhythmic and total" that Chin experiences while reading "the destroyed English language" in which these writers write, does not leave him abject before his predecessors; although he "knew their writing had me as no other ever had," he has the sensation that "[e]verybody I was reading about was likening themselves to me." What he wants most from these paternal figures—what he claims to get from them—are powerful rivals, ideals of yellow literary power against which he can measure his own.

East Meets Western: The Swordslinger and the Martial Artist

The formal similarities between the vernacular subject that Chin heroizes in his aesthetic writings and the ones codified by Ellison, Baker, and Gates should now be quite apparent. The style or sensibility that all of these writers celebrate as racially authentic is one that manifests itself through an appropriation of linguistic materials taken from other racial sources. The agonism upon which it is predicated, moreover, takes the same kind of virilizing shape as that which propels "the strong poet," in Harold Bloom's formulation, to develop his own vision as he absorbs and reshapes the vision of the writers he has been influenced by. Chin's aesthetic theory also shares with Ellison's a claim that *literary* manifestations of the vernacular draw from, reproduce, and refine a popular set of cultural practices that are identified with a particular "folk" community that is demarcated in spatial and class terms. In an earlier chapter, I traced the persistence of these concerns in Ellison's various and successive codifications of the black constituency he claimed to speak for in his writing: in his Marxian phase, he (along with Wright) celebrated the folk forms of the working-class population that became urbanized during the Great Migration; after Wright's death (and as he became intent on separating himself from his former mentor's legacy) Ellison began to focus on the working-class black community of the American Southwest, with the jazz and Renaissance man ideals that were characteristic of *his* "people." It is this evocation of everyday cultural practices such as the blues, the jazz dance, the dozens, and so forth—practices that are claimed as the inspiration and model for his own literary project—that Ellison uses to establish his own credentials as an authentic literary spokesman for the "ordinary" American Negro. They comprise the populist veneer that works to deflect any charges of elitism that may be directed at him.

Chin also evokes a set of folk culture practices as providing the model for his own aesthetic endeavors. In contradistinction to Ellison—and somewhat surprisingly, given the profound disdain with which he generally treats the mass media—the cultural practices he celebrates involve the passionate devouring of popular culture. Indeed, the vernacular for Chin—as befitting the postmodern moment in which he writes—involves an extravagantly parasitic relationship to a racist popular culture. The parasitic relationship between the Asian American "real" and the "fake" images promoted by the mass media is suggested by the title that he and his colleagues assigned to their groundbreaking anthology, *Aiiieeeee!*. This title refers to the voices of those Asian Americans

> who got their China and Japan from the radio, off the silver screen, from
> television, out of comic books, from the pushers of white American culture

that pictured the yellow man as something that when wounded, sad, or angry, or swearing, or wondering whined, shouted, or screamed "aiiieeeee!" (xi–xii)

In lower case, "aiiieeeee!" signifies the voice ascribed to Asian Americans by the stereotypes promoted by a racist culture industry. In upper case, AIIIEEEEE! apparently signifies something else:

> Asian America, so long ignored and forcibly excluded from creative participation in American culture, is wounded, sad, angry, swearing, and wondering, and this is his AIIIEEEEE!!! It is more than a whine, shout, or scream. It is fifty years of our whole voice. (xii)

The scream that this anthology is imagined as voicing—"AIIIEEEEE!!!"—is a near replica, with one crucial exception, of the scream it is supposed to drown out, the "aiiieeeee!" uttered by the yellow man as depicted by the "pushers of white American culture." The only way to read the difference between "aiiieeeee!" and "AIIIEEEEE!!!" is via the hermeneutic mode codified by Gates and Baker, as a kind of "repetition with a difference" or an act of semiotic "guerilla/gorilla warfare." The "authentic" Asian American subject that this inaugural collection attempts to bring into being takes shape not through an utter negation of the stereotype, but through a willful aping of it. This appropriation will be animated by an aesthetic intent shot through with aggression.

In "Confessions of a Chinatown Cowboy" (the title of which also attests to the parasitic relationship to mainstream culture that he consistently maintains) Chin finds a precedent for the adversarial yet appropriative relation to popular cultural forms to which *Aiiieeeee!* gives expression in the decoding practices that he and other Chinatown boys engaged in as they greedily devoured films:

> Like the languages the Chinese brought over 120 years ago that developed into an instrument of a Chinese-American intelligence, making sense of a mess of weirdness and happenings that didn't happen in China, and the kung fu that became high class dirty street fighting, the Chinese movies that I grew up with, that grew me up to figure in the myths of a teacher, a quest, a gang and bloody death, were only academically Chinese. As parts of my life, and the lives of maybe 200,000 like me, second, third, fourth, fifth, sixth, seventh generation, born here, bred here, home here, the

Chinese movies are not foreign entertainments, nor is the meaning we take from them particularly Chinese. (94)

The fact that these films were Chinese seems initially a crucial issue here. But Chin insists that to him and his peers these films "were only academically Chinese," that they were "not foreign entertainments, nor [was] the meaning we [took] from them particularly Chinese."

Chin seems to contradict himself, however, in the very next few sentences when he underscores a crucial difference in the heroic masculinity that these Chinese films endorse and the one popularized in Hollywood films:

> The most popular Chinese movie is the swordslinger, a form comparable to the American western that serves the same popular function of articulating the culture's fantasy of ballsy individuality. The a-man-has-got-to-do-what-a-man-has-got-to-do ethic of gunslinger balls that says the individual rides alone, fights alone and duels man-to-man, is exercised only by fools and the bad guy in Chinese movies. The bad guy, a man invincible in individual combat, goes down under the gang swords of a hero, who's stepped out into life to learn that the lessons of the master's school were right, that a man invincible in individual combat will go down in gang action, that the individual needs friends. (94)

This passage asserts a discrete distinction between the more communal sense of male heroism operant in the Chinese "swordslinger" and the more individualistic one sanctioned by the American Western. This claim would seem, then, to contrast a Chinese heroic ideal to a white American one. It also appears to identify a specifically Chinese meaning that is *encoded* in the swordslinger, which shifts the emphasis away from Chinese American *decoding* practices. But Chin then turns to a number of American films that also heroize a more collectively oriented masculine ideal:

> The balls that the Chinese movie celebrated in Chinatown was gang balls and didn't really clash with John Wayne, who was an extension of the master in *Red River* and *Flying Tigers* and fit right in with street gangs. When Frankenheimer's *The Young Savages* hit the streets, Chinatown had been ready a long time with gangs. His movie just gave us names for our gangs. We discovered names. Names were big. From the dap-down-inspired badass Puerto Rican gang in *The Young Savages*, one Chinatown gang took the name of the Horseman, and was home! That was a good movie. Most were and are fatal doses of white supremacy. (94–95)

Despite its apparent logical inconsistencies, Chin's account of the viewing practices he and his boyhood friends engaged in asserts that they were able to engage in rather selective and empowering acts of identification, which could occur both intra- and interracially. What they somehow were able to make coherent was a specifically *Chinese American* ideal of masculinity that was figured in "myths of a teacher, a quest, a gang and bloody death," that was predicated on the possession of "gang balls" rather than on "a-man-has-got-to-do-what-a-man-has-got-to-do ethic of gunslinger balls." It is, then, a virilizing capacity for mimesis that comprises the very heart of the Chinese American masculine ideal that Chin was drawn to as a boy; as such, it comprises the populist counterpart of the *literary* sensibility he champions, one that is driven by a competitive desire to "cap" those men who function as one's teachers, one's literary "fathers"—those men who constitute both one's rivals and one's "gang."

Chin's remembrances about growing up in Oakland's Chinatown are reminiscent of Ellison's account of his boyhood in Oklahoma City. The mimetic hunger that Chin and his peers were able to satisfy through their devouring of popular culture has its counterpart in Ellison's reminiscences about "the voracious reading of which most of us were guilty and the vicarious identification and empathetic adventuring which it encouraged."[13] The ideal of Renaissance man worked to set the black boys of Oklahoma City on a quest for "examples, patterns to live by," and so they created "[f]ather and mother substitutes," "fabricated [their] own heroes and ideals catch-as-catch can, and with an outrageous sense of freedom."[14] What made those borrowings expressive of this distinctly Negro American sensibility, Ellison insisted, was the "reckless verve" that glowed through each appropriation;[15] the sense that behind these boyhood acts stood "a traditional sense of style" that was shared by bluesmen, jazzmen, and certain novelists—"a yearning to make any- and everything of quality *Negro American*; to appropriate it, possess it, re-create it in our own group and individual images."[16]

Ellison was quite comfortable asserting the basic similarities between this distinctly Negro American style of appropriation and a more broadly American one, since he explicitly believed the two traditions were interwoven. Chin's initial formulation of the imitative style he claimed was expressive of authentic Chinese American manhood also had a nativist emphasis: the "Chinaman sensibility" he celebrates is emphatically Chinese *American*; it is only "academically Chinese." As some critics of Chin have remarked, however, a certain "turn" is apparent in his polemics that dates roughly from the late eighties—a shift in rhetoric that may have been prompted by his anger at the "falsified" view of Chinese culture that he saw writers like Maxine Hong Kingston and Amy Tan promoting in their popular and well-received works.[17] There seems to be lessening emphasis on the nativist—which is to say, U.S.-centered—focus of his earlier polemics and an increasing attention to what might be termed a diasporic Chinese or even global-Asian sensibility. The canonical articulation of Chin's revised account of an *Asian*—as opposed to Asian American—authentic tradition is contained in the prefatory essays that were included in a sequel to the first anthology, *The Big Aiiieeeee!*, which was published in 1991. Much as Henry Louis Gates, Jr., offered in his work a diasporic genealogy for the African American cultural practice of signifying—finding precursors to the figure of the signifying monkey in various African and Carribean cultures—Chin identifies in his later polemics an "authentic" Asian heroic tradition; the Asian American writers he validates as authentic allegedly draw from this tradition.

The texts that comprise the origin of all "authentic" Asian *and* Asian American literature are a set of Chinese classic texts: *The Art of War, Water Margin, Romance of the Three Kingdoms, Journey to the West,* and *Chushingura.* Their plots, by and large, feature the same elements as the sword-slingers he described in "Confessions of the Chinatown Cowboy": "myths of a teacher, a quest, a gang and bloody death." In a 1988 interview with Robert Murray Davis, Chin insists that this heroic tradition is a populist one: "This is not high culture. This is real low down comic book, cookie tin, calendar art kind of culture."[18] In describing the highly conventionalized form that characterizes the popular form of Cantonese opera, Chin places emphasis on its orality:

> Chinese opera, Cantonese opera is like that [oral]. A Cantonese opera
> would open with someone coming out and making a general statement,
> a rephrasing of the mandate that kingdoms rise and fall, nations come
> and go, and this play that we are going to see is at a point in history where
> everything is falling apart and fucked up and we are going to see what hap-
> pens. Each character would come out and introduce himself, depending on
> the stature of the character, with a couplet, a quatrain, or pages of couplets
> and quatrains. Giving their history, setting their voices. And the form of
> the classic novels of the heroic tradition, every Asian kid has known for a
> thousand years, is oral. (92)

Chin concludes from these conventions, moreover, that

> The form is Saturday matinee serials. All action. Nouns and verbs. Our hero boom boom boom to the brink of doom and whoops! Live or Die? You wanta know, friend? To find out, read on . . . modeled on professional storyteller's chat notes. The exact telling of the story depended on the storyteller's sense of money and rapport with the audience. (92)

This orality, then, this emphasis on action, and therefore this proximity to the formulas of "Saturday matinee serials"—all of these are elements that Chin has attempted to incorporate into his own works:

> In *Three Kingdoms, Water Margin,* and *Monkey,* the novels and the operas there is always an exuberance in the language and the style I tried to transfer to my work. I write to be heard. So, if you read my stuff silently and your lips are moving, that's good. It helps if you sit in front of your TV set tuned to a Western. (92–93)

By aligning his own work with this Chinese folkloric tradition, one that is wholly compatible with the staple forms of American popular culture, Chin characterizes his own writings as populist, however avant-garde or experimental—however elitist—they might seem. His is a writing that attempts to speak to those readers who—like him—have learned a particular mode of reading through an immersion in these Chinese classics and also in U.S. mass media.

At another point in this interview, Chin explicitly defines his ideal audience—the only one that wholly understands what he is trying to do—as immigrants:

> Immigrants who know *Three Kingdoms* and *The Water Margin* have enjoyed my work. There are bilingual puns and little plays on the heroic tradition to let them know exactly what my characters are stupid about. So my ideal audience would be composed either of immigrants fluent in American English and history or, as I would prefer, American born who were knowledgeable about the basic works of a universal Asian childhood. (91)

When Davis wonders whether such an audience might be "a little hard to get," Chin points to the recent influx of Chinese immigrants: "new Chinese coming in from Cambodia, Thailand, Laos, Viet Nam, Singapore, mainland China, everywhere" (91). The hope he sees in this potential audience derives from the fact that "They are bringing the real stuff with them, the stuff that the original immigrants brought over, the literature, the civilization, the values—all in translation and comic books" (91).

The subjectivity that is gained through this immersion in the key texts that comprise "the basic works of a universal Asian childhood" is one that is potentially inoculated against the more pernicious effects of a white racist American popular culture. It is, moreover, a subjectivity that knows how to absorb and appropriate from other cultures—even those steeped in an anti-Asian racism—those elements conducive to the development of a racially authentic form of Asian American manhood. It is, therefore, a subjectivity that is defined by—to rephrase Ellison's formulation—"a yearning to make any- and everything of quality [*Asian*] *American*; to appropriate it, possess it, re-create it in our own group and individual images."

What lies at the heart of the classic tradition Chin codifies is, in fact, a subject whose essential Asianness and virility is indexed by an extraordinary capacity for mimesis—a mimesis that bespeaks a combative will to power. In an essay entitled "Come All Ye Asian American Writers of the Real and Fake" (1991), Chin describes what he identifies as the Chinese "real." He claims that the "authentic" Chinese subject is basically a martial subject—a subject steeped in a heroic tradition that teaches him that "life is war and behavior is strategy and tactics," that "Living is fighting" and "Life is war."[19] Within this tradition, "All art is martial art. Writing is fighting" (35). The essence of Chinese identity can thus be detected in the *pedagogical* structure of the martial arts: "One learns tai chi, kung fu, and martial art by *memorizing* a set of poses, stances, and movement in a specific order and rhythm. Then one recites the moves of the set" (36). The Chinese subject begins as a passively mimetic subject—a disciple—imitating movements scripted by others. But later, this memorization enables a sort of creative play. Eventually one moves "from recital to internalization. One is no longer reciting the set from memory; the set is now an animal in one's instinct" (36). Instead of being a group of formal movements exterior to the subject, the set becomes something *inside* the subject. According to Chin, this is "the way Chinese learn everything: [through] memorization, recitation, and internalization" (36). Chin calls this "the internal process" (36).

But what is it, exactly, that gets internalized by this process? It turns out to be the master. As one employs "the internal process" to master a set, one also internalizes the master who invented the set. One learns to become a "real" Chinese individual by learning to imitate another, by internalizing the identity of the master to such a degree that his "sets" become "an animal in one's instinct." One's identity itself is an improvisational copy of an original. And if Chinese civilization is coterminous with and equivalent to "Confuciandom," as Chin claims, then insofar as we express this heroically mimetic power, we express our essential Chinese identity by turning ourselves into copies of Confucius, who Chin identifies as a "strategist, a warrior" (34).

The essentially martial Chinese subject Chin celebrates in his more recent writings is nothing less, I am arguing, than an Orientalized version of the "chameleon Chinaman" he had championed in his earlier writings. If the very essence of Chinese identity is expressed by "the internal process" through which "we" "learn everything," then Chineseness comes to be defined as a prodigious capacity for imitation. The heroic individual, the fighter, is a subject whose ethnic identity is expressed through mimesis. What it means to be Asian is to always be in the process of becoming an other. Within the terms of this logic, it becomes possible to retain one's essential Asianness even if one follows the teachings of a white or black "Master," because such an imitative disposition is, after all, the very expression of the Asian individual's martial soul.

The Dream of the Vernacular

In my analysis of Chin's aesthetic writings, I have attempted to draw out their resemblance to those of Ellison, Baker, and Gates—a resemblance in the centrality they accord a certain conception of the vernacular subject in their evocations of an authentic and racially distinctive literary tradition. As Diana Fuss has suggested, the "dream of the vernacular" that haunts such writers has much to do with the ultimately *fantasmatic* sense of reconnection to *working-class* communities that it enables: by claiming an allegiance to the vernacular, professionalized writers of color can affirm an organic link to a "people" that they are—economically speaking, at least—no longer actually a part of.

There is, however, another aspect of the fantasmatic allure that a vernacular conception of the literary holds for *male* writers of color. The various codifications of the vernacular subject that I have been examining all insist on a certain modality of homosocial assimilationist desire that is both racially distinctive and wholly virile. The "perverse" version of this desire is the debasing self-abnegating desire for whiteness that is depicted with disturbing ease and persistency through a certain homophobic symbolism—a symbolism that turns the "faggot" of color into the master signifier of the idolatrous and libidinally charged desire for white masculinity that a racist and patriarchal social order encourages men of color to harbor. The antidote, as it were, that a certain conception of the vernacular proffers does not work by alleviating this debilitating and debasing desire; rather, what the domain of the literary promises to engender is an altered way of experiencing and expressing this desire. The aping of white literary and discursive modes apparent in vernacular literary works can be seen as an act of semiotic "guerilla/gorilla warfare"; as the expression of a "yearning to make any- and everything of quality *Negro American*; to appropriate it, possess it, re-create it in our own group and individual images"; as products of "the internal process" through which the mimetic martial artist develops his own style.

Given the fact that this vernacular subject is a kind of linguistic cannibal—promiscuously devouring and mangling whatever languages and discourses may come his way—it would seem that the orality with which he is identified is not simply aural but also alimentary. For Chin, at least, the vernacular subject he champions is one that has no taste; he is defined instead by an immensely unfinicky appetitive urge:

> Hungry, all the time hungry, every sense was out whiffing for something rightly ours, chameleons looking for color, trying on tongues and clothes and hairdos, taking everyone else's. . . . Everything [is] copycat. Hunger and copycat. ("Confessions," 68–69)

To be a "chameleon Chinaman" is to be driven by this mimetic impulse: one is always on the prowl, looking for objects to cannibalize: "tongues and clothes and hairdos." And since that desire to imitate is likened to a kind of hunger, its objects are always subjected to a digestive violence. In his paean to the digestive prowess of the Chinaman identity, which appears in the aptly titled short story "The Eat and Run Midnight People," Chin celebrates a cultural identity that is defined by a staggering capacity to eat damn near anything:

> Being a Chinaman's okay if you love having been outlaw-born and raised to eat and run in your mother country like a virus staying a step ahead of a cure and can live that way, fine. And that is us! Eat and run midnight people, outward bound . . . we live hunched over, up to our wrists in the dirt

sending our fingers underground grubbing after eats. We were the dregs, the bandits, the killers, the get out of town eat and run folks, hungry all the time eating after looking for food. . . . We eat toejam, bugs, leaves, roots, and smut and are always on the move, fingering the ground, on the forage, embalming food in leaves and seeds, on the way, for part of the trip when all we'll have to eat on the way will be mummies, and *all the time eating anything that can be torn apart and put in the mouth*, looking for new food to make up enough to eat. . . . I'm proud to say my ancestors did not invent gunpowder but stole it. If they had invented gunpowder, they would have eaten it up sure, and never borne this hungry son of a Chinaman to run.[20]

Orality functions for Chin as the means by which he seeks to remasculinize by de-eroticizing the identificatory relationship to men of other races that is at the very heart of the Asian American masculinity he advocates. While this interracial mimetic desire can be seen to resemble a homosexual desire, Chin insists on its virility by emphasizing its oral and appetitive manifestations. The Asian manhood Chin celebrates in his work is embodied by a paradigmatic organ, but not the usual one. It is erected upon an essentially oral foundation: the mouth almighty.

Coda

From the vantage point provided by recent theoretical and critical works that have argued for diasporic and transnational perspectives on race, it would be tempting to write off the kinds of representations I have been examining in this study as relics of a dying ethnonationalism. The nativist emphasis that structures the works of Ralph Ellison and Frank Chin is indeed self-evident, and it might be reasonable to assume that other traditions of black and/or Asian writing—ones that imagine community in terms that exceed the nation—would enact a politics of identity unsullied by the problematic rhetorics of identity so apparent in the texts I have been examining. But as the most careful scholars of race have noted, the emergent dominance of forms of capital and political power that exceed the nation-state and of ideological forms of community that are diasporic have not simply consigned nationalism to the dustbin of history. As Khachig Tölölyan has noted, for instance, in his prefatory essay to the inaugural issue of the journal *Diaspora*, "To affirm that diasporas are the exemplary communities of the transnational moment is not to write the premature obituary of the nation-state, which remains a privileged form of polity"; he further notes that "transnational communities are sometimes the paradigmatic Other of the nation-state and at other times its ally, lobby, or even, as in the case of Israel, its precursor."[1] I would like to end this study, therefore, by suggesting the afterlife of the rhetorics of identity I have been examining by briefly considering two literary texts that self-consciously attempt to move beyond a nation-focused framework. My point in broaching this issue is not to weigh in against the recent emergence of transnationalist or diasporic modes of analysis in African American or Asian American studies. It is, rather, to argue preemptively against a conclusion that some readers might be tempted to draw from the analyses I have offered in this study: namely, that cultural texts that mobilize an imaginary that moves beyond the nation would automatically leave behind the racial and sexual rhetorics of identity that have been my primary focus.

One author who has achieved literary prominence in recent years for a body of work that ranges across the African diaspora—and that explores the concept of diaspora from Jewish perspectives as well as Afro-Caribbean ones—is Caryl Phillips.[2] Bénédicte Ledent begins her monograph on this author's works by describing him as "one of the best-known and most talented British writers of his generation," and identifies his primary concerns as "displacement" and "exilic issues."[3] Phillips was born in 1958 in St. Kitts, part of the West Indies, but was raised in Leeds, England, a predominantly white working-class area. His literary career began during his college years at Oxford, where he began writing and directing plays. In the introduction to *The European Tribe* (1987), a collection of essays that recount his travels through Europe, the United States, Africa, and the Caribbean, he offers an anecdote about an event that apparently solidified his aspirations to become a professional writer, a story that also pays tribute to the influence of Ralph Ellison. He describes a five-week-long bus trip across the United States he took during the summer after his second year at college:

> There was a three-hour wait for the bus to San Francisco, but I preferred to shelter from the streets of Salt Lake City. I bought an out-of-date copy of the *Los Angeles Times*, and settled into the number two berth in the queue. An hour or so later, I looked at my watch and started to plan what I would have to do when I returned to Oxford. Behind me, a hunch-shouldered man of about sixty leant forward to address the man in front of me, whom he had clearly never met before. "Lot of niggers on the streets today." The recipient of this information, who had earlier offered me a cigarette and borrowed my *Los Angeles Times*, looked horrified. "In my day," continued the man at my rear, "if we saw too many niggers in the streets we'd shoot 'em." My nominal ally ignored my nominal enemy. I burst out laughing. The absurd ritual of it all had finally reduced me to hysteria.[4]

As a result of this encounter in Salt Lake City, he further recounts, he "had already discovered what it meant to be invisible in America" (7). Phillips's description of his response—which was to laugh at the absurdity of white

American attitudes toward blacks—has clear Ellisonian resonances, and it works to foreshadow the crucial, though somewhat curious, role that *Invisible Man* plays in his account of how he came to discover his calling as a writer. Five days later, in Los Angeles, Phillips came across Ellison's novel and *Native Son* in a book store. He spent the next day and much of the evening at a beach reading Wright's novel.

> When I rose from the deck chair it was dark and I had finished my reading by moonlight. I felt as if an explosion had taken place inside my head. If I had to point to any one moment that seemed crucial in my desire to be a writer, it was then, as the Pacific surf began to wash up around the deck chair. The emotional anguish of the hero, Bigger Thomas, the uncompromising prosodic muscle of Wright, his deeply felt sense of social indignation, provided not so much a model but a possibility of how I might be able to express the conundrum of my own existence. Even before I had opened Ralph Ellison's *Invisible Man*, I had decided that I wanted to try to become a writer. (7–8)

While this passage appears to render Ellison somewhat superfluous to a momentous encounter with Wright, it also describes the author of *Native Son* as providing Phillips with "not so much a model" but with a sense of "possibility of how I might be able to express the conundrum of my own existence." For it appears that Phillips's own existence—or rather his experience of how it went unacknowledged by those who, like the white man in the Salt Lake City bus station, refused to even see him—was more aptly described by the writer whose novel he had, at this point, not even read: Ellison, whose phraseology (laughter, absurdity) Phillips suggests is the appropriate one for understanding his earlier encounter.

At other points Phillips more explicitly aligns himself with an aesthetic stance often associated with Ellison and against one conventionally linked with Wright. In an interview with Frank Birbalsingh, in which he cites Ellison as a writer who was "initially important to me," Phillips offers this rather Ellisonian explanation for why he does not focus exclusively on British subjects in his fiction:

> I think it would be impossible or, at the very best, extremely difficult for me to address the situation in Britain only. To limit myself to Britain only for my subject matter would make me a protest writer, merely an extension of the university sociology faculty. . . . I am not prepared to limit myself to

the British situation, because eventually there will come a time when the idea of rage—which is what Baldwin was talking about when he criticized Richard Wright—the idea of rage would become my theme.[5]

The novel of Phillips's that seems most Ellisonian is *Crossing the River*, which was first published in England in 1993, a legacy that is suggested by the author's own characterizations of this work. In an interview with Carol Margaret Davison, he remarks that he wanted this novel "to make an affirmative connection, not a connection based upon exploitation or suffering or misery, but a connection based upon a kind of survival. This is an unusually optimistic book for me."[6]

This affirmative orientation toward the slave trade, the Middle Passage, and the reverberations of that exploitative and violent history across the African diaspora is an aspect of the novel that critics and reviewers also emphasize. Gail Low characterizes *Crossing the River* as recounting "a redemptive and affirmative history of survival."[7] Like Bénédicte Ledent, Low sees Phillips's novel as aligned with the critical project outlined by Paul Gilroy in his influential study *The Black Atlantic*:

> What is especially appealing about *The Black Atlantic* [and also, then, about *Crossing the River*] is its representation of slave history as an interpretive tool that is possibly "redemptive," and perhaps even utopian. In an age when "the concept of nationality" is conflated with that of culture, ethnic cleansing, closed borders, and racial exclusions are local manifestations. Gilroy's chronotope of the ship as an alternative to culture, conceived as an organism, provides a way out the mire of separate homelands.[8]

As it "ranges over a terrain similar to Gilroy's project," Phillips's novel

> grapples with the questions of kinship, social memory, and the renewal of identity; it establishes a unity that is at once fictive and performative, and yet also necessary and real. Furthermore, *Crossing the River*'s inclusive understanding of diaspora is one that offers an alternative conception of freedom and belonging. across and within racial lines.[9]

The "redemptive" quality of *Crossing the River* is directly connected to its compositional structure. Framed by a prologue and epilogue narrated by a kind of mythical African father, the body of Phillips's novel is divided into four sections. Three of these center on the children of Africa whose loss is marked and lamented by the father of the opening and closing chapters. The first of these is Nash Williams, a freed slave who settles in Liberia in the 1830s and works as a Christian missionary. His story is told in the first section of the novel, which is entitled "The Pagan Coast," along with that of Edward Williams, his former master, who journeys himself to Liberia in search of Nash. The second part of the novel, "West," is set late in the nineteenth century. It recounts the experience of Martha Randolph, also a former slave, who attempts to journey from Virginia to California in search of a new life, but who dies in Colorado before reaching her goal. The next section, "Crossing the River," crosses back in time to the 1750s, and its central character is James Hamilton, an English ship captain involved in the slave trade who buys the three children in 1753. The story of the third child, Travis, is set in the twentieth century, and it is told in the fourth part of the novel, "Somewhere in England." This section is narrated by Joyce, an Englishwoman who meets Travis during the Second World War and becomes his wife; he is an African American GI stationed in England. She bears him a son, whom she gives up for adoption after Travis is killed in action. The novel concludes with a reunion decades later between Joyce and her lost son.

The brief summary I have provided of *Crossing the River* indicates some of the parallels that might be drawn between this novel and *Invisible Man*. Both works offer a sweeping, even panoramic, account of African American history, though Phillips's novel situates that history in a diasporic rather than U.S. context. Both novels, moreover, draw attention to the devastating effects of white racism on black subjects, effects that are often produced through the actions of white characters whose motivations are not consciously malicious. Each novel concludes, moreover, with an epilogue that underscores the utopian potential of interracial connection. In Phillips's novel, the African father claims Joyce, a white Englishwoman, as one of his "daughters," giving her pain equal standing with that of the black characters; moreover, her narrative, which is recounted in the first person, is the longest of the novel's four sections and is, arguably, the most moving. In the epilogue, the African father explicitly includes Joyce's voice as part of "the many-tongued chorus of the common memory" that the work as a whole is seeking to record.[10]

The considerable and complex sympathy with which *Crossing the River* treats the character of Joyce, however, suggests a central element of Phillips's literary vision that distinguishes it from Ellison's, which has to do with the later writer's explicit allegiance to a feminist gender politics. If, as I have argued earlier, *Invisible Man* registers only with ambivalence—and, indeed, with a definite misogyny—the analogous function that black men and white women are made to play in a social order that is both racist and patriarchal, *Crossing the River* makes that commonality the basis for an emotional connection that has quite different political ramifications. The affinity that Phillips typically suggests in his fiction between the predicament of white women and black men is something that he has self-consciously sought to depict. He explains in an interview with Jenny Sharpe that "Linking questions of class and gender with the whole question of race has always been important to me."[11] His interest, he conjectures, may be a product of the fact that "I was brought up by my mother."[12] In reference to Emily, a white female character in his novel *Cambridge* (1991), Phillips recalls that he

> was interested in exploring the parallel situations that a woman might find herself in and that black people were definitely in Britain at the turn of the nineteenth century. The power structure operated in a different way, but the power source was the same. At the time I was writing that book, actually, I was thinking about the Brontë sisters. And wondering, What did the Brontës know about slavery? It turns out they knew a lot, they knew a hell of a lot. I was very, very interested in a working-class woman's relationship to slavery.[13]

Phillips's white female characters prove a stark contrast to such characters as Sybil and the white stripper in *Invisible Man*, as his recognition of the analogous disempowerment of black men and white women engenders a sympathy that invites a stitching together of antiracist, anticolonial, and feminist concerns. His progressivism on issues of gender might encourage readers to assume that his work is devoid of the disturbing homosexual symbolism that is, as I have been arguing, central to Ellison's novel. This is not, however, entirely the case. Without wanting to diminish the aspects of *Crossing the River* that have been justifiably lauded as progressive, I want here to indicate briefly the continuing presence in Phillips's diasporic fiction of the disturbingly pervasive representational strategy I have been examining in this study—the symbolic shorthand that makes of homosexuality an apt symbol for white racism. My focus is "The Pagan Coast," the first section of Phillips's narrative, which depicts the relationship between Edward Williams, an American slave owner, and his former slave, Nash, who has journeyed to Liberia to work as a missionary.

"The Pagan Coast" is told in the third person, and the narrative point of view gives the reader access to Edward's thoughts as he commences his own journey into Liberia in search of Nash. The story opens with Edward receiving a letter from Liberia announcing Nash's disappearance. The remainder of the narrative recounts the slave owner's ultimately failed attempt to track down his former slave in Liberia, and it records his reflections on the nature of their relationship. Interspersed throughout are letters—most of them from Nash to Edward—which give further clues about the bond between the two men.

Phillips's characterization of this slave owner, who sees himself as doing God's work by instilling his slaves with Christian values and encouraging them to spread them in Africa, echoes Ellison's depictions of putatively altruistic white men in *Invisible Man*. (The character he most resembles is Norton, the Northern philanthropist who regards the black men he helps to educate as surrogates for and memorials to his dead daughter, though significant echoes of Young Emerson are also to be found.) Edward thinks of himself primarily as a beneficent patriarch to the slaves he educates in the ways of Christianity, and Nash's own letters to him address him as "dear father." The sanctimonious piety with which Edward reflects on his endeavors to civilize the slaves he has owned and on the missionary effort in Liberia—elements of his personality that are apparent from the first few pages of the narrative—are enough to set the reader against him even at the outset. But what works to solidify the reader's initial mistrust of this figure is the accretion of insinuating details that disclose the libidinal motivations behind his putative altruism.

One important example of this is the narrative's piecemeal disclosure of the fracture that his affection for Nash had produced in Edward's relationship to his wife, Amelia. Early on, the narrator suggests that Edward's now-dead wife "would no doubt have been gravely suspicious of the motives which lay behind his projected expedition" to locate Nash (12). The narrative subsequently tightens the reader's focus on Amelia's suspicions as it brings in several poignant letters from Nash to Edward that express an increasing distress over their recipient's lack of reply; it is revealed that a jealous Amelia has intercepted and destroyed any correspondence between the two men she could find (56). The narrative also eventually reveals that Amelia has committed suicide out of outrage over the fact that her husband had begun to direct his affections toward another young black male slave after Nash's departure for Africa (56). When placed alongside slave narratives by Frederick Douglass and Harriett Jacobs, Phillips's depiction of Amelia's actions suggests an inverted form of the sexual jealousy that the wives of white slave owners are often described as harboring toward the black female slaves to whom their husbands had sexual access. And although the narrative never spells it out explicitly, it becomes nearly impossible for readers not to see that, at its core, the relationship Edward enjoyed with Nash was sexual.

Phillips's text is in fact littered with insinuations concerning Edward's desires. It records the prurience with which he seems to gaze upon the bodies of the black men he comes into contact with in Africa. Upon disembarking from the ship, he is described as "examin[ing]" the numerous black men that surround him, "particularly the natives, their semi-clad bodies ensnared by large corded muscles" (47). Edward's interactions with a young black man whom he enlists to help him in locating Nash further intimate his attraction. Upon being left alone with his hire, Edward asks

> the young man whether or not he was in possession of either a wife or a girl. To this the boy smiled shyly, then shook his head. Edward examined the young man, his perfect shape, strong torso, powerful legs, and then sat down on one corner of the bed. The bondsman remained standing, although he moved uneasily from one foot to the next as though unsure of what was expected of him. And then Edward, sensing the young man's discomfort, simply leaned forward and asked after his name. The boy averted his eyes, and, keeping the screen of his lashes low, he whispered the single word "Charles." (49)

This element of the narrative is something that Gail Low touches upon in her reading of the novel, noting how it gradually reveals to the reader Edward's "homosexuality, his sexual abuse of the young Nash, and the tragic death of his wife as a consequence of those passions."[14] The revelation of such details is, Low writes, "startling," and they also render Nash's "perception" of his relationship and "his representation of himself as a 'past intimate' somewhat chilling."[15]

Low also points out the parallel and contrast between this quasi-paternal bond and the other forms of familial connection in the text. She describes Edward's "betrayal" of Nash, his sexual exploitation of him, as

> not simply the betrayal of silence, but a betrayal of trust and kinship. In this, it parallels the betrayal of the prologue—the father who sells

his offspring into slavery. Edward's feelings of love and his desire for "un-conditional affection" may be real, but his realization of them is totally contrary to the spirit that motivates them.[16]

The adjectives Low uses to describe Nash's and Edward's relationship ("per-verse") and the effect that the revelation of its sexual dimension apparently has on the reader ("startling," "chilling") is quite apt. They bespeak the per-sistence in this Black Atlantic text of the kind of homophobic symbolism that I have been examining in this study. For what "The Pagan Coast" re-iterates is the assertion we first encountered in Fanon: namely, that the Negrophobic man is a kind of Negrophile, and that the desire expressed through his interest in black men is, at bottom, homosexual. As a "perverse" couple, Edward and Nash are rendered as emblematic of "the shameful inter-course" of the slave trade (1), and the "chilling" or "startling" effect of the revelation of their sexual bond invites the reader, as Low suggests, to invest in the more utopian forms of interracial connection that are also depicted in the novel. "The Pagan Coast" thus primes the reader to invest emotionally in the fourth and longest section of the novel, which focuses on the more utopian and, notably, heterosexual desire that emerges between Travis and Joyce, the star-crossed lovers who meet in World War II England. While Edward and Nash exemplify an interracialism that is diseased, Travis and Joyce embody a romance that is capable of suspending the obstacles posed by racism, one that is only cut short by a round of mortar fire.

If the sexual dimension of Edward's and Nash's relationship constitutes "an abuse and perversion of [the] kinship" the two men both apparently claim, it provides, through the bond between Joyce and Travis (and also between Joyce and the biracial son she is ultimately reunited with), more "uplifting example[s]" of the "yearning for familial connections [that] is the central theme of *Crossing the River*."[17]

In the reading I have just sketched out, my aim has not been simply to "out" the homophobia of an otherwise progressive Black Atlantic writer; it is rather to suggest that a homophobic persistence of vision can be seen to shape Phillips's rendering of the distinction between forms of interracial con-nection that are "perverse" and those that are "uplifting." It is to point out that even as authors widen the range of their representations to encompass transnational and diasporic concerns, they may still find in the figure of a sexualized coupling of black and white men an apt symbol for racism's perversity—a disturbingly powerful symbolic Other against which more utopian forms of interracialism can be projected. My intent is also to sound a cautionary note to critics who might be tempted to gloss over the less salutary elements of contemporary texts whose progressivism on other fronts is apparent, whose laudable attempts to move beyond the nation as a frame of reference appear to leave behind the more regressive tendencies of cultural nationalism.

Within the context of Asian American literature, one text that has been justifiably celebrated for the ways in which it self-consciously rejects the homophobia and U.S.-focused nativism of the vision of authenticity codified by Frank Chin is R. Zamora Linmark's experimental novella, *Rolling the R's*. Set in Hawaii in the seventies, this work focuses on a multiethnic group of fifth-graders, mainly working-class, who grapple with such issues as racism (internal as well as external forms, directed by whites and from economically advantaged Asians), class division, domestic abuse, and a system of public education that seeks to eradicate their ethnic- and class-based identities. Their confrontation with these interlocking forms of oppression emerges in Linmark's work in relation to their negotiation of sexuality. As in the representations I have been examining in this study, the language of race in this novel is shot through by the language of gender and sexuality; but the sexual politics that animate this writing could not be more different. Linmark is an openly gay author, and his intent in this novel is explicitly anti-homophobic: it is to render with complexity and humanity the experiences of gay male Asian Americans in terms that reject the linkage between authenticity and heterosexuality so powerfully codified in the writings of Frank Chin. But although the inventiveness and playfulness with which Linmark riffs on a Chin-style rhetorics of identity should be (and have been) lauded, it is also important, as I intend to suggest, to grapple with how this reworking also entails a repetition.

In his reading of the novel—which concludes his study *Racial Castration*— David L. Eng describes *Rolling the R's* as a "remarkable" work, one that "brings together queerness and diaspora in innovative, destabilizing, and compelling ways that contest the dominant representations comprising the domestic image-repertoire."[18] He sees Linmark as imagining through his preadolescent characters "a diasporic immigrant subjectivity organized by queerness."[19] The two main protagonists are Edgar Ramirez, who is outspoken and self-assured about what it means to be gay, working-class, and Filipino, and

Vicente de los Reyes, who shares a similar background but is, in contrast, closeted about his ethnic and sexual identities. Their group of friends includes Filipinos, Vietnamese, Okinawans, Japanese, and Samoans, some of whom are recent immigrants and some whose families have been on the islands for generations. As Eng points out, "the disparate ethnic affiliations" of these characters—and, we might add, their different class-locations and relation to immigration and migration—"threaten to divide further their tenuous loyalties"; however, "it is precisely sexuality—an obsessive queer sexuality that permeates *Rolling the R's* from beginning to end—that binds them together as a social group with a common sense of purpose and esprit de corps."[20] Through its depiction of this group of characters, whose internal differences and tensions remain unresolved through the novel, this work suggests how "the coalitional possibilities of 'Asian American' as a viable or even workable group identity are engaged, renewed, and rendered efficacious by this detour through queerness."[21]

Eng's definition of queerness as it functions in the novel is capacious:

> it functions not just in the register of sexuality but as an organizing topos that affirms rather than effaces a host of alternate differences. As a consequence, constitutive differentials of nationality, sexuality, race, and class are rendered heterogeneous, creating complex and shifting rather than singular and static social histories of individual development.[22]

The queer, diasporic, immigrant subjectivity that Linmark's work celebrates is diametrically opposed, in Eng's view, to the cultural nationalist subjectivity prized by writers like Frank Chin. Cultural nationalism itself, moreover, "is a formation in need of queering"—it must subjected to critique not only for its "patriarchal complicities," but also for its "disciplining of the domestic, the forced repression of feminine and homosexual to masculine, and of the home to the nation-state."[23] A text like Linmark's, Eng argues, is tailor-made for such acts of critical "queering."

While there is a tremendous amount of truth to Eng's characterization of Linmark's novel, the reading he offers to support it focuses on a relatively minor character, Orlando Domingo, a senior at Farrington High School who excels at academics (he is fluent in four languages and is the class valedictorian) and is the exemplar of the well-rounded student (he is in the school band and a member of the student body government); he also enjoys dressing up as Farrah Fawcett-Majors. As Eng puts it:

Orlando's outrageous comportment as a Farrah Flip, coupled with his academic achievements as a model minority, forces two disparate and stereotypical images into conceptual overload. This improbable bringing together of the model minority myth with a flagrant and flaming queer sexuality, as well as the stitching together of a racialized diasporic identity with dominant images of the (white) drag queen, mark a novel combination of queerness and diaspora that challenges, resists, and ultimately explodes the dominant representation and expectations that crowd our domestic image-repertoire.[24]

This reading eloquently conveys the aspects of *Rolling the R's* that are genuinely inventive and, indeed, subversive. But the turn toward diasporic queerness in Linmark's text does not, I would argue, constitute a wholesale transcendence of the problematic rhetorics of identity that I have been subjecting to critique in this study.

For underlying *Rolling the R's* playful explorations of the various modalities of identity that populate the local culture of Hawaii is a version of the binary opposition that is the ideological legacy of the homophobic cultural nationalism the novel both challenges and borrows from. Articulated most emphatically by the character of Edgar Ramirez, the novel's politics of identity legislates a division between characters whose relationships to sexual and racial identity are "authentic" and those whose sexual and racial orientations are "inauthentic." We should recall here that in the politics of cultural identity I have been examining, the authentic/inauthentic distinction does not oppose racially hybrid forms of subjectivity with those that are, somehow, racially "pure." As I have been suggesting throughout, what is being championed is a particular modality of racial hybridity—a specific way of negotiating interracial homosocial desire that underwrites claims of racial and masculine "wholeness." Partly due, in this context, to the hybrid nature of Filipino national culture itself, the orientation that Linmark celebrates in his novel is not opposed to but rather mobilizes hybridity as its essential mode. The repertoire of "white" images that his protagonists identify and, indeed, *over*identify with circulate within the U.S. popular culture of the seventies, embodied by a constellation of stars that include not only Farrah Fawcett-Majors but also Scott Baio, Leif Garrett, and Matt Dillon. While all of the preadolescent protagonists enact these identifications performatively—acting out scenes from their favorite movies and television shows and lip-synching along with the singers they idolize—the novel does seem to distinguish between forms that are conducive to the production of "authentic" forms of a queer Filipino identity and those that are not.

This binary operates through the logic of the closet. It opens up a rather stark divide between the two characters who are the work's primary protagonists: Edgar Ramirez and Vicente de los Reyes. Edgar is depicted as a figure who has always known what it means to be gay, working-class, and Filipino, and who has always confronted the world with this knowledge. The second chapter of *Rolling the R's* is entitled "Blame It on Chachi." It opens with the sentence, "Edgar Ramirez is a faggot," and the remaining eight pages of this chapter list everyone who "knows it"—a group that basically includes everybody in the novel.[25] Edgar is probably the funniest character in a novel filled with funny characters, and through his barbed wit he skewers the pretensions of everyone with whom he comes into contact. The first target of his hilarious diatribes is "you," the reader, who is positioned in the novel's opening as one of a number of "closet cases" to whom Edgar is giving his counsel. His message to "you" in this first chapter, "Skin, or Edgar's Advice to Closet Cases," is to stop pretending that "you" do not harbor the same kind of sexual fantasies as he does. He recounts his own dream scenario, which involves a sexual encounter with Scott Baio, Leif Garrett, and Matt Dillon, and then confronts the reader with the following revelation:

> But you know what was so weird? While Matt was piggybackin' me to the bathroom—we was stark naked, of course—we saw you in the corridor givin' Parker Stevenson the Hardy Boys treatment. You actin' like you knew the ropes by trade, spreadin' your legs for spill out the one-and-only clue. You was so grown up, you knew who you was, and was lovin' it too. (1–2)

The closet to which Edgar refers—the closet in which the reader is invited to see himself—is, of course, that in which homosexual men who refuse to acknowledge their orientation hide themselves. To the extent that this opening works to "queer" all of its readers, it simply renders in the most carnal terms the sexual desire that popular cultural representations seek to engender in them. For Asian American male readers, however, an equally salient aspect of the scenarios described is their interracial character. What Edgar's address attempts to "out" is a homosexual desire for *white* men that prevalent images of male desirability in popular culture incite in Asian American men. In this respect, this opening echoes the polemics of Frank Chin: it calls on its Asian American readers to recognize the extent to which they have been encouraged to harbor an eroticized relationship to white masculinity. The key difference—and this difference can not be understated—is that Linmark's writing is intended not to vilify homosexual Asian men, but rather to render their experiences with a complex humanity.

A more unsettling resemblance emerges over the course of the novel as it suggests a link between Edgar's ability to detect the homosexuality of "closet cases" (his "gaydar," if you will) and his ability to tell the difference between Filipinos who, like him, embrace their racial and ethnic identity and those who do not: those who, in essence, inhabit the closet of racial inauthenticity. In a chapter entitled "The Two Filipinos," Edgar humorously—but also with a dose of venom—delineates the contours of an authentic relationship to Filipinoness in terms that echo the rhetoric of the *Aiiieeeee!* editors. It describes a classroom argument over nationality and ethnicity. Nelson Ariola is criticized by his classmates—and most pointedly by Edgar—for insisting that he is American, not Filipino. Nelson's assertions are presented as self-evident proof of a racial self-loathing:

> "I'm sick and tired of being called a Filipino. . . . I'm not like them. . . . I can't be a Filipino. I don't want to be a Filipino because the only Filipino everyone knows is the Filipino that eats dogs or the Filipino that walks around with a broom in his hands." (68)

Edgar's assertions, in contrast, suggest a pride and confidence in his ethnicity that are the counterpart to his solid self-knowledge about his sexuality: "Look at me. . . . I a mestizo born in the U S of A, but my fair skin no stop me from the fact that I one Filipino" (69). The chapter concludes with Edgar's telling off both Nelson and Stephen, a white classmate who has also stepped into the debate:

> Edgar first points his finger to Nelson: "You, Mr. Haole Wanna-be," and then points to Stephen; "and you, Mr. Haolewood. You guys think you so hot-shit, but you know what? The ground you standin' on is not the freakin' meltin' pot but one volcano. And one day, the thing goin' erupt and you guys goin' be the first ones for burn." (70)

The accusation that Edgar uses to call Nelson's relationship to Filipinoness into question—"Mr. Haole Wanna-be"—is a familiar one, though its deployment here is wholly shorn of the homophobia present in many of the texts this study has examined. What must be pointed out, however, is that even in this queer-friendly text, a discrete distinction is being made between an inauthentically hybrid racial identity and one that is, somehow, authentic. This distinction, moreover, is essentially rendered in aesthetic terms. It is not simply that Nelson is embarrassed about his ethnicity and Edgar is not; it is, more crucially, that Edgar's mode of "Haole Wanna-be"–ness is depicted as the expression of a certain queer/Filipino/diasporic *style* while Nelson's is rendered as the absence of one. Though it has shifted from a homophobic register to one that is flamboyantly queer, the rhetoric of identity that is mobilized here still celebrates as "authentic" a certain active, willfull, deforming capacity for imitation. It is, in this novel, never a question of *whether* to imitate white culture; it is, rather, a question of *how*. To do so as Edgar does—with enough verve and style to be fabulously queer and Filipino—is to do so with one's authenticity intact. Because he knows he is and always has been gay and Filipino (and thus what it *really* means to be both), his identificatory and sexual desire for whiteness is rendered as an organic expression of who he is. Because of the authoritative sense of epistemological privilege with which he is endowed in this novel, Edgar can come across in the novel as a gay version of Frank Chin, imperiously drawing lines in the sand between those who are "real" and those who are "fake"—a distinction that is, in the end, no less arbitrary for having been divested of the homophobia with which it had originally been invested.

*

The readings I have offered in closing this study are notably shorter and more cursory than the ones that constitute the body of this study; indeed, they are intended to be gestural. As such they stand in rather stark contrast to the more exhaustive analyses I have been presenting throughout. In giving the two authors who are the focus of this study such detailed attention, this book adopts a very different approach than the one taken by most contemporary works on matters of race and ethnicity—even those by scholars whose training and investments are in literary criticism. In so doing, this study has made an implicit argument on behalf of a mode of close reading that some might view as harkening back to an earlier mode of literary criticism. I would like to end by rendering this argument more explicit.

As I mentioned in the Preface, ethnic studies has often set itself against more traditionally defined fields whose disciplinary parameters are seen as having a narrowing effect on the critical study of race. Partly as a result of the general emphasis placed on interdisciplinarity in this field, cultural studies scholars—and often ones trained in English departments—have assumed a dominant place. This development has come to be regarded by some as having had a number of negative effects, which include: the overvaluing of literary critical methods of analysis, the textualization of experience and history, the aestheticization of politics, and the dissemination of difficult, "jargon"-laden vocabularies that are impenetrable to all but those who have received substantial training in the canon of critical theory. My concern, however, is something different. What I take issue with is not the preponderance of literary critical analyses in the field but rather their abandonment—the leaving behind of a hermeneutic that addresses the cultural specificity of literary objects and subjects. By stating this, I am not advocating a return to a moribund notion of aesthetic culture that sees it as cleansed of political and historical matters; more simply and more modestly, I am asserting the need for literary critics to engage in the disciplined study of the specific kinds of political interventions that writers attempt to make through the act of writing literature.

What I am arguing for is something that Ellen Rooney, in a recent and openly polemical essay, has termed a return to formalism. "Formalism," as she defines it, does not involve the embrace of generalized abstract formulations about the nature of the aesthetic or a depoliticization of literature; what it means

> is any and every exploitation of the text's opacity as it appears in our theoretical fields. The precise work it does in any given disciplinary frame cannot be foreseen from the outside, or from the moment before reading begins. Without such a guarantee, many readers—in cultural and in literary studies—are content to reiterate their convictions, to write them across, over, or into the texts they use as illustrations.[26]

More specifically, formalism points a way from the mode of non-close-reading that constitutes the prevailing method of much cultural studies work. She notes that the dissemination of "theoretical problematics" across an interdisciplinary field—say, the relation of race and gender in ethnic studies—has had the salutary effect of producing "thematization[s]" that can provide a common object of discourse: it "offers scholars unwilling or unable to read theorists or critics working in other fields an intimation of the arguments available elsewhere and the reading effects they engender."[27] Too often, though, as Rooney observes,

> The thematization of critical problematics in this fashion has driven virtually every other formal category from the arsenal of readers in literary and cultural studies. Formalism is a matter not of barring thematizations but of refusing to reduce reading entirely to the elucidation, essentially the paraphrase, of themes—theoretical, ideological, or humanistic. The various modes of thematization that currently dominate critical readings of both the literary and the extraliterary kind are no longer simply inescapable; they are the only game in town. When the text-to-be-read (whatever its genre) is engaged only to confirm the prior insights of a theoretical problematic, reading is reduced to reiteration and becomes quite literally beside the point. One might say that we overlook most of the work of any text if the only formal feature we can discern in it is a reflected theme, the mirror image of a theory that is, by comparison to the belated and all-too-predictable text, seen as all-knowing and, just as important, as complete.[28]

While I might not choose the term "formalist" to characterize my own project, Rooney's assertions do assist me in stating the kinds of issues I have attempted to address here and in identifying some of my aims.

First of all, I have avoided treating the literary texts I have examined in this study as if they were epiphenomenal of a general cultural logic—as if their analysis were merely instrumental to the delineating of that wider logic. While it is true that I have been treating Ellison's and Chin's writings as exemplary and influential, my intent has not been to reduce them to mere repetitions of a larger pattern. I have claimed that their works not only offer us valuable if disturbing insights into the psychic structure of racialized masculinity, but they also enable us to arrive at a highly complex understanding of the fantasmatic allure that the literary domain holds for men of color. To arrive at such an understanding, it is necessary to track the biographical and other trajectories that have shaped their writings, to map, if only provisionally, their literary influences, their intellectual genealogies. It is also necessary to engage in a kind of sustained and individuated close-reading practice that is incompatible with the nonformalist interpretive protocols that Rooney identifies as problematic. As she puts it,

> The effects of the attenuation of the category of form include the reduction of every text to its ideological or historical context, or to an exemplar of a

prior theory (content)—form reduced to an epiphenomenon; the rapid exhaustion of the entire roster of political and theoretical problematics "applied" in this manner, with the attendant miasma theoretical incoherence; the trivialization of the concept of textuality, a process that has quite possibly advanced to the point of no return; and the generalization of reading-as-paraphrase, which robs cultural and literary studies of the power to make any essential contribution to critical work already moving confidently ahead in history, sociology, anthropology, and communications. These are all disciplines that have long since mastered the art of reading-as-summary, reading sans form; cultural studies and literary studies must offer them something more.[29]

What I have been after in the detailed readings I have offered of Chin's and Ellison's works—and something I could only hope to attain by taking the time to give them sustained attention, by, in a sense, living with them for a long time—was an understanding of why, out of a whole range of authors I could have chosen to write about, theirs were the works that have sustained my intense interest over the past decade or so. In the end, the most honest justification I can offer for my admittedly idiosyncratic choice of writers is that they have been the ones who have enabled me the most incisive and also the most difficult and painful insights into how race and manhood converge in constructing the various identities—political and personal—I traverse in my work and in my life. While I might have treated the work of such writers as Chester Himes, James Baldwin, David Mura, and David Henry Hwang (all important figures, in my view), Ellison's and Chin's works have been the ones that have most, as it were, gotten under my skin. Given my training—and my own abiding interest in the specific form of cultural power invested in literature by our culture—the only way I could hope to arrive at some understanding of how and why was to "finger the jagged grain" of their complexity.

Finally, I want to touch upon a point that Rooney raises in the concluding sentences of her essay, as she evokes what literary and cultural studies might gain from a renewed attentiveness to form: "it may help us revise our theories, restore all of our texts to an active place in our thought and our politics, and even, if we can be content with this, give us pleasure."[30] What Rooney is asking her readers to acknowledge is that pleasure comprises part of—and is, perhaps, elemental to—the critical enterprise. The question of how it might come into play in this study is a rather complicated one. For while this is a project that takes its cue from the work of scholars working at the borders of queer and ethnic studies, it is clearly not one that seeks directly to vindicate or celebrate the range of pleasures conventionally (or even unconventionally) associated with gay or lesbian subjectivities. The importance of such work is something I stressed at the outset of the project. But what I have attempted to deploy here is a critical approach that delivers its insights by giving in to the pleasures and desires that are invited by the texts it examines—pleasures that are in no way innocent, and that are as generative of a politics of hate as they are one of love. To understand this seduction is—at least to a certain extent—to give into it, even if the giving in is aimed, ultimately, at a working through, if not a moving beyond.

Notes

Preface

1. Dwight A. McBride, "Can the Queen Speak? Racial Essentialism, Sexuality, and the Problem of Authority," *Callaloo* 21, no. 2 (1998): 377.

2. Johnnella E. Butler, "Ethnic Studies as a Matrix for the Humanities, the Social Sciences, and the Common Good," in *Color-Line to Borderlands: The Matrix of American Ethnic Studies*, ed. Johnnella E. Butler (Seattle: University of Washington Press, 2001), 21.

3. Amritjit Singh and Peter Schmidt, "On the Borders Between U.S. Studies and Postcolonial Theory," in *Postcolonial Theory and the United States: Race, Ethnicity, and Literature*, ed. Amritjit Singh and Peter Schmidt (Jackson: University Press of Mississippi, 2000), 7.

4. Gary Y. Okihiro, *Margins and Mainstreams: Asians in American History and Culture* (Seattle: University of Washington Press, 1994), 34; George Lipsitz, *The Possessive Investment in Whiteness: How White People Profit from Identity Politics* (Philadelphia: Temple University Press, 1998), 209; Vijay Prashad, *Everybody Was Kung Fu Fighting: Afro-Asian Connections and the Myth of Cultural Purity* (Boston: Beacon Press, 2001); Penny M. Von Eschen, *Race Against Empire: Black Americans and Anticolonialism, 1937–1957* (Ithaca, N.Y.: Cornell University Press, 1997).

5. Lipsitz, *Possessive Investment*, 210.

6. Kandice Chuh, *Imagine Otherwise: On Asian Americanist Critique* (Durham, N.C.: Duke University Press, 2003); while the focus of Chu's book is on cultural and political formations that exceed the nation, this study (like the best works on transnationalism, globalization, and diaspora) acknowledges and examines the continuing significance of nationalist ideologies and the political form of the nation-state itself.

7. Butler, "Ethnic Studies," 35.

8. Eve Kosofsky Sedgwick, *Epistemology of the Closet* (Berkeley: University of California Press, 1990), 1.

9. Marlon B. Ross, "Camping the Dirty Dozens," *Callaloo* 23, no. 1 (2000): 290.

10. David L. Eng and Alice Hom, eds., *Q and A: Queer in Asian America* (Philadelphia: Temple University Press, 1998); Dana Y. Takagi, "Maiden Voyage: Excursion into Sexuality and Identity Politics," in *Asian American Sexualities: Dimensions of the Gay and Lesbian Experience*, ed. Russell Leong (New York: Routledge, 1996), 22.

11. Harper, *Are We Not Men? Masculine Anxiety and the Problem of African-American Identity* (New York: Oxford University Press, 1996); David L. Eng, "Out Here and Over There: Queerness and Diaspora in Asian American Studies," in *Racial Castration: Managing Masculinity in Asian America* (Durham, N.C.: Duke University Press, 2001), 204–28.

12. José Esteban Muñoz, *Disidentifications: Queers of Color and the Performance of Politics* (Minneapolis: University of Minnesota Press, 1999), 4.

13. Gayatri Gopinath, "Nostalgia, Desire, Diaspora: South Asian Sexualities in Motion," *positions* 5, no. 2 (1997): 467–89; Eng, *Racial Castration*, 224.

14. Harper, *Are We Not Men?*; Hazel V. Carby, *Race Men* (Cambridge, Mass.: Harvard University Press, 1998).

15. T. V. Reed uses the term *interdiscipline* to describe fields such as American, ethnic, postcolonial, women's, queer, and cultural studies. See T. V. Reed, "Heavy Traffic at the Intersections: Ethnic, American, Women's Queer, and Cultural Studies," in Butler, *Color-Line to Borderlands*, 273–92.

16. Henry Yu's insightful study of the Chicago School, *Thinking Orientals*, illuminates the specific form of *disciplinary* power that both white and Asian American sociologists seek through their intellectual labors; in an analogous manner, *Writing Manhood, Writing Race* examines the disciplinary power that African and Asian American writers lay claim to as writers. See Henry Yu, *Thinking Orientals: Migration, Contact, and Exoticism in Modern America* (New York: Oxford University Press, 2001).

17. Viet Thanh Nguyen, *Race and Resistance: Literature and Politics in Asian America* (New York: Oxford University Press, 2002), 5.

18. Henry Louis Gates, Jr., "Literary Theory and the Black Tradition," in *Figures in Black: Words, Signs, and the "Racial" Self* (New York: Oxford University Press, 1987), 4.

19. Elaine Kim, *Asian American Literature: An Introduction to the Writings and Their Social Context* (Philadelphia: Temple University Press, 1982), 12.

20. Lisa Lowe, *Immigrant Acts: On Asian American Cultural Politics* (Durham, N.C.: Duke University Press, 1996), 86.

21. Ibid.

22. Ibid., 96.

23. David Palumbo-Liu, introduction to *The Ethnic Canon: Histories, Institutions, and Interventions*, ed. David Palumbo-Liu (Minneapolis: University of Minnesota Press, 1995), 12.

24. Ibid., 2.

Introduction

1. Richard Fung, "Looking for My Penis: The Eroticized Asian in Gay Porn Video," in *How Do I Look? Queer Film and Video*, ed. Bad Object-Choices (Seattle: Bay Press, 1991), 148.

2. Ibid.

3. Ibid.

4. Ibid., 153.

5. David L. Eng, *Racial Castration: Managing Masculinity in Asian America* (Durham, N.C.: Duke University Press, 2001).

6. Abdul R. JanMohamed and David Lloyd, "Toward a Theory of Minority Discourse: What Is to Be Done?" introduction to *The Nature and Context of Minority Discourse*, ed. Abdul R. JanMohamed and David Lloyd (New York: Oxford University Press, 1996), 4.

7. The category of "damage"—particularly in the psychological sense—of course played a central role in twentieth-century antiracist, feminist, and gay/lesbian political discourses. Works on this topic pertinent to this study include: Wendy Brown, *States of Injury: Power and Freedom in Late Modernity* (Princeton, N.J.: Princeton University Press, 1995); Anne Anlin Cheng, *The Melancholy of Race* (New York: Oxford University Press, 2000); Daryl Michael Scott, *Contempt and Pity: Social Policy and the Image of the Damaged Black Psyche, 1880–1996* (Chapel Hill: University of North Carolina Press, 1997).

8. Frantz Fanon, *Black Skins, White Masks*, trans. Charles Lam Markmann (New York: Grove Press, 1967), 109, 112–13. All further references to this work will be cited in the text.

9. Stuart Hall, "The After-Life of Frantz Fanon: Why Fanon? Why Now? Why *Black Skin, White Masks*," in *The Fact of Blackness: Frantz Fanon and Visual Representation*, ed. Alan Read (Seattle: Bay Press, 1996), 16.

10. Lee Edelman, "The Part for the (W)hole: Baldwin, Homophobia, and the Fantasmatics of 'Race,'" in *Homographesis: Essays in Gay Literary and Cultural Theory* (New York: Routledge, 1994), 46. Edelman's essay has been an indispensable

resource for my own analyses. Eng argues for a slightly different position, that racial and sexual difference "are *mutually* constitutive and constituted" (*Racial Castration*, 5; my emphasis).

11. See Terry Goldie, "Saint Fanon and 'Homosexual Territory,'" in *Frantz Fanon: Critical Perspectives*, ed. Anthony C. Alessandrini (New York: Routledge, 1999), 75–86. As Goldie notes, when Fanon uses the term *l'homme* in this text, "it is not just the usual casual sexism of using 'man' for 'human': it is very much a male, and it is freedom of males he seeks" (78). "The romance he depicts," Goldie continues, "is that suggested by Eve Kosofsky Sedgwick's wonderful title, *Between Men*" (78). Fanon's focus on male homosociality is also addressed by Ann Pellegrini, in chapters 4 and 5 of *Performance Anxieties: Staging Psychoanalysis, Staging Race* (New York: Routledge, 1997), 89–128. For analyses of Fanon's relationship to feminism see Rey Chow, "The Politics of Admittance: Female Sexual Agency, Miscegenation, and the Formation of Community," in Alessandrini, *Frantz Fanon*, 34–56; Madhu Dubey, "The 'True Lie' of the Nation: Fanon and Feminism," *Differences: A Journal of Feminist Cultural Studies* 10, no. 2 (1998): 1–29; Diana Fuss, "Interior Colonies: Frantz Fanon and the Politics of Identification," in *Identification Papers*, by Diana Fuss (New York: Routledge, 1995), 141–72; T. Denean Sharpley-Whiting, "Fanon and Capécia," in Alessandrini, *Frantz Fanon*, 57–74.

12. There is a certain irony, then, to Fung's use of Fanon's *Black Skin, White Masks* to establish the antithetical ways in which Asian and black masculinities are perceived. For it would seem that regardless of the part to which one is reduced— penis or anus—the masculine experience of being subjected to a racist gaze can be experienced, or at least rendered, as a kind of "racial castration."

13. Benita Parry, "Signs of the Times," *Third Text* 28–29 (Fall–Winter 1994): 31; Hall, "After-Life of Frantz Fanon," 24.

14. Hall, "After-Life of Frantz Fanon," 27.

15. See, for instance, Edelman, "Part for the W(hole)," and Fuss, "Interior Colonies."

16. Fuss, "Interior Colonies," 160.

17. Ibid., 159.

18. Eve Kosofsky Sedgwick, *Between Men: English Literature and Male Homosocial Desire* (New York: Columbia University Press, 1985).

19. Andreas Huyssen, *After the Great Divide: Modernism, Mass Culture, Postmodernism* (Bloomington: Indiana University Press, 1986).

20. Tamar Katz, *Impressionist Subjects: Gender, Interiority, and Modernist Fiction in England* (Urbana: University of Illinois Press, 2000), 2.

21. Robert J. C. Young, *Colonial Desire: Hybridity in Theory, Culture, and Race* (New York: Routledge, 1995), 9.

22. Ibid., 25.

23. In this footnote Fanon announces that he "had no opportunity to establish the overt presence of homosexuality in Martinique" (180, footnote 44). While he acknowledges "the existence of what are called there 'men dressed like women' or 'godmothers'" who "wear shirts and skirts," he is "convinced that they lead normal sex lives" (ibid.). It is only when Martinicans emigrate to Europe that they become "homosexuals, always passive," though he insists that theirs "was by no means a neurotic homosexuality: For them it was a means to a livelihood, as pimping is for others" (ibid.).

24. Henry Louis Gates, Jr., "The Black Man's Burden," in *Fear of a Queer Planet: Queer Politics and Social Theory*, ed. Michael Warner (Minneapolis: University of Minnesota Press, 1994), 234.

25. Amiri Baraka, "American Sexual Reference: Black Male," in *Home: Social Essays*, 1st ed. (New York: Ecco Press, 1998), 216. All further references to this work will be cited in the text.

26. Michele Wallace, *Black Macho and the Myth of the Superwoman* (New York: Warner, 1980), 67.

27. Darryl Pinckney, "The Drama of Ralph Ellison," *New York Review of Books* 44, no. 8 (15 May 1997).

28. Gates, "Black Man's Burden," 234.

29. Frank Chin et al., eds., *Aiiieeeee! An Anthology of Asian American Writers* (New York: Mentor-Penguin, 1991), xix. All further references to this work will be cited in the text.

30. Madhu Dubey, *Black Women Novelists and the Nationalist Aesthetic* (Bloomington: Indiana University Press, 1994), 16–17.

31. Ibid., 19.

32. Ibid., 17.

33. Ibid., 26.

34. Phillip Brian Harper, *Are We Not Men? Masculine Anxiety and the Problem of African-American Identity* (New York: Oxford University Press, 1996), 50.

35. The readings of African American depictions of homosexuality that I will be presenting in this study, though they were arrived at independently, are quite resonant with Lee Edelman's in "Part for the (W)hole." My emphases are different, however, in that my discussion focuses on hybridity and the aesthetic in a way that Edelman does not. Moreover, I extend these analyses to the Asian American context, whereas Edelman's concern is solely with the African American one.

36. For an excellent reading of Baraka's homophobic invective as deriving from—and thus paying a hidden form of tribute—to the camp style of both black and white homosexual subcultures, see Marlon B. Ross, "Camping the Dirty Dozens: The Queer Resources of Black Nationalist Invective," *Callaloo* 23, no. 1 (2000): 290–312. See also the discussion of the homoerotics that subtends Baraka's writings in chapter 2 of Fred Moten, *In the Break: The Aesthetics of the Black Radical Tradition* (Minneapolis: University of Minnesota Press, 2003), 85–169. Both of these works are also important because they provide a much more expansive examination of the homosociality that shapes Baraka's aesthetics than the more selective account I offer in this study.

37. Sigmund Freud, *Three Essays on the Theory of Sexuality*, ed. James Strachey (New York: Basic, 1975), 1–2.

38. Edelman, "Part for the (W)hole"; Leo Bersani, "Is the Rectum a Grave?" in *October: The Second Decade, 1986–1996*, ed. Rosalind Krauss (Cambridge, Mass.: MIT Press, 1988), 303–28.

39. Imamu Amiri Baraka, "CIVIL RIGHTS POEM," in *Selected Poetry of Amiri Baraka/LeRoi Jones* (New York: Morrow, 1979), 115.

40. In contrast to my own reading, Harper suggests that while the meaning of homosexuality in this poem is never specified, its significance would have been self-evident: "Indeed, so well understood was the identification between inadequacies of manhood and black consciousness in the Black Arts context that this poem needed never render explicit the grounds for its judgment of NAACP leader Roy Wilkins, for the perceived racial-political moderation of both him and his organization clearly bespoke his unforgivable 'faggotry'" (*Are We Not Men?* 51).

41. Leo Bersani, *Homos* (Cambridge, Mass.: Harvard University Press, 1995), 78.

42. Ibid., 19.

43. Wallace, *Black Macho*, 67.

44. Edelman, "Part for the (W)hole," 42. For references to this epithet, see W. J. Weatherby, *James Baldwin: Artist on Fire* (New York: Dell, 1989).

45. Eldridge Cleaver, "Notes on a Native Son," in *Soul on Ice* (New York: Delta/Dell, 1968), 97. All further references to this work will be cited in the text.

46. Wallace, *Black Macho*, 68.

47. Ibid. The most influential theoretic elaboration of this psychic predicament—the intimate relationship to femininity that defines African American masculinity as a result of slavery's sexual economy—is, of course, Hortense Spillers, "Mama's Baby, Papa's Maybe: An American Grammar Book," *Diacritics* 17, no. 2 (Summer 1987): 65–81.

48. Ibid., 68.

49. For an exhaustive account of Freud's negative Oedipus complex, see chap-

ter 4 of Kaja Silverman, *The Acoustic Mirror: The Female Voice in Psychoanalysis and Cinema* (Bloomington: Indiana University Press, 1988).

50. See, for instance, Lisa Lowe, *Immigrant Acts: On Asian American Cultural Politics* (Durham, N.C.: Duke University Press, 1996): "By 'hybridity,' I refer to the formulation of cultural objects and practices that are produced by the histories of uneven and unsynthetic power relations; for example, the racial and linguistic mixings in the Philippines and among Filipinos in the United States are the material trace of the history of Spanish colonialism, U.S. colonization, and U.S. neo-colonialism" (67).

51. For an illuminating reading of the significance of the homosexual's "liminality" in such homophobic representations, see Robert F. Reid-Pharr, "Tearing the Goat's Flesh: Homosexuality, Abjection, and the Production of a Late-Twentieth-Century Black Masculinity," in *Novel Gazing: Queer Readings in Fiction*, ed. Eve Kosofsky Sedgwick (Durham, N.C.: Duke University Press, 1997), 353–76. Drawing on the work of René Girard, Reid-Pharr suggests that as a scapegoat figure, the homosexual functions "as the sign of a prior violence, the violence of boundarylessness, or cultural eclipse—to borrow Girard's language—that has been continually visited upon the African American community during its long sojourn in the new world" (354). By attacking this figure, black male writers engage in "a seemingly direct confrontation with the presumption of black boundarylessness" imposed by a long history of antiblack racism (354); such homophobic attacks also enable, however, "a reconnection to the very figure of boundarylessness that the assailant is presumably attempting to escape. As a consequence, black subjects are able to transcend, if only for a moment, the very strictures of normalcy and rationality that have been defined in contradistinction to a necessarily amorphous blackness" (354–55).

52. William L. Van Deburg, *New Day in Babylon: The Black Power Movement and American Culture, 1965–1975* (Chicago: University of Chicago Press, 1992), 2.

53. Quoted in Malcolm X, *The Autobiography of Malcolm X/With the Assistance of Alex Haley* (New York: Ballantine, 1992), 521.

54. Frank Chin and Jeffery Paul Chan, "Racist Love," in *Seeing Through Shuck*, ed. Richard Kostelanetz (New York: Ballantine, 1972), 68. All further references to this work will be cited in the text.

55. King-Kok Cheung, "The Woman Warrior Versus the Chinaman Pacific: Must a Chinese American Critic Choose Between Feminism and Heroism?" in *Conflicts in Feminism*, ed. Marianne Hirsch Keller and Evelyn Fox (New York: Routledge, 1990), 234–51.

56. Jeffery Paul Chan et al., eds., preface to *The Big Aiiieeeee! An Anthology of Chinese American and Japanese American Literature* (New York: Meridian, 1991),

xiii. While this essay was published in 1991, it recycles many of the same arguments that Chin and his colleagues had forwarded in the 1970s.

57. David Leiwei Li, *Imagining the Nation: Asian American Literature and Cultural Consent* (Stanford, Calif.: Stanford University Press, 1998), 212, footnote 9.

58. Gary Y. Okihiro, *Margins and Mainstreams: Asians in American History and Culture* (Seattle: University of Washington Press, 1994), 62.

59. Okihiro illustrates this view of Asians as "near-whites" with a phrase he attributes to the social scientist Harry Kitano: "Scratch a Japanese-American . . . and you find a Wasp" (ibid., 33).

60. Frank Chin, "Confessions of a Chinatown Cowboy," in *Bulletproof Buddhists and Other Essays*, by Frank Chin (Honolulu: University of Hawaii Press, 1998), 61.

61. Ibid., 59.

62. Harper, *Are We Not Men?* 11. See also J. Martin Favor, *Authentic Blackness: The Folk in the New Negro Renaissance* (Durham, N.C.: Duke University Press, 1999).

63. Frank Chin, "Backtalk," in *Counterpoint: Perspectives on Asian America*, ed. Emma Gee (Los Angeles: Asian American Studies Center, University of California, 1976), 557.

64. Ralph Ellison, introduction to *Shadow and Act* (New York: Vintage, 1995), xvi–xvii.

65. M. M. Bakhtin, *The Dialogic Imagination: Four Essays*, ed. Michael Holquist, trans. Caryl Emerson and Michael Holquist (Austin: University of Texas Press, 1981).

66. Young, *Colonial Desire*, 21.

67. Diana Fuss, *Essentially Speaking: Feminism, Nature, and Difference* (New York: Routledge, 1989), 90.

68. Frank Chin, "The Eat and Run Midnight People," in *The Chinaman Pacific and Frisco R.R. Co.: Short Stories* (Minneapolis: Coffee House Press, 1988), 11.

69. Max Scheler, *The Nature of Sympathy*, trans. Peter Heath (Hamden, Conn.: Archon, 1970).

70. Kaja Silverman, *Male Subjectivity at the Margins* (New York: Routledge, 1992), 205.

71. Ibid., 217. Silverman contrasts idiopathic identification with an opposed form that she (also via Scheler) terms heteropathic: "In heteropathic identification one lives, suffers, and experiences pleasure through the other"; this form of identification, moreover, "subscribes to an exteriorizing logic and locates the self at the site of the other" (ibid., 205).

Chapter 1

1. Darryl Pinckney, "The Drama of Ralph Ellison," *New York Review of Books* 44, no. 8 (15 May 1997). All further references to this work will be cited in the text.

2. Ernest Kaiser, "A Critical Look at Ellison's Fiction and at Social and Literary Criticism by and About the Author," *Black World* (December 1970): 95.

3. Larry Neal, "And Shine Swam On," afterword to *Black Fire*, ed. Leroi Jones and Larry Neal (New York: William Morrow, 1968), 652.

4. Clifford Mason, "Ralph Ellison and the Underground Man," *Black World* (December 1970): 21.

5. Ralph Ellison, *Shadow and Act* (New York: Vintage, 1995), 249. All further references to this work will be cited in the text.

6. Gayle Addison, Jr., ed., *The Black Aesthetic* (New York: Anchor, 1971); Hoyt Fuller, "Towards a Black Aesthetic," in *Within the Circle: An Anthology of African American Literary Criticism from the Harlem Renaissance to the Present*, ed. Angelyn Mitchell (Durham, N.C.: Duke University Press, 1994), 119–206; Larry Neal, "Ellison's Zoot Suit," *Black World* (December 1970): 31–52; Kimberly W. Benston, ed., *Speaking for You: The Vision of Ralph Ellison* (Washington, D.C.: Howard University Press, 1987).

7. Two essays particularly asserting Ellison's vernacular credentials are Henry Louis Gates, Jr., "The Blackness of Blackness: A Critique of the Sign and the Signifying Monkey," in *Black Literature and Literary Theory*, ed. Henry Louis Gates, Jr. (New York: Routledge, 1990), 285–321; and Houston A. Baker, Jr., "To Move Without Moving: Creativity and Commerce in Ralph Ellison's Trueblood Episode," in Gates, *Black Literature and Literary Theory*, 221–48.

8. Kerry McSweeney, *Invisible Man: Race and Identity* (Boston: Twayne, 1988), 21. See also Michel Fabre, "From Native Son to Invisible Man: Some Notes on Ralph Ellison's Evolution in the 1950s," in Benston, *Speaking for You*, 187–98; Jerry Gafio Watts, *Heroism and the Black Intellectual: Ralph Ellison, Politics, and Afro-American Intellectual Life* (Chapel Hill: University of North Carolina Press, 1994).

9. Ralph Ellison, introduction to *Invisible Man*, thirtieth anniversary ed. (New York: Vintage, 1995), xx. All further references to this work will be cited in the text.

10. Leslie A. Fiedler, "C'mon Back to the Raft Ag'in Huck Honey," in *The Collected Essays of Leslie Fiedler*, 2 vols. (New York: Stein and Day, 1971), 1: 142–51.

11. One other critic who has also suggested this link between Ellison and the black nationalist writers is Robyn Wiegman, in her book *American Anatomies: Theorizing Race and Gender* (Durham, N.C.: Duke University Press, 1995). She identifies Ellison, along with Richard Wright and the proponents of Black Power, as part of a group of twentieth-century "black male writers [who] have repeatedly

turned to the figuration of the black rapist as both a protest and warning, pur-
posely revising the mythic encounter between black men and white women as
part of a challenge to [a] history of mutilation" (104). She describes *Invisible Man*
as seeking to challenge and reverse a view of black men that had been codified
in the rape mythos by "mov[ing] the focus from the black man's [alleged] sexual
criminality to the white woman's" (104). While my reading echoes Wiegman's
to a significant degree, I do not agree with her basic assertion that it is the white
female characters that are depicted as the primary villains of the novel; in my view,
Ellison's primary object of critique is the "sexual criminality" of white men.

12. I am referring, of course, to Laura Mulvey's influential essay "Visual Pleasure and Narrative Cinema," in her *Visual and Other Pleasures* (Bloomington:
Indiana University Press, 1989), 14–26.

13. Lee Edelman, "The Part for the (W)hole: Baldwin, Homophobia, and the
Fantasmatics of 'Race,'" in *Homographesis: Essays in Gay Literary and Cultural Theory* (New York: Routledge, 1994), 55.

14. Baker, "To Move Without Moving." According to Baker, Norton's fascination with Trueblood's narrative is prompted by its depiction of incest as a means
of fulfilling "a capitalist dream" (339). What Norton glimpses in the incestuous
structure of Trueblood's growing family (his daughter and wife are both pregnant
with his children) is "a productive arrangement of life," one that is "eternally giving birth to new profits" (340).

15. Ibid., 327.

16. It is worth noting some connections between the fictional Norton and the
historical figure of Robert E. Park, the influential liberal sociologist whose writings
I will be examining in the next chapter. Park was connected to the same paternalistic structure of white benevolence with which the novel associates Norton—a structure that provided support for colleges like Tuskegee. Ellison refers to Park as "the
man responsible for inflating Tuskegee into a national symbol, and who is sometimes spoken of as the 'power behind Washington's throne'" (*Shadow and Act*, 307).
While the form of Norton's beneficence is primarily financial (whereas Park's was
primarily political and ideological), Norton is also described in the novel as, like
Park, a "skilled scientist" (37). Furthermore, Norton's own description of his philanthropic work—"my first-hand organizing of human life" (42)—echoes a fundamental conceptual term in Park's sociological writings: "social control."

17. Ralph Ellison, "Stormy Weather," *New Masses* 37 (24 September 1940): 20.
Ellison's critiques prefigure those of Nathan Irvin Huggins in *Harlem Renaissance*
(New York: Oxford University Press, 1971).

18. Ralph Ellison, "Stormy Weather," 20. Certain details in Ellison's depiction
of Young Emerson suggest that this character is partially modeled on the figure
of Charles Van Vechten, an influential sponsor of the artists of the Harlem Renais-

sance: both figures are gay, share an erotic interest in black men, and are collectors of exotic objects. For accounts of Van Vechten's role in this literary movement, his writing, and his overall flamboyance, see Huggins, *Harlem Renaissance*, 93–136; and Ann Douglas, *Terrible Honesty: Mongrel Manhattan in the 1920s* (New York: Farrar, Straus, and Giroux, 1995), 288–92. I will be returning to Ellison's and Wright's references to this homosexual legacy of the Renaissance in a later chapter.

19. Critics have generally focused on this character's name more than on his homosexuality. An exception to this pattern is Alan Nadel, who argues that Ellison, through his portrayal of Young Emerson, is engaging with and seeking to overturn Leslie Fiedler's interpretation of *The Adventures of Huckleberry Finn*. While Nadel thus addresses the homosexuality of Emerson, his main concern is with the intertextuality of *Invisible Man*. See Alan Nadel, *Invisible Criticism: Ralph Ellison and the American Canon* (Iowa City: University of Iowa Press, 1988).

20. Fiedler, "C'mon Back to the Raft," 146.

21. The link between an Orientalist exoticism and the homosexual decadence that Oscar Wilde epitomized I will explore in a later chapter on Frank Chin and the legacy of Sax Rohmer's Fu-Manchu fictions.

22. For an excellent analysis of the composition history of *Invisible Man*, which focuses on the author's increasing disillusionment with the ideals of the Communist Party USA, see Barbara Foley, "From Communism to Brotherhood: The Drafts of *Invisible Man*," in *Left of the Color Line: Race, Radicalism, and Twentieth-Century Literature of the United States*, ed. Bill Mullen and James Edward Smethurst (Chapel Hill: University of North Carolina Press, 2003), 163–82. Roderick A. Ferguson also offers an intriguing reading of an excised chapter of Ellison's novel—one that centers on a black homosexual English professor—as a response to Park's feminizing racial views, in chapter 2 of *Aberrations in Black: Toward a Queer of Color Critique*, Critical American Studies Series (Minneapolis: University of Minnesota Press, 2004), 54–81.

23. Ralph Ellison, "Out of the Hospital and Under the Bar," in *Soon, One Morning*, ed. Herbert Hill (New York: Alfred A. Knopf, 1963), 242–90. All further references to this work will be cited in the text.

24. While no locale is explicitly specified, certain details suggest that this en- counter takes place in the South. The narrator confirms Mary's assertion that he had to "run a long ways" after this encounter, and adds that he "hopped them freight trains and everything" in fleeing (256). The narrator is, moreover, seeking to explain to Mary how he got to this Northern hospital from "down home" (247). Finally, the white man uses Southern terms like *boy* and *mammy* (254–55).

25. Ellison, *Shadow and Act*, xv. All further references to this work will be cited in the text.

26. Ralph Ellison, "A Very Stern Discipline: An Interview with Ralph Ellison," by Steve Cannon, Lennox Raphael, and James Thompson, in *Conversations with*

Ralph Ellison, ed. Marayemma Graham and Amritjit Singh (Jackson, University Press of Mississippi, 1995), 120.

27. Ralph Ellison, "Interview with Ralph Ellison," by Arlene Crewdson and Rita Thomson in *Conversations with Ralph Ellison,* Graham and Singh, 268.

28. In his well-known rejoinder to Irving Howe's criticisms of his work in "Black Boys and Native Sons," Ellison suggests that the seductiveness of the socio-logical view of the Negro taken by many white liberals stems from its capacity to answer to certain psychic needs. Ellison characterizes Howe as being like many white "sociology-oriented critics" who "seem to feel that they can air with impunity their most private Freudian fantasies as long as they are given the slightest camouflage of intellectuality and projected as 'Negro.' They have made of the no-man's land created by segregation a territory for infantile self-expression and intellectual anarchy" (*Shadow and Act,* 108, 123).

29. George O'Meally, *The Craft of Ralph Ellison* (Cambridge, Mass.: Harvard University Press, 1980), 23.

30. "Dr. Robert E. Park was both a greater scientist and, in his attitude toward Negroes, a greater democrat than William Graham Sumner. (It will perhaps pain many to see these names in juxtaposition.) In our world, however, extremes quickly meet. Sumner believed it 'the greatest folly of which man can be capable to sit down with a slate and a pencil and plan out a new social world; a point of view containing little hope for the underdog. But for all his good works, some of Park's assumptions were little better" (*Shadow and Act,* 307).

31. Louis R. Harlan, *Booker T. Washington: The Wizard of Tuskegee, 1901–1915* (New York: Oxford University Press, 1983), 290–91.

32. George M. Fredrickson, *The Black Image in the White Mind: The Debate on Afro-American Character and Destiny, 1817–1914* (Hanover, N.H.: Wesleyan University Press, 1971), 327.

33. Ibid., 102.

34. Ibid.

35. Ibid. The phrase that Fredrickson cites here as exemplifying the "child-stereotype" central to the romantic racialist view belongs to Reverend Orville Dewey, who was a Unitarian clergyman in New York during the antebellum period.

36. For an illuminating analysis of how blackness and queerness are rendered in liberal sociology, see Ferguson, *Aberrations in Black.* Kenneth Warren offers an insightful account of Ellison's antipathy toward sociology that links and distin-guishes it from a comparable disciplinary antagonism in the writings of Houston Baker, Jr., and Henry Louis Gates, Jr.: see chapter 4 of Kenneth W. Warren, *So Black and Blue: Ralph Ellison and the Occasion of Criticism* (Chicago: University of Chicago Press, 2003), 83–99.

37. Fredrickson, *The Black Image in the White Mind,* 327.

38. Fred H. Matthews, *Quest for an American Sociology: Robert E. Park and the Chicago School* (Montreal: McGill-Queen's University Press, 1977), 157.

39. In this, he also resembled his counterpart in anthropology, Boas. For accounts of the debates around Park's and Boas's racial essentialism, see ibid., and Vernon J. Williams, Jr., *Rethinking Race: Franz Boas and His Contemporaries* (Lexington: University Press of Kentucky, 1996).

40. Henry Yu, *Thinking Orientals: Migration, Contact, and Exoticism in Modern America* (New York: Oxford University Press, 2001).

41. Robert E. Park, *Race and Culture*, ed. Everett Cherrington Hughes (Glencoe, Ill.: Free Press, 1950). All further references to this work will be cited in the text.

42. Park cites as the source of this assertion Henry Edward Krehbiel's *Afro-American Folksongs: A Study in Racial and National Music* (New York: G. Schirmer, 1867).

43. Matthews, *Quest for an American Sociology*, 172.

44. Ibid.

45. Ibid., 170.

46. Ibid., 173.

47. Ibid., 172. I noted earlier that even Ellison acknowledged the assistance Park provided to African American sociologists like Johnson and Frazier, as well to Horace Cayton. See Henry Yu's *Thinking Orientals* for an account of the Asian and Asian American sociologists who studied with Park at the University of Chicago.

48. Robert E. Park and Ernest W. Burgess, eds., *Introduction to the Science of Sociology*, 3rd ed. (Chicago: University of Chicago Press, 1969). All further references to this work will be cited in the text.

49. Michael Omi and Howard Winant, *Racial Formation in the United States: From the 1960s to the 1990s* (New York: Routledge, 1994), 16.

50. For a discussion of debates over the "fatalism" in Park's writings, see Matthews, *Quest for an American Sociology*, 80–82.

51. The view of American slavery that emerges from passages like this has led one critic of Park to characterize him as "one of many northern-bred intellectuals who was in sympathy with the Southern perspective on white/black relations." See John H. Stanfield, *Philanthropy and Jim Crow in American Social Science* (Westport, Conn.: Greenwood Press, 1985), 53. Stanfield also asserts that Park "assumed blacks were docile beings who were as they appeared to whites and who trusted whites more than members of their own race" (53). He also cites a passage in Park's unpublished papers that further elaborates the linkage of blackness and femininity that underwrites his racial typology: "Man has got what he wanted by tackling things; going at them directly. The Negro and the woman have

got them by manipulating the individual in control. Women and Negroes have required the machinery of rapid and delicate adjustment to the temper of [white] men" (53).

Chapter 2

1. Ralph Ellison, "A Very Stern Discipline," interview by Steve Cannon, Lennos Raphael, and James Thompson, in *Conversations with Ralph Ellison*, Maryemma Graham and Amritjit Singh, eds. (Jackson: University Press of Mississippi, 1995), 109–10.

2. Darryl Pinckney, "The Drama of Ralph Ellison," *New York Review of Books* 44, no. 8 (15 May 1997).

3. Horace Cayton and St. Clair Drake, *Black Metropolis: A Study of Negro Life in a Northern City* (New York: Harcourt, Brace, 1945); Richard Wright, *12 Million Black Voices* (New York: Thunder's Mouth Press, 1988).

4. Ralph Ellison, *Shadow and Act* (New York: Vintage, 1995), xx. All further references to this work will be cited in the text.

5. This is the title of the interview from which the epigraph to this chapter has been taken.

6. See Michel Fabre, "From *Native Son* to *Invisible Man*: Some Notes on Ralph Ellison's Evolution in the 1950s," in *Speaking for You: The Vision of Ralph Ellison*, ed. Kimberly W. Benston (Washington, D.C.: Howard University Press, 1987), 187–98.

7. George M. Fredrickson, *The Black Image in the White Mind: The Debate on Afro-American Character and Destiny, 1817–1914* (Hanover, N.H.: Wesleyan University Press, 1971); and Nathan Irvin Huggins, *Harlem Renaissance* (New York: Oxford University Press, 1971).

8. Fredrickson, *Black Image in the White Mind*, 327.

9. Ibid.

10. Fabre, "From *Native Son* to *Invisible Man*," 200.

11. Ann Douglas, *Terrible Honesty: Mongrel Manhattan in the 1920s* (New York: Farrar, Straus, and Giroux, 1995); George Hutchinson, *The Harlem Renaissance in Black and White* (Cambridge, Mass.: Belknap Press of Harvard University Press, 1995); Ross Posnock, *Color and Culture: Black Writers and the Making of the Modern Intellectual* (Cambridge, Mass.: Harvard University Press, 1998).

12. Ralph Ellison, "Stormy Weather," *New Masses* 37 (24 September 1940): 20. All further references to this work will be cited in the text.

13. Richard Wright, "Blueprint for Negro Writing," in *Voices from the Harlem Renaissance*, ed. Nathan Irvin Huggins (New York: Oxford University Press, 1976), 396. All further references to this work will be cited in the text.

14. The phrase *open secret* is D. A. Miller's, from *The Novel and the Police* (Berkeley: University of California Press, 1988), 192–220.

15. Douglas, *Terrible Honesty*, 97. David Levering Lewis acknowledges "the limitations of my rather too implicit discussion of gay and lesbian affections" in the preface he added to the 1997 Penguin paperback edition of *When Harlem Was in Vogue* (New York: Penguin, 1997), xxii.

16. Douglas, *Terrible Honesty*, 97.

17. Eric Garber, "A Spectacle in Color: The Lesbian and Gay Subculture of Jazz Age Harlem," in *Hidden from History: Reclaiming the Gay and Lesbian Past*, ed. Martin Bauml Duberman, Martha Vicinus, and George Chauncey, Jr. (New York: New American Library, 1989), 318, 329.

18. Phillip Brian Harper, *Are We Not Men? Masculine Anxiety and the Problem of African-American Identity* (New York: Oxford University Press, 1996), 50.

19. Ibid.

20. Ralph Ellison, "Recent Negro Fiction," *New Masses* 40 (5 August 1941): 22. All further references to this work will be cited in the text.

21. Quoted in Fabre, "From *Native Son* to *Invisible Man*," 211.

22. Ibid.

23. Ibid., 212.

24. Ibid., 210.

25. Ibid., 212; Ellison, "Recent Negro Fiction," 25.

26. Fabre also makes evident how deeply committed Ellison was both to Wright and to socialism, at least through the mid-1940s. The intensity of this commitment is something that Barbara Foley also illuminates in her essay, "From Communism to Brotherhood: The Drafts of *Invisible Man*," in *Left of the Color Line: Race, Radicalism, and Twentieth-Century Literature of the United States*, ed. Bill Mullen and James Edward Smethurst (Chapel Hill: University of North Carolina Press, 2003), 163–82. Through her analyses of early drafts of his novel, Foley helps to expose "one of the best-kept secrets of U.S. literary history"—that "Ralph Ellison was during the late 1930s and early 1940s a fairly close fellow traveler of the Communist Party of the United States of America" (163).

27. Joseph T. Skerrett, Jr., "The Wright Interpretation: Ralph Ellison and the Anxiety of Influence," in Benston, *Speaking for You*, 217–30.

28. Ralph Ellison, "Richard Wright's Blues," in *Shadow and Act*, 78. All further references to this work will be cited in the text.

29. Ralph Ellison, "The World and the Jug," in *Shadow and Act*, 141. All further references to this work will be cited in the text.

30. Ralph Ellison, "Interview with Ralph Ellison," by John O'Brien, in Graham and Singh, *Conversations with Ralph Ellison*, 227.

31. The description Ellison offers in "Richard Wright's Blues" of the "hysterical" forms of expression typical of Negro culture—that it is like "the violent gesturing of a man who attempts to express a complicated concept with a limited vocabulary"—can apply easily to Hemingway's prose style.

32. Ellison, *Shadow and Act*, 140.

33. Ralph Ellison, "Five Writers and Their African Ancestors," interview by Harold Isaacs, in Graham and Singh, *Conversations with Ralph Ellison*, 65.

34. Ibid.

35. Diana Fuss, *Essentially Speaking: Feminism, Nature, and Difference* (New York: Routledge, 1989), 90.

36. Favor, *Authentic Blackness*, 10.

37. Harper, *Are We Not Men?* 11.

38. Fuss, *Essentially Speaking*, 90.

39. Houston A. Baker, Jr., *Blues, Ideology, and Afro-American Literature: A Vernacular Theory* (Chicago: University of Chicago Press, 1984), 8.

40. Houston A. Baker, Jr., *Modernism and the Harlem Renaissance* (Chicago: University of Chicago Press, 1987), xiv.

41. Ibid., xvi.

42. Ibid., 51.

43. Henry Louis Gates, Jr., "The Blackness of Blackness: A Critique of the Sign and the Signifying Monkey," in *Black Literature and Literary Theory*, ed. Henry Louis Gates, Jr. (New York: Routledge, 1990), 286.

44. Ibid., 290.

45. Ibid., 292.

46. Ibid., 293.

47. Ibid., 294.

48. For a discussion of Brooks's and Sapir's cultural nationalism and its regionalist foundations, see Susan Hegeman, *Patterns for America: Modernism and the Concept of Culture* (Princeton, N.J.: Princeton University Press, 1999).

Chapter 3

1. Although these essays are credited as cowritten by all the *Aiiieeeee!* editors, critics have customarily treated Chin as the primary author. My study shares this critical tendency, which seems warranted by the overwhelming similarities of style and substance between these ostensibly collectively authored pieces and those for which Chin is the sole author.

2. Lisa Lowe, *Immigrant Acts: On Asian American Cultural Politics* (Durham, N.C.: Duke University Press, 1996), 11–12.

3. King-Kok Cheung, "The Woman Warrior Versus The Chinaman Pacific:

Must a Chinese American Critic Choose Between Feminism and Heroism?" in *Conflicts in Feminism*, ed. Marianne Hirsch Keller and Evelyn Fox (New York: Routledge, 1990), 235.

4. David L. Eng, *Racial Castration: Managing Masculinity in Asian America* (Durham, N.C.: Duke University Press, 2001), 2.

5. Frank Chin and Jeffery Paul Chan, "Racist Love," in *Seeing Through Shuck*, ed. Richard Kostelanetz (New York: Ballantine, 1972), 68.

6. Cheung, "The Woman Warrior Versus The Chinaman Pacific," 237. For other feminist critiques of Chin, see chapter 6 of Elaine Kim, *Asian American Literature: An Introduction to the Writings and Their Social Context* (Philadelphia: Temple University Press, 1982), 173–213; chapter 3 of Sau-ling Wong, *Reading Asian American Literature: From Necessity to Extravagance* (Princeton, N.J.: Princeton University Press, 1993), 118–65; and chapter 2 of Patricia P. Chu, *Assimilating Asians: Gendered Strategies of Authorship in Asian America* (Durham, N.C.: Duke University Press, 2000), 64–89.

7. Cheung, "The Woman Warrior Versus The Chinaman Pacific," 237.

8. Chin and Chan, "Racist Love," 69.

9. Frank Chin et al., "*Aiiieeeee!* Revisited," in *Aiiieeeee! An Anthology of Asian American Writers*, ed. Frank Chin et al. (New York: Mentor-Penguin, 1991), xxvii.

10. David Palumbo-Liu, "Pacific America: Projection, Introjection, and the Beginnings of Modern Asian America," *Asian/American: Historical Crossings of a Racial Frontier* (Stanford, Calif.: Stanford University Press, 1999), 17–42.

11. This critical focus on U.S. popular culture as the primary source of much anti-Asian stereotyping is evident in Elaine Kim's groundbreaking study *Asian American Literature* (1982), a book that more or less inaugurated the academic field of Asian American literary studies. In her first chapter, "Images of Asians in Anglo-American Literature," Kim explains her focus on "pulp novels and dime romances of varying degrees of literary quality" rather than on texts by more canonical writers like Bret Harte, Jack London, John Steinbeck, or Frank Norris, with the assertion that such representations enable a more accurate sense of the racist stereotypes that Asian Americans have had to contend with (3). Popular culture also constitutes a primary archive for Robert G. Lee's study *Orientals: Asian Americans in Popular Culture* (Philadelphia: Temple University Press, 1999).

12. Chin et al., *Aiiieeeee!* xix.

13. Chu, *Assimilating Asians*, 65. Robert Lee cites a passage from "Racist Love" in his chapter on the historical origins of the model minority myth, echoing Chu's suggestion that a provisional version of this paradigm for understanding anti-Asian racism can be found in this essay. See *Orientals*, 145.

14. Chin et al., *Aiiieeeee!* xvi.

15. Ibid.

16. Jeffery Paul Chan et al., eds., *The Big Aiiieeeee! An Anthology of Chinese American and Japanese American Literature* (New York: Meridian, 1991), xiii.

17. Jachinson Chan, *Chinese American Masculinities: From Fu Manchu to Bruce Lee* (New York: Routledge, 2001), 51–72.

18. Sander L. Gilman, *Difference and Pathology: Stereotypes of Sexuality, Race, and Madness* (Ithaca, N.Y.: Cornell University Press, 1985), 18.

19. Kim, *Asian American Literature*, 8.

20. Lee, *Orientals*, 116.

21. Chan, *Chinese American Masculinities*, 30.

22. Ibid.

23. Ibid., 45.

24. Frank Chin, "Confessions of a Chinatown Cowboy," in *Bulletproof Buddhists and Other Essays*, by Frank Chin (Honolulu: University of Hawaii Press, 1998), 66. All further references to this work will be cited in the text.

25. Chan et al., *Big Aiiieeeee*, xiii.

26. Chin, "Confessions of a Chinatown Cowboy," 66.

27. Contrasting interpretations of the figure of the Asian male villain are forwarded by Elaine Kim and Richard Fung. Like Chin and his colleagues, Kim and Fung argue that the Asian man tends to be portrayed as nonmasculine in Western cultural texts. Kim, however, regards the figure of Fu not as homosexual but rather as "completely asexual" (see Kim, *Asian American Literature*, 8), and Fung, a gay Asian Canadian critic and filmmaker, argues that the Asian male is represented in cinematic texts as "sometimes dangerous, sometimes friendly, but almost always characterized by a desexualized Zen asceticism. . . . the Asian man is defined by a striking absence down there. . . . And if Asian men have no sexuality," Fung asks, "how can we have a homosexuality?" (see Richard Fung, "Looking for My Penis: The Eroticized Asian in Gay Porn Video," in *How Do I Look? Queer Film and Video*, ed. Bad Object-Choices (Seattle: Bay Press, 1991), 148.

28. We find a condensed articulation of this larger cultural view of this desire as "feminine" in Sigmund Freud, "On Narcissism: An Introduction," in *General Psychological Theory: Papers on Metapsychology*, ed. Philip Rieff (New York: Collier, 1963), 56–82. In one of his more regressive moments, Freud describes the "truest feminine type" of woman as one who is restricted in "developing a true object-love" (69). Such a woman can only love narcissistically: "Strictly speaking such women love only themselves with an intensity comparable to that of the man's love for them. *Nor does their need lie in the direction of loving, but of being loved*" (70; my emphasis).

29. Leo Bersani, *Homos* (Cambridge, Mass.: Harvard University Press, 1995), 16–17.

30. See, for instance, Frantz Fanon, *Black Skins, White Masks,* trans. Charles Lam Markmann (New York: Grove Press, 1967); Joel Kovel, *White Racism: A Psychohistory* (New York: Columbia University Press, 1984); and *Joel Williamson, the Crucible of Race: Black-White Relations in the American South* (New York: Oxford University Press, 1984).

31. The model of "homosexual" desire Chin offers here is actually a kind of heterosexuality in drag. It doesn't imagine a man desiring a man, but a man who plays the part of a woman desiring a man. For a rigorous analysis of how theoretical paradigms of homosexual desire tend to give same-sex desire a foundationally heterosexual shape—how they tend to conceptualize that desire as the coupling together of a male and female term—see Judith Butler, *Gender Trouble: Feminism and the Subversion of Identity* (New York: Routledge, 1990), 1–34.

32. Fung, "Looking for My Penis," 148.

33. Lee, *Orientals,* 115.

34. Ibid.

35. Nayan Shah, *Contagious Divides: Epidemics and Race in San Francisco's Chinatown* (Berkeley: University of California Press, 2001), 90.

36. Ibid., 91.

37. Sax Rohmer, *The Insidious Dr. Fu-Manchu: Being a Somewhat Detailed Account of the Amazing Adventures of Nayland Smith in His Trailing of the Sinister Chinaman,* ed. Douglas G. Greene, Dover Mystery Classics (Mineola, N.Y.: Dover Publications, 1997), 24. All further references to this work will be cited in the text.

38. Chan, *Chinese American Masculinities,* 43. Chan also explores how the interest in racial hybridity that governs Rohmer's fictions might refract larger cultural anxieties about miscegenation (41–45).

39. Ibid., 36.

40. Shah, *Contagious Divides,* 91.

41. Ibid., 94.

42. Ibid., 95.

43. As Chan observes, "descriptions of [Fu] reveal that he does not have any sexual attributes and he does not exhibit any sexual needs. Indeed, his desire for elixir vitae and opium overrides all other physical needs" (*Chinese American Masculinities,* 30).

44. Kim, *Asian American Literature,* 12.

45. Rohmer actually wrote twelve more novels in the Fu-Manchu series, many of which were made into Hollywood films.

46. This quote is from chapter 5 of *The Insidious Dr. Fu-Manchu.*

47. Curtis Marez, "The Other Addict: Reflections on Colonialism and Oscar Wilde's Opium Smoke Screen," English *Literary History* 64, no. 1 (Spring 1997): 258. Marez also explores the contradictions of Wilde's identity, placing emphasis

on how he attempted to negate his racialized status as Irishman by constructing himself as a privileged member of an "Aesthetic Empire" symbolically allied with the Union, one that gained its power through its appropriation of non-Western aesthetic forms.

48. Ibid., 264.

49. Ibid., 267–72.

50. Ibid., 272.

51. Ibid.

52. See chapter 3 of Eve Kosofsky Sedgwick, *Epistemology of the Closet* (Berkeley: University of California Press, 1990), 131–81.

53. David Levering Lewis, *When Harlem Was in Vogue* (New York: Penguin, 1997), 197.

54. Richard Bruce [Nugent], "Smoke, Lilies, and Jade," in *Voices from the Harlem Renaissance*, ed. Nathan Irvin Huggins (New York: Oxford University Press, 1976), 100. All further references to this work will be cited in the text.

55. See Amritjit Singh's foreword to Wallace Thurman, *Infants of the Spring* (Boston: Northeastern University Press, 1992).

56. Nathan Irvin Huggins, *Harlem Renaissance* (New York: Oxford University Press, 1971), 241.

57. Ibid.

58. Ibid., 242.

59. George Hutchinson, *The Harlem Renaissance in Black and White* (Cambridge, Mass.: Belknap Press of Harvard University Press, 1995); Ann Douglas, *Terrible Honesty: Mongrel Manhattan in the 1920s* (New York: Farrar, Straus, and Giroux, 1995); William J. Maxwell, *New Negro, Old Left* (New York: Columbia University Press, 1999).

60. Walter Benn Michaels, *Our America: Nativism, Modernism, and Pluralism* (Durham, N.C.: Duke University Press, 1995).

61. Further evidence of the coincident and likely intertwined ways in which the racial difference of these two groups were framed can be found in the topics that were the focus of successive issues of *Survey Graphic* in 1925 and 1926. The 1926 issue of this magazine, which Henry Yu describes as "a periodical published for social workers, reformers, and other interested elites," centered on the Oriental Problem; it included the findings of the Survey of Race Relations, a study sponsored by liberal missionaries and conducted by Chicago School sociologists that concerned itself with Asian-white race relations on the West Coast and in Hawaii. As Yu points out, the preceding issue of this annual, edited by Alain Locke and entitled "Harlem: Mecca of the New Negro," was the one that eventually became *The New Negro*.

62. Chin et al., *Aiiieeeee!* 7; my emphasis.

Chapter 4

1. Patricia P. Chu, *Assimilating Asians: Gendered Strategies of Authorship in Asian America* (Durham, N.C.: Duke University Press, 2000), 67. All further references to this work will be cited in the text.

2. Chu notes that Chin attended college and received his formal education in literary studies during a period—the 1960s—when the paradigm established by critics like Trilling and Fiedler (and subjected to critique by Baym) would have been fully ascendant.

3. Frank Chin, afterword to *No-No Boy* (Seattle: University of Washington Press, 1976), 253–54.

4. Chin's elaboration of an Asian, as opposed to an Asian American, real can be found in Frank Chin, "Come All Ye Asian American Writers of the Real and the Fake," in *The Big Aiiieeeee! An Anthology of Chinese American and Japanese American Literature*, ed. Jeffery Paul Chan et al. (New York: Meridian, 1991), 1–92. See King-Kok Cheung, "The Woman Warrior Versus The Chinaman Pacific: Must a Chinese American Critic Choose Between Feminism and Heroism?" in *Conflicts in Feminism*, ed. Marianne Hirsch Keller and Evelyn Fox (New York: Routledge, 1990), 234–51, and chapter 5 of Chu for a critiques of Chin's account of this heroic Chinese tradition.

5. Elaine Kim, *Asian American Literature: An Introduction to the Writings and Their Social Context* (Philadelphia: Temple University Press, 1982), 189. All further references to this work will be cited in the text.

6. Michael Soo Hoo, review of *The Chinaman Pacific and Frisco R.R. Co.: Short Stories*, by Frank Chin, *Amerasia* 19, no. 1 (1993): 175–76.

7. Ibid.

8. Chu, *Assimilating Asians*, 77.

9. Sau-ling Wong, *Reading Asian American Literature: From Necessity to Extravagance* (Princeton, N.J.: Princeton University Press, 1993), 153.

10. Frank Chin, "Riding the Rails with Chickencoop Slim," *Greenfield Review* 6, no. 1–2 (1977): 85. All further references to this work will be cited in the text.

11. See, for instance, Judith Butler, *The Psychic Life of Power* (Stanford, Calif.: Stanford University Press, 1997), and Anne Anlin Cheng, *The Melancholy of Race* (New York: Oxford University Press, 2000).

12. Sigmund Freud, *Group Psychology and the Analysis of the Ego*, ed. and trans. James Strachey (New York: W. W. Norton, 1959), 48. All further references to this work will be cited in the text.

13. This identification with an ideal that one cannot identify entirely with— that is, "an identification with an unassimilable ideal"—is discussed by Mikkel Borch-Jacobsen as an ultimately impossible structure within Freud's theory, one

that—as Freud's writing itself discloses—cannot hold in check the resurgence of a rivalry that is propelled by a murderous desire to take the other's place. See Mikkel Borch-Jacobsen, *The Freudian Subject*, trans. Catherine Porter (Stanford, Calif.: Stanford University Press, 1988), 127–239. Largely following the trajectory of Borch-Jacobsen's analysis, my analysis will show how the peaceable triangulated relationship of Chin's social group, the brotherhood of the rails, will soon collapse into a murderous (and yet also loving) identificatory dyad.

14. Robyn Wiegman, *American Anatomies: Theorizing Race and Gender* (Durham, N.C.: Duke University Press, 1995).

15. My analysis here of Chin's ambivalent appropriation of this particular image of white manhood is much indebted to Sau-ling Wong's analysis of Chin's "The Eat and Run Midnight People," a short story that recycles much of the material contained in this earlier memoir. Wong focuses upon the historical and ideological determinants of the ambivalence that informs Chin's attempt to create "a Chinese American mobility myth around the symbol of the railroad" through the figure of the brakeman (see Wong, *Reading Asian American Literature*, 146).

16. Borch-Jacobsen staunchly asserts that what lies at the heart of the human subject is an altruicidal, ambivalent, and unquenchable *mimetic desire*, in which love and hate, desire and identification, and sadism and masochism are ultimately indistinguishable. His analysis, however, repeats a shortsightedness of the texts from which it draws: within the Freudian drama as Borch-Jacobsen enacts it, the players are given no gender, no sexuality, no creed, and indeed no color. They are a uniform homogeneous mass in which the differences that seem to matter in the world of history—the "anatomical" differences of sex and race, for instance—play no part in the ahistorical repetitive cycle of madness to which the sum of human experience is quite nearly reduced. We are all, in the end, "sons" of the *same* tribe, who war with each other to usurp the place of the father who never was, and since he never was, he has no color; and the differences and inequalities that predetermine who wins and loses this war between rivals—the unending war that is *human* culture, *human* history—are rendered incidental.

And yet, despite the universalizing pull his theories exert, there is much to be gained from Borch-Jacobsen's insights, for they cast light upon the specific drama of beleaguered *yellow* manhood that Chin plays out. As we shall see, the part Chin's autobiographical protagonist plays is very much that of the fraternal rival/friend/lover, the Freudian subject whom Borch-Jacobsen elucidates so painstakingly and eloquently. But Chin's inescapable knowledge of the difference in skin color between himself and his other self, the white man, and his awareness of the *hierarchical* difference that makes, structures, and determines the specific vicissitudes of his mimetic madness. Although Chin depicts his relation to his white coworkers in terms that echo Borch-Jacobsen's conception of the primal mimetic bond, he sees himself as doubly bound. For as a yellow man, he is not only inextricably tied to the white man as mimetic double—at once hated rival and beloved friend-lover—but, bound as he is by the color of his skin, he knows that the mimetic desire he harbors must always be frustrated in a way that is not true for his white counterpart.

17. In *The Melancholy of Race*, Anne Cheng argues for a much wider application of the concept of melancholia to describe the process of racialized subject-formation.

18. Sigmund Freud, "Mourning and Melancholia," in *General Psychological Theory: Papers on Metapsychology*, ed. Philip Rieff (New York: Collier, 1963), 172. All further references to this work will be cited in the text.

19. In *The Ego and the Id*, after Freud has established his second psychic topography, he makes clear that it is the ego's identification with the lost-object that enables it to court affections that the id once lavished upon another: "When the ego assumes the features of the object, it is forcing itself, so to speak, upon the id as a love-object and is trying to make good the id's loss by saying: 'Look, you can love me too—I am so like the object'" (see Sigmund Freud, *The Ego and the Id*, ed. James Strachey, trans. Joan Riviere (New York: W. W. Norton, 1962), 20.

20. Freud, *Group Psychology*, 37.

21. Freud, *Ego and Id*, 19.

22. Freud, *Group Psychology*, 37; my emphasis.

23. Frank Chin, *The Chickencoop Chinaman and the Year of the Dragon: Two Plays by Frank Chin* (Seattle: University of Washington Press, 1981), 24.

24. Chu, *Assimilating Asians*, 72.

25. Ibid.

26. Ibid., 3. All further references to this work will be cited in the text.

27. In the earlier monologue in which he recounted his boyhood fascination with the Lone Ranger, Tam had also used this mode of address: "Listen, *children*, did I ever tellya, I ever tellya the Lone Ranger ain't a Chinaman?" (31; my emphasis).

28. Frank Chin, *Donald Duk* (Minneapolis: Coffee House Press, 1991).

29. Wong, *Reading Asian American Literature*, 153.

30. David L. Eng presents *Donald Duk* as a much more complex text than Sau-ling Wong allows for in her appraisal. Though he also critiques its masculinism and heteronormativity, he argues that this novel engages in interesting ways with issues of visuality and historical memory. See chapter 1 of *Racial Castration: Managing Masculinity in Asian America* (Durham, N.C.: Duke University Press, 2001), 35–103.

31. Wong, *Reading Asian American Literature*, 145.

32. Ibid., 226, footnote 34.

33. Ibid., 151.

34. Ibid., 148.

35. Ralph Ellison, *Shadow and Act* (New York: Vintage, 1995), 79.

36. Diana Fuss, *Essentially Speaking: Feminism, Nature, and Difference* (New York: Routledge, 1989), 87.

37. Ibid., 89.

38. Kim, *Asian American Literature*, 186, 189.

39. My understanding of Chin's masochism draws upon Kaja's Silverman's analysis of "reflexive masochism." She suggests that this particular form of masochism is "compatible with—indeed, perhaps a prerequisite for—extremely virility" (see Kaja Silverman, *Male Subjectivity at the Margins* [New York: Routledge, 1992], 327). "The reflexive masochist," Silverman suggests, "might indeed as appropriately be designated a 'reflexive sadist'" (324–25). He is a kind of psychic switch hitter, both batterer and battered. He "suffers/enjoys pain without renouncing activity" (325). My analysis is also indebted to the much earlier work of Theodor Reik, who asserts that the sadistic impulse, which Silverman identifies in reflexive masochism, is in fact the central driving force behind masochism in general: see Reik, *Masochism in Modern Man*, trans. Margaret H. Beigel and Gertrud M. Lurth (New York: Grove Press, 1957). For reflexive masochism in contemporary white American masculinity, see David Savran, *Taking It Like a Man: White Masculinity, Masochism, and Contemporary American Culture* (Princeton, N.J.: Princeton University Press, 1998).

Silverman distinguishes reflexive masochism from another form, "feminine," that she argues is subversive of normative masculinity. Her work overall shares with that of other recent psychoanalytic critics and theorists the common political goal of upending dominant constructions of gender and sexuality. Silverman, Leo Bersani, and Gilles Deleuze, among others, assert that male "perversions" like masochism illuminate and resist the oppressive ideological fictions that determine the shape of conventional virility.

Chapter 5

1. Frank Chin et al., eds., *Aiiieeeee! An Anthology of Asian American Writers* (New York: Mentor-Penguin, 1991), 23–24.

2. Ibid., 25. All further references to this work will be cited in the text.

3. Phillip Brian Harper, *Are We Not Men? Masculine Anxiety and the Problem of African-American Identity* (New York: Oxford University Press, 1996), 11.

4. Frank Chin, "Backtalk," in *Counterpoint: Perspectives on Asian America*, ed.

Emma Gee (Los Angeles: Asian American Studies Center, University of California, 1976), 557. All further references to this work will be cited in the text.

5. Frank Chin and Jeffery Paul Chan, "Racist Love," in *Seeing Through Shuck*, ed. Richard Kostelanetz (New York: Ballantine, 1972), 76. All further references to this work will be cited in the text.

6. Frank Chin, "Confessions of a Chinatown Cowboy," in *Bulletproof Buddhists and Other Essays*, by Frank Chin (Honolulu: University of Hawaii Press, 1998), 99. All further references to this work will be cited in the text.

7. M. M. Bakhtin, *The Dialogic Imagination: Four Essays*, ed. Michael Holquist, trans. Caryl Emerson and Michael Holquist (Austin: University of Texas Press, 1981), 279.

8. See my readings in chapter 3 of Houston A. Baker, Jr., *Blues, Ideology, and Afro-American Literature: A Vernacular Theory* (Chicago: University of Chicago Press, 1984), and *Modernism and the Harlem Renaissance* (Chicago: University of Chicago Press, 1987).

9. Chang-rae Lee, *Native Speaker* (New York: Riverhead, 1995), 167.

10. Chin, "Confessions of a Chinatown Cowboy," 104.

11. Kai-yu Hsu, ed., *Asian-American Authors* (Boston: Houghton Mifflin, 1972).

12. Frank Chin, "Afterward," *Multi-Ethnic Literatures of the United States* 3, no. 2 (1976): 16. All further references to this work will be cited in the text.

13. Ralph Ellison, *Shadow and Act* (New York: Vintage, 1995), xv.

14. Ibid.

15. Ibid., xvi.

16. Ibid., xvii.

17. See Patricia P. Chu, *Assimilating Asians: Gendered Strategies of Authorship in Asian America* (Durham, N.C.: Duke University Press, 2000), and King-Kok Cheung, "The Woman Warrior Versus The Chinaman Pacific: Must a Chinese American Critic Choose Between Feminism and Heroism?" in *Conflicts in Feminism*, ed. Marianne Hirsch Keller and Evelyn Fox (New York: Routledge, 1990), 234–51, for discussions of this "turn" in Chin's aesthetic writings.

18. Frank Chin, "Frank Chin: An Interview with Robert Murray Davis," *Amerasia* 14, no. 1 (1988): 91. All further references to this work will be cited in the text.

19. Frank Chin, "Come All Ye Asian American Writers of the Real and the Fake," in *The Big Aiiieeeee! An Anthology of Chinese American and Japanese American Literature*, ed. Jeffery Paul Chan et al. (New York: Meridian, 1991), 34, 35. All further references to this work will be cited in the text.

20. Frank Chin, "The Eat and Run Midnight People," in *The Chinaman*

Pacific and Frisco R.R. Co.: Short Stories (Minneapolis: Coffee House Press, 1988), 11; my emphasis.

Coda

1. Khachig Tölölyan, "The Nation-State and Its Others: In Lieu of a Preface," *Diaspora* 1, no. 1 (1991): 5.

2. *Crossing the River* (1993), the novel I will be considering here, depicts characters who are part of the African diaspora; several of his writings depict the Caribbean, and his novel, *The Nature of Blood* (1997), explores the lives of Jews in Germany, Israel, and Ethiopia.

3. Bénédicte Ledent, *Caryl Phillips* (Manchester, U.K.: Manchester University Press, 2002), 1.

4. Caryl Phillips, "The European Tribe," in *Us/Them: Translation, Transcription, and Identity in Post-Colonial Literary Cultures*, ed. Gordon Collier (Amsterdam: Rodopi, 1992), 7. Further references to this work will be noted parenthetically in the text.

5. Caryl Phillips, interview by Frank Birbalsingh, in *Frontiers of Caribbean Literature in English*, ed. Frank Bibalsingh (New York: St. Martin's Press, 1996), 187.

6. Caryl Phillips, "Crisscrossing the River: An Interview with Caryl Phillips," by Carol Margaret Davison, *Ariel* 25 (1994): 93.

7. Gail Low, "'A Chorus of Common Memory': Slavery and Redemption in Caryl Phillips's *Cambridge* and *Crossing the River*," *Research in African Literatures* 29, no. 4 (1998): 132.

8. Ibid., 122.

9. Ibid., 132.

10. Caryl Phillips, *Crossing the River* (New York: Vintage, 1995), 235. Further references to this work will be noted parenthetically in the text.

11. Caryl Phillips, "Of This Time, of That Place," interview by Jenny Sharpe, *Transition* 68 (1995): 159.

12. Ibid.

13. Ibid.

14. Low, "'A Chorus of Common Memory,'" 134.

15. Ibid.

16. Ibid., 135.

17. Ibid., 135, 136.

18. David L. Eng, *Racial Castration: Managing Masculinity in Asian America* (Durham, N.C.: Duke University Press, 2001), 224.

19. Ibid., 225.

20. Ibid.

21. Ibid.

22. Ibid.

23. Ibid., 210.

24. Ibid., 227.

25. R. Zamora Linmark, *Rolling the R's* (New York: Kaya Production, 1995), 3. Further references to this work will be noted parenthetically in the text.

26. Ellen Rooney, "Form and Contentment," *Modern Language Quarterly* 61, no. 1 (2000): 39–40.

27. Ibid., 29.

28. Ibid., 29–30.

29. Ibid., 26.

30. Ibid., 40.

Index

African American(s): and Asian Americans, 126–27, 141–42, 226–29, 270*n*61; cultural nationalism (*see* black nationalism); feminization of, 4–7, 60, 67–68, 73–74, 79–80, 82, 89; and history, 192, 236; as hybrid, 5; and literacy, xxiv–xxv; and orality, 38; Park on, 69, 70–81; and railroad, 184, 199; vernacular of, 37–40, 44–45, 86, 91–93, 99–100, 105, 109–22; women, 17, 27–28

African American Studies: diasporic approach in, 233; and Ellison, 44; and gay/lesbian studies, xx

Aiiieeeee! See under Chin, Frank, works

anthropology, 70

anti-racism, xxi; homophobic, xxii, 9–10

Apana, Chang, 133

Armstrong, Louis, 115

Asian American(s): aesthetic identity, 190, 195–96, 197, 198; and African Americans, 126–27, 141–42, 226–29, 270*n*61; and asexuality, 268*n*27; and black culture, 186–87, 190, 199, 201–2; and Christian missionaries, 130–31; feminization of, 32, 81, 127, 128–31, 132–34, 136, 161, 188, 213; and history, 196; and homosexuality, 133–34, 136–43, 165, 241; literary tradition of, 161–62, 203–4, 221; language, relationship to, xxv, 207, 208–9, 213–21; and orality, 38, 226–27; Park on, 75–78, 80–81; and popular culture, 131–32, 226–27; 80–81; and sociology, 131; stereotypes of, 32, 35–36, 130, 134–35 (*see also* Chan, Charlie; Fu-Manchu); vernacular of, 198–99, 206–31; women, 145–46

Asian American cultural nationalism, 125; and black nationalism, 31–37, 126; and masculinity, 32–37; homophobia and misogyny in, 16, 32–33, 125; "queering" of, 242

Asian American Sexualities, xxi

Asian American studies: and Chin, 127; diasporic approach in, 233; and gay/lesbian studies, xx–xxi; and globalization, 205; and historicism, 205; multi-racial approach in, 158, 205; and popular culture, 267*n*11

aurality: and blues, 112; and vernacular, 110, 112–14, 122, 216

Baker, Houston, Jr.: on *Invisible Man*, 54, 260*n*14; on vernacular, xxiii, 37, 86, 110–12, 112–14, 199, 206, 208, 216

Bakhtin, Mikhail, 37, 215, 216

Baldwin, James, 23–24

Baraka, Amiri, xxiii; and Chin, 137, 138; and Ellison, 41–43; on homosexuality, 15, 18–21, 21–23, 141–42, 256*n*36; on vernacular, 43, 45. *See also* black nationalism

Baym, Nina, 160, 271*n*2

beatnik, and homosexuality, 19–21

Bersani, Leo, 21, 23, 26–27, 29, 138–39, 274*n*39

Bhabha, Homi, 6

Morning Glory, Evening Shadow: Yamato Ichihashi and His Internment Writings, 1942–1945

EDITED, ANNOTATED, AND WITH A BIOGRAPHICAL ESSAY BY GORDON H. CHANG, 1997.

Dear Miye: Letters Home From Japan, 1939–1946

MARY KIMOTO TOMITA, EDITED, WITH AN INTRODUCTION AND NOTES, BY ROBERT G. LEE, 1995.

Beyond the Killing Fields: Voices of Nine Cambodian Survivors in America

USHA WELARATNA, 1993.

Making and Remaking Asian America

BILL ONG HING, 1993.

Righting a Wrong: Japanese Americans and the Passage of the Civil Liberties Act of 1988

LESLIE T. HATAMIYA, 1993.